BEYOND NAÏVETÉ

Ethics, Economics, and Values

Rohnn B. Sanderson

and

Marc A. Pugliese

University Press of America,® Inc.
Lanham · Boulder · New York · Toronto · Plymouth, UK

4501 Forbes Boulevard
Suite 200
Lanham, Maryland 20706
UPA Acquisitions Department (301) 459-3366

10 Thornbury Road
Plymouth PL6 7PP
United Kingdom

Printed in the United States of America
British Library Cataloging in Publication Information Available

Library of Congress Control Number: 2012940477
ISBN: 978-0-7618-5958-1 (clothbound : alk. paper)
eISBN: 978-0-7618-5959-8

™ The paper used in this publication meets the minimum requirements of American National Standard for Information Sciences—Permanence of Paper for Printed Library Materials, ANSI Z39.48-1992

CONTENTS:

FOREWORD:

ETHICIST'S FOREWORD
KATHRYN D. BLANCHARD

I will begin by letting you, readers, in on a little secret: people with Ph.D.'s feel stupid much of the time. (If you yourself have a Ph.D. you may already be abundantly familiar with the "impostor syndrome" that many scholars suffer; if you don't have a Ph.D. or are hoping to get one, this phenomenon is something you should be aware of from the get-go!) In my case, I have a Ph.D. in Christian theology and ethics, with a minor concentration in economics, and I have written a book on Christian economic ethics. This might cause some to believe that I am able to rest confidently in my knowledge and understanding of both theology and economics—but they would be incorrect.

It has, therefore, been an intellectual treat to read Marc A. Pugliese and Rohnn Sanderson's *Beyond Naïveté: Ethics, Economics, and Values*. Despite my lengthening years of coursework and research, I am nevertheless always grateful to come across a well-organized book that is designed to be helpful to non-specialists, mainly because I myself always feel in need of a refresher course. This clearly-written book is notable first and foremost for its intention to reach readers who do not have equal expertise in philosophy, theology, and economics—which is to say most of us.

The authors' attention to audience is evident, for example, in the book's lack of jargon. Each time a specialized philosophical or economic term is introduced (*a priori*, utility, Pareto optimality, or the like), it is highlighted and defined. This book also avoids the gratuitous name-dropping so common in most disciplinary writing. It does not merely use terms like "Humean epistemology" or "Marxist alienation" as shorthand; instead, the authors pause to tell us about Hume or Marx in enough detail to make their point. Thus, while many books claim to be written for non-specialists, this one actually demonstrates the authors' commitment to accessibility. The book does equally well in explaining both ethics and economics for first-time readers, and it does them side-by-side, discussing, for example, gross domestic product and business cycles together in the same chapter with social contract theory.

Two central ideas are especially important for the book. The first is the early framing of philosophy as the study of "limit questions"—those mysteries that defy the power of empirical science to provide conclusive answers. The second is the distinction between "positive" and "normative" economics: positive economists deal with models based on facts, or "what is," while normative economists venture into the public sphere to make real-life recommendations about "what ought to be." These two foundational ideas about ethics and economics are essential to allowing a philosopher and an economist to write a book together in which one approach does not eclipse the other. The economist here agrees to avoid transgressing into the realm that properly belongs to those who deal in limit questions, while the philosopher agrees to leave the economist's facts and models untouched. Not to allow this boundary to stand would likely push the book too far to one side or the other, making it a work of "economic philosophy" or "philosophical economics" rather than an introduction to, and dialogue between, two distinct disciplines.

Despite—or perhaps because of—the authors' respect for boundaries, they manage to create genuine dialogue in every chapter of the book. The end result is a genuine work of ethics, in which an economist and a philosopher work together, each using his own disciplinary lenses, to try to evaluate economic life. Thus, chapters one through four exist in many ways simply to provide the background necessary to get us to chapter five, in which the book turns its gaze toward the real world. The final chapter—a careful and fair-minded evaluation of capitalism, socialism, and communism—will likely be of greatest interest to readers who are bewildered by the shouting that normally characterizes public conversations about economic ethics. While its evaluation cannot be characterized as entirely unbiased (capitalism looks, unsurprisingly, a lot better than the other two options offered here), the authors nevertheless take great pains to acknowledge and explain the pros and cons of each system. In particular, their discussion highlights the important trade-off between communism's vision of justice as a matter of equality of opportunity on the one hand, and capitalism's vision of justice as freedom to face the consequences of one's own actions, for good or ill, on the other. One might have wished for the authors to move beyond Marx's own understanding of socialism as the gateway to communism, since successful socialist systems today (think of Sweden or Germany) are not designed as temporary way-stations on the road to something more radical. They are rather hybrid systems, designed for long-term stability, that harness the power of markets for the goods they can produce most efficiently; while also harnessing the power of centralized government for other types of goods that markets cannot efficiently allocate. In the 21st century, we might see socialism itself as the ever-elusive "third way" between capitalism and communism, negotiating between the human need for *both* freedom *and* equity—employing *both* economics *and* ethics, *both* markets *and* government—rather than allowing one value to overshadow the other.

As a theologian and a feminist, my main concern about this book is related not to its quality or the expertise of its authors but rather –predictably!—to its primary working assumption, namely that economics is a discrete discipline, and that positive economics deals only in "facts" to which theology, philosophy, and ethics are inconsequential. From a certain point of view, this is a moot point, especially given the traditional organization of universities today. The departmental structure of my own institution provides a fairly typical example: economics is housed in the social sciences division, while religious studies and philosophy are both in the humanities. There is a tidy boundary between these departments—every bit as tidy as the boundary between literature and biology, or sociology and environmental science. But as our authors themselves acknowledge, this was not always the case, which means such a separation is not necessarily "natural." In earlier generations, it was philosophers and theologians who first took an interest in "political economy." Positive economists have long since separated themselves from their more philosophical forefathers (and fathers they were), but such a separation is still worthy of questioning. To be sure, the authors do give brief mention of heterodox lines of thought here and there (such as organicism in chapter three), but overall it is positive economics that has laid the boundaries and set the tone for this interaction.

Take, for example, chapter five, in which the authors reiterate, "The agreed upon laws of positive economics are not malleable. They are analogous to natural laws like electromagnetism and gravity." The deployment of such positivist rhetoric makes it very difficult for anyone to argue against it without being accused of "naïveté." Economics is posited as universally and scientifically true and applicable, regardless of cultural or historical context. But elsewhere in the same chapter they note, "Private property is a necessary assumption of all positive economics." This begs the question: since the "law" of private property has not been written in the stars or revealed on golden plates, who exactly has "agreed upon" its definition? Who has "agreed upon" the idea that property belongs to a private individual rather than to a family or a community? And who has "agreed upon" using the model of private property to analyze people's familial or political interactions?[1]

The rationally self-interested individual agent is another assumption that economics takes to be as natural as water freezing at 32 degrees Fahrenheit; economic science cannot exist without him. But feminist economics has long questioned this masculine ideal of the "separative self."[2] Despite their scientific, fact-based training, feminist economists reject the assumption that a non-normative, value-neutral method of inquiry is possible. "The categories of economic analysis do not express timeless truths. Economic categories and concepts… are embedded in social contexts and connected to processes of social differentiation."[3] Human history, it seems, cannot be reduced to a single model based on *a priori* assumptions posing as natural laws. Markets are people, not chemical compounds or cancer cells. While predictive models and analytical generalizations have limited value and are surely useful if human beings hope to live together in communities, they are nevertheless always provisional and subject to adjustment.

The "naïveté" of the title therefore points in more than one direction. On one hand, it is clearly pointed at people who think positive economic science "should" deal normatively with the "shoulds" of economic life, rather than simply with the "is." But it also points at economists who believe it is possible to create economic models apart from their own cultural biases. Frank Knight, an early master of the "Chicago school" of neoliberal economics, wisely encouraged economists to admit how severely limited was the use of positive economics for the real world. Economics, he argued, "treats of [human] conduct *in so far* as conduct is amenable to scientific treatment, in so far as it is controlled by definable conditions and can be reduced to (natural) law. But this, measured by the standard of natural science, is not very far. *There are no data* for a science of conduct in a sense analogous to natural science."[4] The problem with positive economics is not that it cannot tell us anything; it is rather that so many economists seem to forget that it cannot tell us *everything*. Positive economics is never satisfied to stay in a bubble of positivity; the temptation to normativity is simply too great for embodied, social human beings.

But these comments reflect my own embodied, social, human understanding of the world. In so far as the stated goals of this book are to educate non-economists about economics and non-philosophers about philosophy, and to demonstrate some of the rich ethical conversations that are possible between the two disciplines, it is highly successful. And while I continue to doubt that *any* philosopher or economist (each of whom exists within a culture, speaks a language, has a personality, and lives in a body) can *truly* be "position-neutral," these authors are nevertheless to be congratulated for having done about as well as anyone could possibly be expected to do.

NOTES

1. That the discipline of economics arose among, and has traditionally been dominated by, white males will not surprise anyone; that some women and formerly-colonized persons have adopted its methods does not make it any less of a cultural artifact. The people who agree on such a model are culturally, psychologically, and/or intellectually predisposed to do so; it makes sense to them because of who they are and how they have been educated. In the interest of full disclosure, I should admit that much of economic thought makes sense to me, too. Although I am not male, I am nevertheless a highly privileged white American, the daughter of a CEO; and Marx (via liberation theologies) has taught me that a hermeneutic of suspicion is always warranted when it comes to ideologies that maintain power and privilege for those like me who already have plenty of it.

2. *Beyond Economic Man: Feminist Theory and Economics*, Marianne A. Ferber and Julie A. Nelson, eds. (Chicago, IL: University of Chicago, 1993), 10.

3. *Liberating Economics: Feminist Perspectives on Families, Work, and Globalization*, Drucilla K. Barker and Susan F. Feiner, eds. (Ann Arbor, MI: University of Michi-

gan, 2004), 3. Non-Western economists, too, have questioned the neutrality of positive economic methods. Nobel prize-winner Amartya Sen, for example, argues that the assumption of economic freedom makes sense only within certain social and political contexts. Rather than models that artificially separate economic choice from the settings and limitations within which such choices are made, Sen argues instead for "an integrated analysis of economic, social and political activities, involving a variety of institutions and many interactive agencies." Amartya Sen, *Development as Freedom* (New York, NY: Anchor Books, 1999), xii.

4. Frank Knight, "Ethics and the Economic Interpretation," in *The Ethics of Competition and Other Essays*, ed. Milton Friedman et al. (New York, NY: Harper & Brothers, 1935), 36 (emphasis original).

FOREWORD:

ECONOMIST'S FOREWORD
CRAIG D. BROADBENT

One of the foundational theories of economics is that economic agents respond to incentives.[1] For instance, each day individuals must choose how to allocate their time. Should one work more hours or fewer hours? Introduce the compensation incentive structure for an individual's time, and an economic agent will respond to this incentive and make a decision regarding how many hours to work. Incentive is the fundamental principle that defines how human beings live their lives each day. I was pleased, when reading Pugliese and Sanderson's book *Beyond Naïveté: Ethics, Economics, and Values*, to find this common theme running throughout the book. Understanding how individuals respond to incentives is essential for an aspiring student to understand the fundamentals of economics in conjunction with ethical issues.

It is often thought that economists only concern themselves with studying how individuals respond, or a society responds, to incentives, but do not look at why they respond and how they *should* respond, if the incentive is altered. As Pugliese and Sanderson explain in chapter one, this difference between studying how individuals in fact respond, and being prescriptive about how they should respond, is the difference between positive and normative economics. While the positive economist describes how economic agents do react to incentives, normative economics is prescriptive, explaining how the world ought to be. It is in normative economics that the economist blends ethics into the discipline.

Take, for example, the individual decision to recycle. In order to engage in recycling, an individual must put forth energy to sort recyclable material from non-recyclable material. Further, if one has to take this recycled material to a recycling center the "opportunity cost" of driving to the center must be considered. In looking at the recycling decision, the positive economist can view the individual's choice and see if he or she does engage in recycling, given these costs.

However, there is more to the recycling decision than the mere fact of whether or not the individual chooses to recycle, given the costs. Is recycling the ethical thing to do? Is there some amount of positive "utility" that one receives from engaging in recycling? These questions are examined by the normative economist, who looks beyond why one recycles and asks whether or not one should recycle, and why. Pugliese and Sanderson explain how these economic and ethical issues blend, using the disciplines of both economics and philosophy.

In addition to explaining the difference between these two branches of economics, they also spend time explaining the different types of goods that exist, like public and private. For instance, in chapter one they work to overcome the austere explanation that the market is "up" or the market is "down." In doing this, they note that there is a real difference in the type of goods that are traded in markets broadly defined as private and public goods.

It is in the realm of public goods that many ethical questions arise along with positive economics, such as why we see the overuse of public goods, and should we allow this overuse to occur? It may be that the incentive structure to protect public goods is not properly in place, which can lead to economic agents acting in their own self-interest, so as to overuse the good and ultimately lead to its destruction. This is not a new idea to economists, as it was first explained by Hardin[2] when he defined the tragedy of the commons. Rather than just defining this problem, Pugliese and Sanderson ask the normative question regarding how the incentive structure should be designed to overcome this tragedy. This is an ethical question within the realm of economics, which once again demonstrates the blending of economic issues with ethics.

While raising all of these issues, Pugliese and Sanderson are sure to spend the time required to provide non-specialist readers with the necessary tools for thinking critically about economic issues. In chapter two they take the time to develop the microeconomic theories of supply and demand, utility maximization, and explain how externalities exist in marketplaces that may have improper incentive structures. While explaining these necessary tools for understanding the fundamental principles of microeconomics, Pugliese and Sanderson still take the time to ask the normative questions of how markets ought to operate.

Building upon these foundational principles, they then take readers into macroeconomics in chapter three, again leading readers through the fundamental principles of this branch of economics as a discipline. While they again take care to explain how macroeconomic indicators move, they do not lose sight of the purpose of the book, by asking should the indicators move in this direction? For example, should we allow the unemployment rate to rise or the inflation rate to rise? Should we accumulate national debt, or investigate and consider the consequences of national debt on the investment and savings decision? It is this attention to the book's theme that I find particularly helpful for readers who are non-specialists in economics, ethics, or both.

Once they explain these fundamental economic theories to the reader, Pugliese and Sanderson then dive into specific issues in macroeconomics in chapter four. They tackle questions like: What is the value of liberty or freedom? What are the different types of justice? Can equity and efficiency be in harmony in the marketplace? I particularly enjoyed their examples in applying these questions to specific issues in macroeconomics, such as low income assistance in conjunction with the founding principle of our nation that all people have certain "inalienable rights." Here they investigate whether or not society has a moral obligation to provide for all individuals, in order to sustain life.

As a conclusion to the book, Pugliese and Sanderson spend the time in chapter five to investigate the three general classifications of political systems that we see throughout the world today: Capitalism, Socialism and Communism. After explaining the three different systems, they then take the reader through a set of normative questions allowing the reader to critically analyze each political system. This review of the three political systems along with normative questions allows the reader to ask questions about the morality of each system.

As an economist who spends a great deal of time trying to reach out to the young minds that will shape our world in the future, I find this book particularly fitting for all young aspiring economists and philosophers. After I finished this book I found myself sitting back and asking the normative ethical questions in the classes that I teach, and in the decisions that I make every day. I am appreciative of the time the authors have spent to make sure that the reader understands each economic principle, and to provide so many examples for the reader throughout the book.

Understanding how incentives motivate individuals is critical to understanding how economic agents respond. However, the normative questions about how economic agents should respond in a specified manner, and what is the moral obligation to society of all economic agents, are great questions that must be faced by all individuals as they progress through life. It is the blending of positive and normative economics, in this book, that the authors have accomplished, enabling the reader to critically assess the impact of economic incentives in conjunction with ethical and related philosophical issues.

NOTES

1. A recent popular book, which the reader may find helpful in explaining how economic agents respond to incentives, is: Steven D. Levitt and Stephen J. Dubner, *Freakonomics* (New York, NY: William Morrow and Co., 2005).

2. See, Garrett Hardin, "The Tragedy of the Commons." *Science* 12, no. 3859 (1968): 1243–48.

INTRODUCTION:

From debates between political candidates, to journalism, to the internet, to news sound bytes, to talk shows, to university campuses, to discussions with co-workers, friends, and family; we are engaged by, and in, discussions over whether this or that economic policy is good or bad, right or wrong. We may hear or personally feel that a disparity in income between people is wrong; a certain price is unfair; all people should get a "living wage"; everyone should have healthcare; and it is an injustice that every American does not own a home. Republicans call taxing and redistributing income "glorified theft." Democrats call the free market a "seedbed of vice, avarice, and exploitation." Some say that the pursuit of profit is the essence of evil and reduces fellow humans to mechanical means to selfish ends. Others say that the profit motive is the necessary condition for the advancement and well-being of all. People bemoan a "bad" recession economy and laud the "good" economy of a boom period.

Are minimum wage laws and regulations to benefit workers good and right? Or do regulations inhibit our basic freedoms and are therefore wrong? Is competition good or bad? Is it wrong for the government to intervene in private markets, and is it better to let markets naturally regulate themselves? Is it right to tax consumers or is it right to tax firms? Should those who earn more pay more in taxes? Or should only those who use government services pay for them? Do all have basic inalienable human rights to a job, shelter, food, education, and healthcare? Should the government provide stimulus packages in a poor economy? What defines a "good" or a "bad" economy, and why? Do individuals alone know what is best for them, or does someone else with more knowledge and wisdom know what is best for them? Can we trust people to be concerned about others and society, or are people only self-interested? Is economic justice rewarding contributions and punishing harms brought to society? Or is it providing everyone with equal opportunities, or even equal material conditions?

People offer answers to these questions with conviction and certitude. We may even have our own answers, firmly believing that our answers are right. All of these questions, and more, arise at the intersection of ethics and economics. Quick and easy answers can mask numerous and complex factors. Informed consideration of ethics in economics requires knowledge of two disciplines:

economics as a social science and ethics as a subset of philosophy. Each is a discipline in itself, and addressing questions that arise at their intersection involves both specialized disciplines.

It is not uncommon for popular discussions of ethics and economics to lack consideration of even the rudiments of basic economic theory, for instance, as taught in both introductory college-level microeconomics and macroeconomics courses. Economists are often frustrated when they see non-economists, even highly educated specialists in their own fields, make hasty ethical judgments about economics without evidencing an understanding of the basic agreed-upon principles in the science of economics.

Likewise, philosophers and ethicists are often frustrated when they see non-specialists make ethical pronouncements in economics and other areas without considering the many complex questions of philosophical ethics. Discussions of ethics and economics in the media, by politicians, among religious groups, and on the popular level frequently evidence a lack of even a basic knowledge of the disciplines of philosophy and ethics.

The questions above are a mere sampling of the many questions we can ask about ethics and economics. It is not the purpose of this book to definitively answer these questions. Rather, the purposes of this book are to elucidate the many and complex factors necessary for a serious consideration of ethics and economics, and to demonstrate why people arrive at divergent answers to these questions.

Doing this in one volume necessitates treating the disciplines of economics and ethics at the most basic levels, even including some propaedeutic to both. The breadth and scope of this book in outlining the fundamentals of philosophical ethics and of economics restricts the depth at which any one question or set of questions can be addressed. The hope is that this survey of the host of issues involved will lead others to delve more deeply into specific questions.

The purpose and scope of this book also limits the number of economic and ethical examples included for illustration purposes. For example, in covering consequentialist ethical theories, the authors use the frequent and fairly standard example of utilitarianism. There are numerous versions of non-utilitarian consequentialist ethics, but they cannot include them due to space limitations. Likewise, the authors cannot include all economic theory. For instance, there are many macroeconomic models. However, space and time dictate the examination of only a few while glossing over the breadth of research in macroeconomics.

In addition, this book does not advocate a normative ethical system or normative economic approach to policy. The goal is to provide the basic tools from both disciplines required to begin to think about ethical issues in economics. Our hope is that after reading this book one will be aware of the basic theory and data of positive economics, and the numerous questions and their different possible answers in ethics. These are necessary for understanding why different, even mutually exclusive, answers to questions in ethics and economics are given.

In summary, the specific goals of this book include: (1) educating philosophers and all other non-economists about the basic principles of economics; (2) educating economists and all non-philosophers about philosophical ethics; and (3) showing how the two disciplines begin to interact at a variety of points. The authors do not intend the book to be so technical that it is accessible to only experts in the fields. Rather, it is for non-experts in either or both fields. It is written at the advanced college level so that undergraduates and educated laypersons can read and understand it. The authors try to explain concepts in ways that are easy for the layperson to understand, but, at the same time, strive to be rigorous enough to be used in university-level classes.

There are many books on ethics and economics available, so why write another one? First, a number of the books already available are written by specialists, in *either* economics *or* philosophy, who are not formally trained in both disciplines. Consequently, they often cover one discipline very well but not the other discipline. Professional economists, for example, might fault the monographs on issues in ethics and economics, written by academic philosophers, for lacking robust economic theory.[1]

In contrast to such works, this book is co-authored by specialists in each discipline. It is the fruit of interdisciplinary dialogue that embodies the learning process for each specialist. This has been in many ways analogous to the process of discovering a new world as each specialist learned the parlance, theory, method and content of the other discipline. The book preserves much of that spirit of discovery, and as a result, will help economists and ethicists understand each other better.

Second, a number of works on ethics and economics that are written by specialists in both disciplines tend to focus on a limited set of specific questions or issues. They do not provide a systematic overview of each discipline and discussions of how ethics and economics interact at multiple junctures. For instance, Allen Buchanan's, *Ethics, Efficiency, and the Market*,[2] focuses on assessing the arguments for and against markets as the best way to allocate goods and services. *Economics and Ethics: An Introduction*, by Amitava Krishna Dutt and Charles K. Wilber,[3] has the primary goal of showing how ethics is relevant to the discipline of economics, but not vice versa, and not with an explication of economic theory as agreed upon by positive economists. In, *On Ethics and Economics*, Amartya Sen[4] in three somewhat disconnected sections: (1) questions the thesis that agents in markets should be taken as inherently self-centered; (2) analyzes utilitarianism as a normative ethical theory applicable to economics; and (3) discusses the scope and possibilities of social choice theory for aggregating and measuring welfare. Daniel M. Hausman and Michael S. McPherson's extremely important work, *Economic Analysis, Moral Philosophy and Public Policy*,[5] treats in great depth and technical detail the topics it addresses, with a few good test cases and examples. However, while discussing topics in microeconomics like welfare, efficiency, utility, and rational choice theory, it does not comprehensively cover other fundamentals of microeconomic theory, like supply and demand, and it includes little to no discussion of macroeconomics. The ethical portions are limited primarily to utilitarianism and social ethical questions of freedom, equality, and justice. In contrast, this book covers a breadth of topics in microeconomics, macroeconomics, and philosophical ethics in systematic ways, examining the many ways that economics and ethics intersect, and demonstrates how different answers to questions in moral philosophy yield different answers to ethical questions in economics.

Third, many books on ethics and economics advocate a particular economic policy. Their goal is to argue why one position is correct and alternative positions are incorrect. Some invent a new theory or construct and advance a new thesis. As noted, this book strives to be position-neutral instead, explaining the different possible positions and the reasons for them on a litany of ethical and economic questions. It embarks on a full investigation of many aspects of both economics and philosophical ethics, and examines how they interact at numerous points. Not arguing for definitively right and wrong ethical decisions or normative economic policies, this book instead aims to introduce the hard and fast facts of the science of economics, and the complexities of philosophical ethics. It strives to show that one's answers to a host of questions in ethics determine whether one judges a particular economic action or policy right or wrong, good or bad, and why. A primary goal of this book is to help readers learn more about economics and philosophical ethics, and to develop an informed appreciation of the complexities involved in making and morally assessing economic policy decisions.

The authors also hope that this book will be a helpful supplement to undergraduate and graduate business ethics courses. Business ethics textbooks typically provide brief summaries of major normative ethical theories, like utilitarianism, virtue ethics, Kantian ethics, and the ethics of care. However, due to the amount of material they cover, their discussions of these ethical theories are necessarily brief in contrast to the more comprehensive treatments in this book. Business ethics textbooks also typically cover a wide variety of issues in business and ethics, such as ethics in advertising, workers' rights, affirmative action, whistle-blowing, CEO compensation, sweatshop labor, child labor, the purpose of a business (shareholder vs. stakeholder), and more. Very few include separate discussions of ethics and economics, and if they do, they only address a few isolated questions at the intersection of ethics and economics. For example, *Taking Sides: Clashing Views in Business Ethics and Society*, edited by Lisa H. Newton, Elaine E. Englehardt, and Michael S. Pritchard[6] takes a situational and case-study approach. In addition to numerous non-economic questions in business and ethics, it addresses: "Can Capitalism Lead to Human Happiness?" "Is Increasing Profits the Only Social Responsibility of Business?" "Should Price Gouging Be Regulated?" "Does the Enron Collapse Show That We Need More Regulation of the Energy Industry?" and "Do Environmental Restrictions Violate Basic Economic Freedoms?" with two different essays arguing for a "yes" and "no" answer in each case. Richard T. DeGeorge's *Business Ethics*,[7] is one of the few business ethics textbooks with a separate section on ethics and economics. It is limited, however, to comparing and contrasting free-market capitalism and centralized planning systems, like socialism and communism, examining the pros and cons of each. By contrast, this book is dedicated to ethics and economics specifically and entirely. Through presenting and analyzing in detail the manner in which different answers to the numerous questions in ethics dictate different moral judgments in economics, this book is a comprehensive treatment of ethics and economics, and is an example of applied ethics to a specific area of business and social science.

In view of the goals, scope, and limitations of this book, the authors proceed by introducing and situating the disciplines of economics and ethics in the first chapter. In the second chapter, they cover different theories of normative ethics, microeconomics. Here they show the manners in which each discipline speaks to the other, showing how varying answers to ethical questions produce different judgments in microeconomic issues. The third chapter introduces and surveys social and political philosophy, introduces social ethics, and includes discussion of macroeconomic theory. The fourth chapter begins with a more thorough consideration of social ethics and social values, going on to examine their applications to specific macroeconomic issues. Again the authors here demonstrate how different answers to questions in social and political philosophy and social ethics yield different ethical judgments in macroeconomics. Building on previous chapters, the fifth chapter examines the pros and cons of free-market systems like capitalism on the one hand, and centralized planning systems, like socialism and communism, on the other. Again, the authors show how different answers to philosophical and ethical questions yield different judgments in such a comparison. It is the authors' hope that this book will give readers an appreciation and understanding of both disciplines, and to equip them to *begin* the formidable endeavor of considering economics and ethics together.

NOTES

1. See, for instance, Elizabeth Anderson, *Value in Ethics and Economics* (Cambridge, MA: Harvard University Press, 1993); John O'Neill, *The Market: Ethics, Knowledge, and Politics* (New York, NY: Routledge, 1998); and Debra Satz, *Why Some Things Should Not Be for Sale: The Moral Limits of Markets* (London: Oxford University Press, 2010).
2. Allen Buchanan, *Ethics, Efficiency, and the Market* (Totowa, NJ: Rowman & Allanheld, 1985).
3. Amitava Krishna Dutt and Charles K. Wilber, *Economics and Ethics: An Introduction* (New York, NY: Palgrave Macmillan, 2010).
4. Amartya Sen, *On Ethics and Economics* (New York, NY: Blackwell, 1987).
5. Daniel M. Hausman and Michael S. McPherson, *Economic Analysis, Moral Philosophy, and Public Policy*. 2nd ed. (New York, NY: Cambridge University Press, 2006).
6. Lisa H. Newton, Elaine E. Englehardt, and Michael S. Pritchard, *Taking Sides: Clashing Views in Business Ethics and Society*, 12th ed. (New York, NY: McGraw-Hill, 2012).
7. Richard T. DeGeorge, *Business Ethics*, 7th ed. (Alexandria, VA: Prentice Hall, 2010).

CHAPTER 1:
ECONOMICS & ETHICS—THE BASICS

"Economics must not be relegated to classrooms and statistical offices and must not be left to esoteric circles. It is the philosophy of human life and action and concerns everybody and everything. It is the pith of civilization and of man's human existence." – Ludwig Von Mises[1]

INTRODUCTION TO THE DISCIPLINES OF ECONOMICS AND ETHICS

Since the dawn of man there have been economic systems. Like every science, economics has developed through a process of formulating and testing hypotheses to discover the underlying behavior of economic systems, how and why they work. There is a popular misconception that economists have no valid theories or that economists merely "guess" at solutions to economic problems. This is not so. Economic theory is derived through observation, as are theories in other sciences. College and universities commonly and universally teach this theory. They do so not to legitimize a "pseudoscience," or worse, to indoctrinate an agenda-driven ideology. They do so because this theory best matches the data and makes the best predictions about occurrences in the real world, even with its limitations. Does economics as a discipline have more to discover? Absolutely! Every science does. Economists are just as fallible as any other scientists, but not more so. Through discovery and testing economic theory has developed to show how economic systems function, and their understanding has improved with time. Economic theory allows us to determine what causes and effects are at work in an economic system, and like the technological appropriation of all scientific knowledge, to understand what effects (consequences) will issue from what causes (policy decisions). The modern economic theory taught today is a culmination of theory, development and hypothesis testing dating back hundreds of years. Economics is a social *science.*[2]

This being said, some opponents of modern economic theory criticize it by claiming that economic assumptions are too simplistic and abstract, ostensibly disconnected from the real world. Those opposed to modern economic theory do not challenge the data upon which it is founded, because this is objective and indisputable. Those opposed to modern economic theory challenge its theoretical assumptions, such as those about the rationality, knowledge, and value-seeking of agents in markets, and the assumed values behind the mathematical calculations of efficiency and utility.[3] Like any science, economics must assume and proceed on answers to certain questions that cannot be answered empirically. In this book we call these "limit questions." We indicate the assumed answers economists give to many of these limit questions, explain why they give them, and provide other possible answers to these questions.

That these assumptions can be called into question does not invalidate the objectively verifiable data upon which economic theory is grounded. Human trade always follows the laws of supply and demand, and economic theory can accurately predict the outcomes of actions because of laws like these, regardless of what market agents know, how rational they are, what their motivations are, and how we interpret positive economic efficiency. These attempts to discredit economic theory by criticizing its assumptions sometimes seem like the ways in which religious fundamentalists criticize astronomy, geology, and biology in order to discredit their findings about the age of the earth and human origins. They sometimes do not shrink from imputing bad motives to scientists. They do so because the scientific data challenge what they want to say about these things.

Minority and fringe critics of economic theory seek to undermine modern economics because its findings do not comport with what they want to say about how humans naturally allocate resources through trade. They likewise even sometimes question the motives of economists. Despite its admitted limitations, modern economic theory has a record of remarkable predictive success. This shows that it corresponds to the real world in some way, even though imperfectly. Similarly, some can and do question certain axioms in mathematics on the theoretical level. Yet, despite their weaknesses, the mathematical formulas based on these axioms can and do get rockets to the moon. They pragmatically work and thus do correspond to the real world in some way.

Critics of modern economic theory have yet to proffer an alternative with better explanatory and predictive power. Economists today rely upon— especially at the microeconomic level—*neoclassical economic theory*. This is not because it is flawless, but because it is at present the most mathematically pliable way to model economic systems, best explains the data, and has the most predictive success. Critics of neoclassical economics do not offer a viable alternative that can evoke a consensus among objective observers of economic systems in the social scientific community. Most critics do not even offer an alternative theory, but merely question certain assumptions of neoclassical economics in an attempt to discredit it wholesale. In considering economics, this book takes the generally agreed-upon theory of the current state of the discipline. There simply is no other agree-upon reference point for economics among the few and disparate alternative theories, each claiming few adherents and lacking empirical verification.

Critics also sometimes conflate positive economics and normative economics, according to the current distinction in the discipline. *Positive economics* deals with simply the facts, laws, causes and effects regarding how humans trade and allocate resources in social contexts. It is *descriptive*. *Normative economics* deals with values in terms of what *should* be the case (in distinction from what merely *is* the case), is *prescriptive*, and thus enters the realm of ethics. Confounding positive and normative economics is analogous to conflating biology and bioethics, for example. Some justify doing so by claiming that all human action is value-laden and hence subject to moral assessment. Whether or not this is the case, however, is itself a question in moral philosophy and thus beyond the strictly empirical and descriptive task of positive economics. More about these important distinctions will follow in this and later chapters.

Critics also fail to recognize that, as do all scientists, economists must simplify with models because the real world is simply too complex to comprehend. All sciences, including the hard "physical" sciences, of necessity use models. All scientific models have inherent limitations, and they are constantly being updated.

At the beginning of the twentieth century, scientists modeled the atom as having a nucleus like a piece of fruit, with springs sticking out and electrons at their ends. The springs would shake with energy fluxes. After Bohr's Nobel Prize-winning work on the hydrogen spectrum, scientists embraced his working of model for the atom. This model viewed atoms as tiny solar systems with the nucleus as the center and electrons as planets orbiting the nucleus. Scientists have since abandoned Bohr's model (still popularly embraced), due to developments in quantum mechanics since Bohr. Scientists know and admit the limitations of all such models.

Questions about the relationships of such models to reality are philosophical limit questions of the type to be discussed shortly. For instance, there is the *realist* vs. *anti-realist* debate in the contemporary philosophy of science.[4] No one discredits physics on account of it changing models for atoms. All sciences use models, however, they still explain and predict. Similarly, economists use models with their inherent limitations. However, this does not derogate from the explanatory and predictive power of economic models.

Like all scientists, economists continually add complexity to economic models as their understanding of market phenomena and behavior increases. There is also a difference between *economic models* and *economic theory*. Economic theory involves agreed-upon principles of behavior. For example, all economists agree upon the law of demand. This is one of the foundations of economic theory, stating that there is an inverse relationship between the price of a good and the quantity of the good demanded, as will be explained in more detail later. Conversely, an economic model links the economic theory to how observable phenomena behave, which usually involves formulating a mathematical relationship based on the economic theory.

One of the fathers of modern economics, Adam Smith, claimed that economic systems exist because humans are unique among animals. The human being is *homo economicus*, and economic systems evolve along with us. A key difference between humans and most other animals is that humans are able to divide tasks to make labor more efficient. Since this characteristic predates governments of any real sophistication, it has been argued that economic systems will always exist but governments may not. As Smith put it:

> This division of labour, from which so many advantages are derived, is not originally the effect of any human wisdom, which foresees and intends that general opulence to which it gives occasion. (I.e., it is not the effect of any conscious regulation by the state or society, like the "law of Sesostris" that every man should follow the employment of his father.) It is the necessary, though very slow and gradual consequence of a certain propensity in human nature which has in view no such extensive utility; the propensity to truck, barter, and exchange one thing for another.[5]

Economists study this complex, systematic, behavior in order to understand how it works, and to determine the effects that human beings have on the system via their behavior as individuals and as groups. To that end, economists use the scientific method of formulating hypotheses and testing them to validate economic theory. Again, this is positive economics, more commonly referred to as "what is" (description).

Another aspect of economics involves asking what, if anything, should be done by way of human actions, either as individuals or groups, to produce various outcomes. This is the question of whether certain causes should be applied to generate specific effects, and is where the discipline of ethics begins to intersect economics. Again, this is normative economics, or what we think ought to be (prescription). This is similar to questions about what technologies should be applied, in other sciences, such as whether we should clone other human beings based on our knowledge of causes and effects in biology. The distinction between positive and normative economics is standard in the discipline. It is similar to the distinction between empirical sciences on the one hand, and applied ethics that applies philosophical questions about values to those sciences on the other. An important question regards whether it is possible to move from what is (positive) to what we believe ought to be (normative) in economic systems. This question is discussed in more in detail later.

Questions of what should or should not be done are questions of values, and necessarily involve ethical considerations. They are questions concerning: right and wrong; why humans are concerned with right and wrong; what constitutes right and wrong; how we know right from wrong; why we should do right and avoid wrong, and many others. For as long as we have records, human beings have evidenced a concern with these types of questions. The human being is not only *homo economicus* but also *homo moralis*. It is rare to meet a consistently amoral person who has no value system and acts as if there are no values. In fact, the goal-oriented nature of human activity seems to presuppose values like good and bad, and value judgments like better and worse, right and wrong.

Because humans are social beings, values emerge not only on the individual level but also on the level of groups or social units. These can be as small as children on a playground, families, teams and small businesses, to as large as political entities and groups of people characterized by a particular gender ethnicity, geographical location, or religious affiliation. In addition, if it is true that humans are characteristically economic beings (by dividing tasks to make labor more efficient, always bartering on their strengths), then both values and economics are operative in all human social interaction. Both goal-oriented activity that targets values and economic activity are ubiquitous parts of human experience. This is true on both the individual and social levels.

Ethics and economics are popular topics for many people today. Some are religious and so have strong beliefs about what is right and wrong. Others are quick to offer their opinions about whether a specific activity or behavior is right or wrong. People often debate larger scale issues of social and political ethics that are covered in the media, including those dealing with economic policies and their societal impact.

For example, many economic policies are arrived at socially, like the imposition of a tax derived through governmental representation in voting. This mechanism can easily involve the scenario of a minority group of people imposing their will on the majority of people in a population. Imposition of the minority's preference can easily arise if the total population is larger than the number of individuals who actually vote. We can ask if the imposition of minority will on the majority through representational voting in a democracy—and many unreflectively value representational voting—is right or wrong, should or should not be.

Similar questions about voting can be raised solely on the individual level, too. Assuming the distribution of voters represents the total population exactly, there is still a problem that voting may not capture the intensity of an individual's preferences. A vote of "yes" or "no" for a specific policy excludes the possibility of an undecided individual, or an individual who dislikes either option, to express their preference. This is what economists call Arrow's Impossibility Theorem.[6] Arrow's Impossibility Theorem identifies the problem of ranking individual preferences amidst the potential problem that majority group decisions may not represent the true preferences of individuals in a population. This is why in many cases a minority opinion imposes its will on a majority. Thus, economic and ethical issues are intimately intertwined at both the individual and the social levels.

THE PROBLEM OF SCARCITY

As we consider the rudiments of economics, it is important to grasp what is arguably the most important concept in economics: scarcity. We live in a material world with finite resources. Economics studies how to efficiently allocate scarce resources. In so doing, economics can guide us to what is efficient and what is not. It can also help distinguish between questions of "what is," or how we allocate our scarce resources, (positive) and what "should be," or how we should allocate our scarce resources (normative). Since all resources are scarce, individuals and societies cannot get away from the problem of allocating our resources.

Positive economics studies the systematic mechanisms by which humans have allocated, and do allocate, scarce resources. In normative economics, where ethics comes into play, the questions become: Who gets scarce resources? How much do they get? How should scarce resources be used? These are ethical questions because they deal with values and goal-oriented activity, as we shall see later as we discuss the nature of ethics. Persons who are not economists and not ethicists frequently engage in heated debate precisely at this juncture of economics and ethics. Yet, the fact remains that there are a finite, limited, scarce amount of resources. Normatively, all economists aim to allocate scarce resources as efficiently as possible. They believe that we *should* allocate scarce resources efficiently. Chapter two includes economic models depicting efficiency.

SCARCITY AND TRADE-OFFS

The scientific nature of positive economics means that there are certain facts and laws about economic systems, including the reality of scarcity, which cannot be wished away or violated. This means that from a normative, value-oriented perspective there are certain things that simply cannot be done. That is, in some cases it might not be possible to get an economic system to conform to certain values, just as it is impossible to travel backwards in time or send a message faster than the speed of light.

The fact of scarcity also necessitates what economists call "trade-offs." Certain values, such as spending spare time either watching a movie in a theatre or attending and watching a live basketball game, are mutually exclusive. You cannot do both at exactly the same time. You choose which activity you will do and when you will do it according to the pros and cons of each, or the trade-offs. Economists also study the different pros and cons, benefits and costs, of various courses of action in markets. Any economic goal or policy has clear trade-offs with other options, and cognizance of the trade-offs is necessary for making informed value judgments about which course to choose. No matter how one feels about how scarce goods and services should be distributed, the laws of economics—like scarcity and mutual exclusivity—cannot be violated.

THE CHALLENGES AND PERILS OF NAÏVETÈ IN ECONOMICS AND ETHICS

A common popular normative economic question in the media and among politicians and non-specialist citizens is whether we should let free markets, no matter how competitive or not, allocate scarce resources, or whether a government should control the allocation of goods and services. Both options incur economic trade-offs as will be discussed later. Many who advocate economic choices emphasize certain values but do not clearly understand the trade-offs involved, such as the consequences. A goal of this book is to inform in this regard. In addition, even economists can disagree about complex economic issues because the systems and behavior involved are very complicated. While economic theory may not be able to always accurately quantify all causes and effects, they guide us in understanding the consequences of the choices we make.

Yet, economist Friedrich Hayek has spoken of the "fatal conceit" considering how positive economics has grown and continues to grow in understanding economic systems. Economic systems are highly complex natural systems that antedate our scientific study of them and our attempts to manipulate them. The fatal conceit is that in our limited understanding of economic systems we can manipulate causes to infallibly attain the positive effects we want and avoid the negative consequences. This is related to the question of technology in any science. Until relatively recently in human history, the practice of medicine, predicated on the biological knowledge of the day, was riddled with fatal mistakes, such as bloodletting and poisoning. Even something as simple as building a dam on a river to make a reservoir can result in the dam breaking, because of unknowns that were not factored in. In such a case we do not blame nature or the river, but rather the engineers. The same is true, perhaps more so, given the complexity in engineering economic systems. When economic engineering fails, should we blame the elaborate workings of natural human economic activities or the engineers?

Nonetheless, because human beings always act with goals informed by values, the question of economic engineering in normative ethics is real. Many people act on their values but do not seriously reflect upon them on the level that philosophical ethics does. Philosophical ethics can seem, as we shall see, almost as complicated as natural economic systems. Further, there is even a tradeoff in deciding to implement a normative economic policy based on some value or values, despite potential ignorance of the consequences from the standpoint of positive economics.

Next begins the discussion of ethics by situating ethics as an academic discipline in the broader context of academic philosophy in general. Ethics is also within the purview of religious claims handled by the beliefs, norms and practices of different religious traditions. This section surveys the types of questions that philosophy, and in many cases religion, deal with, the reasons for them and their importance, all with a view to situating ethics as a discipline. This will also frame how individuals' arrive at their beliefs and why others may disagree.

SITUATING ETHICS: PHILOSOPHY AND LIMIT QUESTIONS

Philosophy, in addition to the doctrinal aspects of religious traditions, deals with "limit questions." These are valid questions that cannot be answered using the methods of other areas of inquiry such as the physical, life and social sciences, the arts and the humanities. They are "limit questions" because they arise at the extremes or boundaries (limits) of other disciplines. Those working in other disciplines assume answers to these questions and act upon these answers without justifying or proving them. The questions that philosophy and religion address are broad, universal, and all-encompassing, compared to the restricted areas or subsets of human experience that other areas of inquiry address. What are some specific examples?

Limit Questions about Being

All disciplines study a subset of things or "beings" in human experience. Chemists study atoms. Biologists study the beings exhibiting organic life, usually specializing in a subset of life forms (fish, pine trees, bacteria, marine mammals, eagles, etc.). Geologists study the beings of which the earth is composed, while astronomers study the beings in space. Mathematicians study the beings we call numbers and historians study the beings of past persons, places, and institutions. Linguists study the beings called languages, some specializing in one language or a group of languages. Sociologists study human societies, anthropologists study the behaviors (also things or beings) of humans, and psychologists study the being we call the human mind. Economists study the types of beings involved in human exchange in an effort to understand the allocation of scarce resources (the beings called markets are one of them). All of these disciplines have sub-disciplines in which specialists study subsets like: organic chemistry, nuclear physics, electromagnetic waves, noble gases, dwarf stars, volcanic rocks, sea anemones, trigonometry, Hellenistic Greek, modern Spanish, the Elizabethan history, international corporations or the markets for precious metals.

Yet, all of the disparate things studied in various disciplines, have one thing in common: they are things, entities or "beings." We may say they all share "being in general." Any conceivable thing that we can be curious about, ask questions about, or examine and study, is a being. It is a being as opposed to a nonthing or nonbeing. All beings have certain traits. They exist, in some sense, as opposed to not existing. There are conditions for the appearance of beings and for their disappearance from the realm of things that exist. All beings endure, to some extent, across time but change. They fall into categories in which the different disciplines specialize. While we can ask questions about particular types of beings, we can also ask questions about being in general. These questions may or may not have ever occurred to us, and they may or may not interest us. There are those who are interested in these questions, however, and they are real questions that can be asked.

There is a litany of questions we can ask about being in general. Why are there beings that exist? Why is there something rather than nothing? That is, why is there "stuff" or "things" at all instead of nothing? What does it mean to "exist" or to "be?" What makes something "real?" Is it physical existence perceptible to our five senses? Are ideas like the number two and circularity, or internal mental experiences like joy or anxiety real, even though they are not physically perceptible?

These questions are broad, universal and all-encompassing because they apply to all beings whatsoever, and are not limited to one being or group of beings. They are limit questions because a historian typically does not ask if Hannibal existed or was real. A mathematician typically does not ask if the number two exists or is real. A chemist typically does not ask if the element sodium exists and is real. A Flemish scholar typically does not ask if Flemish exists and is real, and an economist does not ask if the market that she is studying exists and is real. Moreover, an economist does not ask if supply, demand, utility, or systems of individuals engaged in trade exist or are real. Adam Smith assumed that the "invisible hand" guiding the free market exists and is real. Studying any particular being or subset of beings presupposes their existence and reality, and that such a belief is justified. When we begin to ask if a being exists or is real and how we know this, we are entering another level of inquiry with methods and procedures quite different from those employed in the many various disciplines that study specific subsets or types of beings.

Another set of questions about being in general regards the continuity of beings across time. Not only do we constantly assume that beings exist, but also that they are the same beings at any given time despite the many changes they undergo. But what gives a being self-identity across time despite all of the changes it experiences? Why do we assume that the baby picture of a now full-grown forty year old woman depicts the same being now that existed the day she was born? She has undergone many physical and mental changes in the past forty years, and biology tells us that all of the cells in her body have been replaced every seven years. So, why is she the same being today that she was forty years ago?

At what point did this human being begin to exist? When she was conceived, prior to the conception, at some point in her mother's pregnancy, or the moment she was born? When does a being cease to exist? If and when, God forbid, she is brain dead and on life support from an accident? Does a person cease to exist and new one appear when his legs are amputated legs and he has a heart transplant? Similarly we could ask when your car came to exist. When the engine was installed? When the tires were added? When it left the factory? When does your car cease to exist as the same car? When there are a few miles on the odometer? When it begins to rust? When the tires are changed? When it is repainted? When the engine is replaced after years of wear and tear? From an economic perspective, when do markets start? If they constantly change over time, then are they the same market? When does a market appear and when does it cease to exist?

These questions about what makes a being the same across time despite perpetual change (when a being begins to exist, and when a being ceases to exist) are broad, universal and all-encompassing because they apply not to just one being or group of beings, but to all beings whatsoever. They are also questions arising at the limits of all other areas of human questioning. A biologist studying elephants typically does not ask whether the full-grown elephant she is studying is the same being it was on the day of its birth. She just assumes that it is, despite any changes it has experienced. She assumes answers to these questions and acts on them without reflecting on those questions and how to answer them. When we begin to ask what are the criteria or conditions for identifying a being as the same across time despite changes, we are entering a different level of questioning with different methods and procedures than all other areas of human inquiry involving a specific being or specific groups of beings.

Another group of questions we can ask about beings in general involves classification. Every being has similarities with every other being, at the very least the fact that it exists or is real. Yet, every being is different from every other being, including other beings of the same type. No two dogs are the same, and in fact no two dogs of the same species, even a litter of puppies, are the same. They are made of different "stuff" (matter-energy). They are different sizes, shapes, have different numbers of cells and hairs on their body, are in different locations, and have different personalities. Thus we can ask why two beings are dogs and not cats, why two German shepherds are German shepherds and not poodles, and why the German shepherd, Otto, is different from his brother, Wilhelm. Why do beings fall into groupings like living as opposed to non-living, plant as opposed to animal, trees as opposed to flowers, deciduous as opposed to evergreen, and maple as opposed to oak? Are these groupings natural or merely creations of the human mind trying to organize a chaotic world of experience? Are there certain traits that make two beings the same type? Why or why not? What are they?

In economic discussions two common terms are middle and upper class. Where does the middle class begin and end? Where does the upper class begin? What makes these two groups different and how do we define them? So far we have mentioned the term "market," but what is it? Why do we generalize? Why are what we call the market for automotive gasoline and the market for jet fuel both "markets?" While we will get to the definition of markets in economics later, these are important limit questions to ask.

Again, those in other disciplines assume answers to these questions but do not usually reflect in detail on how they arrived at these answers. A nuclear physicist does not usually ask how he knows electrons are electrons and not positrons. He just assumes they are and acts on this assumption. And again, the universal, general, all-encompassing nature of these limit questions about classifying beings is seen in how they are not questions about just one particular thing or group of things, like *this* electron or *these* dogs. Rather, questions about how and why we classify beings into types and sub-types apply to all beings and groups of beings whatsoever.

Another set of questions we can ask about beings in general involves what *causes* bring about beings. Are the causes of things purely physical matter and energy working in a linear series of cause and effect? Are ideas necessary for a specific type of being to come into existence, such as the ideas we use to classify different types of beings? Can we explain how an oyster came to be purely in terms of prior physical things that are also explicable in by prior material causes? Or, do we need mental concepts that classify the types of material that compose an oyster? Can we explain the shell of an oyster without reference to the idea of a shell? Can we explain the material constituting its shell without reference to the conceptual grouping of the element calcium in distinction from the groupings of the other elements? Are other beings that already actually exist necessary to make a new being?

We can also ask whether or not beings always have a necessary purpose or goal for their existence. For example, many organisms have hearts that pump their vital fluid. Can we explain the appearance of a new heart in a new animal with or without reference to the purpose of a heart, namely to pump vital fluid? Do markets have a purpose? To an economist a market is the institution or arrangement in which buyers and sellers come together to trade. Trade itself only takes place if both parties involved gain some benefit from the transaction. So we can ask if a market presupposes actual individuals already existing, and if the mutual benefit of parties engaged in trade is necessary for the existence of a real market as its purpose.

Questions about the causes of beings, whether they are material or conceptual, involve other actual beings, and purposes, are similarly universal, broad and all-encompassing. This is because questions about the types of causes necessary for the appearance of any new being can be asked not only of one specific being (e.g., *this* planet) or group of beings (*trees* in general), but about any and all beings whatsoever. While those studying any one being or subset of beings might ask questions their antecedent causes, a detailed analysis of the number of and types of causes is typically lacking.

Again, many people have never considered these types of questions about being in general. Maybe they do not find these questions interesting, just like they do not find information about the Cyrillic alphabet interesting. Nevertheless, these are valid questions and there always have been, are, and always will, be people interested in these types of questions. As we shall shortly see, questions about being in general, and our answers to these questions, are intimately bound up with our answers to other types of limit questions.

The study of being in general, which raises and tries to address these types of questions, is called *ontology*. *Ontos* means "being" and *logos* means "word" in Greek. Thus ontology literally means "words about being," and more generally means the study of being. Traditionally, in western philosophy going back to the ancient Greeks, ontology has been called *metaphysics*. Aristotle coined this term, meaning "beyond" (*meta*) nature or the physical (*physika*). In the modern period of western history—the last five or so centuries—metaphysics has also come to connote other questions, specifically about *human* beings. To these we now turn.

Limit Questions about Human Beings

Because we are *human* beings and we are concerned with ourselves, we ask ourselves limit questions about human beings. Human beings have many features that other beings do not have and which we typically use in our classification of human beings as *human*. Limit questions arise about these aspects of human beings, too. What are we, exactly? Why are we so similar yet so different from everything else in our world? Are we merely complex animals composed of highly organized matter and energy, or is there part of us that is mental or spiritual, like a soul or immaterial mind? Do we survive in any way after death? Why are we here? Where are we going? Do human existence in general and my life in particular have any purpose? Is there something wrong with human beings? If there is, then what is the solution?

Humans are very much part of the natural world on the one hand, but very different from the natural world on the other. We share many traits with other animals. Yet, we also have memory, dreams, longings, hopes, despair, think at a level of rationality much higher than animals, and are able to transcend and manipulate the natural world in ways that other animals cannot. While economists today do not typically contemplate limit questions about humanity, the founding fathers of modern economics, who were also frequently philosophers, did. Smith explicitly noted the differences of humans from other animals, including economic activity:

> By nature a philosopher is not in genius and disposition half so different from a street porter, as a mastiff is from a greyhound. . . . Those different tribes of animals, however, though all the same species, are of scarce use to one another. Among men, on the contrary, the most dissimilar geniuses are of use to one another; the different products of their respective talents . . . are being brought into common stock, where every man may purchase whatever part of the produce of other men's talents as he has occasion for.[7]

One set of limit questions about humans regards what, precisely, humans are made of. Are we only complex configurations of matter and energy so that all of our unique features can be explained by reducing them to their material elements? Or, is there part of us that is immaterial and that explains our unique features, like a mind, soul or spirit? Our high intellectual capacity has led many philosophical and religious traditions to identify reason as what makes humans unique, perhaps even divine in some sense. We will see that economics as a discipline assumes that people in markets engaging in transactions are "rational." We must ask what this means, however, and whether perhaps in some ways they are irrational. The answers to these questions have implications both for the science of economics and ethics in economics.

One scientist studying humans may assume they are only matter and energy, while another assumes they have an immaterial mind or soul. Neither on a regular basis asks how they know this. Neither could they use the methods and procedures of their own discipline to answer these questions, which makes them limit questions.

Because we are involved in the physical world we are subject to chains of physical causes and effects. Yet, again, we seem to rise above the physical world in important ways. We constantly act and make choices. Are our choice fully determined by physical and / or mental events in a chain of causes and effects, so that our choices are ultimately determined despite any feeling of freedom we may have? Or is there something unique about us that frees our choices from the iron chains of causes and effects we see everywhere else in nature? Do we have "free will?" If so, then what makes it free?

The question of free will has enormous consequences for ethics and economics. If all of our choices are determined by prior causes then can we really be held morally responsible for them? Most people regularly assume their actions are free in some sense and that therefore they are responsible for their actions. When we praise or blame a person for a particular action we assume this without proving it. Others, probably a small minority, assume human choices are determined by prior causes. They may claim that we are therefore not responsible for our actions or, perhaps inconsistently, assume that we are responsible without justifying this belief.

The question of free will or determinism arises in political and economic systems as well. As a discipline, economics assumes people in markets are "willing and able" to enter into the transactions they make. Does this mean that they somehow are exempt from the pervasive chains of causes and effects in nature, or does this mean something else? Does willing mean a determined choice but still somehow in the control of the individual? Some people have a fatalistic view of economic systems. They believe that our abilities and choices are determined by prior physical, mental, social, and cultural causes, so that we do not have any real choice. In this case, a person's economic situation is ultimately determined unless there is substantive intervention by the government or some other central economic planner. Others believe we have a freedom that transcends the causes and effects of nature so that individuals are masters of their own destinies, including their economic situations.

Reflecting on free will and determinism involves methods different from the methods of all other areas or disciplines of inquiry. This makes it a limit question. Questions about free will, determinism, and personal responsibility are broad, universal and all-encompassing because they apply to all people and economic systems whatsoever, not just one person or group. It is not a question of whether this particular criminal had a bad upbringing that forced him into a life of crime. It is a question of whether the choices of all people everywhere are free or determined, and whether people, as a whole, can be held responsible for their actions or not.

Another limit question we can ask about humans regards the goals and meaning of human existence. We can wonder about why we are here, where we are going, and what happens after death. We wonder if our existence has an overarching purpose or goal. Is our uniqueness in the universe merely an accident, or is it the result of rational and purposeful activity? Most people have answers to these questions and base their actions, even their lives, on these answers. Yet, they usually do not reflect on how and why they have their specific answers to these questions. Reflection on the meaning and purpose of human existence goes beyond other areas of inquiry and requires other methods. It is general, universal and all-encompassing because the answers apply to all human beings, not just one person or group.

Another limit question about human beings regards whether or not there is a problem with which all humans are confronted, and if so, what is the solution? Throughout history we find people vexed with the awareness that there may be something wrong with themselves, and with their pain and suffering. We are apparently the only sentient beings that contemplate death, its meaning and consequences. We rise to pinnacles of hope and depths of despair apparently absent among other animals. While all sentient beings experience pain and suffering and try to avoid it, we reflect on this pain and suffering to a degree seemingly inaccessible to other living things. Why do we suffer? Why do we, and indeed all beings, come into existence and perish? Is this just the way things are, or is there something wrong with this? Economically speaking, is the fact that there are scarce resources for which we compete and with the result that some go without even enough to survive part of a human "problem?"

While pain, suffering and death are everywhere, we also seem responsible for it to a degree that no other beings, living or non-living, are responsible. We are even capable of doing things most consider horrendously evil to our fellow human beings, like torture and extermination (e.g., genocide like the Nazi holocaust). These seem to go far beyond the types of "evils" we might witness in the natural world. We can ask why this is the case. Is there something wrong with the world in general and us in particular? If so, then is it a moral problem, a lack of knowledge, or something else?

Again, many of us have, and operate daily, on answers to these questions without reflecting on how or why we have them. And again, answering these questions requires methods not used in addressing most other questions we normally ask. If there is a problem and solution for humans in general, then they apply to everyone always and everywhere, not just one person or group. These, too, are limit questions.

These limit questions about human beings are typically classified as philosophical or theological anthropology. They clearly differ from questions in other disciplines that study humanity, such as the social sciences of anthropology, sociology, political science and economics. They are real questions, though, that can be and are asked.

Limit Questions about Truth and Knowledge

Other limit questions revolve around truth and knowledge. These questions are intimately related to the other types of limit questions surveyed here. Two very important questions are "What is truth?" and "Why do we value truth over falsehood?" Almost all of us take for granted specific answers to these two questions and continually act on those assumed answers. On closer reflection, though, we can see how the question of what truth is and why we assume it is better than falsehood are real questions with different possible answers. All areas of human inquiry, from the arts, sciences and humanities to everyday questions we ask, assume there is such a thing as truth and that truth is better than error. What exactly do we mean, though, when we speak of truth?

A commonsense intuition is that truth is a property of statements that reflect the way things are. For this reason, many have argued that truth is when a statement or claim corresponds to being. The word "fact" is derived from the Latin verb for being. If it were raining outside right now and I say "It is not raining now" then my statement would not correspond to the way things are. The statement "It is raining outside right now" would match-up with the way things are.

We can question this commonsense view of truth. What if it is only drizzling a few droplets? Is it raining then? We can also ask if statements and concepts can match-up with reality. There is no intrinsic connection between the words "It is raining" and what is or is not happening. The German phrase "*Es regnet jetzt*" uses different sounds and characters to make the same claim about the weather now. Further, the word "raining" is general, not specifying *what* is raining. We assume the speaker means "water from clouds" but the unspecific nature of the word "raining" leaves it open to meaning "raining" cats and dogs, volcanic lava, or something else. Also, there are many statements and concepts that are not as cut and dry as the statement "It is raining outside right now." If I say "that is exciting" or "that is painful," or "that is wrong," or "that movie was a good one," then others can disagree with me. I am expressing my own private, subjective feelings and responses, but the private feelings and responses of others might vary from mine. Because of these considerations we can ask if truth really is "out there" in objective reality or whether it varies between individual people and groups. We can also ask if we are able to construct statements of beliefs that are true or false in any meaningful sense.

In economics, is truth only that which can be quantified, or not? In view of what we said about the limitations of models, are economic theories true? With the amount of complexity involved, can we ever measure such complexity? The question of whether mathematical models can be true because they work but are also abstractions from reality is a pressing question not only for economics but for many disciplines.

In addition to asking what truth means, we can also ask why we value truth over falsity. At times falsehood seems more valuable than truth. What if we lie to save someone's life? Consider a German hiding Jews during World War II and being interrogated by Nazis. Knowing those he is hiding will be killed if he tells the truth, he might lie to deceive the Nazis, saying "I have not seen any Jews." Most would value falsehood over truth in this case. When someone lies to cover a wrong they have done they value falsehood over truth. Lying to one's self in order to feel better, psychologically, values falsity over truth.

Examples of valuing falsity over truth exist in popular economics. Do politicians value dissemination of economic error over truth? Do we ourselves want to believe something that is not true, economically? For example, there is a tradeoff with minimum wage laws. While some workers will receive a higher wage there is always the consequence of putting more people out of work than without the law. The exact number depends on the specific market, but this always happens. Yet this fact is frequently ignored or denied in policy debates. Does our wanting to help individuals or feel good cause us to want to be deceived?

On account of such examples we can legitimately ask why we usually value truth over falsehood. Friedrich Nietzsche, in challenging non-religious scientists of his day, said that they have as much unproven faith as religious persons because they believe without proof that truth is better than falsehood. He asks:

> We see that science also rests on a faith; there simply is no science "without presuppositions." The question is whether *truth* is needed must not only have been affirmed in advance, but affirmed to such a degree that the principle, the faith, the conviction finds expression: "*Nothing* is needed *more* than truth, and in relation to it everything else has only second-rate value. . . . But why not deceive? But why not allow oneself to be deceived?"[8]

Questions about what truth is and why we value it are limit questions. They arise at the limits of all other areas of human questioning and cannot be answered by the methods and procedures of those disciplines. Those asking any specific question assume answers to such limit questions about truth, without proving them. The historian does not wake up and say: "I want to be deceived about the American Revolution today." The mathematician does not say: "I want my equations to be wrong or erroneous." The economist does not say: "I want measurement error in my economic model." When a salesperson asks her colleague if a big potential client accepted her bid on the new project, she assumes that her colleague's answer can be either "true" or "false" and does not want the answer to be "false." These questions are universal, broad and all-encompassing because they apply to every statement or belief about anything whatsoever, and are not limited to one or a group of statements and beliefs.

Other limit questions revolve around knowledge. Practically all people everywhere have assumed that there is such a thing as knowledge, they can know certain things, and knowledge is better than ignorance. Upon closer reflection on what precisely knowledge is, how we obtain it, and why we value it, limit questions arise. These limit questions about knowledge and the answers we give them are intimately bound up with the limit questions and answers about truth.

What knowledge is may seem obvious. A commonsense view is that knowledge is correct beliefs, or beliefs that match up with reality. This view complements the view of truth that sees truth as corresponding to reality. If it is actually raining outside right now and I believe it is raining, then I know that it is raining.

But take this example. Say I want to learn to play the piano. I go to the library and read many books on piano playing. I go to piano recitals and listen to piano music. Do I now know how to play the piano? Probably not, unless I am as precocious as Mozart was. Examples like this lead some to argue that knowledge is the ability to successfully do something. It is not a set of propositions, concepts or beliefs. They further argue that I have gotten knowledge from my misguided piano study, just not the ability to play the piano. I can identify the names of the keys on a keyboard, and recognize a Baroque tune when I hear one. This is being able to successfully *do* something, and so it is a type of knowledge. Sir Francis Bacon forever enshrined the view that knowledge is the ability to *do* something by saying "knowledge itself is a power."[9]

Even if knowledge is having correct beliefs that match-up with reality, there are additional questions. I might have a belief corresponding to reality, but how I obtained that belief and what proof I have for it might determine whether I know or believe or do not know. How do we justify our beliefs, and what makes our beliefs knowledge instead of mere belief or opinion?

Say I am playing a shell game where an entertainer puts a ball under one of three shells, moves them around with dizzying speed, and then asks me which shell it is under. Say I guess shell number three and the ball really is there. Did I really know in that case where the ball was? My guess matched match up with reality, but some would say I did not have knowledge because I had no justification for it. It was just a lucky guess. Had I managed to keep track of which shell the ball was under then perhaps I really did know. Why? I saw it with my own eyes and so had proof.

But consider this: I followed the shells as best as I could and I was convinced I correctly kept my eye on the shell with the ball. I trusted my eyes and my ability to follow the quick hand motions, resulting in a firm conviction that I really did know where the ball was. I said shell number two but was wrong. I thought I had a good justification for my belief but it proved faulty.

Can we ever trust our economic "eyes?" Economists base their knowledge and theories on observation, but the question of justification of knowledge arises for economics as for any other science. The correspondence or lack thereof of theories to what is observed is a pressing question in the philosophy of science.

In economics, there is also the problem of knowing how successful policies are, because of the problem of not having counterfactuals from which to benchmark. If policy Y is implemented we cannot definitively know that policy Y is better than policy X because we cannot roll back time and see what policy X would have done instead. These questions about what types of proof or justification we have for our knowledge are closely related to another set of limit questions about *how* we know things.

Must we be absolutely certain about something in order to know it? Some things we know seem necessary because the opposite is inconceivable. Suppose I tell you about three of my friends. I say the first, Jane, is shorter than the second, Joe. I then say the second, Joe, is shorter than the third, John. If I went on to ask you if John is shorter than Jane, you would say: "No, of course not." You would claim to certainly *know* John is taller than Jane, and you would know this without ever having seen Jane or John. You have absolute certainty based solely on the relationships between the ideas in your mind, without reference to anything you perceive with your senses. It is impossible to hold the following three ideas in your mind at the same time: (1) Jane is shorter than Joe, (2) Joe is shorter than John, and (3) John is shorter than Jane. It is inconceivable. Thus some argue that we only truly know things that we know with absolute certainty, through the relationships between ideas and apart from sense experience.

Others argue that the vast majority of our knowledge is never absolutely certain, but is rather based on probabilities. Do you know that the sun will rise tomorrow? You would probably say yes. Yet, you can conceive of a situation in which the sun does not rise tomorrow. The planet earth could be destroyed by some freak cosmic accident, and we know at some point the sun will actually burn out. This might sound absurd but the possibility must be granted. However, the probability is extremely low, so low that most would argue it is practically non-existent. Considering the high probability that the sun will rise tomorrow, many argue that we know the sun will rise tomorrow, or that extremely high probability constitutes knowledge.

Consider another example. Suppose you are reading this at 11AM on a Wednesday morning in October. Suppose you know an eight year-old girl, Sophia, who is an elementary school student at Pleasant Valley Elementary School. Now, I ask you if you know where Sophia is right now. There is a high probability that she is sitting in a classroom but perhaps she is at recess, a school assembly, or even got sick and went home. Would you say that you know she is in a classroom right now or would you say that you are fairly certain but don't know for sure? The point is that, although the vast majority of things we believe are based on probabilities, our beliefs lie on a spectrum of probability from practically certain to highly probable, to fairly probable to slightly less probable, to slightly more improbable to fairly improbable, to highly improbable to practically impossible. If probability, not certainty, "is the very guide of life,"[10] as Bishop Butler said, then where do we draw the line between probability that is knowledge and probability that does not constitute knowledge? Economics is faced with much uncertainty regarding outcomes, and economists typically act on the belief that high probability of occurrence constitutes knowledge.

So how we obtain knowledge is an important question. Is knowledge worthy of the name only obtained by our five senses so that we must see it to believe it? Sometimes our senses deceive us, as in the shell game example. Our sense experience depends on our perspectives. You see a billboard as long and rectangular while I see it as thin and flat, depending on our perspectives. The grass is bright green if we look at high noon, but it is black if we look at it at midnight. As the ancient Greek philosopher Zeno of Elea pointed out, if you drop a bag of seeds you will hear a thump but if you drop one seed you will not. Does a dropped seed make a noise or not? Hearing must deceive us in one of these instances. In economics the distinction between observable and unobservable data can call into question the accuracy of what is observed, resulting in competing interpretations. Therefore, some question whether or not sense experiences gives us the best type of knowledge, if any knowledge at all.

Another type of knowledge comes from the relationships between ideas, apart from sense experience. This is the case in the example of the relative tallness of Jane, Joe and John. If in addition to telling you Jane is shorter than Joe I tell you Jane is a trial lawyer, you know things about Jane without ever having experienced her with your five senses. For example, you know she went to law school and she is frequently in the courtroom dealing with legal cases.

Another limit question about knowledge is, as with truth, its value. And as with truth, the value of knowledge may seem obvious. Of course it seems that to *know* is better than to be ignorant. Yet we can question this, too. Many thinkers have indicated that knowledge brings negatives as well as positives so that we can legitimately question its value. The author of the biblical book *Ecclesiastes* writes: "For with much wisdom comes much sorrow; the more knowledge, the more grief,"[11] a sentiment frequently echoed in every age and in every place. The popular saying "Ignorance is bliss" encapsulates this sentiment.

Like questions about truth, questions about knowledge are limit questions. Questions about what knowledge is, how we obtain it, and why we value it, arise at the limits of all other areas of human study and demand different methods to answer them. As with other limit questions, most people engaging in other areas of investigation, formal or informal, assume answers to these questions without rigorously examining them. They also constantly act on their answers to these questions without consciously thinking about the questions and their answers.

The cancer researcher typically assumes that she can know things about cancer, perhaps even know what the cure is (if she or someone else is fortunate enough to discover it) without reflecting on what knowledge is. Despite the complexity of economic systems, most economists still assume that they can still know things about economics. Anyone watching the news and seeing a story about how scientists have definitively discovered life on Mars would probably say they now know there is life on Mars. They would probably do so without asking: "How can I *know* this is true?" "Must I be certain?" "Must I see it myself or can I go on the testimony of the scientists and the reporter?" Are these sensible questions to ask? The fictitious *War of the Worlds* story about a Martian invasion aired on the radio in 1938 for an uninterrupted sixty minutes with fictitious news bulletins and most took it as fact, which resulted in public outrage afterwards.

The possibility of any formal area of study, as well as the possibility of our everyday endeavors to know and to act on our knowledge, assumes that there are truth and knowledge, that we should strive for them, and that it is possible to arrive at them. Typically, though, we don't ask whether what we perceive with our five senses is true, or whether the way we relate our ideas leads to truth and knowledge. These questions are universal, general, and all-encompassing because they are not questions about specific instances of truth and knowledge, like two plus two equals four or that summers are hotter in Florida than in Maine. Rather, they are questions about all truths and every instance of our claiming to know anything. What is characteristic of all truths? What is involved in knowing anything? The area of philosophy called "epistemology" (*episteme* meaning "knowledge" or "understanding," in Greek) deals with limit questions about truth and knowledge.

Limit Questions about Values

Other limit questions concern values. We have already made reference to values and value judgments in surveying other limit questions. All types of limit questions are interconnected so that the answers given in one area, like ontology or epistemology, bear on the answers given in another, like values, and vice versa.

Limit questions about values are more immediately germane to a book on economics and ethics. Yet all other limit questions are not far behind, lingering in the background and pressing on ethical concerns in economics. Here we briefly survey the types of limit questions about values in general, reserving for later discussions more detailed examinations of the different answers given to them, especially as they bear on the ethics and economics.

Why are there limit questions about values? Although frequently disagreeing on the details of what constitutes goodness and badness, humans at all times and places have distinguished between "goodness" and "badness." That is, they have made judgments of value, deeming certain things, persons, and actions as better ("more good") or worse ("more bad") than other things, persons, and actions. We say things could be better or worse. We frequently aim to move things, situations, states of affairs, and even ourselves, from what we call worse to what we call better. We constantly do this with economic systems too, feeling the need to make economies better. We often say economic situations are bad, desiring to improve them.

Questions about goodness and badness involve more than questions about morality. We make value judgments not only about human existence and activity, but about practically all things. They include claims as diverse as: "Dogs are better pets than pigs," "The Rolling Stones are better than The Who," "Chevy trucks are better than Fords," "Money now is better than money later," "Today's society is worse than it was fifty years ago," "It would be better for you to break-up with Bill and start dating Cliff than to stay with Bill," "Socialist governments are better than Libertarian governments," "Leadership by the few is better than leadership by the many," "It is better to give than to receive," "Jane a better lawyer than John, but John is better at quilting," "It is always better to tell the truth than to lie," "Freedom of speech is better than censorship," "It is better to steal from the rich to feed one's family than to let one's family starve," "The gold standard was better than the Federal Reserve system," "The CEO who extorts money is worse than the CEO who does not," "It is better to oppose an injustice than to endure it," "It is better to have fun and die young than to lead an austere but boring life to a ripe old age," "It is better to kill in self-defense than to be killed," etc. The list could go on *ad infinitum*. Any time we compare things and judge one as *better* than another we make a value judgment. Value judgments presuppose concepts of "good" and "bad," and some means to judge which of at least two things is better than the other.

What are some limit questions about values? One fundamental question about values is: What do we mean by good and bad? What exactly is goodness? How do we recognize it when we see it? Is goodness a property that beings can or cannot have, or is it a state of being? Can only human beings or activities be good or bad, or can non-human things and their activities be good or bad? Typically, questions of value asking how we ought to be and behave is the realm of ethics and morality, but we have seen that questions of values arise that are not the same as moral questions. Can only things be good or bad, can actions also be good or bad, or can both things and actions be good or bad? Is goodness equivalent to usefulness in accomplishing some goal? Is goodness the degree to which a thing accomplishes its reason for existing? Is goodness only that which promotes pleasure or happiness? Is goodness something defined by God or ultimate reality? Is goodness only an idea that humans and societies create?

A key limit question about values is why we value good over bad. Just as we can ask why we value truth and knowledge over falsehood and ignorance, we can ask why we value goodness over badness. We have ideas of good and bad, and we value good over bad, but why? Again, this question might seem pointless and the answer obvious. There are, as usual with limit questions, considerations and counterexamples that make things more complicated.

What if we benefit from something being bad instead of good? I might prefer my tennis opponent to be bad, or at least worse than I, so I can win. Frequently, we benefit from the hardships of something being worse than better. One who struggles to rise to success in business from a poor, lower-class, underprivileged background might have as a result developed positive character traits that a person from a wealthy, upper-class, privileged background did not have the opportunity to develop. What about benefitting by committing an act considered bad? If one had absolute certainty they could get away with stealing enough money so they would never have to work again for the rest of their lives, would they do it?

This question of why we value good over bad is intimately bound up with why we should, ethically speaking, strive to be good and avoid evil. Why should we try to do right and avoid wrong? Are we somehow happier if we do well and avoid evil? Should we be good to avoid God's wrath and go to heaven when we die? Should we do right and avoid wrong only because of pressure from others and from society? Should we be good only to avoid jail?

Another set of limit questions about values in general and ethics in particular is: How do we know what is good and bad, right and wrong? Do we know right and wrong from God's commandments? If so, then how does God know right and wrong? Does God know right and wrong on some other grounds, like an eternal principle of goodness alongside of or inside of God? Or does God freely determine what is right and wrong, so that God could have made it right to lie, murder, cheat and steal, and the paragon of virtue to hate God? Did God create human beings so that every person has a right to food, shelter, education and healthcare because they are made in God's image?

Do we know right and wrong by examining the natures of things, looking for their purposes and inherent goals that tell us how things should be? Are economic systems natural so that their natural state without intervention is the way they should be, as Adam Smith claimed? Or can we discern a natural way economic systems should be so that humans, as part of nature, need to modify those economic systems that do not meet this standard? Or are right and wrong wholly independent of the way the world is, so that we can never discern ethical principles by observing the world and studying it scientifically?

Do we know right and wrong by considering the consequences of each possible action in any given situation? Is lying wrong in one situation, such as to avoid punishment, but right in another situation, such as to save lives? Or do we know right and wrong prior to considering consequences, perhaps in a timeless moral code, God's commandments, the dictates of reason, or of conscience? Does good economic policy change, based on different consequences in different situations, or are there universal principles that must guide policy in every situation regardless of different consequences?

Another related limit question about values is whether values are absolute, universal and timeless, or whether they are relative, contextual, and conditioned by history, different people, and different cultures. That is, are good and bad, right and wrong, relative, being different for different individuals and groups? Or are good and bad, right and wrong, universal and absolute, applying to all individuals and groups at all times and places?

These questions about values and value judgments are all limit questions because, again, they arise at the limits of all other areas of inquiry, cannot be answered by the methods of those disciplines, and everyone constantly assumes and acts on answers to these questions. On a day-to-day basis everyone has and operates on assumptions about values, most frequently without examining these assumptions in detail.

A historian of colonial America may see the fact that Europeans captured and sold millions of Africans into chattel slavery, but the methods of her discipline do not help in passing moral judgment on this action. She may very well believe this was wrong, but there is nothing about history as a discipline that can lead to this judgment. A nuclear physicist may study fission and fusion, knowing their scientific causes and effects. However, there is nothing about the scientific method in general or nuclear physics in particular that helps determine whether we *should* only manipulate atoms to produce energy for humans, or whether we *should* make nuclear weapons to attack other humans. They similarly cannot answer the environmental ethical question of whether or not we should use nuclear power at all. A nuclear physicist might have strong ethical views on these questions, but she did not obtain them from the methods of her discipline. An economist, politician, and citizen might have strong views on whether everyone is entitled to a living wage, but their views did not and could not come strictly from the disciplines of economics and political science.

Questions about values are also limit questions because they are broad, universal and all-encompassing. They are not only about one instance of an ethical judgment. It is not a question of whether it would be wrong for me to tell a white lie by saying a colleague's new haircut looks good when it really does not. It is a question of how we can know if lying in any circumstance at any time or place is ever morally justified.

The Relevance and Complexity of Limit Questions

Surveying limit questions can lead one to wonder if philosophy is merely an exercise in irrelevant and impractical abstraction, a mental game for ivory-tower and armchair thinkers. Concentrated focus on specific limit questions does seem abstruse and pointless to some. This is probably because: (1) limit questions cannot be addressed with the methods of other areas of human inquiry alone; (2) many have not engaged in rigorous consideration of the limit questions formally or informally; studying philosophy, if it happens at all, usually begins at the college level; and (3) many are not interested in these questions and their answers, at least initially.

Limit questions and our answers to them are, however, extremely practical. All human existence and activity presupposes answers to the limit questions. Many do not consciously or regularly think about their answers to the limit questions. If and when they do, however, they realize that how they live their lives would be different if they answered limit questions differently. Ideas have consequences. Belief that God has revealed moral commands and belief in an afterlife will greatly affect one's life and behavior in different ways than disbelief in God and an afterlife. How we classify beings, including human beings, has enormous practical consequences. Not considering minorities as the same type of being as the majority has resulted in innumerable crimes against humanity in history, such as slavery and the Holocaust. How they answer limit questions in general and those about values in particular will greatly shape how an individual or group allocates scarce material resources.

Many make claims about what is right and wrong in general, and what is right and wrong economically, in particular. Yet, they have never been confronted with and thought about the limit questions addressed by ethics, the different possible answers to them, and the reasons for these different answers. When they are, they can see how making ethical pronouncements in any realm, including economics, is more complicated than it initially seems.

WORLDVIEWS

Due to their all-encompassing, general, universal character, all limit questions we have surveyed are interrelated. The answer to one question has implications for all others. It would be inconsistent to say all knowledge comes through the five senses on the one hand, but then to affirm that humans have an immaterial soul that endures after death, on the other, because we cannot perceive such a soul with our five senses. It would be inconsistent to say that God has revealed what is right and wrong for us so that we can be happy in heaven and avoid hell, but then to say different people should choose for themselves what is right and wrong. It would be inconsistent to say that individual freedom is a higher social value than equality, but then to advocate an economic policy that restrains individual freedom to ensure greater equality among members of society. Similarly, it would be inconsistent to say the highest economic value is the most efficient allocation of resources, but then to say we must interfere in the market to ensure everyone has shelter, food, healthcare and education because economic systems should guarantee basic human rights (assuming that non-market interference is most efficient). This is because, as we will see later, most economists agree that almost any intervention in a properly functioning market causes loss of efficiency.

All of this means that answers to limit questions are *systematic*. They come in large systems in which the answers must be consistent with each another. These comprehensive systems answering the limit questions are sometimes called "worldviews." Everyone has a system of answers to the limit questions, or a worldview, and operates on it. No one can daily live and act without assuming answers to the limit questions that worldviews address. But just as many do not normally reflect on limit questions, many do not normally reflect on their worldviews. Most people have not systematically thought through their worldviews for themselves. Rather, they have gotten their worldviews from others: parents, religious traditions, education, and culture.

Philosophy and Religion as Addressing the Limit Questions

We might not find these limit questions addressed in worldviews interesting or important. They are valid questions that can be asked, however. Why not ask them? There have always been people who have found these questions interesting and important, namely, philosophers and theologians. Both philosophers and theologians rely on reason and their experience to address these questions. The difference between philosophers and theologians lies in whether or not they also give a place for some purported authority to help answer these questions, too. Religious people typically also trust some sort of authority to help address limit questions. The authority might be some supposed revelation from ultimate reality, God, the gods, or spirits. This might be a special text (scripture), tradition, person, body of teachers, or some combination of them. Some might give the Bible such authority. Some might give the Qur'an such authority, or the Vedas. Some might trust their tribal shaman and his or her experiences. Philosophers jettison questions about an authoritative answer to these questions, instead relying on their own reason and experience, and the reasoning and experiences of others, to address these questions.

ETHICS AND ECONOMICS TOGETHER

Positive economics deals with the "what is" of economic systems. For example, a positive economic statement would be: "the unemployment rate is 9 percent." Normative economics speaks from a values perspective, such as: "the unemployment rate is too high." Efficient allocation is frequently the highest value among economists. Economics is a practical and important science because allocation of scarce resources is something we must do and something we are all concerned about. Because of its practicality, economics intersects with ethics. To ask how we *should* allocate scarce resources, and how society *should* be organized economically and politically in order to do so, enters the realm of values and, hence, ethics.

As a science, positive economics seeks knowledge about a particular subset of things in human experience, asks questions about them, and applies specific methods to discover the answers. Economics is not equipped, by itself, to address the limit questions that philosophy and religion address. Whenever economics journeys into the realm of values, it begins to ask different types of questions that must be addressed in different ways, namely, limit questions.

Normative economics involves what *should* be done to an economy, if anything, thus involving value judgments. Here economists can learn from philosophers and theologians who have long addressed limit questions. Generally economists value market efficiency, but questions arise about what this means and why it should be valued most. Philosophers and theologians can elucidate the limit questions normative economics deals with, their complexity, related questions to be addressed, and the reasons for the various answers. Thus economists benefit from dialogue with philosophers and theologians.

Conversely, economists have specialized knowledge about how markets behave and the laws of cause and effect in our perennial effort to allocate scarce resources. Philosophers and theologians engaging ethics frequently have an elementary understanding of economics and are therefore handicapped in developing moral theories bearing on economics. Being wrong about the facts of how markets behave inevitably leads to errors in constructing ethical theories about how economics and political entities *should* be arranged. Therefore, it is imperative that ethicists learn more about the content and findings of the science of positive economics.

An increase in mutual understanding to help economists and ethicists practice their trades well is thus a chief goal of this book. This is not the only goal, however. Many people stigmatize economics in general as amoral or even immoral, and even more people judge certain economic policies to be moral or immoral. The typical person in any walk of life usually has a rudimentary grasp of the laws of economics. The typical person in any walk of life usually assumes answers to a host of limit questions and acts on those answers, without addressing those questions on their own terms and by methods appropriate to them.

Therefore, another goal of this book is to help those who want to think about economics and ethics together by providing them with some tools for doing so. The book presents the basic laws of economics agreed upon by most economists, many of which are unknown by those thinking about ethics and economics. The book also examines in depth the many limit questions of value that arise in ethics in general and in applying ethics to economics in particular. Throughout, the authors seek to link the relevant limit questions about values to the agreed upon facts and laws of economic theory and market behavior. One goal is an increased understanding of both the science of economics and the discipline of ethics for all interested readers. Another goal is to show that there are no easy answers to ethical judgments in economics given the number and complexity of considerations involved in any such judgment.

A limited understanding of both ethics and economics leads many today to claim that modern economics is an uncertain science not reflecting reality, even a failure, and that it is a cold, amoral, even immoral, discipline. Economists find these claims difficult to believe. As in any science both progress and mistakes are made, but economists continually work to learn from mistakes and progress more. There have been many mistakes, great and small, in every natural science. Although we once thought that water covered all of Venus, no one uses this to discredit astronomy as a scientific discipline. Physicists once concurred that light waves propagate through a material "ether." Neither this mistake nor the problems with pre-relativity and pre-quantum physics are used to discredit physics wholesale. Entire paradigm shifts can and must take place for progress in any science.[12]

Economists have always tried to consider ethical questions in the normative aspect of economics. The values of their times certainly influenced economists like Smith, Walras, Jevons, Marshall, Samuelson, Mises, Hayek, Keynes, Menger and many others. They contemplated ethical considerations nonetheless. Many fault economic models for making simplistic assumptions about human behavior and values. As frequently happens, though, it is easier to naysay than to construct a modeling alternative that both incorporates these concerns and has the predictive power of the standard models in modern economics.

So, although books on economics and ethics abound, this text seeks to examine ethical issues in economics through the lens of neoclassical economics. There is of yet no other rigorous mathematical formulation for understanding economic events with such empirical verification. As in any science, the reduction of variables makes economic models viable. The fact that economists use simplifying assumptions does not make economic models erroneous. Economists of all normative persuasions agree that neoclassical economics works best in explaining and predicting economic data, especially on the microeconomic level. With few exceptions, teaching economists all teach neoclassical economics in their respective educational institutions. This book seeks to educate readers about neoclassical economic models while examining and applying the relevant ethical concerns.

Trade-offs in Economics and Ethics

Again, at the heart of economics is the problem of scarcity. This means we do not have infinite resources to fulfill unlimited human wants. This limitation entails mutually exclusive trade-offs due to scarcity. Economists study trade-offs, and in many cases seek the most efficient way to use our scare resources. A common term economists use to describe trade-offs is *opportunity cost*. This is the value of the next highest alternative mutually exclusive with what is actually chosen. For example, you can go either to a baseball game or a basketball game that take place at the same time, but not both. If you choose the baseball game then you are indicating your preference that the baseball game is worth more to you than the basketball game. The opportunity cost is the basketball game. Opportunity costs arise when timeframes are the same, which makes choices mutually exclusive. If the games were not simultaneous then one game would not be the opportunity cost of going to the other.

Trade-offs are the innumerous and ubiquitous facts economics deals with, as individuals and societies are forced to make choices about scarce resources. For example, when hurricane Katrina struck the Gulf Coast and people made donations for hurricane relief, other charities did not get as much money that year. In more general terms all choices entail trade-offs, be they choices of individuals, groups or governments. No one has unlimited resources due to scarcity and so we all face trade-offs individually and as societies.

Choices involving trade-offs and opportunity costs involve value judgments. When forced to choose either the baseball or basketball game and the choice is made, an individual reveals that he values one more than the other. Economists call these revelations of value in choices *preferences*, which are value judgments from a limit questions perspective.

Similarly, governmental policy choices involve opportunity costs and trade-offs because of finite resources. Every policy, no matter what its benefits, involves costs. Something is always given up in any policy decision, frequently in the form of negative consequences. For example, the government cannot give money to someone on unemployment or disability without someone else, the taxed citizen, bearing the cost. Another value question arises here, too, because the taxed citizen might not agree with the choice that she should bear the cost in this policy. Someone else makes the decision for her based on the value judgment that citizens should sacrifice some of their finite material resources for the disadvantaged. In fact, the question of whether individuals in society should be free to make their own decisions, or whether someone thought to be more competent should make some decisions for them, is another limit question in social and political philosophy that we will discuss later. Who knows best, the individual or someone else, and why?

A complication for value judgments expressed in revealed preferences is that opportunity costs often remain unknown. This means trade-offs are made that might not have been had there been more information about the costs. For example, many value electronic media such as emails and electronic documents over paper copies because they value conserving the trees used to make paper. A frequently unrealized opportunity cost, however, is that non-renewable carbon fuel is required to run electronic devices. On the other hand, paper is renewable since it can be recycled and new trees can be planted. Our knowledge or ignorance of the consequences of our actions is an important factor in the limit questions addressed by various ethical theories, as we shall see.

ETHICS AS AXIOLOGY AND SOCIAL ETHICS

Earlier we situated ethics in the context of limit questions addressed by philosophy and the teachings of religious traditions. We surveyed some limit questions about being, truth, knowledge, and values. Ethical questions fall under the study of values, called *axiology*. *Axios* means "worth or value," in Greek, and "ology" comes from *logos* meaning "word," in Greek. Thus axiology literally means "words about values" but connotes the general study of values. Axiology tries to answer the many limit questions concerning values. It is more than the study of right or wrong human behavior, since, as we have seen, we value all sorts of things. We value beauty, for instance, and so philosophical aesthetics falls under axiology.

Ethics ascribes value to certain human states of being and activities, about which there are many limit questions, as we have seen. Because humans are social animals, there are social as well as individual values. These include justice, equality, freedom, and discussions of rights. Thus, social ethics and political philosophy also deal with axiological questions. In fact, precisely because economics is the scientific study of trade between human beings, social values must also be considered in addition to individual values.

In the next section, we examine, in more detail, questions involved in ethics or moral philosophy, both in their individual and their social dimensions. One goal is to show how the issues involved in making ethical judgments in general are complicated, let alone making ethical judgments in economics. It is prudent to avoid hasty ethical pronouncements. Our ethical judgments in economics largely depend on how we answer important fundamental questions about good and bad, right and wrong. In fact, the way we answer these questions can lead to completely opposite judgments in any particular economic scenario.

Whence the Idea of "Good?"

An important limit question is how the ideas of good vs. bad arise and why we make this distinction. One's answer has important implications for all other ethical considerations. Does the distinction between good and bad arise merely from individual and / or social preferences? Does it arise from our bodily experiences of pleasure and pain? Does it come from our more distinctively human features, like mental and emotional happiness? Does it come from practical necessity, such as keeping people who live together from getting into conflicts? Some argue that we consider stealing property and killing other humans bad, only because they work against keeping social groupings of humans together, while not taking others' property and not killing others allows people to live together in harmony. Who would remain in a group where their property and life were constantly threatened by others? Or does the distinction between good and bad come from something built into the nature of the world that determines goodness and badness, such as a the natural purpose of a given being? Do we look at an albino mammal and say there is something *wrong* with it because it goes against the purpose of that species' normal hair coloring to help the animal blend in with its environment in order to avoid predators, and to protect it from the sun's radiation? Does the distinction between good and bad, right and wrong, ultimately come from a personal God?

Economists look at how individuals reveal their preferences as they participate in markets. Thus economists usually say that markets "reveal" social preferences and values through the price of the good and the quantity of the good demanded and supplied. Why do individuals in markets have values expressed through preferences? Why do economists say that market efficiency in allocating goods and services at the equilibrium price and quantity is good and inefficiency is bad? Whence the distinction?

Value Judgments

One reason for the concerns of ethics is the fact that humans constantly make value judgments. We continually judge some things to be good, some to be bad, and some to be better or worse in comparison to other things. We constantly say things like: "Football is a *good* sport," "Ford pick-ups are *better* than Chevy pick-ups," "Payment in cash would be *better* than check or credit," "It is *good* to tell the truth and *bad* to lie," "The job at the San Francisco firm would be *better* than the job at the Boise firm," "Mother Theresa is a *good* person but Vlad the Impaler was a *bad* person," "Mother Theresa was a *better* person *than* Ivan the Terrible," "Macs are *better than* PCs," and "It is *better* to turn the other cheek *than* to seek revenge."

Examples of value judgments are practically limitless because we make them all of the time, usually without verbalizing them. Value judgments are inherently economic, too, because they inform trade-offs and opportunity costs.

Not only do we make value/economic judgments all of the time but we are constantly acting on them. Say you want to pick up lunch while driving and you see McDonald's, Subway, and Taco Bell. You pull into the Taco Bell drive-thru and get some burritos. You have made a value judgment even though you probably did not verbalize it, and you acted on it. If you decide to meet a friend for coffee instead of doing some housework, you have also made a value judgment. Both are economic in that there is a tradeoff of time and / or money, and the options you forfeited were the opportunity costs of the choices you made.

Economists add that your choices of Taco Bell and coffee with a friend gave you the highest net *utility*. Utility is an economic term that captures value judgments, roughly equivalent to satisfaction, but still requiring analysis from an axiological perspective. Now you may say, "I got Taco Bell because that's what my friend wanted." An economist would say you are still maximizing your utility, but that you value your friendship and thus factor their preferences into your lunch decision.

Moral vs. Nonmoral Value Judgments

A question arising from some of the above examples is whether or not all value judgments have a moral element. We typically think of morality as dealing with specifically *human* ways of being and acting. While it might be bad for my computer to crash before I saved my work, we would not hold my computer morally culpable for doing so. We would impute blame to someone who intentionally unplugged my computer before I saved my work, though.

Some of the above examples of value judgments, however, do seem related to morality. Most would consider judgments about telling the truth versus lying and being merciful instead of seeking revenge to be *moral* judgments. Most would consider judgments like which job or kind of pick-up truck is better to have little or no relationship to morality, and so be *nonmoral* judgments.

However, this may not be the case. Some believe that all value judgments are related to moral considerations. Assuming that humans are inherently *moral* beings, they reason that all of our value judgments are moral judgments, and that all of our actions following from them are morally assessable. Some, also, base this claim on ontology. Recall that ontology deals with limit questions about being in general. If part of what it means to be a specific type of being includes the purposes or goals for that kind of being (technically called "teleological" or "final" causes), then the degree to which a being fulfills its purposes involves a value judgment. If a ballpoint pen actually writes with ink very rarely then we make the value judgment that it is bad, since it fails to fulfill its purpose as a ballpoint pen, namely, to write. Since some believe that human beings have proper purposes and goals, they believe that the degree to which a person fulfills their specifically human purposes and goals is subject to moral appraisal.

For example, say we assume that part of what it means to be a *human* being is to show mercy to others. Say a particular person is ruthless, showing little mercy. Then our moral judgment that they are "bad" is based on ontological final causes, since they "fall short" of one of the purposes of a *human* being. Using the possible distinction between a being's real purpose and how well it attains that purpose, some see morality as a subset of ontology or the study of being in general. They believe that morality is what it means to be a human being in terms of the ontological purposes of human beings. Hence, they argue that all human value judgments are moral and that all human actions are subject to moral assessment. Conversely, if one's ontology denies that all beings have inherent purposes or goals for their existence and activity, then she could deny that all human value judgments are moral and that all human actions are morally assessable.

Economists, too, have a way to interpret seemingly nonmoral acts morally through what they call *signaling*. Maybe you value a certain kind of pick-up truck partly based on how you feel others will perceive you. That is, you are sending a "signal" to others about who you are. Another example is the purchase of a "green" product. Maybe you chose it because you think it will help the environment or maybe because you want others to think that you are environmentally conscious. We will discuss the related limit question of whether or not all human actions have selfish ulterior motivations later. These considerations raise the limit question: Are all value judgments moral, or are some value judgments *moral* and some *nonmoral*?

Descriptive Value Judgments vs. Normative/Prescriptive Value Judgments

Another observation about value judgments is that some describe the way things are, like: "Ford pick-ups *are* better than Chevy pick-up trucks" and "Honesty *is* better than lying," while some describe the ways things *should be*, like: "You *should* buy a Ford pick-up instead of a Chevy," and "You *should* always tell the truth and never lie." Value judgments about what *is* good or bad, and what *is* better or worse, are sometimes called descriptive value judgments. They are judgments about facts, the ways things are, and are related to the *indicative* mood in language. "The car *is* good" describes a state of affairs, like: "The earth *is* round, not flat." Both statements are indicative. Value judgments about what *should* be the case are sometimes called normative or prescriptive value judgments. They are about how things *should* be and are related to the *imperative* mood in language: "Your car really *should* start every time you try to start it" describes what should be the case, like: "People *should* treat others as they want to be treated (the "Golden Rule")."

Just as we can potentially distinguish *moral* from *nonmoral value judgments*, we can potentially distinguish between *descriptive moral value judgments* and *descriptive nonmoral value judgments*. "Mary's humility is a very good thing for such an excellent tennis player" could be a descriptive moral value judgment, while "Mary has an excellent tennis swing" could be descriptive nonmoral value judgment.

Similarly, just as we can possibly distinguish between *moral* and *nonmoral value judgments*, we can likewise distinguish between *normative/prescriptive moral value judgments* and *normative/prescriptive nonmoral value judgments*. "You should be as humble as Mary" could be a normative/prescriptive moral value judgment, while "You should swing your tennis racket like Mary" could be a normative/prescriptive nonmoral value judgment.

We have already indicated the distinction between positive and normative economics. Positive economics concerns the facts or what *is the case* in economic systems. Normative economics concerns what people say or believe *should be the case*. Sometimes, we shall see, it is near impossible to reconcile the two. For example, saying the unemployment rate is ten percent is a positive economic statement. It is merely a statement of what is the case. Saying the unemployment rate is too high is a normative value judgment, namely, that it should be lower. Some even add a moral aspect to this value judgment by saying it is morally wrong to have such a high unemployment rate. A hasty jump to a normative/prescriptive value judgment, bypassing the positive (descriptive) statement and a potentially nonmoral value judgment, can confuse the technical analysis of economic systems.

To summarize what might be a confusing taxonomy, first, there are value judgments in general. Second, value judgments can be either *descriptive* (describing the way things are) or *normative/prescriptive* (prescribing the way things should be). Third, if there is a distinction between *moral* and *nonmoral* value judgments, then there are distinctions between: *descriptive moral value judgments, descriptive nonmoral value judgments, normative/prescriptive moral value judgments* and *normative/prescriptive nonmoral value judgments*.

Table 1.1: Types of Value Judgments

VALUE JUDGMENT TYPES	Moral	Nonmoral
Descriptive	Our mechanic *is* good because he charges a fair price.	Our mechanic *is* good at repairing automobiles.
Normative/Prescriptive	A mechanic *should* charge a fair price.	A mechanic *should be* good at repairing automobiles.

Is There Any Connection Between Being and Value Judgments? Does "Is" in Any Way Imply "Ought?"

As discussed, positive economics deals with the description of economic facts. Normative economics deals with evaluating economic facts as actually good or bad (descriptive value judgments) or how they should be (normative/prescriptive value judgments). The distinction between mere descriptions of facts and evaluations in value judgments raises another important question, touched on above: Is there any connection between the way things are, or facts, and values? This question arises from the possibility of a relationship between the type of being that something is and the value judgments made about that being.

Some argue that we can discern how a specific being should be or act from the purpose of the type of being that it is. They argue that there are connections between what something is (being), how good it actually is (descriptive value), and how it should be (normative / prescriptive value), based on how well it fulfills its purpose for existing.

Say a cardiologist has two male patients. She says to one: "You have a good heart," and to the other: "You have bad heart." How does she make these descriptive value judgments? In saying one heart is good she means it is fulfilling its function of pumping blood at the volume and rate that healthy human hearts are supposed to. Its parts exist and work together in harmonious integrity to reliably and efficiently pump blood at a certain volume and rate. In saying one heart is bad she means it is not fulfilling its function of efficiently and reliably pumping blood at the volume and rate of normal human hearts. Perhaps the man with the bad heart has weak heart muscles, a clogged artery, or a malfunctioning valve. How a heart is pumping blood depends on its "way of being." This "way of being" means having or not having the integrity of parts required to efficiently and reliably pump blood at a certain rate and volume.

Likewise, a good automobile reliably and comfortably transports human beings, while an automobile is bad to the degree that it does not do this. We do not say a heart is bad because it does not comfortably and reliably transport human beings. Nor do we say a car is good because it efficiently and reliably pumps blood at a certain volume and rate.

We can look at economies in the same way. For example, Adam Smith said the purpose of economic systems is to allow people to exchange goods and services to the benefit of all: "Among men, the most dissimilar geniuses are of use to one another; the different products of their respective talents are being brought into a common stock, where every man may purchase whatever part of the produce of other men's talents he has occasion for."[13] For Smith, this propensity for exchange arises in man alone, not coming from any government or organization. It exists naturally, has a specific function, and has been evolving in a natural progression from barter to money since the dawn of humankind. In this view, a "good" economy is one that allows exchange of goods and services to the benefit of all, since that is an economy's function or reason for existing. In a "bad" economy, this does not occur. We can raise additional values questions about what the "benefit of all" means, and why this view of an economy's function does not include, as would some others, the alleviation of societal ills.

In these ways, some argue that value judgments about how good something is, and how it should be, are based on the function of the type of thing it is. The degree to which something fulfills its purpose is the degree to which it is good. The degree to which something does not fulfill its purpose is the degree to which it is bad. These thinkers see an intimate connection between limit questions about being (ontology) and limit questions about value (axiology).

The claim that being and value are thus connected has been a major theme in much of western philosophy and religion for over two millennia until the last few centuries. The often misunderstood and oversimplified "natural law" tradition of medieval Christian thought maintained a strong connection between the purposes of beings and our value judgments about them. Belief in a personal God who created the world and gave each created being a purpose was conducive to forming this connection. Many pre-Christian thinkers of classical antiquity also saw similar connections between purposes of beings and our value judgments about them. Because human beings are *beings*, this line of thinking can reason from supposed purposes of human existence to value judgments about human beings.

Conversely, there are those who argue that there is no connection whatsoever between how things are and how they should be. Historically, the separation of religious explanations from those offered by the sciences, history, philosophy, and other disciplines, has strengthened this view in the last few centuries, called the "modern" period (in distinction from medieval and ancient). So, belief in a personal God who created all things with specific purposes has become less common. If we do not invoke God to explain the world's existence in general and specific beings in particular, then we can raise questions as to whether there are purposes for specific beings, or whether specific beings are entirely the result of purposeless, arbitrary, chance.

There was also a shift in the modern period toward fascination with limit questions about knowledge (epistemology) over those about being (ontology). This also weakened any supposed link between ontology and values. Philosophers more often contemplated limit questions, like: Does our internal experience gained through our senses actually correspond to the world outside of us? Can raw sense experience tell us anything about values, or do we merely bring value judgments to the raw data of our sense experience? Questions like these led many to question whether we can discern the purpose for a particular type of being, assuming that there even is one.

The British philosopher, David Hume (AD 1711 – 1776), famously said there is no way to move from *is* to *ought*.[14] Say, we walk into a room, find a man dead on the floor in a pool of blood, and another man next to the body with a smoking gun in his hand saying: "I shot him but he got what he deserved." We can stare long and hard at the gun, the body, the blood, and the shooter, but there is nothing about our sense perceptions of those objects that enable us to make a value judgment about the rightness or wrongness of the mere fact of the shooting. There is nothing inherent in the perceived facts that cry "This is right!" or "This is wrong!" Rather, we bring something to the situation that moves us to make a value judgment.

Some draw the same distinction between the facts of positive economics and the value judgments of normative economics. There has been much recent debate about healthcare. Some argue that whatever system of healthcare we have is a valueless fact. There is nothing about the facts that tell us it is right or wrong. The raw data of the facts tell us nothing about value. We bring our values, perhaps the belief that healthcare is a human right, to the facts. This line of thinking argues that the way things are tell us nothing about the way they should be, as Hume said, "*Is* does not imply *ought*."

For Hume and others, value judgments are merely expressions of facts about our inner feelings. The claim that "the shooting of that man was wrong" translates to the *fact* that we feel bad about the shooting of that man, or that we do not like it. The value judgment is translated into an account of another state of affairs or fact, another "is." This translation of the value judgment merely states a fact about how we feel. It is an indicative statement about what is the case, without any inherent value one way or the other.

In light of these considerations, many question whether values, goodness, and badness, are in any way tied to being. Is the way things should be really based on the purposes of specific types of beings? Or are beings and facts about them utterly valueless?

Questions about the Goal-Oriented Nature of Human Activity

Intimately connected to values is the fact that human actions are always goal-oriented. Ethical considerations also arise partly because of the observation that human beings are always acting, and, in their acting they aim at goals. Everything we do freely and voluntarily is with an end, goal, or purpose in mind. Getting a cup of coffee in the morning is goal-oriented. We want to wake up, have a happy attitude, or just experience the pleasure of drinking coffee. Looking in our briefcase for our flash drive is goal-oriented. We want to find our flash drive. Lying down in bed and turning off the lights is goal-oriented. We want to fall asleep. Talking to someone is goal-oriented. We want to get information, share information, feel a different way, or motivate them to do something. Even refraining from acting is itself an action. We might refrain from gossiping about a co-worker simply because we think gossiping is bad, and our goal is to be good. When we act with purpose we prefer one state of affairs over other states of affairs. We want to wake up instead of being half asleep, experience a pleasure instead of not experiencing it, have our flash drive instead of not having it, have someone else know what we know instead of not knowing it, fall asleep instead of staying awake, or be good instead of being bad.

All economic action or non-action is also goal-oriented, expressing a preference for one state of affairs over another. Often, they are mutually exclusive and we want both. Then we aim for the state of affairs we want more and forgo the other states of affairs we want less, which are the opportunity costs. If we pull into Taco Bell instead of MacDonald's for lunch then we prefer eating burritos for lunch over hamburgers, and not eating hamburgers for lunch is the opportunity cost. If we get coffee with a friend instead of doing housework, we prefer coffee with a friend and less housework done is the opportunity cost. In a sense all action is economic, because every action is goal-oriented and involves opportunity costs, due to finite limitations or scarcity.

All action is goal-oriented, trying to move from one state of affairs, valued less, to another state of affairs, valued more. Thus, some argue that the goal-oriented nature of human action is related to values and ethics. Limit questions about the value-oriented nature of human activity include: What values should we pursue in our actions? Should we pursue self-interest, pleasure, happiness, material goods, justice, love, something else, or a combination of these? Why? How do we know what values we should pursue in our actions? Does the fact that humans pursue a goal automatically make it a value, or good? Or is there possibly a disparity between the values people *are* pursuing and what they *should* be pursuing? If so, then why?

The goal-oriented nature of activity pertains to societies as well. Groups, too, try to attain things judged to be good and better than existing states of affairs and other possible goals. Societies constantly pursue peace, security, material prosperity, comfort, pleasure, health, education, aesthetic and cultural value, greater respect for rights, following the divine design for societies, and many other values. Normative economic policies of societies are goal-oriented. Possible societal economic values include: market efficiency, freedom, equality of condition, equality of opportunity, a just distribution of goods and services, reward and punishment based on merits, and fair exchange in the marketplace.

Limit questions arise about which values social groups should pursue: What is the highest social value? Efficient distribution of scarce resources, the greatest happiness for the greatest number of people, health, knowledge, peace and security, justice, freedom, equality of condition among members, equality of opportunity among members, greater honoring of individual rights, or following God's design for societies? How do we know what values societies should aim at, and why? Are the things societies pursue automatically right just because they pursue them? Or can we differentiate between the values societies *are* pursuing and what they *should* pursue?

Are Values Absolute or Relative?

As mentioned, an important ethical question is whether values are absolute, applying to all people at all times and places, or whether they are relative to different individuals, groups and cultures. It is a fact that cultures at different times and places have had different, in some cases contradictory, ethical norms and practices. Does it follow from this fact that values are relative and not absolute? Or among conflicting ethical claims is one right and others wrong?

Some indigenous peoples believe it is right to let a male visitor sleep with the woman of the house even if she is married. Elderly Inuits voluntarily freeze themselves in order to allocate scarce goods to the younger and more vital. In western culture some believe aborting human fetuses is always wrong, while others believe it is morally justified in some cases. Some believe we should never execute a criminal but others believe capital punishment is sometimes morally justified. Some believe we should allow homosexuals to marry and raise children while others do not. Some believe free markets should allocate scarce resources without interference, saying their efficiency makes everyone better. Others believe central planning and market interference—taxation, regulations, market stimuli—are morally justified, even demanded. Of course there has been much ethical agreement in and between various cultures. Most people at most times and places have believed it is wrong to take someone else's property, or to kill an innocent person.

There is, though, the fact of moral relativism historically and in our own day. We can ask whether the fact of ethical differences makes all values, even mutually exclusive ones, right. If so, then, cannibalism is *wrong* for people who do not believe in and practice it, but it is *right* for those who do believe in and practice it. Some argue, though, that the mere fact of different ethical norms and practices among different peoples does not mean that the same thing is right for one and wrong for another. This means that at least some things are right and some things are wrong for all people at all times and all places, regardless of whether or not they believe in and practice them. If this position is correct, then cannibalism could be wrong, for instance, for all people everywhere, even though some people believe it is good and practice it.

The former position is *moral relativism* and the latter is *moral absolutism*. Moral relativists argue from the fact of different values to the legitimacy of different, even contradictory, values. They also appeal to social theories of the origins of ethics, which claim that ethics and values are only social phenomena with the function of preserving human societies. In this line of reasoning, ethics and values are human constructions. They can and do differ, but when they do, each is right for the society that has developed them.

Moral absolutists indicate that many things in the world, natural and manmade, are not right. They say there are times when we see what *is* the case and judge that it *ought not* to be that way. Humans have committed and still commit mass genocide of others, but this fact about what *is* does not mean that it *should* be this way or that it is right. The fact that some people are born with congenital diseases, such as sickle-cell anemia, does not mean that it *should* be this way.

Moral absolutists also raise the point that different individuals and groups who differ on ethical questions must live in the same world and interact. This unavoidably leads to conflicting ethical norms that cannot both be applied. Say, someone, who believes that wife-sharing is right, is my guest. He thinks I should let him sleep with my wife but I do not. A moral relativist must say that both he is right and I am right. But how can we both practice our conflicting ethical beliefs? At the end of the day, figuratively as well as literally, he will either sleep with my wife or he will not, and one of us will think it right, but the other will think it wrong.

A more realistic example would be that some elected officials, with policy-making power in New York, think it is right to put a ceiling on rents, so that those who cannot afford housing will be able to get it. Others, though, think a price ceiling is wrong because it will result in more people not having housing due to the shortage that will ensue according to the laws of supply and demand. These are mutually exclusive alternatives, since it is impossible to both have a rent-ceiling and not have one at the same time. But they must act. Even if they do not act they are acting because there is currently either a rent ceiling in place or there is not. Thus, not acting is acting for the status quo. When they do act, some are forced to do what they think is wrong while others do what they think is right. A moral relativist must say that both sides on this issue are right, even though it is impossible for both sides to do the right thing as each sees it. On the level of the whole nation, economically speaking, it is impossible to have both in the same country at the same time a *laissez-faire* free market economy and a strong centralized planning system of the government intervening in the market.

Moral absolutists also point to our intuitions about certain horrendous evils. An ethical relativist is committed to saying that, for most people, Hitler's holocaust of the Jews was gravely wrong, perhaps the essence of evil itself. At the same time they are committed to saying that for Hitler, and those who agreed with him, the holocaust was the right thing to do. We have a profound intuition that it is seriously wrong to say that the holocaust was, in any sense, right.

Many moral absolutists nuance their position by saying that differences between people, including their situations, can result in opposed ethical norms that are both right. However they maintain there are right and wrong methods to answer ethical questions in different situations, and these right and wrong methods are absolute, regardless of the circumstances or contexts.

Metaethics, Normative Ethics and Applied Ethics

One limit question about ethics and values that we surveyed earlier was: How do we know what is good and what is bad, or what is right and what is wrong? This question refers to what means, procedure, or steps we should follow in order to determine whether a particular way of being or acting is good or bad, right or wrong. It is a question about what method we use to identify good and bad, right and wrong. This is the realm of what philosophers call *normative ethics*.

Normative ethics tries to determine uniform principles and rules for differentiating between good and bad, morally speaking. Part of the task of normative ethics is to defend one's principles and rules for determining good and bad, right and wrong, over other possible rules and principles. Normative ethics does not address whether a specific human action or way of being is right or wrong. Rather, it seeks a systematic way to determine whether any particular human action or way of being is right or wrong. In fact, people often agree *that* a particular action is right or wrong but still disagree on *why* it is right or wrong. Most agree *that* it is wrong to steal, for instance. They often disagree on *why* they believe stealing is wrong, however. This is because their normative ethical systems are different. In other cases different normative ethical systems lead to different answers as to whether or not a specific action is right or wrong. Later, we will see how different normative ethical systems can lead to different moral judgments of economic facts.

Metaethics considers values, good and bad, right and wrong, at a higher and more general level than normative ethics. It addresses questions about the nature of normative value judgments, such as whether a value judgment like "You should not lie" can be true or false. It seeks conceptual clarity of terms like "good," "bad," "right," "wrong," and "rights." It also asks whether or not we can justify moral judgments. Metaethics also inquiries into the most fundamental moral principles, and seeks how many there are (one or more). It thus looks for answers to the most fundamental questions of value and morality that we must answer before developing a way to determine what is right and wrong in the task of normative ethics.

Applied Ethics deals with specific ethical questions in a given area, and presupposes normative ethics. It is the practical task of determining whether or not a specific action is right or wrong. Different ethical questions arise for different areas of human study and activity. For instance, in healthcare there are specific ethical questions about abortion, euthanasia, and cloning. Seeking to address these specific ethical questions, bioethics is a type of applied ethics. Business ethics tries to answer specific ethical questions about business operation and practice. In economics we can ask about good and bad ways to allocate scarce resources. Is it ethical for a central government to transfer and redistribute wealth more equitably? Is it better that all people have their basic needs met, like food, shelter, clothing, healthcare and gainful employment? Or is it better to reward the contributions to, and punish harm inflicted upon, society by individuals with a strict system of merit-based distributive justice? As we consider specific economic policies for their moral value, we enter the realms of applied and social ethics.

Table 1.2: Fields of Ethics

CATEGORY	QUESTIONS	SAMPLE QUESTION	LEVEL
Metaethics	Most fundamental and universal limit questions about values	"Can we justify saying a person 'should' do something, and if so, then can such a statement be 'true' or 'false'?"	Most abstract and general
Normative Ethics	A system or method to answer ethical questions	"How do we know if a person should or should not do something?"	More abstract than one specific ethical question but assumes metaethical answers

Applied Ethics	Consideration of a specific ethical question	"Should Dr. Doppel clone that person or not?"	Most concrete and practical

Thus, before applying ethics to economics we must survey some metaethical questions and some normative economic systems. Here we survey some basic considerations that all normative ethical systems face. Later we will survey some common normative ethical systems, including their pros and cons.

How Many Fundamental Moral Principles Are There?

We have already seen how ethics can be related to limit questions about being or ontology, classically called metaphysics. An important metaphysical question is: Is there is only one ultimate principle, or multiple ultimate principles, underlying everything else? If matter and energy are the same thing, as Einstein's $E=mc^2$ formula indicates,[15] and if one holds that matter-energy explains everything else, then she is a metaphysical monist. If one holds that there are multiple fundamental principles, whether material principles (e.g., elements or subatomic particles) or a non-material mental "stuff" in addition to matter, then she is a metaphysical pluralist. The question of whether there is one or there are multiple fundamental moral principles is comparable to the metaphysical question of monism or pluralism.

Are Descriptive Values and Normative / Prescriptive Values Connected?

We have already touched on the question of whether descriptive value judgments and normative / prescriptive value judgments are somehow connected. We might see someone give time and money to the poor and say, "Her action is good." This is a descriptive value judgment about the way things are: her behavior *is* good. We can then ask how the *fact* that her behavior is good is related to the statement: "People should give time and money to the poor." This is a normative / prescriptive value judgment about what people *ought* to do. It might not occur to us to ask this question because we often assume a connection between descriptive and normative / prescriptive value judgments. Yet, we can question this assumption. We can ask if there is really such a connection, and if so, then, what the nature of this connection is.

For example, assume it is the evening of April 14th and you haven't submitted your federal tax return. A friend calls and asks if you would like to go out to eat and catch a movie. If you do, you will not complete and submit your tax return on time. There is a tradeoff due to the finite resource of time. You would enjoy a night out and so judge that to be good. You also judge that it would be good to complete your tax return to avoid a penalty. Therefore, you descriptively judge both to be good. Now we can ask: "What *should* you do?" The answer is a normative / prescriptive value judgment. You must choose. Say you stay home and finish your tax return, because the opportunity cost of the night out is less than that of missing the tax return deadline. You judge finishing and submitting your tax return on time to be a greater good. Then the *descriptive value judgment* that going out would be good does not issue a command about what you should do, a *normative value judgment*. This means we can ask about the potential gap between what is judged to be good, descriptively, and what is judged good normatively. In economics, we can see how the descriptive *fact*, that two mutually exclusive options are both good, does not tell you which you *should* choose. You ultimately choose the one that will give you greater satisfaction after an opportunity cost comparison.

So we can ask if there is any connection between what *is* good and what we *should* do. Some conclude upon further analysis that there is no connection. They argue that normative principles, commands or rules, are independent of the prospect of good or bad results. This might seem counterintuitive but there are reasons for arguing this, which we will consider later. In the example of completing your tax return, one could say there is a rule that you should always obey your country's laws. That would make it automatically right for you to stay home and finish your tax return, regardless of the good that would result from your going out to eat and seeing a movie.

Others conclude there is a connection between what *is* good and what we *should* do. If so, then what is the connection? Some argue that the human will is drawn to what is good so that we desire what is good naturally. When there are mutually exclusive good things, the will is drawn to what it judges to be the greater good. The greater desire for a good underpins the imperative about what we should do. Others argue, based on the definitions of "good" and "right," that the ideas of good and right imply each other and are involved in one another.

Is Morality General or Particular?

Another question is whether or not there are moral commands or rules that apply regardless of specific situations. Can something be the right thing to do always and everywhere, or can it be the right thing to do in one situation but wrong in another situation? Is there, for example, a universal ethical command to "Never lie" that applies in all situations whatsoever, or is lying actually the right thing to do in some particular situations? Sometimes lying produces good, like not hurting someone's feelings or even saving someone's life, but telling the truth results in something bad, like hurting someone's feeling or someone losing their life. Does this mean that particular situations dictate the rightness or wrongness of lying? If so, then by what means do we know the rightness or wrongness of lying in any given situation?

Normatively speaking, economists usually value seeking the most efficient allocation of scarce resources as good and right in all situations. They define what they mean by "efficient" and they have good reasons for this value, to be discussed later. This value often causes consternation among many non-economists and bothers them a great deal, leading them to view economists as "cold" or "non-caring." We can ask, though, if efficiency should always be sought, or whether something else, like equity, should be sought in some contexts. As we will see, there is usually a trade-off between efficiency and equity.

Normatively, economists also highly value *Pareto optimality*, saying it should always be sought. Pareto optimality says that we should take an economic action only if it makes at least one person better off and no one else worse off. "Better off" means satisfying the individual's *preferences*, which are expressions of what they want. "What they want" means what will give them the most satisfaction, or what economists call *utility*. This is the usual extent of philosophical reflection by economists on the important concept of utility.

We can, however, ask if Pareto optimality is an absolute, universal, normative principle that should be applied in every situation, or if in some cases it should not be applied. In fact, attaining Pareto optimality is almost always an impossible ideal because of the large trade-offs and transaction costs of trying to make a system Pareto optimal. So, one might fairly ask: Can we make something that is at best an unattainable ideal a universal principle to always apply?

Is Morality Rule-Based or Consequence-Based?

A related question is whether morality is based on rules prior to any consideration of an action's consequences, or if an action's consequences partially or wholly determine its goodness or badness. Some normative ethical theories argue that we must consider the value or lack thereof, good or bad, resulting from an action in determining its rightness or wrongness. These theories are called *consequentialist* ethical theories. Because actions often have multiple consequences, some good and some bad, consequentialist approaches often try to weigh the costs and benefits of an action's consequences, in order to estimate its net goodness or net badness. Others argue that morality depends on rules, principles, or commands known prior to any consideration of the value of an action's consequences. These are *deontological* ethical theories. There are combinations of rule-based and consequence-based theories. However, any theory that considers the consequences of an action is considered consequentialist.

Return to the example of the good German hiding Jews during World War II and being interrogated by Nazi officials. On a deontological approach if there is a rule that we should "always tell the truth," then the right thing to do is to tell the Nazis he is hiding Jews, regardless of the consequences. On a consequentialist approach, the fact that much good would result from lying and much bad from telling the truth must be considered and could lead to the conclusion that lying in this situation is right, and telling the truth is wrong. Similarly, in economics, possible rule-based ethical norms include profit maximization or equilibrium, while possible consequence-based norms include efficiency or equity.

Another consideration is that value might not only lie in the universal rule or in the consequences of the action. Value might lie in the person doing the action. If so, then this value must be considered as well. This leads to the next question.

Does Value Lie in the Actor or in the Action?

In addition to the values of specific actions, which we have been focusing on, we can also ask if the condition, attitude, disposition, or motivations people have when they perform an action bears on the goodness or badness of the action. Consider an elected senator in office who repeatedly votes for legislation providing more governmental assistance for the poor. Whether or not enacting such legislation is the right thing to do is, economically speaking, as we will see, determined answers to a host of ethical questions. Assume for the moment that governmental assistance for the poor is good and valuable, better than not helping the poor. A strict consequentialist would say that the goodness of the result, helping poor people, makes the senator's actions right. Assume for the moment that a deontological ethicist believes there is a universally applicable rule that we ought to help the poor. This person, too, would say that the senator did the right thing.

Having established the goodness of the act, we can now ask: *Why* does the senator help the poor? Let's add to the scenario the fact that this senator comes from a very poor state. It could be that she has a genuine concern for the poor, and this is why she supports legislation for welfare and other means of helping the poor. However, it could also be she votes in favor of legislation helping the poor in order to please her constituency, because she wants her home state to re-elect her. Now discerning individuals' motivations is notoriously risky business. But assume we know with certainty the senator's motivations, and say that she was voting to help the poor in order to get re-elected. This would probably affect our moral assessment of her action in voting.

A common assumption is that stinginess is bad, although later we will see an argument for why it is good economically. We would probably praise less a habitually stingy businessman who, under the influence of alcohol, gives money to the homeless on the street than had he shown such liberality while sober. Thus it is possible that conditions, attitudes, dispositions or motivations bear on the goodness or badness actions, and not just the actions themselves.

Why Be Good?

Another limit question is that, assuming there are good and bad ways to be and act regardless of how we know what they are, why should we be good? Why do what is right and avoid what is wrong? If we believe that being good and avoiding evil ultimately gives individuals or groups more pleasure or happiness, then that could justify seeking the good and avoiding evil. If we believe that being good and avoiding evil ultimately gives us more happiness, then that could be the justification for doing good and not evil. If we believe that seeking good and avoiding evil will help us pragmatically better accomplish things, then that could justify seeking the good and avoiding evil. If the dictates of reason and of being rational lead to an inviolable duty to do what is right, then that could be the justification for seeking the good and avoiding evil. If we believe there is a personal God who has issued positive commands and negative prohibitions, then that could be the reason for seeking to do the good and to avoid evil.

Several of these reasons could be combined to explain why we should seek the good and avoid evil. For instance, if there is a God who has given commands that, when obeyed, lead to happiness and flourishing in this life and the next, then there are multiple reasons for seeking good and avoiding evil. If ethical principles are social constructions to help us live together and accomplish common goals, then avoiding the unhappiness of societal ostracism or punishment, coupled with the happiness of security among one's companions and the greater ability to accomplish shared goals, would provide multiple reasons for being good according to societal standards.

Do Human Beings Have "Rights" that Should Be Honored in Social Contexts?

The United States' founding fathers said in the *Declaration of Independence*: "We hold these truths to be self-evident, that all men are created equal, that they are endowed by their Creator with certain unalienable rights that among these are life, liberty and the pursuit of happiness." The question of "rights" is another consideration in ethics. The idea behind rights is that individuals, groups, or all people have just and proper claims on certain things that should be honored. The founding fathers believed it was self-evident that the Creator endowed on all, the just claim to life, freedom, and the pursuit of happiness. There are many candidates for rights: life, freedom, equality, justice, happiness, education, healthcare, a living wage, self-expression, freedom of speech, participation in government, choice of religion, etc.

In discussing rights, we enter the realm of social values and therefore social ethics. Some values, like justice and equality, assume groups, not individuals. Rights and social values are essential to the intersection of economics and ethics since the markets that economists study involve two or more individuals engaged in trade. Another layer of complexity arises because social values, rights, and markets also involve social and political entities. This means that we must also consider the limit questions addressed by social and political philosophy. Here we survey some issues surrounding social values in general, and consider rights specifically. A later chapter on social ethics will cover social these topics in more detail.

Consideration of rights seems "right" and "good" in itself. Most, today, would say that humans have certain rights. We sometimes even hear of rights of non-humans, like animals, plants, the earth and the environment. "Rights" is a loaded term. The term of itself carries much power but on closer examination it leaves so many questions unanswered that it can seem vacuous and meaningless.

"Liberty" or "freedom" has been an important American value since the founding of the United States. The founding fathers championed freedom and saw it as a God-given right. The word, "Liberty," is on all U. S. currency (just a century ago "Lady Liberty" was depicted in some way in most U. S. coinage). But what exactly do we mean by "freedom?" Do we mean the license to do anything we want, such as take others' property, physically harm others, do things that only affect ourselves but do not impose harm on others unless freely chosen by others (so called "victimless crimes" like taking drugs and prostitution), freedom to drive as fast as we want, freedom to marry multiple people, freedom to say things that offend others, etc.?

Practically all societies have imposed some limits on freedom, so that in no society have individuals had unlimited freedoms. The nineteenth-century British philosopher, John Stuart Mill (AD 1806 – 1873), claimed that in a free society, "That the only purpose for which power can be rightfully exercised over any member of a civilized community against his will is to prevent harm to others."[16] This is called the *harm principle.* The question arises, however, as to what constitutes "harm?" Is it merely physical bodily harm?[17] Is it mental, psychological or emotional harm? Can we harm a person by harming another person or thing to which they are intimately related? Is harm to one's property harm to the individual, in Mill's sense? Is economic harm the loss of material resources, loss of health, loss of mental well-being, or what? In addition to the difficulties with defining "harm," in order for humans to successfully live together in societies it seems there must be *some* limitations on their freedom. Otherwise, insecurity and fear would lead most reasonable people to abandon the society.

We can ask similar questions about the social value of "equality." Saying that all humans are or should be "equal" sounds good, but what precisely do we mean by "equality?" Do we mean equality of condition so that all are the same in every way? What did the founding fathers mean when they said "all men are created equal?" Do we mean a right to equality of condition in society so that all have the exact same amount of income, possessions, wealth, housing, and material goods? Do we mean that everyone gets the same healthcare and has the same say in the government? Does equality mean removing all distinctions of class, status and authority?

Perhaps instead of equality of condition we mean equality of opportunity so that all have exactly the same opportunity to succeed or fail, depending on their will and effort. Is it sufficient for everyone to start at the "same place," so that whatever one achieves is due to their own ingenuity and hard work? Is economic equality merely equal division of a nation's product to all citizens, or should each person get an amount equal to the proportion of their efforts?

No matter how we define and value equality, we can also ask if equality in any of these senses is ever possible. Most would admit that by nature people are not equal in every way. Some are taller than others, and some are stronger than others. Some are healthier than others, and some are more intelligent. Even if we say that equality means a right to an equal position in society in terms of material goods, income, healthcare, education, status, rank or position (i.e., *some* form of equality of condition), we can still ask if this is even possible given the scarcity of resources due to finite metaphysical limits. The facts of economics regarding the allocation of scarce resources could be used to cast doubt on this possibility. Similarly, regarding equality of opportunity, we can wonder if getting everyone to the same "starting point" on a "level playing field" is ever really possible.

What about the social value of "justice?" Does "justice" mean rewarding and punishing individuals based on the contributions they make, or harms they bring, to society? This view of justice presupposes that individuals are responsible in some sense for their actions. Again, other limit questions impinge on questions of value here. If one believes metaphysically that all things are the determined effects of prior causes in an inexorable chain of causes and effects then she might conclude that individuals are not really responsible for their actions. Do genetics and environmental conditions determine an individual's behavior? If so, then perhaps the just thing to do is to not hold them responsible for their actions, but rather to alter their situations and living conditions (manipulate the causes) so as to produce good and desirable actions (effects).

Alternatively, if one believes that humans have some sort of freedom independent of deterministic causes and that makes them responsible for their actions, she can consistently hold that justice means distributive justice, dispensing of rewards and punishments based on good and bad behavior, contributions and harms, brought to society.

When Social Values and "Rights" Come Into Conflict

Talking of social values and rights is easier than thinking long and hard about what, specifically, these values mean and what, precisely, these rights entail. Yet, even once we have more clarity and precision about social values and rights there is the additional consideration that social values and rights can be mutually exclusive, and conflict. Then, there are trade-offs in which we must prioritize one over the others. These trade-offs are often unrecognized or even unknown.

Consider liberty and equality. Often exercising freedom necessarily results in disparities among individuals. If at Thanksgiving dinner I exercise my freedom to take a second helping of stuffing and there is not enough for everyone to have a second helping, then I have introduced an inequality, albeit a trivial one. On a larger societal level, if one worker exercises her freedom by applying it to more industrious work than another she may very well end up with more material goods than the other person. The extra goods she earned cannot go to the other worker. They are no longer available. Later, though, we will see how, over time, one person's industriousness can mean that all have more than they have now, albeit still in unequal amounts. On certain understandings of distributive justice this would also be just. The inequality of economic disparity results, though. Therefore, we must choose between valuing freedom or equality.

Now say we value equality over liberty. On Thanksgiving we impose a restriction on my freedom, in economic terms a "regulation," to take a second helping of stuffing. We might even divide the remaining stuffing, maybe only enough for one helping, into equal micro-units and give everyone a spoonful more. On a larger societal scale, we could limit the amount of work that our industrious worker freely chooses to do. She can earn only a limited amount of material goods so that there is more left for the other person. This is what market regulations do, in effect.

Another consideration is that perhaps not everyone wants more stuffing. If not, then the regulation does not help everyone attain their individual wants. Indeed, it now causes inefficiency in attaining the economic value of satisfaction or utility, because those who do not want more stuffing get it and those who wanted more have less. Economists have found that this is most often the effect of regulation as a law of markets. Here, valuing equality involves a tradeoff with the social value of freedom and the individual economic value of utility, due to inefficiency. On certain views of justice this would be just, although freedom is limited.

Now, say those who got extra stuffing did not it but rather wanted more sweet potatoes, so they trade their stuffing for sweet potatoes. Economists find that people generally find ways to freely trade for goods and services they prefer, even when there is market regulation. Free markets, legal or illegal, always exist. Yet we can ask if the fact that people naturally seek the freedom to get what they want means that they should freely seek what they want. Again, is "what *is* the case" also "what *should* be" the case? Some argue equality is a higher value on the basis of saying that what individuals prefer may not be what is really best for them, as we shall see.

Some even argue that wealth itself is freedom because it allows more possibilities to choose from. One with more wealth can choose to eat out more, buy a more expensive car, or take a vacation, compared to one with less wealth. There is a disparity not only of material goods but also in freedom since the wealthier have more freedom than the less wealthy. If we value equality over freedom, however, we might redistribute the material goods of those with more to those with less. Again, there is a tradeoff. The results are more equality of material condition and more freedom for more people, except for those from whom the wealth is taken. Their freedom is actually less. This is what taxes do, in effect. On certain views of justice this is just. Yet, someone's freedom must be limited to make way for equity or justice so conceived.

The Basis of Social Values and Rights

Another question about social values and rights is their source, which is similar to that regarding the sources of values in general. If one believes in a personal God then perhaps one claims that all human beings have certain rights in virtue of being created by God. The founding fathers held this. Christian thinkers have similarly argued that humans have basic fundamental rights on account of their being created in the image of God:

> It is not possible for one to be wealthy and just at the same time. Do you pay such honor to your excrements as to receive them into a silver chamber-pot when another man made in the image of God is perishing in the cold?[18]

Or one could hold that by nature human beings have natural rights according to the way the world is. This is similar to the more general theories of values rooted in being discussed above. One could argue that social values arise purely for the practical reason of human beings successfully living together, so that rights are a necessity for social groupings.

A related question is whether or not all humans are entitled to the same rights. What if these are privileges instead of rights? Not all people living in the United States have the right to vote. There are many residents of the United States who are foreign citizens. In order to vote, those not currently citizens but residing in the United States would have to become citizens.

We have briefly visited numerous limit questions about ethics and values bearing on all human existence and activity, including economic entities and activities. Finitude or scarcity necessitates trade-offs among mutually exclusive options both in our actions and in our values. How we answer these limit questions determines what the trade-offs and opportunity cost are for us in contemplating any possible economic activity. As we continue, we will see how the discipline of economics typically assumes that certain answers to these ethical limit questions are correct, and acts on them. We will also see that one's answers to the limit questions about values affect the values one assigns to opportunity costs and one's consideration of trade-offs when contemplating different possible economic situations and activities. Just as actions reveal individual preferences, whole economic systems reveal societal preferences about values. To understand this we must first understand how trade occurs.

MARKETS

The term "market" is frequently misunderstood in economic discussions. The media says the market is up or down. This ambiguous statement annoys many economists, who need and have a precise definition of a "market." In economics a market is a group of buyers and sellers, and the institution or arrangement through which they have to come together to trade. This ostensibly simple definition is loaded with many questions. What constitutes a group of buyers and sellers? How large is the group? What good or service is being traded and where is the group located? Answers to these questions have important consequences for the behavior and outcomes of a particular market.

When the media uses "market" in an all-inclusive sense, such as the "market" is up, they usually mean all individuals who are buying and selling stock.

Surely this group comprises different individuals in diverse locations trading heterogeneous goods. Economic analysis requires specificity and particularity. Every year in New Mexico green chilies are grown in the southern part of the state, are harvested in the fall, and many are sold in grocery store parking lots after being roasted. There are a lot of people in New Mexico who want roasted green chili in the fall. Would not the scenario be quite different if instead of New Mexico the location were New York? Would not the buyers be different? Of course they would, and the market for green chili in New Mexico is very different from the market for green chili in New York. The difference is vital because it leads to different price and quantity outcomes.

Combining all green chili buyers and sellers everywhere lessens the specificity requisite for meaningful description and analysis. Markets can and must be described by their scope and scale for the descriptions to have meaning. How many people are we talking about? Where are they? Do they have different tastes and preferences? These details are usually lacking in the media's discussions of markets. Should we be surprised if people in New Mexico are willing to pay more for green chili than people in New York? People in New Mexico have many more uses for green chili than those in New York, so they are willing to pay more than New Yorkers.[19]

The arrangement question is also important for description. How do buyers and sellers come together for trade? For example, we go to car dealerships expecting to haggle, but we do not haggle over prices at Wal-Mart or Best Buy. Different institutions result in very different means of trade, which is also important to consider. Why do people expect to haggle at a car dealership? Diverse markets evolve with different rules tacitly defined by traders over time. Yet, depending on the market, some may feel it is necessary to change the rules due to ethical considerations.

Consider healthcare in our country today. There are opposed ethical views as to how this market *should* behave. We have introduced many regulations that change the natural way that the market would function unregulated. Some would love to haggle with their physician to get the best deal, but others would find this vulgar. Financial gurus, like Dave Ramsey, advocate haggling in markets with tacit rules against haggling. Here there is a disparity between how the market might naturally evolve and interference in the market, in part due to societal mores.

Whether this is good or bad depends on different values and different answers to ethical limit questions. Because we can regulate, should we? Can we produce the effects we want by manipulating a natural system of causes and effects? This is the question of applying scientific knowledge through technology in any natural domain. Ethical considerations are usually close behind such questions, such as when we ask whether or not we should dam rivers, mine and change natural oil into gasoline, or clone human beings, just because we can. Are not human beings and their capacity to transcend and change nature themselves part of nature?

We must also ask if we even have the scientific knowledge to obtain the effects we want, regardless of ethical considerations. Neoclassical economics views economic systems as so complex that numerous and frequently undesirable unintended consequences can result when we interfere in markets. This is the case despite our current knowledge of positive economics. Economics is a social science, as explained above. Unlike the hard "physical" sciences, however, the systems that economists study cannot be studied in a controlled environment, such as a laboratory. Complexity and lack of controlled testing mean that the degree and specificity of economic predictions predicated on economic laws are less than in the hard sciences. This does not gainsay the claim that economics is a science. It does mean, however, that, precise and exhaustive predictions are difficult. Economists, as a rule, agree, though, that market regulations introduce many new chains of causes and effects into market systems. Regulations result not only in what economists know will result due to positive economic laws, but also in many unintended consequences as well.

For many neoclassical economists, then, market regulations are roughly equivalent to trying to grow bananas in Antarctica. Should we be surprised when it doesn't work? In this case we know bananas need a warm climate so we do not even try to grow bananas in Antarctica. Likewise, many neoclassical economists claim that societies constantly attempt market manipulations that are destined to fail due to the complexity of economic systems. Since there are more unknowns than knowns, societies embark on ill-informed quixotic quests. Other more optimistic judgments of our knowledge of economic systems say, usually on the basis of values concerns, that we can and must transcend and control markets to get the results we want. Yes, mistakes will inevitably occur, but has not all science and technology ultimately progressed through trial and error, and learning from our mistakes? It is the dignity and glory of humanity that human ingenuity will triumph over obdurate nature.

TYPES OF GOODS

Not only is the market important but so are the characteristics of goods. We must realize the importance of differences between goods, and why they are important. Economists classify goods by how a change in a variable, like the good's price or people's income, affects its consumption. Major classifications include "normal" and "inferior" goods. Consumption of these types is inverse and in proportion to changes in income. As income increases so does the consumption of a *normal* good, and as income decreases so does a normal good's consumption. For an *inferior* good it is the opposite. As income rises people consume less of an inferior good, but consume more as their income falls.

The preferences of many people dictate that as their income increases they buy more steak, but as it decreases they buy less (normal good). Conversely, as their income increases they buy less ramen noodles, but as it decreases they buy more (inferior good). For them, steak is a normal good and ramen noodles an inferior good. Yet, some people's preferences dictate that ramen noodles are actually a normal good for them. Everyone has different preferences, which is also an important consideration that we will discuss in more detail later.

Another category of goods, varying with income, is *luxury* goods. These are a special type of normal goods. Further, some goods may be *substitutes* or *complements* to one another. In this case their prices are inversely or positively correlated. For many, Coke and Pepsi are substitutes, meaning that they are indifferent, to a certain degree, about which they have. If the price of Coke goes up and Pepsi is a substitute for someone, then she will buy more Pepsi. For complements, such as peanut butter and jelly, the effect is the reverse, because the goods are tandem to one another. If the price of peanut butter rises, many also buy less jelly.

Substitutes are especially important when it comes to the effects of taxation and reallocation. Goods we tax may have many or few substitutes. Gasoline usually has few substitutes. Most need it to use their cars, without which they cannot get anywhere. The result is that their demand for gas is *inelastic*. This means they are not very sensitive to changes in the price. When gas prices increase for any reason, taxation or otherwise, they buy about the same amount as they did when the price was lower. This does not necessarily mean that oil companies are "evil." It is simply because there are no substitutes for gasoline for many people.

Conversely, goods with many substitutes are *elastic*. This means many respond to price increases by buying something else. A tax on soft drinks increasing their price will probably cause a reduction in the quantity people buy, as they will substitute another beverage. Economists often call taxes on a good or service *distortionary*, since people change their behavior due to the tax. The term "distortionary" does not imply a value judgment in positive economics, but rather a mere factual description. More on taxes will come later. It is important to realize now, however, that whether a good or service has a substitute or is a compliment is necessary to anticipate how certain changes in an economic system will inevitably affect economic activity.

SUMMARY

This chapter has introduced the disciplines of economics and ethics, and surveyed a variety of rudimentary concerns of, and issues in, both disciplines. The next chapter examines how consumers and firms interact, and how that interaction determines market prices, according to the economic model of supply and demand. These are the principles of microeconomics. We will also examine in more detail the most common normative ethical theories.

NOTES

1. Ludwig on Mises, *Human Action, A Treatise on Economics*, Scholar's Edition (Auburn, AL: The Ludwig von Mises Institute, 1998).

2. *The Oxford American Dictionary of Current English* defines economics as: "1. (a) the science of the production and distribution of wealth. (b) the application of this to a particular subject (the economics of publishing). 2. the condition of a country, etc., as regards material prosperity" ("economics *n.pl.*" *The Oxford American Dictionary of Current English*. Oxford University Press, 1999. *Oxford Reference Online*. Oxford University Press. Brescia University. 30 January 2012 http://www.oxfordreference.com/views/ENTRY.html?subview=Main&entry=t21.e9730).

3. These concepts are explained in detail later, but are noted now simply to identify specific points of economic theory that critics try to attack. For some examples, see, Steve Keen, *Debunking Economics: The Naked Emperor Dethroned?* 2nd expanded and revised ed. (London: Zed Books, 2011); Rod Hill and Tony Myatt, *The Economics Anti-Textbook: A Critical Thinker's Guide to Microeconomics* (London: Zed Books, 2010); Jonathan Aldred, *The Skeptical Economist* (New York, NY: Routledge, 2010); and Moshe Adler, *Economics for the Rest of Us: Debunking the Science That Makes Life Dismal* (New York, NY: The New Press, 2011). These critiques of economic theory routinely criticize assumptions that we will discuss later, such as, that: (1) agents in markets act rationally; (2) agents in markets operate on full knowledge; (3) value can be quantified; (4) individual market agents are the best judges of what they need and want; (5) positive economic "efficiency" calculations do not really measure value, and many others. We discuss all of these non-empirical claims in the book, but where they belong: in a discussion of the philosophical assumptions of the science of economics and in normative economic questions of value, not in a discussion of the validity of positive economics as a science and its findings.

4. For a good survey of the realist vs. anti-realist debate in contemporary philosophy of science, see, Martin Curd and J. A. Cover, eds., *Philosophy of Science: The Central Issues* (New York, NY: W. W. Norton & Company, 1998), 1049 – 1289.

5. Adam Smith, *An Inquiry into the Nature and Causes of the Wealth of Nations,* Vols. 1 – 2, ed. John Ramsay McCulloch (Edinburgh: Adam and Charles Black, 1863), 8.

6. K. J. Arrow, "A Difficulty in the Concept of Social Welfare," *Journal of Political Economy* 58, no. 4 (1950): 328 – 46.

7. Smith, *Wealth of Nations*, 8.

8. Friedrich Nietzsche, "The Gay Science, Book V (1887)," in *The Nietzsche Reader*, ed. Keith Ansell-Pearson and Duncan Large Dallas, 362 – 83 (Oxford: Blackwell, 2006), 363.

9. Sir Francis Bacon, *Meditations Sacrae and Human Philosophy* (Whitefish, MT: Kessinger Publishing, 1996), 71.

10. Joseph Butler, *Analogy of Religion* (Memphis, TN: General Books, 2012), 2.

11. Ecclesiastes 1:18.

12. Thomas S. Kuhn, *The Structure of Scientific Revolutions*, 2nd ed. (Chicago, IL: The University of Chicago Press, 1970).

13. Smith, *Wealth of Nations*, 8.

14. "In every system of morality, which I have hitherto met with, I have always remark'd, that the author proceeds for some time in the ordinary ways of reasoning, and establishes the being of a God, or makes observations concerning human affairs; when of a sudden I am surpriz'd to find, that instead of the usual copulations of propositions, *is*,

and *is not*, I meet with no proposition that is not connected with *an ought*, or an *ought not*. This change is imperceptible; but is however, of the last consequence. For as this *ought*, or *ought not*, expresses some new relation or affirmation, 'tis necessary that it shou'd be observ'd and explain'd; and at the same time that a reason should be given, for what seems altogether inconceivable, how this new relation can be a deduction from others, which are entirely different from it" [David Hume, *A Treatise Of Human Nature* (Oxford: Clarendon Press, 1896], 469 [italics original]).

15. Energy [E] is equal to matter [m] times the speed of light [c] squared.

16. John Stuart Mill, *On Liberty* (London: John W. Parker and Son, 1859), 22.

17. Commentators typically interpret "harm" here for Mill to mean physical harm and harm to personal property. Of course harm can mean other things, too, as seen in the questions raised here.

18. St. John Chrysostom (ca. AD 347 – 407), quoted in, J. H. W. G. Liebeschuetz, *Barbarians and Bishops: Army, Church, and State in the age of Arcadius and Chrysostom* (Oxford: Clarendon Press, 1990), 175 – 76.

19. This is not a reference to what the actual market price will be. Chapter 2 explains the concept of actual market price.

CHAPTER 2: MICROECONOMICS & NORMATIVE ETHICS

The first chapter introduced economics and ethics as disciplines, with their methods and contents. This chapter examines the heart of economic transactions: markets and the supply and demand model illustrating allocation. Here we also visit some common normative ethical theories, and we will see different ethical theories lead to different conclusions about ethics and economics.

PLEASURE AND HAPPINESS AS VALUES

A prime economic value is satisfaction or "utility," defined loosely as happiness or pleasure. Philosophical ethics has long considered pleasure and happiness as values. Is pleasure or happiness the greatest value? Some normative ethical theories say that it is, but certainly not all. It may seem that valuing pleasure or happiness in ethics is misguided since it implies selfishness, but many value selflessness. Value judgments like "You should share," "You should give to charity," and "Treat others as you want to be treated," seemingly dictate selfless behavior.

Yet, we can ask *why* we should act in seemingly selfless ways. Often the answer is some benefit, like, "Your life will be better," "People will like you and reciprocate kindness," "God will be pleased and bless you," "You will go to heaven when you die," or "You will accumulate good karma." Such benefits imply pleasure or happiness. Would we do any of these actions if there were no benefits for us, or worse, if we would only experience pain and unhappiness as a result?

We often do painful things. Some say that we only do so for greater happiness in the long-run, as a payoff. Pain now is the opportunity cost of more pleasure later. Exercising every day involves pain, but the goal could be greater health or attractiveness. A root canal or getting tonsils removed is painful, but the goal is the happiness of health. Going to college involves pain and sacrifice, but the goal might be to get a degree and a better job, as a result. Doing what we believe God wants can involve suffering and sacrifice, but our goal is happiness in the afterlife.

If we ask why someone pursues a goal like a career, marrying a certain person, or living in a specific place, they might respond with other goals like, "to make more money," "he or she is a nice person," or "to be closer to loved ones." Eventually, though, the chain of goals ends in the goal of "being happy." Although we seek all sorts of things we value, every value can be reinterpreted as a means to the end of happiness. Pleasure and happiness, though, are ends in themselves. We seek them for themselves alone, not as means to other ends. These thoughts lead some to say that happiness is the greatest, even the only real, value.

While the means of attaining it vary according to different policies, normative economics values a form of happiness that economists call *utility*. In normative economics the goal is to maximize the welfare of society as a whole by maximizing net utility. Thus economists are often mystified when indicted for being cold, hard advocates of selfishness, while many non-economists value happiness with virtual impunity. Is not seeking the "good life" or "well-being," with the end goal of pleasure or happiness, the same? Normative economic utility, and its roots in early modern philosophical ethics, are discussed below.

The descriptive question of whether or not we always *do* seek happiness directly bears on the normative question of whether or not we *should* always seek it. We have noted the distinction between indicative/descriptive statements about the way things *are*, and normative or prescriptive statement about the way things *should be*. Regardless of whether the way things are is related to the way things should be, if we always pursue happiness and cannot do otherwise, then ethical systems denying that happiness is the only value, seem wrongheaded. It seems foolish to say we should, at least sometimes, act without pursuing our own happiness, if we cannot. We would then be asking people to do something that they simply cannot.

Psychological Egoism vs. Psychological Altruism

One limit question of philosophical anthropology relevant to these considerations regards whether or not we always and necessarily act selfishly. This question is not about values, but about the ways things are, the facts. In considering this question, by itself, we do not make a descriptive value judgment about whether selfishness is good or bad. The question is only if people do, in fact, always act self-interestedly. The answer does bear on value judgments, though, because it seems foolish to say selfishness is bad and we should be unselfish, if we cannot. If we are capable of being unselfish, however, then, possibly we should be unselfish.

Psychological egoism says that we do always act selfishly and cannot do otherwise. This seems counterintuitive because of counterexamples of unselfish allocations of scarce resources. If I give money to a charity or pay for a friend's dinner, I allocate money for others, instead of myself. If you talk on the phone with a friend in crisis at 2AM then you allocate your sleep time to someone else. If you stop to help the victims of car accident then you allocate time and energy to them instead of yourself. If you get Chinese with your significant other because they want Chinese, even though you want Mexican, then you satisfy their preferences over yours.

A psychological egoist reinterprets such counterexamples to find selfish motives, perhaps hidden, underlying apparently unselfish actions. They say we allocate money to others because it makes us feel good, or we want others to think we are nice, or we want some other benefit like a good afterlife, as in religious almsgiving. They say you bought your friend dinner because you want them to like you more, or because it made you feel good. You allocate time to your friend at 2AM because you want them to think you are a good friend, or you hope they will one day return the favor. Perhaps your feelings toward them means their pain brings you pain. The apparently selfless act of sacrificing sleep for a friend is really a way to eradicate your own unhappiness, replacing it with happiness. Such suspicious reinterpretations that look for hidden selfish motives can be used on any counterexample of apparently selfless acts.

What about examples involving no benefit to the actor? Some sacrifice their lives for others. In 1941 in the Auschwitz concentration camp the Nazis punished ten innocent prisoners with death by starvation for the escape of another prisoner. Maximilian Kolbe, a Polish Franciscan friar, offered to take the place of Franciszek Gajowniczek who cried: "My wife! My children!" when selected. Kolbe gave his life for Gajowniczek, who survived. What of such examples?

A psychological egoist still posits hidden selfish motives. She might say that Kolbe subconsciously feared criticism for shirking his duty as a man of the cloth, had he not volunteered to take Gajowniczek's place, or that he could not live with the guilt he would have felt had he not. Such reinterpretations seem cold and harsh in the face of such self-sacrifice. Psychological egoists make no secret of their conviction that all people in all times and places always act out of selfish motives and cannot do otherwise. If they are right, then it would be inconsistent for any normative ethical system to say that people should, at least sometimes, act unselfishly.

Are there responses to psychological egoists? Advocates of *psychological altruism* say so. Psychological altruists claim that even though we do, maybe even often, act selfishly, we act unselfishly, at least sometimes. They point to how psychological egoists generalize from a sample, even a large sample, of selfish actions to the conclusion that *all* human actions are selfish. This is a strong generalization. Strong generalizations are precarious, however. Merely one example of a selfless act would defeat psychological egoism. No person or group can examine every action of every person who has ever lived. The set of such actions is astronomically large. One would have to be all-knowing to do this. Psychological altruists, then, question the strength of the large, all-encompassing, generalization that psychological egoists make.

Psychological altruists also point to how it is impossible in some cases to know the inner motivations of others. We can posit a possible selfish motive for any act, but this does not mean the act is really motivated by self-interest. Some psychological altruists go so far as to say that the psychological egoist projects his own selfish motives onto others, which is unfair. If psychological altruists are right that some people can and do sometimes act unselfishly then normative ethical theory can possibly include the value judgments that people should be unselfish or act unselfishly. In this case we would not demand of people something they cannot do, as would be the case if psychological egoism were correct.

Economics, as a modern discipline, began in the eighteenth and nineteenth centuries, and its fathers engaged philosophical questions more so than economists today. They were influenced by current philosophical trends, like modern philosophical arguments for egoism over altruism. Inheriting this tradition, neoclassical economics today mostly assumes egoism as the answer to this philosophical anthropological limit question, without much philosophical reflection. It assumes that individuals in markets act with self-interest but in an enlightened way, since trade benefits all parties involved. Some economists today advocate or even argue for altruism. Many economists, though, see altruistic behavior as a way of increasing one's own happiness, and thus, at root, egoistic.

Ethical Theories Involving the Pursuit of Pleasure and Happiness

Psychological egoism and psychological altruism consider how people do act without passing a value judgment on this fact. *Ethical egoism* and *ethical altruism*, however, make value judgments. Ethical egoism is the normative claim that we *should* always act self-interestedly, and ethical altruism is the normative claim that we *should*, at least sometimes, act unselfishly. The debate between psychological egoists and psychological altruists shows how this question of whether or not pleasure and happiness are the greatest or only values is related to whether or not people always *do* pursue pleasure or happiness. This is not the only point in favor of the normative value judgment that we *should* always act to increase our pleasure and happiness.

In addition to saying that every act is a means to the end of pleasure or happiness, which are the only ends in themselves, many add that we know by experience that pleasure and happiness are values. We feel the goodness of pleasure and happiness, directly. This experiential argument leads many with empirical epistemologies, theories addressing limit questions about knowledge that prioritizes experience, to claim that pleasure or happiness is the greatest or only value. Those prioritizing or confining knowledge to sense experience often conclude that we know pleasure and knowledge are values because we can directly experience their goodness.

We have already seen how theories, saying pleasure or happiness is the greatest or only value, are criticized for reducing ethics to selfishness. Some critics add that because animals always seek pleasure, such theories put us solely on the level of other beasts, despite our apparent transcendence of and differences from the natural world. There are those who do say we should only seek physical pleasure and pleasant feelings, which fits well with empirical epistemologies. This is called *ethical hedonism* from the Greek word *hedone*, meaning "pleasure." Yet hedonism in our day connotes something inferior, even base and bestial.

In response, ethical egoists distinguish between pleasure and happiness. This was the ancient Greek philosopher and ethical hedonist Epicurus' (342 BC – 270 BC) strategy, and that of many ethical egoists today. Admitting that only pursuing sensory pleasure is animal behavior, they say that happiness is different from mere sensory pleasure. We are different from other animals, and this precisely is why we can have enjoyable states of well-being, or happiness. Complex emotions like friendship, love, the joys of thinking abstractly and rationally, and aesthetic beauty are examples of joys, unique to humans, which transcend simple physical pleasure. They urge that humans should pursue these types of joys, too, and not only base physical pleasure.

While some ethical hedonists do advocate pursuing bodily pleasure alone, many others formulate ethical theories that say we should pursue the more complex value of happiness. They see an intrinsic connection between goodness and happiness. Plato (429 BC – 347 BC) and Aristotle (384 BC – 322 BC) argued that by developing an ethical character, or proper set of virtues, we become happy. Some religious traditions like medieval Christianity have argued that God, as the supreme good, is also supreme joy. This means that seeking union with God, by being and doing good brings, supreme happiness (or beatitude), to which no created thing can compare.

Those saying pleasure or happiness is the greatest or only value face other difficulties. What is happiness? People define happiness differently. Some say it is having money. Others say it is having close friends and meaningful relationships. Others say it is fishing on a remote lake on a summer's day. Some say it is doing exciting things, like playing sports or riding roller coasters. Others say it is sitting at home watching a movie and cuddling with a loved one.

The fact that different things make different people happy poses a problem for identifying what, exactly, happiness is. It seems that if there is such a thing as happiness, as opposed to mere bodily pleasure, then all experience of happiness must have something in common. Is happiness a state of mind? Is it an emotion? Is it attaining one's goals, even though people have different goals? Is it peace and the absence of anxiety? Those making the normative value judgment that we should pursue happiness usually try to define it somehow, but others argue it is really just a vacuous term we use to label many disparate things. Economists value, and therefore want to maximize, utility, which they loosely define as satisfaction. This definition faces a similar problem because different individuals in markets have and express different preferences.

Utility Maximization and "Real" vs. "Apparent" Goods

Even if happiness is a real thing and not a vacuous term, this does not mean all have the right notions on how to attain it. Three year-olds might think eating an entire jar of cookies will make them happy, but adults know better and stop them. College students might think that partying every night will make them happy, but if they do, they risk the unhappiness of flunking out of college. We can envision numerous examples of people pursuing what they think will make them happy but they are apparently wrong. Yet, many individual's choices are predicated on the assumption that they alone know what will make them happy.

Thus, there is a potential distinction between *apparent goods*—what people *think* will make them happy and *real* goods—what will really make them happy. If valid, this distinction is crucial for economics and ethics. Neoclassical economics assumes that individuals in markets know what is best for them. The preferences that they act on are assumed to be what will really, not only apparently, maximize their utility. Only they can judge what will maximize their utility, and therefore *no one should* interfere with their choices. This can normatively lead to a free market with minimal regulation. Other economic approaches claim that some or most people do not know what is best for them. They need guidance in their preferences and choices. If they are incorrigible, then perhaps their choices must be forced. This can normatively lead to more regulation and central planning, where the government fixes the choices of agents in markets.

The problem of who is qualified to judge real and apparent goods applies to all normative ethical theories, not only those that prioritize happiness as a normative value. No matter what the normative values are, we can always ask if individuals are qualified to identify that value and the proper means to attain it. Some argue that only some, not all, people are thus qualified. Some argue that only a wise and benevolent monarch can do this. Plato famously argued in the *Republic* that only philosophers can do this, and so they should lead. Others point to the limited knowledge and power of even the wisest persons, indicating that no one person is qualified to judge what is best and how to attain it for everyone. Some of these same people argue that self-interest overtakes even the wisest and most powerful people. So, when policy decisions are limited to a few, their selfishness inevitably jeopardizes the well-being of the many.

We have spoken thus far only of individuals pursuing pleasure and happiness. Yet, we are social beings our actions affect others. We have already surveyed some social values like justice, freedom, and equality. Assuming a life of their own, groups might act with a greater and more dangerous self-interest than individuals, some contend.[1]

In economic markets the actions of individuals affect others. Sometimes agents in a market know the consequences of their actions for others, sometimes they do not. If pleasure or happiness is the highest normative value, does the individual's happiness matters most, or does the happiness of all matter most? If we *should* pursue happiness, *should* we pursue first and foremost our own happiness? Or *should* we pursue the happiness of everyone in our social group, or the happiness of every human being? We can extend this question to even non-human organisms capable of pleasure and pain. Many animal rights activists, for instance, condemn certain behaviors on the grounds that they inflict needless pain on animals. Further, if we should pursue the happiness of all then there is still the economic problem of aggregating individuals' utility to calculate sum totals when comparing different possible policies to implement. We will see that this is difficult and requires using simplifying assumptions, such as that all people are risk-averse. We will discuss risk-aversion later. The validity of these assumptions is valid and is a concern. Some economists believe most individuals are risk-averse, but are uncomfortable assuming everyone is risk-averse.

Earlier, we discussed ethical approaches that try to consider an action's consequences, at least to some extent, in determining its rightness or wrongness. This means that the same action can be right in one situation but wrong in another. These consequentialist approaches correspond to theories of knowledge that depend on our examination and experience of the world (empiricism) instead of ideas and the reasoning about the relationships between those ideas (rationalism). Empiricism and consequentialism are *a posteriori* (literally, "from the end" or "after") approaches to knowledge and value, because truth and value are known only *after* examination of the world. Ethical systems that see pleasure or happiness as the highest or only normative value say we *should* seek pleasure or happiness as the consequences of our actions. Thus, pleasure and happiness-based ethical theories are forms of ethical consequentialism.

Earlier we also examined ethical systems that bring and apply to specific situations pre-established rules, principles, or judgments determined apart from any consideration of situations or consequences. These are *a priori* (literally, "from the beginning" or "before") approaches, and hold that we know right and wrong *before* any consideration of a specific situation or consequences. These correspond to epistemologies valuing ideas and reasoning (rationalism) over the world of our sense experience (empiricism). In these approaches, if telling the truth is always right and lying is always wrong, then even lying to save someone's life is still wrong, no matter how stark the consequences of telling the truth. There are pros and cons to both *a priori* and *a posteriori* approaches to ethics, with arguments made by advocates of both. We will examine some of these as we survey common theories of normative ethics, to which we now turn.

NORMATIVE ETHICAL THEORIES

Normative ethics involves systematic theories that aim at a coherent way to make value judgments about good and bad, right and wrong. It involves seeking a systematic and consistent method to be applied to any question of right and wrong. Normative ethics, then, is not concerned with specific ethical decisions, whether doing "x" or "y" is right or wrong. Rather, it involves theories applicable to any and all ethical decisions whatsoever. As we explicate more economic theory we must note how different normative ethical theories answer questions of good and bad, right and wrong, that arise in economics.

Utilitarianism

As explained above, an ethical theory is consequentialist if it considers, to any extent, the consequences of actions in determining right and wrong. There are many varieties of consequentialism that combine rules and principles with consequences to various degrees. In this survey we do not have time and space to consider their main types, however, we will examine perhaps one of the most well-known consequentialist theories, utilitarianism. *Utilitarianism* is a consequentialist normative ethical theory based on pleasure and happiness. It has been adopted in a modified form by modern economics to normatively analyze markets and policies. That pleasure or happiness is the highest or only normative value, is a very old idea. More recently, British philosopher and empiricist Jeremy Bentham (AD 1748 – 1832) developed utilitarianism as one of the most formidable normative ethical theories based on pleasure as the only value.

Bentham observed that we directly perceive with our senses the value of pleasure, and that all other values are means to the end of pleasure, the only end in itself. He thus concluded that pleasure is the only normative value toward which we should strive. Yet Bentham was not an ethical egoist who would say individuals should seek only their own pleasure, because all sentient creatures can experience pleasure. Pleasure, not the individual, is the value, and it does not play favorites. Bentham was one of the early animal rights activists in the west.

This means for Bentham that in any situation an action is right to the degree that it promotes pleasure. The right thing to do is that which will result in the greatest pleasure for the greatest number, and an action is wrong to the degree it will result in pain. This is called the *principle of utility*. The greatest net pleasure for the greatest number is the value, not the pleasure or pleasure of the individual alone. Bentham admits that attaining the greatest net pleasure might mean pain for some, but the greatest net pleasure for the greatest number, once opportunity costs have been weighted, is what matters. He even developed a *hedonistic calculus* based on types of pleasure and pain resulting from any given action, and advocated using it to determine right and wrong in any given situation. Modern economics adopted and modified this concept of utility analysis. Because it is impossible to sum every person's utility, economists now use utility in a strictly ordinal sense. They assume individuals always act so as to maximize their own utility, always preferring a higher indifference curve, as will be explained later in the chapter.

John Stuart Mill (AD 1806 – 1873) further refined Bentham's utilitarianism and responded to criticisms. Bentham focused more on pleasure and pain than the more nuanced ideas of happiness discussed above. He also viewed pleasure and pain in the hedonistic calculus mostly *quantitatively*. Mill included *qualitative* judgments as well, so that certain types of pleasure or happiness are worth more than equal amounts of other types. For example, spending time in good company and stimulating conversation might outweigh an equal quantity of physical pleasure. Economists account for these qualitative differences by allowing individuals to rank their preferences and index them.

Mill also responded to criticisms of utilitarianism. The complex calculation of the net pleasure of all possible actions is burdensome. How can we do this for every decision? Mill said that there are many tried and true actions that produce the greatest net happiness, others before us have performed the calculus, and so we need not do it again. Human history has repeatedly confirmed, for example, that people in societies are happier if they respect each other's property rights and do not steal. This general rule is derived from the principle of utility, but we need not perform a hedonistic calculus for every question of theft vs. respecting property rights.

Utilitarianism, then, explains our many general ethical rules and norms by saying they are ultimately based on the principle of utility. The Ten Commandments, in this view, came from the practical concern of promoting the greatest happiness for the greatest number. Murdering lessens the victim's happiness he would have by living longer. Stealing increases general unhappiness. The rule to forgive rather than seek vengeance helps alleviate the pain of guilt and conflict between parties at odds. Analogously, economists formulate general rules by knowing that certain policies always increase utility or disutility (lower utility), without doing the math in every new situation.

There are questions about some rules utilitarianism tries to explain. What about the rule against adultery? Does this not stifle pleasure and happiness? Would not free love bring more pleasure to more people? Utilitarians reply that although there is short-term pleasure in free love, there are longer-term negative effects resulting in greater pain and suffering for more people in the long-run. People can get sexually transmitted diseases. Children born outside of wedlock and without stable family units can have worse lives. Free love can cause emotional and mental pain by bonding intimately, but not permanently, with numerous sexual partners.

One strength of utilitarianism is its ability to account for diverse ethical norms. Another is its flexibility in accounting for unique situations. *A priori* theories are inflexible, at times forcing us to go against our moral intuitions. Consider, again, the example of a good German hiding Jews under Nazi interrogation. In this situation it seems that lying is the right thing to do. Say a poor man's family is starving, so he steals a few dollars from a rich person to get food. On the frequent economic assumption that most people are risk-averse, the rich person will not miss these few dollars. Losing them causes him little pain. These few extra dollars will, though, bring great happiness to the starving family. The principle of utility could lead to saying it is *right* for the poor man to steal the few dollars. Some rule-based theories would say that stealing is always wrong, and so the man's theft to feed his family is wrong. Our intuitions tell us, though, that it is not wrong but right for the man to do this.

This example is similar to the normative economic question of redistributing wealth from the rich to the poor through taxes and other means. Those advocating redistribution frequently say that the rich suffer very little pain by giving up a small portion of their wealth, but the poor receive much happiness. But this is true only on the assumption that the rich are risk-averse.

As a normative ethical theory, utilitarianism is a method to arrive at the right course of action in any situation. It does not prescribe specific courses of action. In fact, utilitarians and those advocating rule-based normative ethical theories might very well agree on the right action in the same situation. Mill agrees with many of the same norms that we see in *a priori* ethical systems. The difference lies in the *method* for arriving at the right course of action.

Take the soldier who throws himself on a grenade to save his platoon members. One might say this is the right thing to do using divine command theory, which we will examine shortly. It is right because God commands us to love our neighbors as ourselves, and many of us would want someone else to save our lives by sacrificing their own. Thus on the basis of divine authority the soldier is obligated to save his fellow platoon members by sacrificing himself. God's commandment makes throwing himself on the grenade to save his mates right.

A utilitarian examining this situation would say the same thing. It is right for the soldier to throw himself on the grenade to save his platoon members. The *reason* for why it is the right thing would be very different from the divine command theorist's, however. If the grenade kills a whole platoon then more people suffer pain and lose the opportunity to experience more pleasure and happiness than if only one person dies. Someone has to die. The question is whose dying will insure the greatest net happiness for the greatest number of people. Even though the soldier sacrificing himself suffers pain and happiness loss, the net result is greater happiness for the greater number. Not a divine command, but the calculation of net happiness based on the principle of utility makes the self-sacrifice right for a utilitarian. We can ask, though, if every member of the platoon would get the same amount of utility by staying alive, and how we could possibly know this.

Utilitarianism is an important example of a contemporary consequentialist theory. There are other objections to consequentialism in general and utilitarianism in particular. We will see some of these as we turn to a diametrically opposed approach to normative ethics, *a priori*, rule-based ethics. Immanuel Kant's ethics is one of the purest examples of such an approach.

A Priori, Rule-Based Ethics: Immanuel Kant's Deontological Ethics

Utilitarianism demonstrates well consequentialism in normative ethics. Considering an action's consequences before determining its rightness or wrongness, it is an *a posteriori* approach that determines value only after examining the world. There is a very different approach relying on rules, duties or obligations derived *a priori* ("from the beginning") or prior to our experience of the world, without considering an action's consequences. As with consequentialism, there are many variations of this approach. Perhaps one of the purest examples is the ethics of the eighteenth-century philosopher, Immanuel Kant (AD 1724 – 1804).

Kant embarked on ethics after reading an earlier eighteenth-century British philosopher, David Hume (AD 1711 – 1776). Hume was a radical empiricist in his epistemology. Wanting to abide by the empiricist principle that *all* knowledge begins with experience, he questioned even basic beliefs that we hold that cannot be derived from experience, like cause and effect. Hume argued that since we never experience with our senses what we call "causality," but only correlated events happening in regular succession, causality is only an idea in our minds with perhaps no basis in reality. Maybe causality is a convenient fiction we fabricate to help us make our way in the world. Hume similarly questioned the existence of an individual self, or "soul," in older metaphysical parlance. He argued that all we ever experience is a succession of thoughts, feelings, and emotions, but never a unified self. As with the idea of causality, he said that perhaps we have constructed the idea of a self as a useful fiction.

In ethics, Hume's radical empiricism led him to question the idea of normative value judgments in general. All we know from our sensory experience are states of affairs or facts. There is nothing in our experience giving us value judgments about right and wrong. We can stare long and hard at a masked bandit pointing a gun at an elderly woman demanding her purse, but there is nothing in our sensory experience of that event that tells us the masked bandit is doing something *wrong*. For Hume, values are not built into our experience of brute facts in the world.

Focusing on experiences of facts alone, he went so far as to say that value judgments translate to indicative states of affairs. There is nothing right or wrong with the bandit's activity. Rather, for some cultural, religious, social, instinctual, or other reason, experiencing this event causes us distaste or displeasure. When we say: "The bandit robbing the elderly woman is wrong" we really mean: "I have an unpleasant feeling of disgust when I see the bandit robbing the elderly woman." By such an analysis, Hume drove a wedge between our empirical experience of the world and our value judgments.

Applied to economic policy, Hume would say that the facts of positive economics just are what they are. They are neither right nor wrong. Providing healthcare for all is neither just nor unjust. Efficient allocation of scarce resources is neither right nor wrong. Individuals just have different subjective feelings about these economic states of affairs, and there is nothing inherently right or wrong about the states of affairs themselves. Saying: "It is just for all to have healthcare" really means: "Everyone having healthcare makes me feel good." "Efficiency is good" means: "I like efficiency."

Hume's radically empirical arguments "interrupted my dogmatic slumber," says Kant.[2] Kant had long believed in cause and effect, the individual self, and right and wrong, but Hume challenged these beliefs. This set Kant on the path to revolutions in epistemology, ethics, and the philosophy of religion.

In situating ethics earlier we surveyed different limit questions addressed by philosophy, and we mentioned how all limit questions and their answers are related. Focusing on the priority of sense experience as the best or only form of knowledge, empiricism is tied to contingency, probability, uncertainty, difference, and inconsistency. Our senses can deceive us, offer different information at different times and places, and only draw tentative conclusions pending more experiences. What we now believe based on our sensory experiences might change, perhaps into something inconsistent with what we earlier held.

Conversely, focusing on definitions, ideas, and the relationships between ideas, rationalism is tied to necessity and certainty. Relationships between ideas are frequently necessary, certain, and consistency. The ideas that: (1) "x is greater than y" and (2) "y is greater than z" make it certain that (3) "x is greater than z." Denying proposition (3) would be an impossible rational inconsistency because of the relationships between propositions (1) and (2). Ideas (1) and (2) infer the certain, necessary, and consistent idea that (3) "x is greater than y," apart from any sensory experience.

We have also already seen the connections between *a posteriori* consequentialist ethics and empiricism, and between *a priori* rule-based ethics and rationalism. Hume was a radical empiricist, but Kant was optimistic about rationalism. In his ethics, as in so many other areas of his philosophy, Kant advocated rational consistency as of highest value: "Consistency is the highest obligation of a philosopher, and yet the most rarely found."[3] Agreeing with Hume that there is an unbridgeable gulf between experience and ethics, between fact (is) and value (should), Kant still did not abandon the idea that humans are necessarily ethical beings, and for more than personal and social reasons.

Kant used Hume to refute consequentialism. Hume denied that causes and effects are in our empirical experience. Kant added that although we anticipate *probable* consequences of our actions we cannot be *certain* about their happening. The good German can lie to the Nazis to save the Jews hiding in his house, but the Nazis still might search the house, find, and kill them. The lie's intended consequence would thus be thwarted. Our utilitarian soldier who tries to save his platoon mates might fail and die with them. Thus his self-sacrifice would fail in its intention. Similarly, an ethical egoist might fail in attaining her own happiness, no matter how hard she tries.

For Kant, these examples show that our experience is too contingent and unpredictable to base values on consequences. There is too much beyond our control, so that intended good consequences are never certain. Kant's argument here is of import to normative economics. Since economic systems are so complex it is difficult to know all of a policy's consequences, and whether its intended results will issue. For example, Estonia pays women to have babies to increase the nation's birth rate.[4] While this does attain the good goal of increasing the population, an unanticipated negative result has been more unwed single mothers whom society must support. The impact of this unintended consequence is difficult to measure, but it certainly necessitates adjusting the policy in the future to correct unwanted outcomes. F. A. Hayek spoke of the "fatal conceit" by which those who advocate interfering in economic systems to get "better results" can never account for all of the unknown results of such policies.[5] He believed the presumption that we can fully understand markets and control them with precision is false and fatal.

These considerations led Kant to claim that ethics cannot be based on anything in our experience: "Is it not thought to be of the utmost necessity to work out for once a pure moral philosophy, completely cleansed of everything that may be only empirical?"[6] He proceeded to construct an ethics dedicated entirely to the supremacy of the universal principles of reason. Reflecting on why we might do the right thing, Kant concluded that duty, or what he calls a "good will," alone determines an action's value. Duty is the desire to do the right thing for no other reason than it is right. Duty alone is good without qualification. If goodness depends on the success of our actions, then it is as contingent and uncertain as the desired results, not necessary and certain. Any ethics, basing goodness on our empirical examination of the world, is uncertain and changeable because sense experience is uncertain and changes. If "lying is wrong in situation X but is right in situation Y," then the command to tell the truth is contingent, and, therefore, good only with qualifications. Also, if an action's goodness is based on its consequences then its goodness is only a secondary means to some other desired goal, like happiness. Its goodness is not an end in itself. Ethics therefore needs what is absolutely and unchangingly good, not contingent. Ethics needs what is "good without qualification."

Kant even denied that an action's goodness is based on the actor's intentions. While we can make informed guesses concerning others' motivations, we can never be certain of them. This is due to both the uncertainty of empirical knowledge and the fact that others' motivations are interior, hidden from view. We can also misjudge our own intentions by deceiving ourselves into thinking we have good ones when we really do not. If we say an action's goodness is determined by the actor's intentions, then its goodness is as contingent and uncertain as the actor's intentions. It is only a qualified goodness, not goodness "without qualification."

Consider some examples. People do not steal for many reasons: to avoid punishment, avoid disapproval and disdain, please God, or feel like a good person. Remember the egoist. All of these can be reinterpreted as selfish reasons. Does not one who refrains from theft solely because it is his duty, and only because it is right, deserve our praise? Suppose someone gives to a charity for the homeless because it gives her a good feeling, a "warm fuzzy" inside. Another does so because she believes it is her duty, and she is even aware of the painful fact that she is sacrificing her own money for others. Will we not praise the one who sacrifices out of a sense of duty, not in order to gain some benefit, like feeling good? Notice, too, that all of the reasons given in these two examples, apart from duty, are based on consequences that will benefit the actor: people will like me, I will feel good, I will not get in trouble, or I will go to heaven. If goodness depends on intentions then goodness is contingent on elusive good intentions. Even if benefiting one's self is good, the intended consequences may fail, and with them the action's goodness.

In these ways Kant argued that acting out of duty, doing what is right solely because it is right, is the only action worthy of the name "good." A "good will" is the only unqualified goodness. Even if one's action fails to achieve its intended purpose, the good will of this person "then, like a jewel, it would still shine by itself, as something that had its full worth in itself."[7] Its value would not go up or down depending on how useful or fruitless it was. Acting on duty alone makes an action good for Kant.

How do we know our duty then? First, understanding duty as a rule or obligation, as what *should* be done, Kant spoke of duty as an imperative. Second, as a rationalist ethically, Kant believed that we *know* our duty from reason and logical consistency. Third, metaphysically, duty is one and universal, applying to all people at all times and places. Duty rises above the plurality of the flux and flow of the constantly changing external world of our empirical knowledge. Duty is entirely self-contained, not depending on anything else.

Kant made a distinction between independent imperatives and imperatives dependent on something else, like attaining a goal or consequence. For example, an ethical hedonist might issue the imperative: "Eat your dessert first." Imperatives of this form are dependent on uncertain consequences and on empirical knowledge. The ethical hedonist aims at the pleasure of the actor and bases his imperative on his belief, right or wrong, that eating dessert first will attain that goal. Kant said that imperatives like this can be rephrased as: "If you want to have more pleasure then eat dessert first." He calls this a *hypothetical imperative* because it depends on something, in this case the goal or consequence of pleasure. The "If . . . then" structure of this and other such imperatives makes them contingent and qualified, and thus hypothetical. For Kant, true goodness is entirely independent of anything else, or unqualified. There cannot be any condition, any "if." This type of absolutely unqualified imperative, depending on nothing else, he calls a *categorical imperative*. The categorical imperative determines our duty.

How do we know what the categorical imperative is? The universality of duty apart from the plurality and flux of experience led Kant to define the categorical imperative as: "I ought never to act except in such a way that I could also will that my maxim should become a universal law."[8] Our duty, or the categorical imperative for any given action, is capable of being made into a universal law for all persons at all times and places, without logical inconsistency. We can universalize a categorical imperative to cover all possible situations, without a rational inconsistency.

What would be an example? A common rule of manners says: "At the dinner table you should let others serve themselves before serving yourself." Many believe this is the right thing to do. Not Kant. For Kant, this is a rationally inconsistent pious platitude. Why? Could we consistently universalize this imperative? No. Why? Always letting others get their food before we do is logically inconsistent because then *no one* would get food. It is logically impossible for everyone to pass the food and anyone to get food. Everyone must pass the food, so no one gets served. The ideas (1) "*everyone* go second" and (2) "others go first" are logically incompatible. They cannot be held together in our minds at the same time, just as the ideas that (1) "x > y" and (2) "y > z" cannot be held together in our minds with the idea that (3) "z > x."

The possibility of consistently universalizing a rule is how we discern our duty, says Kant. He argued that rules like telling the truth and treating other people as ends instead of means to ends can be consistently universalized. Many common moral rules we accept as right are, according to Kant, derived from this rational consistency principle. In some cases, however, this leads to counterintuitive conclusions, such as it is wrong to lie to save lives. Consider the economic question of the rightness of giving to charity, which many agree is good. If *everyone* should give a certain amount of money to charity then those who receive charity should also give the amount they received. No one gets to keep the charitable giving if the rule is universalized.

Some criticize Kant with inconsistency himself, because the mental exercise trying to universalize the rule relies on what would happen in the real world. Kant wants to avoid empirical knowledge and the consideration of consequences in ethics. Yet, is not the exercise about the dinner table based on the consequences of everyone passing the food? Kant says no. The ideas in our minds are in some sense derived from experience of the world, but the relationships between ideas are processes of logic independent from the world. We may get the idea of the number two from seeing instances of two things in the world, but the idea of the number two is not an object in our experience. It is rather an idea, and we can perform mathematical exercises in our mind apart from any connection with the world of experience. We can manipulate ideas in our minds to know their certain and necessary relationships, like, "If St. George killed the dragon then it is not the case that St. George did not kill the dragon," without the ideas of St. George and the dragon having any connection to anything in our experience.

Divine Command Theory

Since all limit questions and the answers we give them are interrelated, ethics and the philosophy of religion intersect. This is clearly seen in *divine command theory*, a normative ethical theory used by some traditions within the western monotheistic religions of Judaism, Christianity and Islam, but with analogies in some non-western religions. Recall that both philosophy and religion address limit questions. The difference is that philosophy relies on reason and experience alone, while religions appeal to supposed religious authorities in addition to reason and experience.

Divine command theory assumes belief in the personal God of *monotheism*. "Monotheism" comes from two Greek words, *mono* meaning "one" and *theos* meaning "God" or "deity." As with many etymologies, the etymology of monotheism tells us precious little other than it is belief in only one God. What does this mean? Monotheism is metaphysically monistic regarding ultimate reality. Ultimate reality is that which ultimately explains everything else, and beyond which there is no other explanation. Monotheism asserts that ultimate reality is only one thing, not many. Some philosophical and religious traditions are metaphysically dualistic or pluralistic regarding ultimate reality. They believe in two (dualism) or more (pluralism) ultimate realities that account for everything else, but which are not accounted for by anything else. They believe in two or more fundamental and irreducible elements of reality. Even though monotheism is monistic regarding ultimate reality, other philosophical and religious traditions are metaphysically monistic regarding ultimate reality, but not monotheistic. One who believes that matter-energy is ultimate reality is monistic, for instance.

Pantheism and Deism are similar to, but not identical with, monotheism. Pantheism claims that ultimate reality is identical with the universe as a whole. Deism claims that a personal ultimate is responsible for the universe, but is not intimately present and involved in the universe. For monotheism, ultimate reality is both very different from ("transcendent"), and intimately present and involved in ("immanent"), the universe, and the universe depends on this ultimate reality for its own existence and activity.

Monotheism calls the one ultimate reality it believes in, "God." This one God is self-existent, having existence only from itself and requiring no prior principle, cause, or explanation. This God's existence is independent from everything else, while everything else depends on this God for its existence. This God is believed to be all-powerful (omnipotent), all-knowing (omniscient), all-good (omnibenevolent), and all-present (omnipresent). Monotheists believe this God is in some sense personal, with subjective consciousness, reason, freedom, and a will.

Divine command theory is only one normative ethical theory used by monotheists. It is not the only one. Divine command theory says that: (1) all that God commands is obligatory or morally right; (2) all that God prohibits is morally wrong; and (3) all that is neither commanded nor prohibited by God is morally permissible, neither obligatory nor prohibited. If God commands that we should give at least some money to the poor, then giving money to the poor is morally right. If God prohibits stealing the possessions of others, then stealing is morally wrong. If God says nothing about the type of clothing we should wear and the food we should eat, then we are permitted to wear any type of clothing and eat any type of food. What we wear and eat is not subject to value judgments of right and wrong. In normative economics many believe that God commands governments to insure the good of citizens. Thus, regardless of economic impact, it is always right for a government to do things like redistribute wealth and have a welfare safety net to help the poor and needy.

Thus, in divine command theory, God's commands and prohibitions alone determine right and wrong. These are expressed as rules, so divine command theory is a rule-based *a priori* theory, not a consequentialist or *a posteriori* theory. Prior to any specific situation in which stealing could occur we know that stealing is wrong and honoring property rights is right. Any good consequences of stealing, like feeding starving children, have no bearing on the rightness or wrongness of stealing. If God commands it, then taxing the rich and redistributing their income to the poor is right. This is so regardless of its impacts on a society, such as lesser well-being for the individuals being taxed and for all persons in society, considered collectively.[9]

Divine command theorists make several arguments. If individuals or groups come up with ethical rules they can and do differ in some cases. They can even be mutually exclusive and contradictory. Some mandate monogamy as morally right but others do not, allowing polygamy and / or multiple sexual partners. Some mandate that the wealth a person earns in a free market is rightfully theirs, but others mandate the redistribution of some earned wealth to those who have less or none as morally right. Some divine command theorists even argue that Kant's attempt to base ethics on universal rational principles common to all is insufficient, because what seems rationally consistent to some does not seem rationally consistent to others. God alone, they argue, can provide a truly *universal, absolute* and *ultimate* justification for morality.

Divine command theorists also argue that an authority is required for moral principles to be absolutely binding. In order for moral principles to have force, they must be imposed by an external authority. If, as some say, morals are only rules invented by individuals and societies, then they are like the rules of a game. Those same individuals or societies can change the rules or exempt themselves from them at some point. Two groups playing an informal game of baseball might agree that three strikes is an out, but they could conceivably both agree that only two or four strikes make an out. When those bound by rules also make the rules, they are above the rules. If rules cannot impose absolute force, they do not have the strength of moral authority. Frequently divine command theorists add religious arguments. They will say that following God's rules is necessary for a happy existence in this life, and / or a blessed afterlife—to go to heaven and avoid hell when one dies.

As with all normative ethical theories, there are problems with divine command theory. A primary concern is where to find God's commands and prohibitions. Many believe they are in sacred texts, but which ones? Are they in the Tanakh, Old and New Testaments, Vedas, Qur'an, or some other text? Others believe they are in the teachings of a religious leader, group of religious leaders, or specific religious tradition. How do monotheists know where to find God's commands?

Even if monotheists agree on where to find God's commands and prohibitions, they differ in their interpretation. Biblical monotheists disagree over whether God sometimes allows capital punishment, whether God requires pacifism, and whether God mandates worship on Saturdays or Sundays. Some biblical monotheists think God mandates private property and a free market economy, while others believe God mandates a form of socialism or communism. They also disagree over what is commanded and prohibited as opposed to what is permissible. Some think God prohibits drinking of alcoholic beverages, while others do not, thinking alcohol is permitted. Some think God requires believers to give ten percent of their income to the religious community, but others think this is not explicitly mandated, so any amount is permissible.

Another problem is that some divine commands go against our moral intuitions. If God really commanded the Israelites to kill all of their enemies in the Promised Land, including women and children, that would go against our deepest moral intuitions. In Genesis chapter twenty-two God commands Abraham to sacrifice his son, and in Hosea God commands the prophet to marry a prostitute who will certainly be unfaithful to him.[10] These go against our moral intuitions, but divine command theory says they are right simply because God commanded them.

Other problems involve how some criticisms divine that command theorists level against other theories may apply to divine command theory, too. The problems are just pushed back onto God. Take the problem of the rule-makers changing the rules. Divine command theorists argue that people cannot both make and absolutely obey moral rules, because they can change them. If the sole basis of right and wrong is God's commandments and prohibitions, then what if God decides to change these? God could possibly change the rules? If so, this jeopardizes the absolute and binding nature of moral rules demanded by divine command theorists. The problem of possibly shifting moral commands is merely pushed back from humans to God. What if God suddenly mandated the torturing and killing of innocent children? Like the examples above, this goes against our deepest moral sensitivities. Yet, divine command theory says that our ideas and feelings about right and wrong have no bearing on actual right and wrong. God alone determines right and wrong. So a divine command theorist is forced to admit that if God did make such a rule, then it would be right simply because God commanded it.

This problem of God possibly changing the moral rules, perhaps into ones contradicting the current ones, is related to another problem with divine command theory. In Plato's dialogue the *Euthyphro* Socrates asks Euthyphro: "Is what is holy, holy, because the gods approve it, or do they approve it because it is holy?"[11] Although asked in a polytheistic context, the same problem arises for monotheists. The profound question asked here is this: "Does God command what is a good action *because* it is good, or is an action good simply *because* God has commanded it?" The *Euthyphro Dilemma* asks whether God's will alone is the ultimate source of right and wrong, or if something else, independent of God and to which God's will corresponds, is the ultimate source of right and wrong.

Consistent divine command theorist opt for the answer that God alone determines right and wrong. Why? If God's rules merely communicate right and wrong as determined by something else, then God is not the ultimate source of right and wrong. If there is some eternal standard of right and wrong alongside of God, and which God merely communicates to us, this jeopardizes monotheism, which says God is ultimate reality, dependent on nothing else. An eternal standard of right and wrong, alongside of God, threatens the claim that God is the sole ultimate reality. If we reply to Socrates: "God commands what is good *because* it is good," then God is dependent on something else, as indicated by the location of "because." Therefore, divine command theorists tend to say

God's will alone determines right and wrong. They answer Socrates: "An action is good simply *because* God has commanded it."

This raises again, though, the problem that God could change what is right and wrong, perhaps in ways that go strongly against our moral intuitions. Some divine command theorists say God has a good nature that determines that God will only ever command what is good. They say God could never command the torturing and killing of innocent children because God has an inherently good nature. This poses a problem similar to positing an eternal standard of right and wrong alongside of God. It does not matter if the eternal law of right and wrong is outside or inside of God as part of God's nature. Either way, there is something distinct from God that limits God's freedom to determine right and wrong. In either case something other than God ultimately determines right and wrong.

A perhaps obvious problem is that divine command theory assumes belief in God. What about those who do not believe in the God of monotheism or in any God at all? Divine command theory works only if monotheism is true, but many doubt this. Divine command theorists respond that our opinions have no bearing on right and wrong, and that monotheism is true regardless of one's belief or unbelief. Nonetheless, someone who is not a monotheist cannot accept divine command theory. Also, modern secular societies that separate religion from the state cannot appeal to divine command theory in questions of ethics and normative economics.

Related to the problem of God's existence is a more generic criticism of religion. Many religious scholars view the development of religious beliefs and practices in an evolutionary way, including the development of religious explanations. A common theory is that religious explanations arose out of human ignorance of natural explanations for phenomena. Early humans did not understand the scientific causes and effects of natural events, like the fruitfulness of trees and what produces the weather required for good crops. In the absence of natural explanations they believed that trees, the sky, and many other things have "spirits" acting as agents to explain their changing and otherwise inexplicable behavior. As humans learned more about the natural world they required less spirits to explain things. Spirits decreased in number but humans still explained abstract aspects of their experience like love, war, wisdom, fecundity, etc., with personal gods. With more time, some humans developed belief in only one God as the simplest explanation for the variety of phenomena they still did not understand.

With the rise of modern science, Deism arose as the belief that God is required to explain the origin and laws of the universe, but is not necessary to explain the many causes and effects in nature as explicable by science. Some religious theorists hypothesize that as human knowledge of the natural world grows and becomes more complete, belief in God to explain the inexplicable will disappear entirely.[12] The theory that belief in God is merely a way to explain the inexplicable is sometimes called the *God of the Gaps* theory. This theory can be used to criticize divine command theory as using God to explain human moral rules and behaviors, which really exist on other grounds.

Virtue Ethics

The normative ethical theories examined so far deal with the goodness and badness, rightness and wrongness, of actions. Another approach focuses on the goodness or badness of persons. We speak of good people as well as good actions. The value judgment here is not about actions but about persons. Persons and their character are also subject to moral value judgments. *Virtue ethics* is a normative ethical theory focusing on persons instead of actions. "Virtue" comes from the Latin, *virtus*, meaning "strength." We can view the characters of virtuous people as "strengths" and the characters of non-virtuous people as "weaknesses."

How can character be strong or weak? Just as we can distinguish between moral and non-moral values we can distinguish between moral and non-moral strengths or virtues. A good computer is "strong" because it works well, is fast, easy to use, rarely locks-up, etc. A good knife possesses the "strength" or virtue of easily cutting, while a bad knife lacks this strength or virtue. These are examples of what we might call non-moral virtues. Moral virtues are states of being and dispositions for acting that can be judged morally. Some have character traits and dispositions for acting that we judge as morally "strong" or valuable. Generosity, humility, courage, piety, honesty, mercy, self-sacrifice and service are common morally valuable traits.

Virtue ethics is similar to consequentialism in that becoming virtuous is rarely an end in itself, but is the means to an end. In ancient Greek philosophy one value of being virtuous was functioning well individually and in society. The Greeks viewed virtue as integrity of the parts of the person leading to good functioning. A new car accomplishes its purpose, comfortable and reliable transportation, because all of its parts fit and work together as a harmonious whole. As cars get older and wear down, some of their parts no longer function properly. They no longer fit harmoniously into the overall whole. The car's integrity is diminished, and as a result the car no longer accomplishes its purpose of comfortably and reliably transporting people.

In ancient Greek virtue ethics the person's integrity was not the only end aimed at. Having integrity was requisite for a happy life. A virtuous person would be happier than a non-virtuous person. When adapted by major western religious traditions, virtue ethics saw the goals of virtue as a right relationship with God, others, and a happy afterlife. Insofar as virtue is required by any type of being to attain its reasons for existing, it can be said that the virtue of any given being depends on the type of being it is. Because a being's virtue is based on the purpose of the type of being it is, human virtue is based on the purpose of the *human* being.

Plato's virtue ethics began by saying that humans are unique among beings in the world. In addition to our material bodies, we have immaterial souls distinguishing us from everything else. Plato also thought the physical world is inferior, to and less real than, the mental or spiritual realm of reason and ideas. This goes contrary to our way of viewing the physical world as the most real, which is largely due to major developments of the last five hundred years in science. Why did Plato believe this? The answer requires some explanation.

Following some before him, Plato said the physical world is in constant change. Material things exist only for finite periods. They appear to be the same across time, but as a rationalist, Plato distrusted the senses. Physical things constantly change despite appearances. Our bodies are not the same day by day, or even moment to moment. Plato reasoned from these things that physical things are not truly real. He also said the perpetual change of the physical world causes pain and suffering. Only what changes can suffer, because feeling pain is a change from non-pain to pain. Sickness and death occur because of the changes in matter. The limitations of space and time in the physical world introduce competition. Living things compete for food, land, water, and other finite material resources. They must eat other living things to survive. In fact, Plato would answer the limit question about why there is scarcity for economists to study in the first place by saying scarcity is due to limitations of the physical world.

On the other hand, Platonists have argued that eternal and unchanging immaterial ideas are superior to physical things. Following the Pythagoreans, they say math and geometry are clear examples of this. Where is the number two located? It is an immaterial idea that will never change. While the fact that your hair is black may change as you age, the fact that 2 + 2 = 4 will never change. There is no perfect circle in the imperfect physical world, only approximations that come and go. The idea of a perfect circle exists and will always exist in the mental realm. Likewise, ideas, or "forms" in some Platonic parlance, of things never change. The idea or form of your cat persists even after its body dies. The same can be said for any physical thing. It is mentally conceivable before it physically exists, like the plans for a new house not yet built. It exists only for a finite time in the physical world, like the hundred years the house stands. When it physically disappears, its idea continues forever. We can always still think and talk about the house after it is torn down. Thus, in Platonism, the immaterial world of the eternal and unchanging ideas is more real than the world of finite and changing physical things. This is a dualistic metaphysics, holding that reality has two fundamental components, mental and physical. It decidedly sees the mental realm as superior and the physical realm as inferior.

Platonism is decidedly rationalist in its epistemology. Plato argued that only the unchanging truths of reason, known with certainty through their relationships, are worthy of the name "knowledge" (*episteme* in Greek). Facts known by empirical experience are contingent, uncertain and change (*doxa* in Greek). They are therefore only opinions. For Plato, the fact that human beings are aware of and can think in the mental realm of ideas proves that human beings are unique among other beings. Humans have a physical component, their bodies, but their minds or souls are of the mental realm of the ideas. Just as the mental realm is truly real and the physical realm less real, the mind or soul is the real person, for Plato. The body is only a temporary and inferior vehicle for the soul. Because the realm of ideas is eternal, the human soul is eternal, he reasoned. Plato believed in a form of pre-existence of the soul and reincarnation.

Because the soul and reason make humans uniquely *human*, human virtue depends on the soul and rationality for Plato. The soul's purpose is to direct the whole person through rational deliberation, and to ultimately elevate them to pure contemplation of the ideas in the mental realm. It functions to order all the parts of the person (body, living or animal soul, and mind) in a harmonious state that he called justice, rightness, or integrity (*dikaiosune* in Greek). The result is that the person will be happy, because they are living according to the purpose for the human being.

Plato forged his ethics in response to the Greek *sophists*. Numerous and contradictory opinions about truth and values, as witnessed in the growing international and cosmopolitan Mediterranean basin at the time, had led the sophists to say that there are no absolute truths and values. That is, the sophists were ethical relativists. Plato was, in part, responding to this ethical relativism.

Plato responded that only ideas (e.g. "treeness") are eternal and unchanging, but their physical manifestations (e.g., physical trees) are imperfect and changing. There is also an eternal unchanging idea of the Good (*agathos* in Greek), which is perfect and unchanging in the mental realm. The idea of the Good is exemplified, to various degrees, in the physical world. Ideas are absolute, universal and unchanging truths, despite the changing and relative physical world of sense experience. The idea of the Good is an absolute, universal and unchanging value. This is so despite changing and different values in the world, such as the divergent values of different individuals and cultures.

As the most exalted state of being, able to know the Good, the rational soul's role is to order and control the whole person. Rational persons put their lower animal desires in check. When the soul subjugates and orders all parts of the person properly, the whole person is in a state of justice (rightness) or integrity. Such a human being has good and valuable traits lacking in others, or the virtues. Knowing just how much to eat, drink and have sex—not too much and not too little—is the virtue of temperance. Knowing what to fear and what not to fear is the virtue of courage.

Due to his close association of truth and value, reason and goodness, Plato believed that when people know the Good they will necessarily do the Good; just as one cannot deny what one knows to be true. The human moral problem for Plato is that not everyone knows the Good. The dualistic metaphysics on which it relies is a weakness of Plato's ethics, if one does not accept this dualism. A practical problem is that we can ask if a person can truly know the Good but still not do it (for whatever reason). Plato's view of goodness as universal and rational recalls Kant. There are parallels between them because both claim reason alone, not sense experience, must ground ethics. Both say the physical world and empirical experience can only provide relative, changing and uncertain values, but we need absolute, unchanging and certain values. Some criticisms of Kant's ethics are thus, in modified form, applicable to Plato's.

Aristotle was Plato's most famous student and his close friend. Taking much from his master, he also disagreed with Plato on points, saying: "While both are dear, piety requires us to honor truth above our friends."[13] Aristotle's philosophy has been called more "down to earth" than Plato's. Aristotle valued the material world, and his epistemology was empirical. He saw the "form" or "idea" of a being as its principle of order and organization, residing *within the being itself*, not in an abstract and separated mental realm of ideas or forms.

Aristotle took from and modified Plato's ethics. He believed all beings have a purpose, and that value corresponds to how well a being attains its purpose. He agreed that humans have rational souls, animal souls, living souls, and physical bodies. For Aristotle, the rational soul is the principle of organization for the whole person, as its form. Believing that forms are inherent in beings themselves, Aristotle denied the immortality of the soul. He held that when a human being ceases to exist then their rational soul ceases to exist as well.

Aristotle divided the rational soul's function of ordering and guiding into two parts: theoretical and practical reason. *Theoretical reason* involves abstract knowledge and thought, while *practical reason* guides a person's conduct in the world. He agreed with Plato that the rational soul should govern and guide a person's lower animal, sentient, and bodily parts. But this is guiding and governance in what they *do*, their conduct or the realm of practical reason. What we know through theoretical reason is the domain of the rational soul alone.

Like Plato, Aristotle held that if the rational soul properly governs and guides the person, then success in living and happiness results. He believed all people strive for happiness in all of their choices and actions. The goal of every human act is happiness. However, many act in ways that do not make them happy, due to ignorance and the rational soul's lack of control.

As for Plato, for Aristotle, true happiness results only from developing a virtuous character and acting virtuously. How do we know virtue? Aristotle observed that any way of acting properly (virtue) can be both overdone and underdone. Acting excessively or too little, in any one way, causes unhappiness. Therefore, virtue, in any type of acting, is what he called the *golden mean*, the right balance of acting and not acting. The virtue of courage is the mean between being foolhardy and cowardly. The virtue of temperance is the mean between eating and drinking too much and too little. Modesty is the mean between false humility and arrogance. Generosity is the mean between the profligate giving away of wealth and miserliness. We can also ask if there are other economic virtues besides generosity. Is there a golden mean between giving to charity and saving for capital investment? Is there a mean between private property and communal property? Is there a mean between individuals deciding and acting to maximize their own utility (welfare), and special groups deciding how individuals must act to maximize their utility?

How do we become virtuous, according to Aristotle? In good empirical fashion, he says we become virtuous by observing the virtuous person. We perceive the mean by seeing the virtuous person act according to the mean. Then we try to act according to the mean ourselves. As we repeatedly do what is virtuous, we develop a disposition of character inclining us to act virtuously. Repeatedly doing what is virtuous changes our character, making it easier to act virtuously in the future. This acquired habit of virtue predisposes us to act virtuously, but does not necessitate it. A virtuous person can act out of character by not acting virtuously. A non-virtuous person sometimes acts out of character by acting virtuously, perhaps to our surprise.

More so than Plato, Aristotle incorporated relevant differences between varying circumstances into his ethics. Practical reason must also learn how the details of each specific situation affect the appropriate mean in each situation. The way to apply the mean can change, as circumstances change. This focus on how to act virtuously in multiple, sometimes disparate, situations is an advance upon Plato's virtue ethics.

Virtue ethics is an important normative ethical theory, similar to, but also different from, those we have already surveyed. The focus, on a universal Good known by reason, has affinities with *a priori* rule-based ethics, and the focus on happiness and success has affinities with consequentialism. A major difference is the focus on the state of the person as the subject of the normative value judgment (i.e., a "virtuous" person), instead of the person's actions. Applied to economics, virtue ethics involves discussions of virtuous societies and markets, what exemplifies virtue in economies, how we recognize it, and how we attain it. It also includes discussions of the purposes of economies, and how well economies do attain, or fail to attain, those purposes.

Natural Law Ethics

A final theory of normative ethics we should address is *natural law ethics*. The complexities and nuances of natural law theories are often oversimplified and misunderstood in summaries of normative ethics. Even the name, "natural law," gives the false impression that these normative ethical theories are characterized by only one of their many aspects. We will use this name, however, as it is the standard one in the discipline.[14]

Natural law ethics developed in ancient Greece, and, with virtue ethics, heavily informed medieval Christian ethics. It is a substantive part of the Roman Catholic Church's moral philosophy, and has influenced many other aspects of the western philosophical and religious traditions. St. Thomas Aquinas (AD 1225 – 1274) is often taken to be one of the best examples of this normative ethical theory. Although heavily shaped by religion, natural law ethics has deep philosophical moorings. Incorporating aspects of virtue ethics, rule-based ethics, consequentialism, and divine command theory, natural law ethics is complex and nuanced. While all ethical theories interact with limit questions of being, knowledge and truth, natural law theories perhaps show most lucidly how axiology is tied to metaphysics and epistemology.

In the monotheistic religious traditions adopting it, natural law ethics claims that human beings, as created by God, can discern principles of right and wrong by examining the natural world God created. This claim is related to the points we examined earlier about the possible connections between a being's purpose and value, and whether or not the way things should be is in some way grounded upon the way things are. If God designed individual things we might be able to discern from their purposes their good and proper, and their wrong and improper, uses.

Take a human artifact. When Native Americans first saw a chair brought over by the Europeans, they probably concluded certain things about its purpose by merely examining it. They probably quickly realized it was not a type food intended to nourish. They probably realized it was not a mortal weapon, unless they exercised great creativity of imagination. From its size and shape they probably concluded that its purpose was not shelter. From the flat seat they might have concluded that its purpose involved supporting some thing or things, and perhaps even compared it to a table. Even though they had never seen a chair before, it would not surprise us if one of them had eventually sat down on the chair properly, and realized its purpose.

Natural law theory holds that just as we can discern the good and proper use of a human artifact by examining it closely and long enough, we can discern the good and proper use of things in nature, be examining them. We have already used the example of the heart organ in living organisms. Scientists eventually realized that a heart's purpose is to pump vital fluid. Natural Law theory also ties value to a being's use or function. We would probably make the value judgment that using a chair for shelter or as a mortal weapon is wrong. If a cardiac surgeon tried to attach a donor heart to the patient's respiratory or digestive system instead of their circulatory system, we would probably say that is "wrong."

Natural law theorists further agree with those who claim that we can make value judgments about any being itself based on how well it fulfills its purpose. A chair with a broken leg or missing seat so that it cannot support someone is worse than a (better) chair with four legs and a good seat that can support someone. A weak heart, not pumping blood to its full capacity, is worse than a healthy heart pumping to its full capacity. These value judgments about specific chairs and hearts are based on the functions of chairs and hearts in general. Similar examples—in fact, as many examples as there are types of beings—could be adduced.

There are criticisms of basing value on purpose and use. As we have seen, Hume and others argue that we cannot move from the way things are (indicative) to the way they should be (imperative). They raise important questions about whether value can come from fact. If not, then natural law ethics crumbles. However one answers the question about moving from fact to value, they will do so on the basis of their metaphysical philosophy of being, or ontology.

Natural law theorists have an ontology that sees goals, purposes and proper uses as essential parts of any being. From these, they make value judgments about how well a particular being fulfills its purpose and how well it is being used. The fact, that often things do not fulfill their purpose and are not properly used, takes nothing away from the fact that they still have a purpose and a proper way they ought to be used. In such cases natural law theorists invoke the old legal axiom: *abusus non tollit usum* ("Abuse does not remove use").

Another criticism is that, like divine command theory, natural law theory assumes God's existence. While certainly true of versions of natural law theory adopted by western monotheistic religions, this is not true of all natural law theories. In fact, natural law ethics largely developed in the Greek philosophy of Stoicism, founded by Zeno of Citium (ca. 334 BC – 262 BC). Stoicism was non-dualistic and naturalistic in its metaphysics, so that ultimate reality in Stoicism was very different from the God of western monotheism. It is true that western monotheists like St. Thomas Aquinas have argued that only an ultimate reality like the personal God of western monotheism, in certain key aspects, can fully account for order and purpose in the universe. They have argued that the order and purpose, upon which natural law ethics relies, require an omnipotent (all-powerful), omniscient (all-knowing), intelligent, and personal being. There is a difference, however, between arguing that order and purpose in the cosmos require such a being, and that natural law ethics requires such a being. If the former is false then natural law ethics, which relies on order and purpose, can be established on other grounds, as in Stoicism.

Natural law theory is complicated with many facets. Assessments of natural law theory in contemporary ethics largely limit themselves to its claim that purpose and proper use are inherent in all beings, and that on this basis we can form value judgments. There are other features of natural law theory with analogues in other normative ethical theories. Natural law theory typically incorporates virtue ethics by linking human action with the goal of attaining happiness. Some, like Hume, deny any connection between the way things are, including the way humans do act, and the ways things should be, including the way humans should act. Many natural law theories argue that because all human action is goal-oriented toward happiness, and assuming the value judgment that happiness is good and should be sought, all human actions are already value-laden and already moral.

Early Christian thinkers, who used Greek philosophy to explain, understand and defend their Christian faith, modified the philosophical systems they adapted and used. They agreed with Greek virtue ethicists that humans aim at their own happiness, but that many pursue what they wrongly think will make them ultimately happy (apparent goods) instead of what will really make them happy (real good). For Greek virtue ethicists happiness, was something primarily concerned with existence and life in this world. With their belief in God as the supreme good and supreme blessedness (happiness or beatitude), Christian philosophers claimed that the real good all of us seek, without necessarily knowing it, is God, who is supreme good (*summum bonum*) and supreme happiness. Because of a moral problem with humans, explained in terms of original sin and sinful acts, we frequently aim at apparent goods we think will make us supremely happy, instead of the supreme good that will really make us happy. Because everything, other than God, depends on God and is not eternal, happiness derived from anything other than God is temporary, not eternal. Being eternal, only God can bring eternal happiness.

Christian virtue ethics also incorporates aspects of divine command theory. It holds that, although we do a fairly good job of discerning the moral principles of natural law by examining God-given purposes and uses for things, the effects of sin result in mistakes in doing so. To make fundamental moral principles unequivocally clear, God has supernaturally revealed right and wrong in commandments and prohibitions.

Natural law ethics was used by some early modern economists, and it is a viable model for doing normative economics. Some economists have argued that we can discern a natural purpose for markets and human exchange. Adam Smith and F. A. Hayek are examples of many economists who have argued that free trade in human societies has the purpose of making everyone happier, as people benefit from each other's talents and skills. I cannot build my own car and I do not know medicine to the point of healing many of my ills, but free trade allows me to contribute my skills, and what I do know, to society by exchanging my contributions to society for things like cars and healthcare.

Either on theistic grounds or naturalistic grounds, others have argued that societies and their governments have the purpose of securing the common good of all, despite natural harms. They say that free uninhibited trade inevitably introduces harm to some, so societies and governments must insure the good of all by attenuating some of these harms through measures like wealth redistribution and welfare safety nets. On religious grounds some claim that because all people are created in the image of God, all individuals have inherent dignity and rights, which it is the natural purpose of good human societies and governments to honor and secure.

SUPPLY & DEMAND

Returning to basic economic principles necessary for understanding economics and ethics, *supply and demand* are fundamental realities driving natural markets. Economists define *demand* as what someone is *willing and able* to pay for a good or service. Demand is determined by opportunity cost in the form of price in money-driven markets. The various price/quantity combinations one is willing and able to pay constitute their demand curve, as shown here:

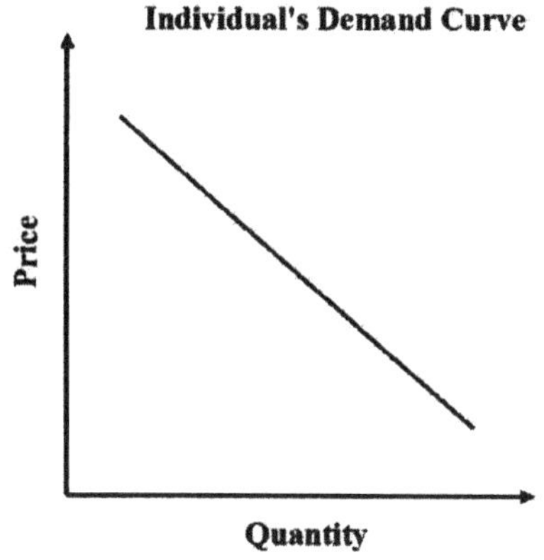

Figure 2.1: Demand Curve

A demand curve graphically represents the price/quantity relationship and demonstrates the *law of demand*. The quantity demanded for a good or service is inversely correlated to price. As price increases, the quantity demanded decreases, and as price decreases, the quantity demanded increases. The concept of demand is frequently misunderstood by non-economists, including the media.

Price does not influence the demand curve. Lower price does not change "demand," but only the point along a person's demand curve, or the quantity she demands. Lower price only increases quantity demanded, which represents a movement along her demand curve. "*Demand*" is her entire demand curve, which represents all of the combinations of quantities she demands at different prices. Preferences and ability to pay, not price, change a person's demand as a whole, or her demand curve. Price itself does not change consumer facts like a person's preferences and her ability to pay for a good. For example, if she hates sardines then she would never buy them, regardless of price. Thus, a change in price does not change a person's "demand," but rather the quantity she demands. It is important to remember that a good's price does not move the demand curve—which would be a true increase or decrease in demand—but instead changes only the quantity demanded.

Since every individual has a demand curve, the market demand curve is the sum of the demand curves of individuals in a particular market. As with individuals, a market demand curve shifts due to factors other than a good's price. Indeed price is not the cause, but the effect, of economic forces. Quantity demanded, not the demand curve, changes due to price. Demographics, tastes, preferences, income, price of substitutes, price of complements, expectations of future prices, and timing cause a demand curve to shift either "in" or "out." A shift "out" is called an *increase in demand*, as show graphically here:

Figure 2.2: Demand Increase

A demand curve shift outward means individuals in this market are willing and able to pay more for the good at all price/quantity combinations. Demographically, the market demand curve shifts out when more individuals are in the demand curve. This can result from population changes, like more people moving into a particular geographic area. Shifts in tastes and preferences also shift the demand curve. These shifts result from natural changes in what people want. Fads and other cycles where goods become popular, as happened with bell bottom jeans and "MC Hammer" pants, can do this. Some fads come back and others do not, which may cause the demand curve for some goods to shift in and out over time.

We must also remember one other thing about demand: It provides information to others in the market. For instance, suppliers were willing to supply bell bottom jeans because there were consumers who wanted them. This is crucially important to economic systems. It means information passes between buyers and sellers in markets. This helps market agents socially arrive at decisions regarding what goods to produce, and how many to produce. Demand is half of the information puzzle, as market agents seek to answer these questions.

An increase in income can also shift the demand curve out for normal goods. Take steak for example. Most people consider steak a *normal good.* This means that as their income increases, so does their demand for steak. In other words, they are willing and able to buy more steak at all price levels as their income increases. Demand curves for *inferior goods* can also shift out when people's income falls. Demand for inferior goods increase as people's income decreases. If someone considers ramen noodles an inferior good, then their demand for them increases as their income falls.

Prices of *substitutes* and *complements* also affect demand. If a good's price rises and there is a good that is a substitute then people will buy more of its substitute. For example, assume Coke and Pepsi are substitutes for you, meaning you are indifferent about which you have. If Coke's price goes up while the price of Pepsi remains the same, your demand for Pepsi increases (shifts out). The opposite is true for complements. For example let's assume that to a particular individual peanut butter and jelly are complements, when the price peanut butter decreases causing an increase in the quantity demanded of peanut butter it also causes that individual's demand curve for jelly to increase (shift out).

Expectations also shift demand curves because we not only choose *what* to buy, but *when* to buy. If people expect gas prices to double next week, they might buy more gas this week, which shifts the demand curve for gas this week. Time is a vital but easily neglected factor in considering economics and ethics together. A correct understanding of demand is often neglected in ethical considerations, too, such as in discussions of "just" or "fair" prices. Remember, a price change only causes the quantity demanded to change, but not the demand curve itself. Demand curves depict the salient facts of quantities people are willing and able to buy at any given price, and are determined by demographics, tastes and preferences, income, prices of substitutes and complements, expectations and timing. So, if a large mass of individuals feels that a certain price is "unjust," then this would certainly be reflected in the demand curve for that particular good.

These factors determine the quantity people are willing and able to pay at a given price. While price-setting is possible, the normative ethical question to ask is whether the collective preferences and abilities of those in the market *should* set the price naturally, or whether some person or group should set the price, regardless of market factors. If the latter, then any consequentialist ethical theory employed must consider the consequences of price-setting. We will see that one consequence of price-setting is almost always market inefficiency in producing the greatest net utility or satisfaction (as understood in positive economics) for all in the market. Perhaps we know this and set prices anyway, either because we value some other consequence more or because another ethical theory dictates we do so, regardless of the consequence of inefficiency.

The same forces that shift demand curves out can also shift them in:

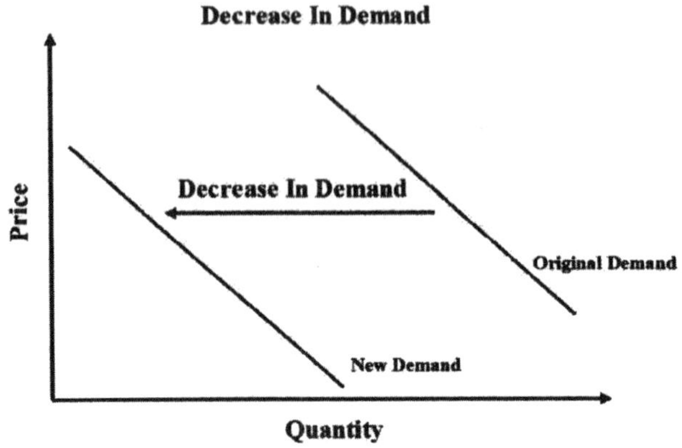

Figure 2.3: Demand Decrease

Demographics, tastes and preferences, income, prices of substitutes and complements, expectations of future prices, and timing can *decrease demand*, or shift the demand curve in. Now, however, these factors work in reverse of what we saw before. Fewer people, the end of a fad or a change in taste, fall in income and a normal good, increase in income and an inferior good, decrease in prices of substitutes, increase in prices of complements, and expectations of lower prices in the near future can all cause the demand curve to shift in.

We must now consider the other part of the economic equation, *supply*. Producers supply quantities of goods and services based on what price they are willing and able to accept in return for offering the good or service. The different price/quantity pairs constitute what economists call the *supply curve*, shown here:

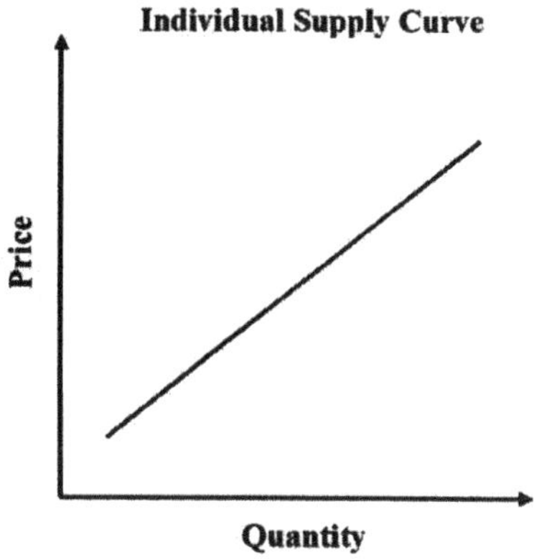

Figure 2.4: Supply Curve

The *supply curve* depicts the *law of supply*, which simply states a positive correlation between a good or service's price and quantity supplied. Just as demand curves shift, supply curves shift. Just as demand, quantity supplied changes, based on price, but again different factors shift the supply curve itself. These include: prices of inputs, technological change, prices of substitutes in production, number of firms in the market, and expectations of future prices. An increase in the price of dough, an input for pizza, causes suppliers to supply less quantities of pizza at every price. Because more money is required to produce a pizza, the supply curve shifts in. If technology makes it cheaper to produce a pizza, or a substitute for a pizza ingredient decreases in price, or more pizzerias open in the neighborhood increasing competition, then suppliers supply more pizzas at every price. The supply curve shifts out. These natural market factors, not price, dictate supply at all prices, or the supply curve. Again, we can fix supply, but then we must be fully cognizant of the consequences. If we are and still do, then perhaps we value another consequence more highly if we are consequentialists, or maybe we do so on the basis of some other, non-consequentialist, normative ethical theory.

Depicting supply and demand together shows what economists call *equilibrium*, or the price and the quantity dictated by the current supply and demand curves, as seen in Figure 2.5:

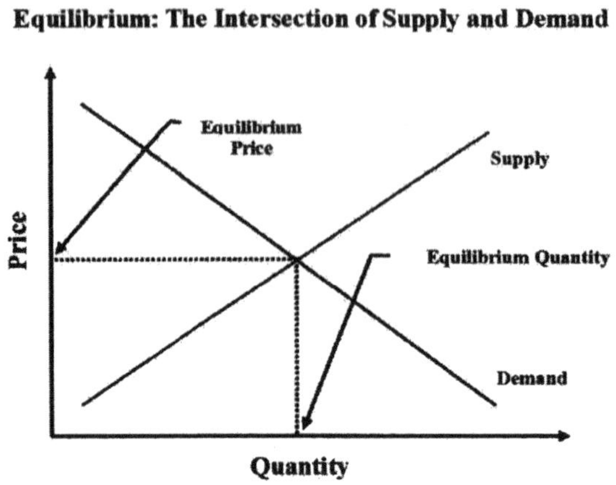

Figure 2.5: Market Equilibrium

Prices and quantities are the results of an economic system, not the causes. They naturally arise from the interaction of the buyers' demand curve, and the sellers' supply curve. Equilibrium is important because it is the point at which a market efficiently allocates scarce resources. At equilibrium, a market naturally and automatically produces the most efficient quantity and price to allocate a good or service, given the preferences of all buyers and sellers in the market.

As described above, supply and demand curves shift. Such shifts change equilibrium price and quantity. Consider a market with the equilibrium depicted in the graph below. Assume the income of buyers, in this market, increases, shifting the demand curve to the right. This results in a new equilibrium at a higher price and quantity.

Equilibrium: The Intersection of Supply and Demand

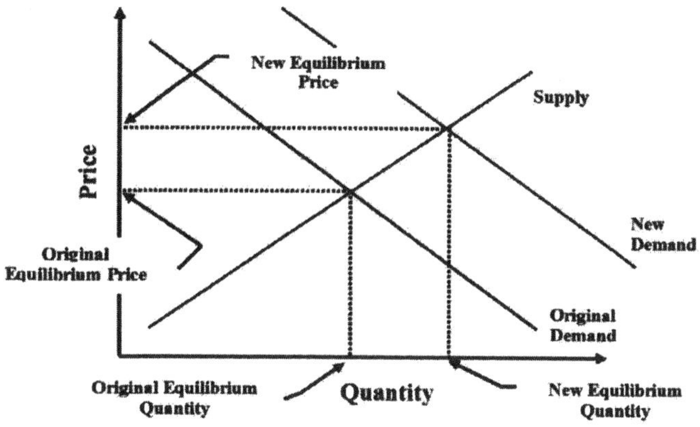

Figure 2.6: Effect of an Increase in Demand on Equilibrium

Increased income causes the good's price to rise. A key point is that prices, as determined by the intersection of supply and demand, naturally ration goods according to individuals' preferences. This is the unmanufactured genius of a natural market. Without the price increase there would not be enough of this good for everyone who now wishes to purchase it.

We can graphically see what happens if the price is not allowed to adjust when the demand curve naturally shifts due to increased income. Assume an initial equilibrium point of a $6 price and quantity of eight units, but the demand curve shift causes a new equilibrium of an $8.50 price and a quantity of thirteen units (Figure 2.7):

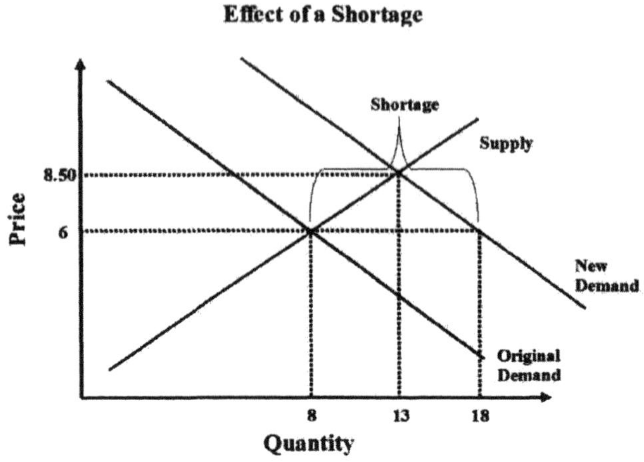

Figure 2.7: Shortage

If the price stays at $6, then there is a shortage of ten units, since more people want the good (18) than suppliers are willing and able to provide (8) at $6. Unconstrained, the market would naturally raise the price to $8.50 as sellers run out and produce the quantity they are willing and able to supply at $8.50. If we force the price to stay at $6, then eighteen people want it, but only eight can have it. This is why, as mentioned earlier; price-setting can cause inefficiencies in a market's allocation of resources according to individuals' preferences.

Natural laws of supply and demand set prices and quantities so as to ration scarce resources most efficiently, and interference almost always introduces inefficiency. There are indeed some exceptions, as we will discuss later. Yet, it is impossible to have demand increase (with no change in supply) and not have increases in price and quantity. As market forces work, firms cannot raise prices at will without causing surpluses in quantities, a condition that cannot persist. Conversely, if prices are artificially lowered, shortages necessarily result.

Also, price does not indicate a good's quality. Price is the result of the interaction of current supply and demand for the good. Think of the strawberry market in your area. Do you not pay more for strawberries in the winter? Do you not get the best strawberries in the summer, but for lower prices? These prices are the result of supply and demand changing over the seasons.

If oil drilling decreases for environmental or ethical reasons, then the oil supply decreases and the supply curve shifts in. However, the demand will, at least for a time, remain the same. This means the equilibrium point necessarily moves to a higher price and lower quantity. Oil price and quantity are effects, not causes. Again, if the price is forced to stay low, then a shortage results and some, who are willing and able to buy oil at the higher price, will not get it. There is no way to effectively choose who will get the good and who will not.

Inefficiency, or not getting resources to those who want them the most, inevitably results.

This all means that if a person or group does not like, or passes a negative value judgment on, current price or quantity, there is not necessarily a problem from an economics standpoint. This is because efficient allocation of scarce resources is what matters most. Prices and quantities set naturally by supply and demand almost always allocate resources most efficiently (with the exception of externalities which we will discuss in a moment). What does this mean?

Since economics involves utilizing our scarce resources efficiently economics values efficiency, or utility maximization. Utility maximization (individuals maximizing their "happiness") means getting as much of what individuals want to those who want them the most, as judged by the choices they make in markets (buying and selling). In economic parlance, to the degree that a market does this it is *efficient*, and to the degree that a market does not do this it is *inefficient.*

Utility maximization (which we shall see later) is the formal model of consumer choice in economics. With it individuals' utility can be modeled and measured and we can see how individuals are affected in an economy and why they behave the way they do. Market agents make choices about buying and selling, and these choices are measurable. Economists say that these choices reveal individuals' *preferences*. Supply and demand curves model preferences, or the choices agents *will make* in the market at various prices and quantities. Because market agents would, and actually do, make these choices at different prices and quantities, economists say they are "willing and able" to make them.

Economists view utility as a vague form of satisfaction in attaining preferences, without much further philosophical reflection, as discussed earlier. Because utility is measurable and because economists assume that attaining preferences is valuable, economists typically value utility maximization.

Some critics of the neoclassical economic theory that economists use question assumptions about what utility measures. Perhaps the choices of market agents, or their revealed preferences, do not reveal what they *really* want and / or are able to do in markets. That is, we could possibly distinguish between the choices they make, called revealed preferences, and what they really want or are able to do. Maybe their choices are forced against their will. Maybe they are able but unwilling. Maybe they are willing to buy or sell, but are unable. In such cases, the choices of market agents would not reveal what they actually value. Thus utility measurement would not measure what people really value.

Some critics grant that preferences accurately reveal what market agents value the most. Maybe market agents really do value most what they are pursuing through their choices, or revealed preferences. Perhaps their choices reveal what they are really willing and able to do, and these choices reflect what market agents really value the most. However, perhaps they are pursuing apparent value (apparent good) instead of real value (real good). Perhaps their value judgments, as revealed in their preferences, are inaccurate. In this case utility measurement would measure what people *think is most valuable*, but not what is *really most valuable.*

These are all legitimate questions. However, the fact remains that utility measurement still measures *something*: the attainment of goals that market agents would and do pursue through their choices in markets. Because they make these choices, they are in some sense willing and able to do so. This is true even if in another sense they are unwilling and / or unable. This is also true if their choices reflect what they mistakenly think is most valuable, but is actually not most valuable. Because economists judge the attainment of goals pursued by market agents through their choices to be valuable in some sense, and because this attainment is measurable, economists value utility maximization.

For many economists, then, the highest value is the allocation of resources so as to maximize the net utility or satisfaction of all, based on their preferences. This does not mean that individuals do not want a higher level of utility that is currently unattainable to them, but rather given the current constraints the net utility of all is maximized. As we shall see what is more problematic is how government and individual actions in economic systems can drastically change the utility of others.

Often, even pure consequentialists who are non-economists do not realize that market interference almost always introduces inefficiency, or utility loss, economically speaking. When we choose to regulate markets, three things almost always result: some winners, some losers and a loss of economic efficiency. If economic utility is the same as what utilitarians call "utility," then informed utilitarians must judge free unregulated markets to be best. All transactions between willing and able buyers and sellers at the equilibrium price and quantity produce a net utility greater than the utility lost by those unwilling or unable to buy and sell at equilibrium. Strict consequentialist utilitarianism dictates that market equilibrium *should* be the price and quantity at that time.

Psychological egoists argue that because we cannot do otherwise than act out of self-interest, a free market with no interference is usually the best way to maximize everyone's self-interest in an enlightened way. Psychological altruists, believing that we can and should help others, might argue for price- or quantity-setting to help those who are unable to afford a good. If they are consequentialists at all, though, they must consider the fact of inefficiency. Just because a consequentialist helps some who are currently unable to get a good and sees them get it, this is not necessarily what is best. Such a *tactile fallacy* does not consider all the unseen people harmed by inefficiency through surpluses and shortages. Psychological egoists might even say that those committing this tactile fallacy do so selfishly. They get the satisfaction of feeling good about themselves by seeing those whom they are helping, while those being harmed remain unseen.[15]

Even those aware of the consequence of inefficiency might still conclude that price and quantity regulations are best, given considerations from other normal ethical theories. Virtue ethics might dictate that good markets should provide for a certain number who cannot afford the natural cost of a good, and value this more than utility maximization. Perhaps a rule-based or divine command theory ethicist would say the same. It is still important, however, to know the consequences and trade-offs of doing so.

Also, since different people are at different points in the total supply and total demand curves for any market, we must ask who will set the current price and quantity. Some individuals' demand curves are such that they would buy none of a good at *any* price, as in the earlier sardine example. If they could choose, they would set the price and quantity at zero. Thus judgments about "fair" prices can be unique to each individual, differing from person to person.

WELFARE MEASUREMENT

Economists use supply and demand to measure welfare in an economic system. Demand is what someone is willing and able to pay for a good or service. If a consumer pays less than they are willing to pay, then they have what economists call a *surplus*. Assume you want a new laptop. You have decided on the model you want, and that you are willing to pay $1000 for it. Assume you go to the store and they have it for $800. Since this is less than the $1000 you were willing to pay, you buy it and thus you get a $200 *consumer surplus*. You now have $200 extra to spend on something else. From a behavioral point of view we can note one more thing, which will become important later. When you see that the laptop you want is only $800, you would not say to the checkout clerk: "Please charge me $1000, because that is what I am willing to pay." Interestingly, consumers often expect suppliers to engage in this very behavior.

Economists call the other side of surplus, supplier welfare, *producer surplus*. This is the difference between what a supplier is willing and able to accept and what they actually receive for a good or service. Now assume you are the laptop producer and are willing to accept $600 for it, but instead are able to get $800. Like the consumer, you would take the $800 and you would not say you are willing to take less. Psychologically speaking, consumers often pass negative value judgments on producer surplus, but not on consumer surplus.

The total economic surplus or *welfare* in a specific market is the sum of the consumers' and producers' surpluses. In a supply and demand graph, this is the area under the demand curve and above the supply curve up to the point of equilibrium, where no more of the good is bought or sold. Specifically, consumer surplus is the area below the demand curve and above the equilibrium price, and producer surplus is the area above the supply curve and below the equilibrium price:

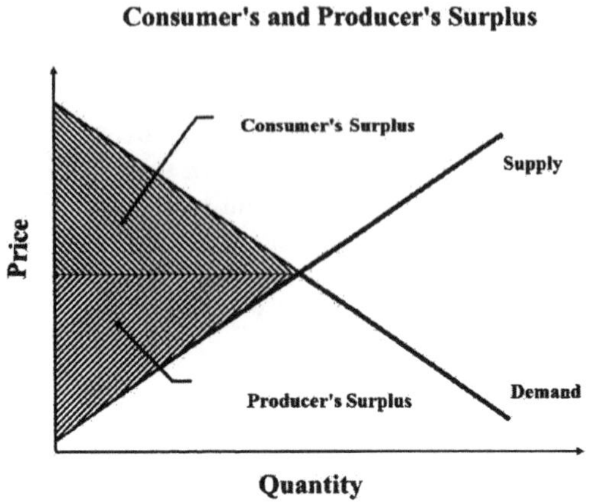

Figure 2.8: Consumer & Producer Welfare

It is important to understand that for private goods (about which more comes later), equilibrium results in an efficient allocation of the goods, leading to maximum welfare for all in a market.

Taxation of private goods and services without externalities (about which more follows), causes welfare loss both for consumers and producers. Economists call this a *deadweight loss*, which cannot be captured by any party. In the graph below the equilibrium point is eight units at $6. Assume a tax of $4 per unit applied to producers. This false increase in input costs causes the supply curve to shift in, resulting in a "new" equilibrium of four units at $8. Notice that both consumer and producer surplus go down. Part of this reduction is the $16 tax revenue. The triangle to the right of the tax revenue is the deadweight loss, the loss of welfare that nobody receives, which in this case is $8. This is because the quantity demanded at the new price is only four.

Consumer and producer surplus can enlighten us on another fallacy, that producers burden consumers with tax increases. This is not true. Both parties pay part of the tax. Economists call this *tax incidence.* Consumers would pay all of a tax only if the demand curve were completely vertical. While theoretically possible, economists have yet to find such a beast, a kind of "Bigfoot" in economics. In this case, since the supply and demand curve slopes are equal, both parties pay equal parts of the tax. Both buyers and sellers pay $2 of the tax. Now buyers pay $8 per unit and sellers only receive $4 per unit.

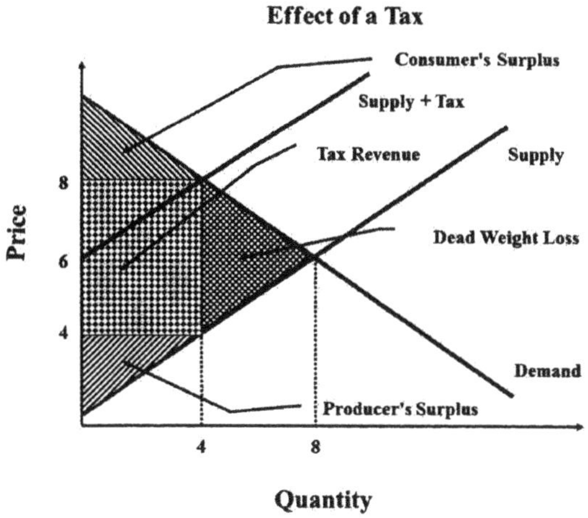

Figure 2.9: Effect of a Tax

Because of the deadweight loss they create, all economists call systems with taxes, "second best." They can never be as efficient as systems without taxes.

Tax incidence is also often misunderstood. In this example, the tax incidence is $2 for both buyers and sellers. Depending on the slopes of the supply and demand curves, tax incidence varies between parties. Yet, it is very rare that only one party bears it. This is true no matter whom we tax. Taxing buyers or sellers makes no difference on the new equilibrium, as any tax causes tax incidence for both. This is surprising for many who feel that it does matter who is taxed. Indeed, political debates evidence that many candidates are ill-informed regarding whom to tax. From a purely economic point of view it does not matter. Both parties will bear some of the tax burden.

Another issue is where the tax revenue ends up. Most goes into a general fund that local, state, and federal governments use for operations and programs. It is difficult to know who gets a surplus from tax revenue in the form of a *subsidy* (negative tax), and how to compare the surplus gain for one party to the surplus loss for another. We discuss this more in the utility section later. Having examined efficiency, let us compare efficiency with equity.

EFFICIENCY VS. EQUITY

Many non-economists struggle with efficiency and equity. Equilibrium demonstrates efficiency, since at equilibrium there is no surplus or shortage of a good. Just enough is produced and sold. This is *allocative efficiency*. Everyone willing and able to pay the equilibrium price gets the good, while those who are not, do not. Also, if the market is competitive, meaning there are many buyers and sellers, then the market is also *productively efficient*. Competition causes the good to be produced at the lowest possible cost. Intuitively, we may have no problem with this. A person who is not willing and able to pay the price of an iPhone does not get one. From a purely economic standpoint this is good, since it leaves an iPhone available for someone who is willing and able to buy one.

Assuming that revealed preferences express how individuals value goods, economists usually value the result that those who value goods the most get them. A good's value is measured by price, and price is the result of individuals acting in a market, not the cause. Economists also assume that a buyer is both *willing* and *able*. As mentioned, some may *want*, even *need*, a good but cannot afford it. They may be *willing* but not *able* to buy it. If one inclines more toward the *determinist* answer to the philosophical limit question of *free will vs. determinism*, then she may disagree with the assumptions and value judgment made by economists that goods *should* get to those who value them the most as, evidenced by their *willingness* to pay for them. Someone could value a good, even highly, but be unable to buy it due to circumstances (causes) beyond their control (freedom). Also, those who want, but cannot get, a good suffer *disutility*, or lack of satisfaction by not getting it.

At equilibrium, society does not get too many or too few iPhones. Those who judge this fair by focusing on freedom and willingness, may however judge productive efficiency unfair for other goods or services, like healthcare. What makes healthcare different from any other good or service? Maybe natural law, a divine command, or a right of human beings that says all people have a right to healthcare. If our ethics dictate this, we must remember that the fundamental laws of economics do not change. Any intervention in the market almost always introduces allocative and productive inefficiency. No amount of wishing, hoping, or legislating can change this positive economic fact. We cannot change the law of gravity, nor can we change the laws of economics.

That being said, we can modify economic systems through intervention, just as we can transcend other natural systems to change them, with technology, for instance. Perhaps our ethics says that we have an obligation to provide healthcare for everyone, so we intervene in the market. We can dam a river to make a reservoir. If the dam breaks and floods a town, however, we do not blame the river. Nor should we blame markets or economics when we get results that we do not like from market interventions, like regulations. If we intervene in the natural market allocation mechanisms, to provide healthcare for all, then there will be a trade-off. The opportunity cost of the value of equity is inefficiency and deadweight loss. Ethics-based economic policy-making must realize that there is often a trade-off between equity and efficiency.

Equity and justice are social values that will be discussed in a later chapter. To anticipate, however, there is problem in defining them. One definition of equity is that everyone gets the same amount of a good or service. Is that just or fair? Suppose you hate sardines. Believing it is not equitable that only some get sardines, society divides them up evenly. Now you are stuck with sardines that you do not want. What will you do with them? You will probably try to trade them with someone who likes them for something you prefer. Trade, based on preferences, is natural and is the source of black markets, when we try to regulate any good or service. Individuals will always have different preferences, and this complicates discussions of equality. What is just, fair, or equal to one is not to another. Who decides? A further complication (also covered more later) is that perhaps some individuals prefer what is really not the best for them. Perhaps they prefer an *apparent*, not a *real*, good. Also, although we can alter economic systems with laws and regulations, it is difficult to measure whether or not they have really improved society. Economists value utility because satisfaction in attaining goals aimed at through market choices based on preferences is measurable. Equity and other values are not so easily measured.

Rent control is a good example of the trade-off of efficiency for equity. Its goal is to lower housing costs so that some, who are unable to pay for housing at a market equilibrium price, can get it:

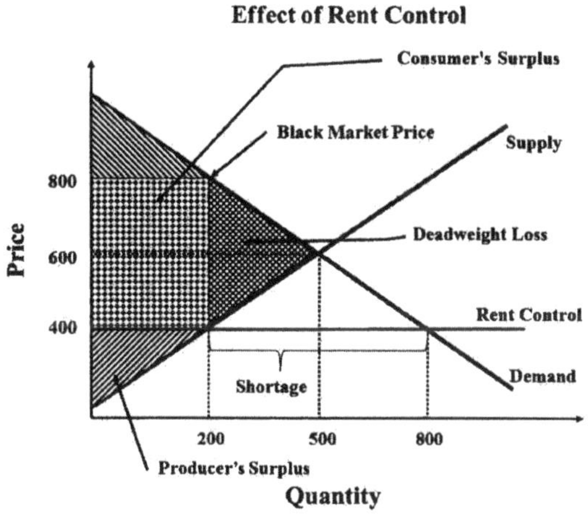

Figure 2.10: Effect of Rent Control

Assume that equilibrium for a town is at five hundred apartments supplied at $600 per month. Some cannot afford this, so we limit sellers to taking only $400 per month. This is a rent control, or what economists call a *price ceiling*. This causes a housing shortage. There are now eight hundred individuals who want apartments, but, at $400, sellers are willing and able to supply only two hundred. This causes a shortage of six hundred apartments and deadweight loss. While making housing affordable for some who are unable to pay $600, this regulation has the trade-off of inefficiency and deadweight loss, making more people homeless. As mentioned before, there are some winners, some losers and a loss of economic efficiency. Two hundred get to stay in their apartments at a lower rate (win). Three hundred, who were in apartments, now are homeless (lose). Three hundred who now want an apartment at $400 cannot get one (lose).

Plus, suppliers lose some of their producer surplus (lose). Also, we have the deadweight loss, which no one gets (inefficiency).

Also, natural market forces still persist. The newly created homeless will not want to stay homeless, so this regulation can also introduce a black market. From the quantity of two hundred on the supply curve up to the demand curve, we see the black market rent is $800. If a black market results, then new renters now pay $800 and the gain in consumer surplus is transferred back to the producers, while the deadweight loss still persists. So, the total effect of the policy could be fewer apartments supplied at a higher price. Another example is minimum wage laws:

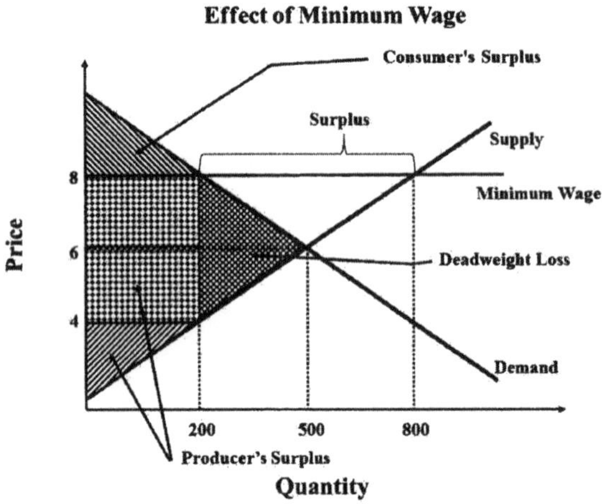

Figure 2.11: Effect of Minimum Wage

Assume equilibrium is five hundred workers at $6 per hour. Judging this to be unjust, society imposes an $8 minimum wage. Economists call this a *price floor.* A surplus of six hundred workers results, since more are willing and able to supply their labor but firms demand only two hundred, due to higher costs. The regulation causes deadweight loss and a surplus transfer from firms to workers. Notice that, now, suppliers of labor who are still working get both the small producer's surplus in the lower triangle, as well as the rectangular-shaped surplus above it. Thus minimum wage laws cause more unemployment, and only those who get to keep their jobs at the higher wage benefit (gain surplus).

In summary, most economists value allocative and productive efficiency with respect to resources, because it is measurable. Other values, like equity and justice, are not only difficult to measure, but also raise many philosophical questions, as we shall see. One's ethics may dictate valuing something more than efficiency, but there are always opportunity costs and trade-offs. Consequentialists, utilitarian or otherwise, must be cognizant of these trade-offs. Those less familiar with economic laws can easily miss unintended consequences. Even non-consequentialists must know the trade-offs, as they might affect their deliberations. Kantian ethics, for instance, must consider the impossibility of universalizing an imperative that all workers should *both* make more per hour *and* continue working. The economic and mathematical model, which does reflect the real world, as seen in its explanatory and predictive power, cannot work. This is akin to the logical contradiction in asserting that one is less than two, which is less than three, which is less than one.

UTILITY

As already explained, economists must use what they can measure. This is why most value maximizing utility. Demand reveals consumers preferences. Because demand can be measured, preferences are measurable. Economists assume that attaining their preferences makes people happy in some sense, and they call this "utility," which is a form of satisfaction. Philosophically we have seen that we can question this assumption with the distinction between seeking *apparent* versus *real* goods. Economists do not specify further what utility is, but philosophically there are questions about what happiness is. Incipient modern economics used the utilitarianism of Bentham and Mill for its theory of utility.

The economic theory of consumer choice assumes that consumers optimize their utility subject to a budget constraint. As described earlier, utilitarianism argues that societies should try to achieve the greatest happiness for the greatest number of people. Bentham and others tried to measure utility across individuals to calculate the net sum of utility for a society. Early modern economists tried to do the same with *cardinal utility*, the summation of individual units of utility called *utils*.

Economists soon realized that different things make different people happy, which is one of the philosophical problems in defining happiness. Thus, for economists, there was no standard measure for an additive summation of utility. However, they did realize that individuals know what they prefer and rank their own preferences, so *ordinal utility* is now used. This does not concern numbers of utils but instead means that utils represent an index to an individual. In addition, since utility is not additive, economists consider *consumption bundles*. An example would be a whole hamburger, consisting of a bun, meat, cheese, etc., and not each item individually. We will later see how a person's demand curve reveals their utility, but now we will examine utility in general.

In modern economic theory of utility, there are *six axioms of consumer preferences*. The first four are properties of real numbers:

> Axiom 1: Preferences are complete. For any two consumption bundles X and Y a consumer can make one of the following three comparisons:
>
> > X is preferred to Y, Y is preferred to X, X is indifferent to Y. Axiom 1 means that individuals can rank their preferences and can compare all possible consumption bundles.

Axiom 2: Preferences are reflexive. If an individual is presented with two identical bundles so that X=Y then X and Y are indifferent to each other.

Axiom 3: Preferences are transitive. If an individual prefers X to Y and Y to Z then the individual also prefers X to Z.

Axiom 4: Preferences are continuous. If bundle X is preferred to bundle Y and bundle Z is very close to bundle Y then X is also preferred to Z. That is, in an infinitesimal division, what is called a limit in mathematics, Axiom 3 remains true. Or in other words, consumer preferences are represented by smooth curves.

Axiom 5: Preferences exhibit nonsatiation. More of a good or service is preferred to less.

Axiom 6: Indifferent bundles of goods exhibit diminishing marginal rates of substitution. As individuals give up more of one good then more of another good (a substitute) is required to keep them indifferent.

Philosophically we note that, while necessary, axioms can be questioned.[16] Although the axioms of consumer preferences concerning real numbers are perhaps less questionable, axioms five and six are questionable insofar as they assume answers to certain limit questions in philosophical anthropology. For example, axiom five might assume psychological egoism and thus, some psychological altruists could question it. With these caveats, positive economics posits these axioms, from which they graph utility. Here we compare two bundles of goods X and Y:

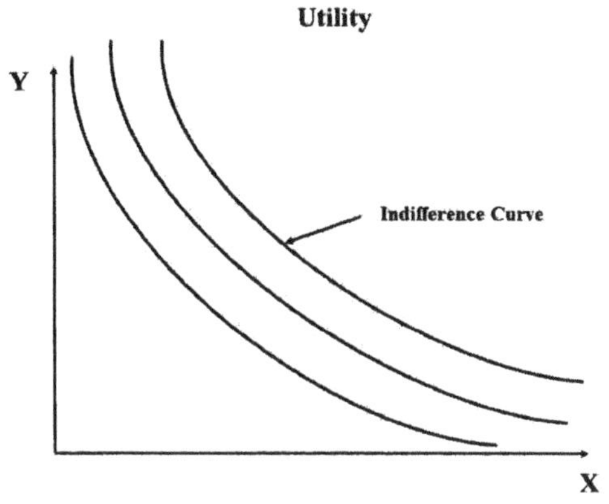

Figure 2.12: Utility

Here are three *indifference curves*. This individual has many more, in fact an infinite amount. An indifference curve represents all combinations of X and Y that give the individual the same level of utility. Now we add the numbers to these same indifference curves:

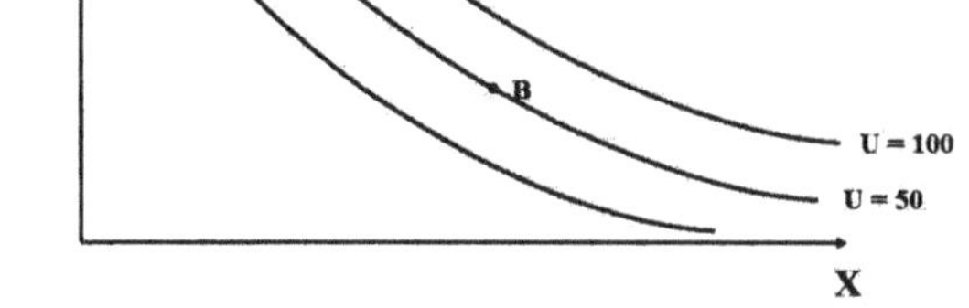

Figure 2.13: Multiple Indifference Curves

Both points A and B give the individual a satisfaction level of fifty utils. This means they are indifferent to bundles A and B. That is, they derive the same level of satisfaction from bundles A and B, even though they represent different amounts of the goods X and Y. Point C, however, gives the individual one hundred utils of satisfaction. Therefore they prefer C over A and over B. Economists assume that individuals always choose higher levels of utility, higher and higher points, even higher than those pictured here. Infinite utility is impossible, given finite resources. A person's budget constraint limits the amount of utility she can maximize. *Consumer demand* is what a consumer is willing and able to pay for a certain amount of utility.

Mathematically, the budget constraint for two goods is the amount of money one has or has budgeted (M). This must be equal to the price of good X multiplied by the quantity of good X purchased, added to the price of good Y multiplied by the quantity of good Y purchased. For two goods the equation is: $M = P_xX + P_yY$. P_x is the price of good X, P_y is the price of good Y, X is the quantity of good X, and Y is the quantity of good Y. The budget constraint is graphed here:

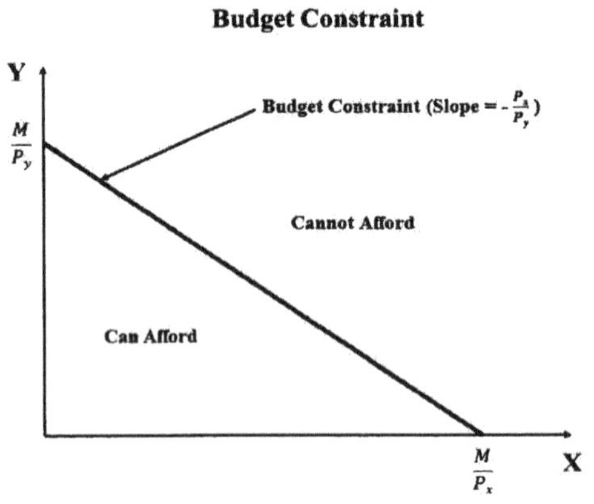

Figure 2.14: Budget Constraint

The intercepts are equal to the budget divided by the price of only one good because at the intercepts the person buys zero of the other good. The slope of the budget constraint, which will be important later, is the ratio of the prices between the two goods. The individual can afford any consumption bundle on or under the budget constraint. It is thus attainable. She cannot afford any consumption bundle above the budget constraint, which is not attainable. We now put the indifference curves together with the budget constraint. The axioms dictate that there will be one unique point where the individual maximizes their utility subject to their budget:

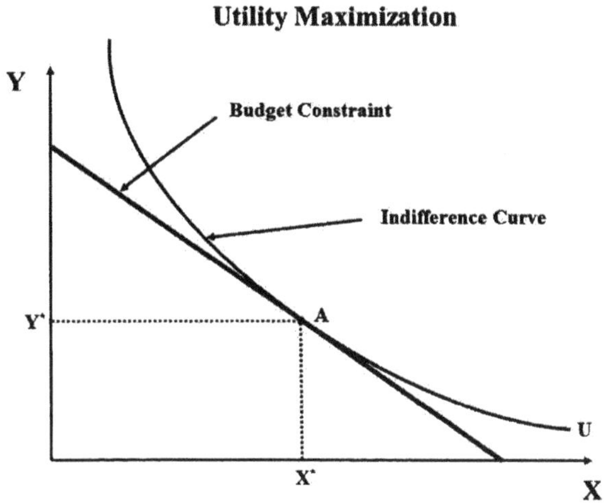

Figure 2.15: Utility Maximization

At point "A" a consumer's utility is maximized based on her preferences and budget. The indifference curve depicts her preferences. This consumer will pick a bundle that contains a quantity of X that is X^* and a quantity of Y that is Y^*. The asterisk (*) denotes the optimal combination. She would never choose a bundle below the budget constraint, because that would violate the axioms of consumer preferences. She will never choose a bundle beyond A, because she cannot currently afford it. Assuming consumer preferences remain fixed, only a change in the good's price or consumer income will change her choice. If her income increases, then her budget constraint increases, so shy can buy more of both goods, and M shifts out:

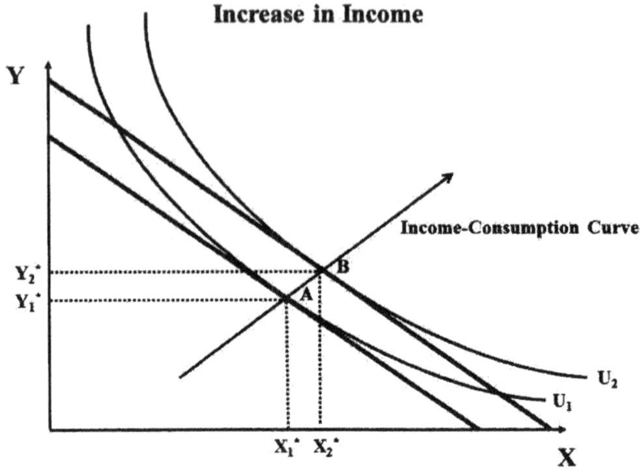

Figure 2.16: Effect of Income Increase on Utility Maximization

In this graph, an increased income shifts the budget constraint out, causing the consumer to re-optimize to consumption bundle B. Now bundle A is inferior to bundle B, as B now produces more utility than A. The line through all optimal bundles is the *income-consumption curve*, which holds prices and preferences constant across changing income. In a world of uncertainty, income changes, and how uncertainty affects utility is discussed later. The same is true in reverse for income reductions. Starting with a higher income at bundle B, a decreased income causes re-optimization that makes consumption bundle A preferable, despite its lower utility level.

Many things, like taxes, reduce income. The reason many do not like taxes is that taxes reduce their utility level. Strictly speaking, this applies only if the tax is not subsidized back into the price of good X or Y. Even with a subsidy on one of the prices, though, the person can never get back to the same bundle, only a different bundle on their original indifference curve U_2. This is why economists say most taxes, except in special cases, distort an economic system. Here they have a special rule for implementing Bentham's ideal, *Pareto optimality.* This states that something should not be done unless it makes at least one person better off (higher utility) without making anyone else worse off (lower utility). Economists use this as a cardinal rule for weighing policy choices. It is a stiff benchmark, however, so, sadly, most policies do not meet this standard.

We can finally see where the demand curve comes from. Consider a minor change, such as X decreasing in price. As seen below, this causes the budget constraint to shift out, causing the consumer to re-optimize from bundle A to bundle B. The curve connecting the points between the optimal quantities of X and their respective prices is the demand curve. This is why economists say that the demand curve is individuals revealing their preferences. Of course economists can also get demand data, and then work backwards to utility.

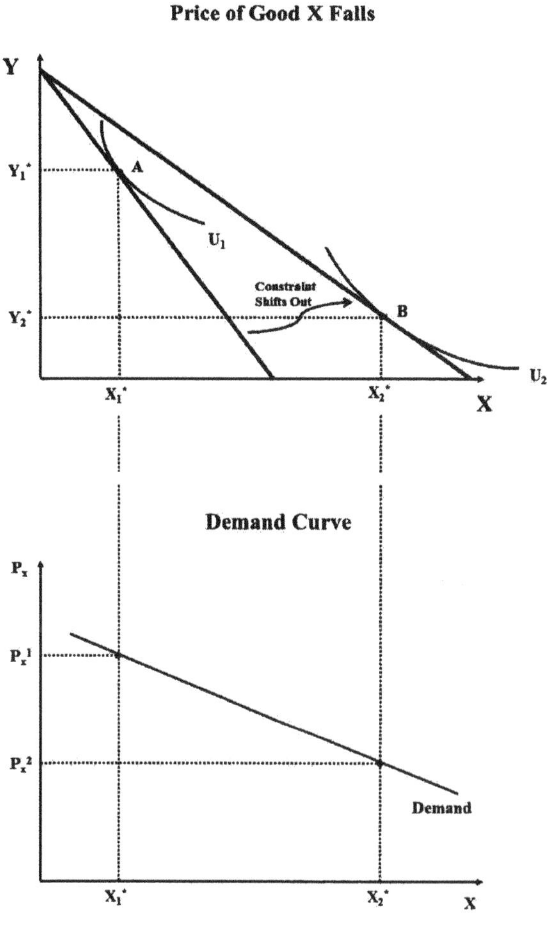

Figure 2.17: Demand Comes From Utility

This shows the theoretical link between utility theory and the visible demand curves. As with income change above, the price change here could be the reverse, an increase in the cost of X. Similarly, we could also add a tax on X. A tax would pivot the budget constraint in and cause utility loss. In discussing consumer surplus earlier we were really referring to utility, because the demand curve monetizes utility, or welfare. While we will not discuss this topic further, due to the shapes of indifference curves, when government projects change the prices of normal goods for consumers, they tend to overstate social gains and underestimate social losses. The opposite is true for inferior goods, because there are really two effects going on with utility: income and substitution. The income effect changes the budget M. The substitution effect changes the shape of the indifference curve between two goods. Now we consider uncertainty.

While we will not broach the complexities of probability theory, we must consider how uncertainty affects the picture. Economists specify three types of individuals in considering uncertainty: risk-averse, risk-loving, and risk neutral. Given some level of wealth (W), individuals are *risk-averse* if they always prefer a certain outcome over a risk with the same expected outcome as the certain outcome, but with some positive variance as to its outcome. Individuals are *risk neutral* if they are indifferent to the certain outcome and the risk. Individuals are *risk-loving* if they prefer the gamble of the risk to the certain outcome. Assume a risk-averse individual works on commission with three possible outcomes for her salary (wealth), and thus her corresponding utility as well, for the year as follows:

Outcome 1: $50,000 with a utility of 40
Outcome 2: $100,000 with a utility of 90
Outcome 3: $150,000 with a utility of 120

Given this data, we have the following graph of wealth vs. utility.

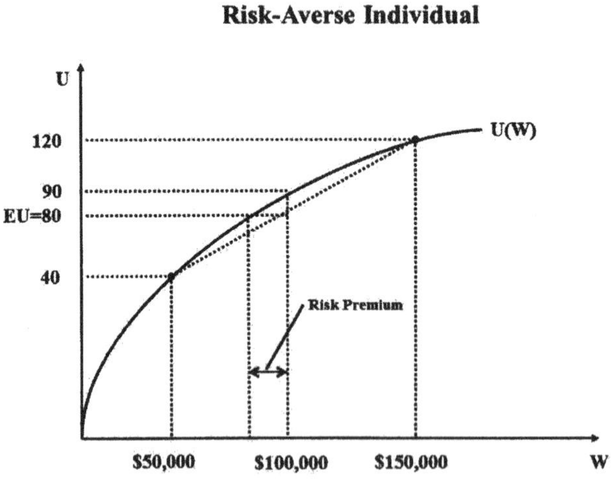

Figure 2.18: Expected Utility of Risk-Averse Individual

If she earns \$150,000 then she gets one hundred twenty utils of satisfaction. If she earns only \$50,000 then she gets forty utils. Consider two possible actions available to her. The first yields \$100,000 with certainty, or ninety utils of satisfaction. The second yields either \$50,000 or forty utils at 50 percent probability, or \$150,000 or one hundred twenty utils at 50 percent probability. The *expected utility* of the second action is: EU = 0.5(40) + 0.5(120) = 80. The expected utility of eighty of the second action is less than the ninety certain utils of the first action. If she is risk-averse then she chooses the first. What if she could not take the first action and had to choose the second? Then she would be willing to pay a *risk premium* to mitigate the risk and get a certain outcome. This is akin to buying insurance. In fact, she would be willing to pay up to the distance between the double arrows to avoid the risk, as she gets more utility from certainty. What if she were risk-loving instead of risk-averse? She might have these wealth and utility combinations:

Outcome 1: \$50,000 with utility of 10
Outcome 2: \$100,000 with utility of 30
Outcome 3: \$150,000 with utility of 100

Again, she could take the first action, providing certain income of \$100,000 and thirty utils, or the second action yielding either \$50,000 or forty utils at 50 percent probability, or \$150,000 or one hundred twenty utils at 50 percent probability. If she chooses the second, her expected utility is: EU = 0.5(10) + 0.5(100) = 55. Being risk-loving, she prefers the second with fifty utils as opposed to thirty. Thus we see Figure 2.19.

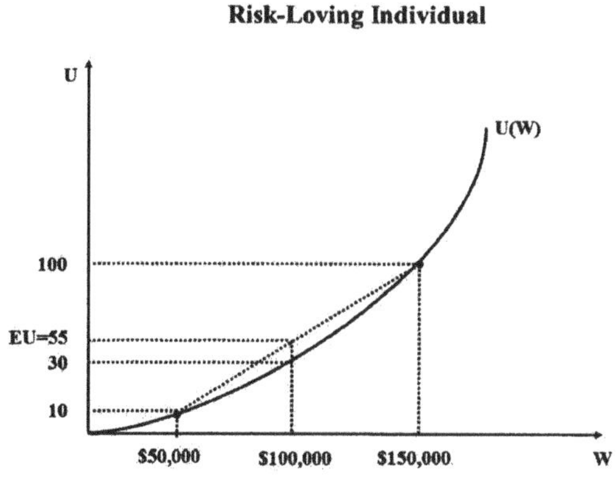

Figure 2.19: Expected Utility of Risk-Loving Individual

This is important, because it affects many social policies. If everyone is risk-averse, then things like social security can be justified from a utility standpoint, since all are willing to pay a risk premium to avoid uncertainty in income. Although it is plausible that *many* individuals are risk-averse, that *all* are is a very strong assumption. If even one person is risk-loving then a program like social security could violate *Pareto optimality*, since it makes someone worse off. If there are a mix of risk-averse and risk-loving individuals in an economy, then taxes to support programs like social security only transfer harm (disutility) from one party in order to give utility another.

The normative value judgments that welfare *should* be maximized and harm minimized in economic utility theory, are derived from utilitarian ethics. They more generally rest on the belief that pleasure or happiness is the greatest value. We have seen that this is philosophically and ethically questionable. In this regard, they are subject to the criticisms of all ethical theories prioritizing pleasure or happiness, like ethical hedonism, utilitarianism, and many forms of consequentialism, discussed earlier.

The complexity of economic systems might make it impossible to predict, with probability, let alone certainty, desired consequences. We have seen that whether individuals are risk-averse or risk-loving affects welfare and harm, but we do not know how many, if any, individuals are risk-loving. There are also questions about what constitutes things like happiness and harm (physical only, mental and / or emotional, etc.).

Even assuming the strength of consequentialist ethical theories specifying happiness or welfare as the highest value, this discussion of utility theory provides important data to consider. As the analysis of imposing risk premiums on markets in which there are at least some risk-loving individuals shows, there are times when policies intended to help some also bring harm to others, often unwittingly by policy-makers. There are many more such examples. We can legitimately ask who is qualified to judge to whom utility should be transferred and who will suffer disutility as a result. Some might argue that some basic human rights require this, or that equality is the highest social value and that equity can be insured only through more intervention in markets. Even if this is the case, economists have difficulty with this because, unlike utility that is measurable through revealed preferences, equity is not so easily measured. Further, there are different conceptions of equality, as we will later see. On these different conceptions, some would argue that increasing the utility of some at the expense of others' utility is not equitable, but in fact inequitable.

PRIVATE VS. PUBLIC GOODS

Another important distinction, between kinds of goods, is that between *private goods* and *public goods*. In economics, two subtypes divide these: rival and excludable. A good *rival in consumption* prevents others from consuming it. If Bill eats a cheeseburger then no one else can eat that cheeseburger. Goods *non-rival in consumption* do not prevent others from consuming it. Listening to the same radio station by one person does not prevent others from doing so.

Goods can also be *excludable*, which means that suppliers can prevent someone from consuming it. Bill can be excluded from a cheeseburger. The cheeseburger supplier will not give him one unless he pays for it. Other goods are *non-excludable*. A classic example is a light house. No one can stop people from seeing the light from a light house. The following table summarizes these types of goods.

Table 2.1

	Rival	Not Rival
Excludable	Private Good	Natural Monopolies
Non-Excludable	Common Resources	Public Good

Rivalry and excludability cause allocation problems in economics. Markets cannot produce public goods since they are non-excludable. Suppliers cannot charge for consumption. National defense, for instance, is a public good that is non-excludable. That is, even those who do not pay their taxes benefit by national defense, and the government cannot exclude them from doing so. Yet these distinctions can be blurred in discussions of ethics and economics. If ethically a person or society believes a good or service should be provided to all, this still does not change its nature. Proper understandings of these distinctions allow for solutions to allocation problems. The problem economically, again, is the most efficient allocation of scarce resources.

Take the issue of universal healthcare. Many normative ethical systems could lead to the value judgment that all in a society should have healthcare. This could result from using natural law-type or divine command theory-type reasoning to conclude that every human being has a right to healthcare. Defining a good or service as a right does not solve the allocation problem, however. Healthcare is excludable, as it can be withheld for non-payment. It is also rival, since consuming resources like doctors, medicines, and hospitals prevents others from doing so.

The situation is similar with education. Many intuitively believe that everyone should have education, and many normative ethical theories can be used to argue this. Perhaps it is a natural or divine right of humans. Even a utilitarian-like consequentialism could argue that education makes people successful, and therefore happier. Yet, education is rival, as it is well-known that more students per instructor decreases education's quality. Limits on how many students one instructor can teach also necessitate more instructors. Education is also excludable, as school doors can be closed to not allow people to consume educational resources.

Different uses of a term can confuse. Merely calling primary education in state-funded schools, "public education," does not make it a public good, economically speaking. That we might get a positive externality (covered in the next section) from education can be considered in ethical deliberations, but this still does not make it a public good. The problem of scarcity, for economists, leads them to value the most efficient use of scarce resources. These categories exist to attain this goal. Deadweight loss in a system hinders this goal. Barring the presence of externalities, if a good is rival and excludable then a competitive market is the most efficient way to allocate it.

The non-excludability of public goods, like national defense, causes allocation problems. The military still protects those who do not pay their taxes. The problem is that a private company could not provide this good, since, although all in society require and use it, individuals would not pay for it. Economists call this *free riding*, and it causes market failure. *Market failure* occurs when a competitive market fails to efficiently allocate a resource, because of the nature of the good. This is the argument for governments providing public goods. An economic misconception is that market failure means getting a competitive market result that we do not like. Market failure is merely the inability of a market to efficiently allocate the good or service.

The rival and excludable traits of goods can cause other problems as well. For example, fish in the ocean are a *common pool resource*. Catching fish is non-excludable but rival. Apart from a regulation, no one is excluded from fishing. Nothing naturally stops one from fishing in the ocean, so it is non-excludable. If someone stops fishing, then someone else catches the fish they would have caught, so catching fish is rival. These two facts can incentivize overfishing, since people might fear that others will catch fish they could catch while they are not fishing. This means that non-excludability can cause resources to be overused, which is inefficient.

The problem here regards property rights. Neo-classical economics assumes the right to private property, as much early modern social and political philosophy argued for private property rights, as we will see. Most modern people agree with private property rights. Private property grounds neo-classical economic theory but some very different economic theories, like communism, do not assume this right. Most economists today insist on the right to private property and find serious problems with rejecting it, as we also will see.

In most cases there is not just one person who owns a stream, lake, or ocean. This lack of property rights causes the *common pool problem*. This is what causes the market failure, but the private market has not failed. Rather, a private market cannot exist without defining property rights. There are many solutions to this problem. Some include regulations, like permits. These may work, but there is still the problem of the cost of enforcement. Fishing permits and rules about fish sizes and fish amounts, as solutions to the common pool resource problem, rely on credible enforcement. Without enforcement, the common pool problem still exists.

In some cases, simply defining property rights solves such problems for economists. Take air pollution. Some have defined pollution as a right and have sold permits allowing firms to pollute.[17] Firms installing equipment that lowers their pollution can then sell some of their permits to other companies who, for whatever reason, need to pollute more. Each year the government reduces the number of permits available, which thus reduces the total amount of pollution. While this idea is still in its infancy, we may someday see a market-based solution to this issue.

When a good or service is not rival but is excludable, like media broadcasting, natural monopolies can result. *Natural monopolies* are the reverse of the common pool problem. They usually result from the large investment required to produce the good or service, causing few firms to be in the market. Sometimes competitive markets solve this problem. Media firms make money through advertisements, which are excludable. One cannot get an advertisement without paying for it. Also, some economists believe natural monopolies are always temporary, because any profitable industry eventually attracts competition, resulting in multiple competing firms.

The point regarding these different types of goods is that economists need these distinctions as they seek the value of efficient allocation of scarce resources. Ethical systems may lead to valuing certain rights and obligations more than efficiency. However, calling goods public does not change their nature and consequent categorizations, by economists, used to determine their effects on markets. Also, any ethical considerations used in judging economic policies must take into account that inefficiency is often the cost of honoring rights or meeting other obligations, as dictated by various normative ethical systems. Inefficiency will certainly be a consideration of any consequentialist theory. It does, however, behoove those using non-consequentialist theorists, like deontological or divine command theories, to at least be cognizant of the opportunity costs of inefficiency involved in the trade-off for other values in economic systems. Perhaps governments should provide some private goods like healthcare and education. There may even be positive economic reasons for doing so, as in the case of externalities, which we will now consider. However, these facts do not change the basic nature of a good or service.

EXTERNALITIES

Externalities are by-products of economic activity. A common example is pollution. Suppliers are in business to sell their products, not their pollution. Externalities can be positive and negative, meaning they can have extra benefits or costs. Again, they usually stem from property rights issues. Regarding pollution, we can ask who owns the air. Markets rely on property rights as discussed earlier, so they cannot incorporate the costs and benefits of these by-products. Without well-defined property rights, markets cannot transfer an externality's costs or benefits.

Not all externalities are negative. Assume you live in an apartment complex and your next door neighbor buys a fire extinguisher. His purchase makes you safer from the risk of fire in your apartment, which is a benefit. You probably would not give him money for making you safer. This again shows how an externality is not captured by a market. There are many externalities, but many are trivial, like noise pollution and leaf-burning. It is inefficient to solve everyone's trivial externality problem. Economists care about externalities because they cause inefficiency, and, again, economists value efficiency.

The graph below depicts a market with a negative externality, an electricity market. Pollution is a negative externality of producing electricity, but due to the property rights issue, no one pays for it. Assume we know the cost of the externality (E) and we impose the cost on the producer, although, as with taxes, it does not matter upon whom we impose the cost. Thus, in this market the cost to produce electricity is the supply curve (S) plus the externality (E), or S+E.

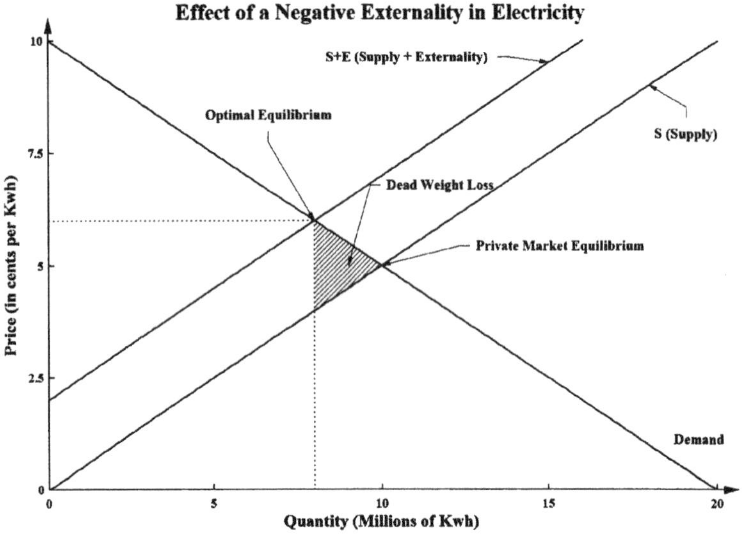

Figure 2.20: Effect of a Negative Externality

With externalities, the deadweight loss is at the private market equilibrium and is removed by including the externality. One way to do this is with taxes. A tax equal to E, then, would remove it. This is the one instance in which taxes do not generate a deadweight loss.

Education, also discussed earlier, produces positive externalities. As people are educated they become more efficient. Assume your neighbor goes college. Going through school she becomes more knowledgeable, and upon graduation she gets a higher paying job. This benefits you as well as her. She has additional money to redo her yard and improve her home. Again, you probably would not financially compensate her for making you better off by improving the neighborhood. In this case, giving a subsidy could move the market to efficient equilibrium.

Economists have difficulties estimating an externality's size. Both economically and philosophically there are problems in both defining what constitutes "help" and "harm," and in determining whether or not they are trivial or non-trivial. Philosophically, who decides what constitutes help and harm, and whether or not it is trivial or significant? Private markets can identify help and harm, and can quantify them. Help and harm are revealed in trade, through the decisions of consumers and suppliers who reveal their preferences. Yet, property rights are needed for private markets to work, which is the problem with externalities. Also, the market model assumes buyers and sellers who are both "willing and able," but the preferences revealed in decisions only capture the "willing" aspect. What if someone is very willing, but unable, to buy or sell?

Assuming an externality is deemed non-trivial, there are solutions to externalities other than taxes or subsidies, which are negative taxes. One is to assign a property right so that the externality is incorporated into a private market. This was the solution offered by R. H. Coase in his groundbreaking research. He also first identified the property rights issue. Coase also stressed that harm goes both ways. Of his many examples, consider that of a psychiatrist and candy maker next to each other in a strip mall. The candy maker must make noise to make candy, which is a negative externality to the psychiatrist who needs quietness for his business. If the psychiatrist sues the candy maker and the court rules that the candy maker cannot make noise, then harm has been transferred from the psychiatrist to the candy maker. That is, the candy maker is out of business to the benefit of the psychiatrist. That harm goes both ways means that "solving" harm always only shifts harm from one party to another.

Coase explains that this is a property rights issue, as we do not know who owns the right to make noise.[18] Coase suggests that to solve this problem we must assign the property right to one party—which party does not matter—and then let the parties buy and sell the property right. If we allow the parties to transact the right then it will go to the party who values it the most, and the party who values it the most will also compensate the other party for the harm. Suppose we give the candy maker the right to make noise but the psychiatrist wants it more. Then the psychiatrist will pay the candy maker for the right. This will compensate the candy maker, who now needs to move his business. This is called *Coasian bargaining*, but it only works if the costs of the transaction are low and few parties are involved. While an elegant example of how we can solve externality problems without regulations or taxes, it stresses the "willing" adjective in the posited "willing and able" buyers and sellers in neoclassical economics. What if for some reason the psychiatrist wanted to buy the noise right, but were unable to do so?

Solutions to externality problems are varied and situation dependent. For economists, taxation and regulations are not necessarily the only possible solutions, and the goal is always to maximize the value of efficiency. As we have said, different normative ethical approaches could lead to valuing something greater than efficiency. In those cases the problems are different and require different solutions. Again, economists can only measure efficiency.

MARKET FAILURE & GOVERNMENT FAILURE

Market failure is often discussed in economics, but many do not fully understand its meaning in economics. Market failure does not occur when there is an equilibrium price and quantity that someone or some group does not like. Judging the price of gas to be "too high," and therefore claiming "market failure," is erroneous. As with externalities and public goods, market failure is a private market's failure to achieve efficiency because of property rights or the public nature of a good. It is incorrect to use normative economic judgments to determine market failure, which is a positive economic term. Again, economists value the most efficient allocation of resources because it alone is measurable. Attaining this may mean an equilibrium price we do not like, but this does not imply a problem that needs to be fixed from a positive economic perspective.

Similar to this is *government failure*, which is a government's failure to most efficiently provide a good or service. Governments use tax revenues to provide resources. As seen in the sections on utility and *Pareto optimality*, taxes are almost always inefficient. This means that almost anything the government provides is inefficient. There will always be some unhappy with the distributions and amounts of government goods and services, or inefficiency in terms of utility.

Governments often provide both public and private goods. A government-provided good or service is not necessarily a public good, economically speaking. Again, clear examples are education and healthcare. Education is not a public good but a private good by definition, since it is both rival in consumption and excludable. "Public" education is really the public provision of a private good when the government provides it. Healthcare is also rival, in consumption, and excludable, so, "public" healthcare provided by a government is really the public provision of a private good.

Government attempts to fix education and healthcare have been largely ineffective, since they are private goods, and policy-based intervention in the natural market allocation system introduces inefficiency. However, just because education and healthcare are private goods does not mean that real problems do not occur due to externalities. Both education and healthcare involve externalities. The education of one helps all, and the healthiness of one helps all, even if it is as simple as not making other people sick. In neither case is there pecuniary compensation for these positive externalities.

From a positive economic perspective, the only hope for market efficiency is to discover the correct amount of these externalities, if that is even possible. Again, there are both philosophical and economic problems in determining the triviality or non-triviality of externalities. Further, the size of externalities could inform judgments about their triviality or non-triviality.

Sometimes critics of neoclassical economics appeal to the difficulties in determining the triviality or non-triviality, and size, of externalities, in attempts to undermine economic theory as a whole. They claim that there are too many externalities that go unconsidered, and so the model of a competitive market predicated on property rights is a dismal failure. Economists respond that, yes, there are many, perhaps innumerable, externalities, but the vast majority of externalities are trivial and small enough to be of negligible import. It has been said that contemplating the problem of externalities is like holding a hammer, which makes everything looks like a nail. Thus, some, with an agenda to undercut positive economic theory, appeal to the problem of externalities. They have yet to proffer a viable alternative model to neoclassic economic theory, with equal explanatory and predictive power.

Questions about the triviality or non-triviality, and size, of externalities also feed policy debates with political agendas. In such cases, limit questions that economics does not purport to address are appealed to in conjunction with externalities, in order to advocate more or less market intervention by governments. Philosophical questions in defining "hurt" and "harm" inform value judgments about what are and are not externalities, and what are the "best" ways to handle them. These are not mathematical and scientific, but philosophical, questions. Indeed, questions about externalities and how to best handle them exhibit well yet another way in which economics, at the limits of its scientific purview, ineluctably broaches philosophical limit questions:

> This is not science; it is metaphysics: value judgments and political goals will enter into the determination of whether externalities occur in our world. You cannot show analytically that the government, in principle and in all cases, handles externalities better than the market; nor can you prove the opposite: it all depends on what point of reference you choose. And that is not a question of positive economics. By choosing the appropriate point of reference, the 'conclusion' is reached that government intervention (or no government intervention) is optimal. . . . This is not positive economics; it is a political discussion, at least until we better justify the choice of appropriate reference points. It is doubtful whether the term 'externality' has any meaningful interpretation, except as an indicator of the political beliefs and value judgments of the person who uses (or avoids using) the term.[19]

There are thus philosophical issues involved in defining hurt and harm that cannot be measured in terms of utility, and normative (not positive) economics may at times value something else more than measurable efficiency. In the latter case there will certainly be a trade-off of economic efficiency for some other value, but it is necessary to be aware of the trade-off. All technological applications of scientific knowledge to modify natural systems have pros and cons. The risk of unintended consequences and the extremely large and complicated nature of markets is perhaps greater in economics than in many other areas, however.

SUMMARY

This chapter surveyed some of the most common normative ethical theories, and the reasons for them. In doing so, it considered at points how they might apply to discussions of normative economics. This chapter also surveyed basic principles of microeconomics as positive economic theory. In doing so, it highlighted, at points, ways in which ethics, and in some cases broader philosophical questions, bear on the assumptions of positive microeconomics.

Macroeconomics and social ethics expand the economics and ethics discussion beyond smaller units, comprised of individual parties acting in markets, to larger social groups. Although we have, of necessity, already broached social values, it is now necessary to enter a detailed discussion of social values and social ethics. As we do so, we must also survey the basic principles of macroeconomics. To these we now turn.

NOTES

1. One such example of the argument that groups act with even greater self-interest than individuals is: Reinhold Niebuhr, *Moral Man and Immoral Society: A Study in Ethics and Politics* (New York, NY: Simon & Schuster, 1995).

2. Immanuel Kant, *Prolegomena to Any Future Metaphysics* (Charleston, SC: Forgotten Books, 1951), 6.

3. Immanuel Kant, "Selections from *Critique of Practical Reason* [1788]," trans. Thomas K. Abbott, in *Basic Writings of Kant*, ed. Allen W. Wood, 223 – 72 (New York: Modern Library, 2001, 231).

4. Marcus Walker, "Population Control: In Estonia, Paying Women to Have Babies Is Paying Off; As Low Birthrates Threaten Growth, Developed Nations Watch Incentive Effort; $1,560 a Month for Annaliisa," *The Wall Street Journal* (New York), October 20, 2006, Eastern edition, sec. A.

5. F. A. Hayek, *The Fatal Conceit: The Errors of Socialism*, ed. W. W. Bartley III (Chicago, IL: University of Chicago Press, 1991).

6. Immanuel Kant, *Groundwork of the Metaphysics of Morals*, ed. Mary J. Gregor (New York, NY: Cambridge University Press, 1998), 2.

7. Kant, *Groundwork of the Metaphysics of Morals*, 8.

8. Kant, *Groundwork of the Metaphysics of Morals*, xv.

9. The *a priori*, rule-based, tendency of religious ethics based upon some variation of divine command theory is seen, for instance, in the Hindu concept of doing one's duty, regardless of consequences: "You have a right to perform your prescribed duty, but you are not entitled to the fruits of action. Never consider yourself the cause of the results of your activities, and never be attached to not doing your duty" (*Bhagavad-gītā* 2.47) (A. C. Bhaktivedanta Swami Prabhupādā, *Bhagavad-gītā As It Is* [Los Angeles, CA: The Bhaktivedanta Book Trust, 1986], 121).

10. Genesis 22:1 – 18 and Hosea 1:2. In his classic work on the divine command for Abraham to sacrifice Isaac, *Fear and Trembling* (AD 1843), Søren Kierkegaard (AD 1813 – 1855) argues for the rightness of the action solely based on the divine command, and evidences the concern with the universal *a priori* principles apart from consequences in rule-based ethics like divine command theory: "The ethical as such is the universal, it applies to everyone, and the same thing is expressed from another point of view by saying that it applies every instant. It reposes immanently in itself, it has nothing without itself which is its *telos*. . . . By his [Abraham's act] he overstepped the ethical entirely and possessed a higher *telos* outside of it, in relation to which he suspended the former . . . It was not for the sake of saving a people, not to maintain the idea of the state, that Abra-

ham did this, and not in order to reconcile angry deities. . . . Why then did Abraham do it? For God's sake, and (in complete identity with this) for his own sake. . . . What ordinarily tempts a man is that which would keep him from doing his duty, in this case the temptation is itself the ethical . . . which would keep him from doing God's will" (Søren Kierkegaard, *Fear and Trembling* [Radford, VA: Wilder, 2008], 39, 43 – 44). Yet, Kierkegaard evidences the counterintuitive, even scandalous, effects of such a divine command, when he says: "Therefore, though Abraham arouses my admiration, he at the same time appalls me" (Kierkegaard, *Fear and Trembling*, 44).

11. Plato, *Euthyphro*, 10a2 – 3. In *Plato: The Collected Dialogues*. Edited by Edith Hamilton and Huntington Cairns, 169 – 86. New York: Pantheon Books, 1964, 178.

12. For instance, Sir James George Frazer theorized that humanity has developed through two stages of three: (1) primitive magic, (2) religion, (3) science. See, James George Frazer, *The Golden Bough: A Study in Magic and Religion*, 1st ed., 2 vols. (London: Macmillan, 1890).

13. Aristotle, *Nicomachean Ethics*, 1096a15, ed. W. D. Ross, rev. J. O. Urmson, in *The Complete Works of Aristotle*, vol. 2, ed. Jonathan Barnes, 1728 – 1867 (Princeton, NJ: Princeton University Press, 1984), 1732.

14. For a good introduction to what is typically called "natural law ethics," see, Ralph M. McInerny, *Ethica Thomistica: The Moral Philosophy of Thomas Aquinas* (Washington, DC: The Catholic University of America Press, 1997).

15. See: Frederic Bastiat, *The Bastiat Collection* (Auburn, AL.: Ludwig von Mises Institute, 2011).

16. For instance, in the nineteenth century some geometers questioned Euclid's axioms to develop geometries with alternative axioms in order to make geometric properties invariant under projective transformations. See, for instance, Alfred North Whitehead, *The Axioms of Projective Geometry* (Cambridge: Cambridge University Press, 1906), and idem, *Process and Reality: An Essay in Cosmology*, corrected and revised edition, ed. David Ray Griffin and Donald W. Sherburne (New York: Free Press, 1978), 294 – 336.

17. Wikipedia contributors, "Emissions trading," *Wikipedia, The Free Encyclopedia*, http://en.wikipedia.org/w/index.php?title=Emissions_trading&oldid=4742 19477 (accessed September 30, 2011).

18. R. H. Coase, "The Problem of Social Cost," *Journal of Law and Economics* 3 (1960): 1 – 44.

19. Carl J. Dahlman, "The Problem of Externality," *The Journal of Law & Economics* 22 (1979): 156.

CHAPTER 3: MACROECONOMICS & SOCIAL ETHICS

As should now be evident, ethics, economics and their intersection are complicated. Ethics invokes ideas of an individual acting and our passing value judgments about such actions' rightness or wrongness. Ethics does deal with people acting individually. Yet, important aspects of ethics are *social* values and *social* ethics. *En masse*, this is of particular concern in macroeconomics, as the actions or inactions of all individuals in an economy affect the outcome.

Humans are not only individuals but are also social. As far back as we know, very few of our species have been born, lived, acted, worked, loved, fought, played, been religious, and died alone. The solitary hermit has been, for the most part, the exception and not the rule. And even hermits have frequently lived together, for instance, in religious communes. In units of family, tribe, clan, neighborhood, community, city, state, and the world, we are thoroughly social beings.

Our social and communal nature has numerous implications for the intersection of ethics and economics. It greatly complicates, even exponentially, the limit questions regarding ethics and morality. We can, of course, contemplate an individual all alone along with his actions, which we can analyze ethically. Yet, the vast majority of our ethical and economic considerations deal with two or more people, which make ethics and economics a social affair.

Recall economics as we have defined it is the "study of the allocation of scarce resources." "Allocation," here, implies that there are more than one person to whom the resources are allocated. Hence economics is social by definition. Further, transactions, as the basic unit of the science of economics, are between two or more people or groups. Indeed, economics is often considered a "social science," like sociology and political science. It is a *science* due to its empirical methods and procedures, but it studies the social phenomena that we call economic activities between people and groups. Because economics is a *social* science, when we contemplate the relationship between economics and ethics we must, of necessity, consider values in social contexts.

Although we have touched upon social ethics, in this chapter we examine more thoroughly the numerous concerns of social ethics. Social ethics presupposes and builds on the axiology, value theory, metaethics, normative ethics and applied ethics already considered. Here we consider limit questions about values as they emerge in social contexts. Discussions of "rights," prominent in considerations of ethics and economics, are also social ethical issues.

Things are further complicated, by the necessity of considering aspects of social and political philosophy, when discussing ethics and economics. Social and political philosophy raises and tries to answer the limit questions about the social entities in our experience. These include limit questions about being, knowledge, truth, and values. As we have said, all of the limit questions addressed by philosophy and religious doctrines are inextricably connected. Thus, here, we examine the intersection of economics, social ethics, and social and political philosophy.

MACROECONOMICS THE BASICS

Many people are interested in ethical questions concerning economic policies. To consider these we must understand macroeconomics. Demand and supply curves can be extended to analyze the aggregate level of activity at the macroeconomic level. There are several key concepts with specific definitions for measuring macroeconomic activity.

Macroeconomic activity in an economy is measured by GDP (Gross Domestic Product). GDP is the current market value of all newly produced final goods and services during a fixed time period. Chiefly for convenience, GDP is usually considered over a single calendar year.

The phrase "all final goods and services" means goods and services sold to an end consumer. For example, if you were to purchase new tires for your car then the new tires would be considered a *final good*. If, however, Ford bought the tires to put on a vehicle produced on their assembly line, then the tires would not count as a final good. Rather, the tires would then be an *intermediate good*. The distinction between final goods and intermediate goods avoids double counting of goods in a GDP. The tires as final goods are counted only once, in the car's sale price to the consumer once it is completed. Similarly, the sale of a used car is not counted in GDP because the car was not produced in the current year.

Why do economists call GDP a nation's income? For simplicity's sake, hypothetically consider a society with only one economic transaction for the entire year. Say the transaction is your getting a haircut for $20. Your $20 expense is $20 of income to your hairdresser. This is why economists say that a nation's expenses must equal its income. Economists represent the equation of a nation's income, or GDP, with a nation's expenses by defining the expenses:

$$Y = C + I + G + NX$$

Where:

Y	=	GDP (National Income)
C	=	Consumption
I	=	Investment
G	=	Government Spending
NX	=	Net Exports (Exports – Imports)

In order to understand this equation we must examine in more detail what each variable entails.

Consumption is the total spending for newly produced goods and services in a given year. Currently, consumption is the biggest component of the GDP of the U. S. There are three subcategories for consumption: consumer durables, nondurable goods and services. *Durable goods* are goods that last a long time, like cars and washing machines. *Nondurable goods* are short-lived goods, like food and gasoline. *Services* are items like haircuts, air travel and banking.

Investment in GDP does not mean stocks in the various stock markets. Investment here is spending on capital goods used as means of production of other goods, like machines in factories. There are three basic categories of investment in capital goods: fixed, inventory, and residential investment. *Fixed investment* is spending by businesses on equipment like machines, furniture and computers. *Inventory investment* is the change in inventories held by firms. If inventories rise it is positive, but if they fall it is negative. *Residential investment* is purchases of new houses. Recall that sales of used homes are not included.

Government spending is spending by the federal, state or local government on currently produced goods and services. It is important to note that much of what the government does in terms of transferring income from one person to another, as in taxation for welfare, is not included in this measure. This is because transferred money is not spent on a current good or service. Also, whatever money the government spends will fall into either consumption expenditures or investment expenditures, such as roads, arms, government offices, etc.

Net exports are: NX = X – M, where X = exports and M = imports. Exports are produced domestically and sent abroad. Imports are produced in another country and brought in for sale.

With these definitions in mind, let us examine some of the U.S.'s current GDP figures:

Table 3.1[1]

GDP by Category for 2009	Billions of $	Percent GDP
GROSS DOMESTIC PRODUCT (GDP)	14119	
Consumption expenditures (C)	10001.3	70.8
Durable goods	1026.5	7.3
Nondurable goods	2204.2	15.6
Services	6770.6	48.0
Investment (I)	1589.2	11.3
Fixed investment	1716.4	12.2
Nonresidential	1364.4	9.7
Residential	352.1	2.5
Change in private inventories	-127.2	-0.9
Net exports (NX)	-386.4	-2.7
Exports	1578.4	11.2
Goods	1063.1	7.5
Services	515.3	3.6
Imports	1964.7	13.9
Goods	1587.8	11.2
Services	376.9	2.7
Gov. consumption exp/gross investment (G)	2914.9	20.6
Federal	1139.6	8.1
National defense	771.6	5.5
Nondefense	368	2.6
State and local	1775.3	12.6

Here, consumption represented the largest portion of U. S.'s GDP for 2009 at 70.8 percent. The largest component of consumption in 2009 was services, representing 48 percent of the U. S.'s GDP. This reveals a possible reason our latest recession was so volatile. Individuals tend to cut back most on services when they fear a fall in their income. Also, service jobs tend to be more flexible in an economy in that service businesses are both easier to start and easier to close.

After consumption, government spending was the second largest component of GDP in 2009 at 20.6 percent of the GDP. Notice national defense was 5.5 percent of the GDP. While many target national defense for cutting expenses, it is not the largest component of government spending. Also, as mentioned above, transfers are not included in these numbers, and roughly 70 percent of all government programs are transfer programs of some kind.

Economists call such a break-down the *stylized facts* of our nation's current GDP. Economists derive GDP from all of these components. Although consumption is currently our largest component, this does not mean consumption must or will necessarily remain the largest component of the United States' GDP. Only when the limit questions about values are considered in conjunction with the facts, do normative or prescriptive value judgments emerge, like: "We *should not* spend so much on national defense" or "We *should* spend more on fixed investment." Differences in normative macroeconomic policies frequently involve varying value judgments about which components of GDP should be larger and smaller.

For example, some economists believe that consumption should not be the largest GDP component, and so see a difference between what it currently is (indicative) and what they believe it ought to be (imperative). This is adding a consideration of the limit questions concerning values to the bare facts of how much has been spent on different components of the GDP.

Value judgments about GDP also take into account the components of GDP across time. The figure below shows how the components of GDP have varied from 1925 to the present.

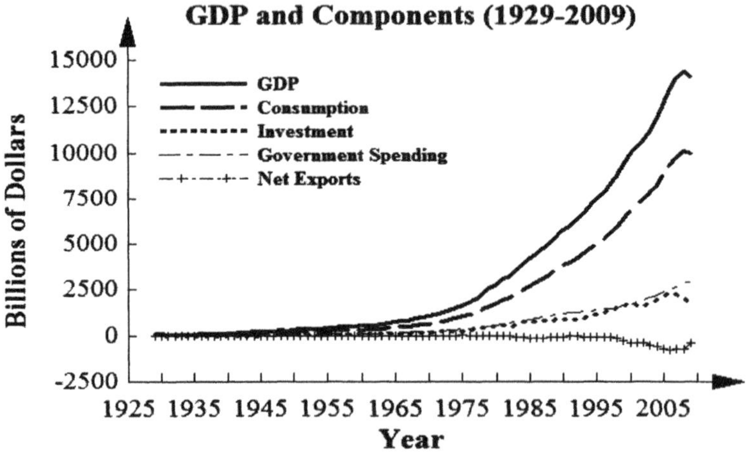

Figure 3.1: GDP by year 1929 – 2009[2]

We see that there has been an exponential growth in consumption, and since it is the largest component of GDP, the GDP has also grown exponentially. Investment has fallen in the last few years, and government spending appears to be starting an exponential trend upward. As a percentage of GDP, the components over time from 1929 to 2009 are as follows:

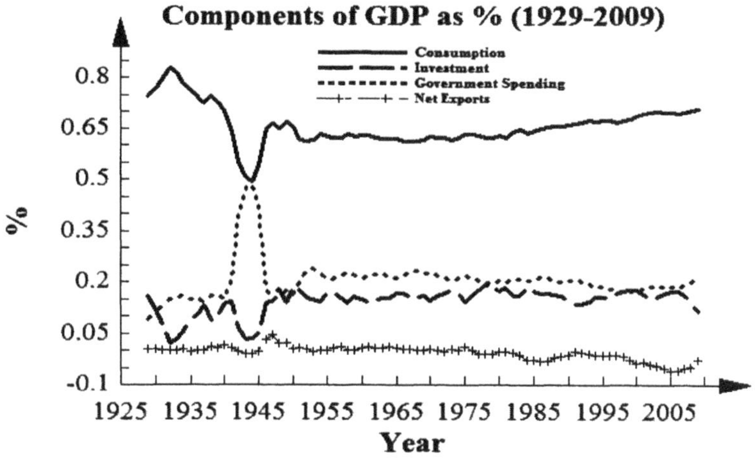

Figure 3.2: GDP by Percentage 1929 – 2009[3]

Notice that after World War II there were structural changes in the components. Government spending as a percentage of GDP has not fallen back to where it was prior to World War II. Also, net exports have been in a slow continual decline. Again, these are merely what economists call the stylized facts, before ethical considerations are brought to bear upon them. More economic theory is required in order to know what, exactly, these facts mean.

We have said that a nation's income is equal to its expenses or aggregate expenditures. Therefore, it is not only true that Y = C + I + G + NX but it is also true that a nation's aggregate expenditures (AE) is AE = C + I + G + NX. This means aggregate expenditures are equal to GDP, or AE = Y (GDP). The macroeconomic model of AE is called the *Keynesian cross*.[4]

Understanding the *consumption function*, the *marginal propensity to consume*, and the *multiplier* are necessary for understanding the Keynesian cross. There is a functional form for consumption, which is the essential component of the Keynesian framework. In a linear form consumption is defined by: C = a + bY. Here, "a" is *autonomous consumption*, which is a fixed amount that an individual will consume, regardless of their income. Here, "b" is the slope of the consumption function, which varies according to one's income. Other forms of the consumption function add the individual's expectations, which influence their consumption as well.

Using the linear consumption function, economists have estimated consumption using real income and consumption figures from 1929 to 2009. The term "real" reflects that inflation has been accounted for in the calculation. Economists find it important to distinguish between "nominal" values (current values) and "real" ones adjusted for inflation.

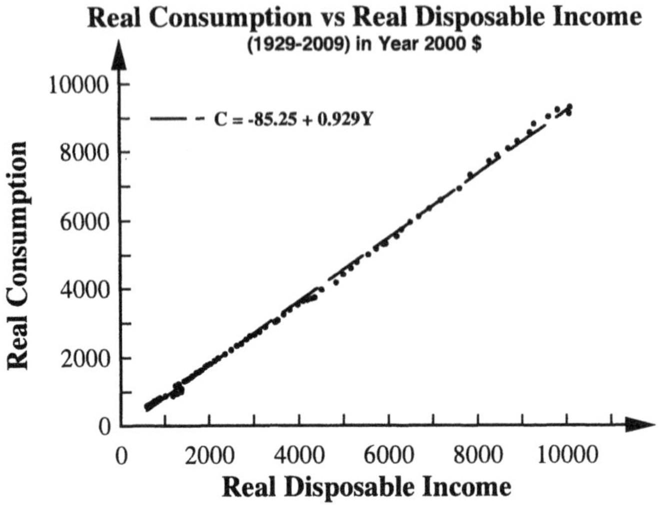

Figure 3.3: Real Consumption vs. Real Disposable Income[5]

This graph indicates a strong relationship between income and consumption. The slope of the equation 0.929 represents the *marginal propensity to consume* (MPC). This slope demonstrates the fact that, for every additional dollar earned, approximately ninety-three cents will be used in consumption.[6] From MPC is derived the concept of a *multiplier*. The formula for the multiplier is:

$$\textit{Multiplier} = 1 / (1 - \text{MPC})$$

Given the MPC of 0.929, the multiplier is 14.08. The multiplier describes the iterative effect of income changing hands in an economy. The multiplier of 14.08, here, means that with a $1 increase in income to an individual in the economy, there will be a total increase in GDP of $14.08. In view of this summary of the consumption function, marginal propensity to consume, and the multiplier, a graph of the Keynesian cross appears immediately below.

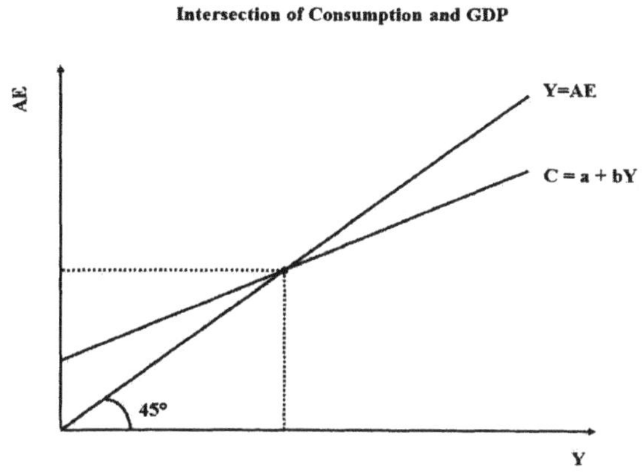

Figure 3.4: Intersection of Consumption and GDP

The Keynesian cross is the basic benchmark of macroeconomic equilibrium, but we have not yet added investment, government spending and net exports. The forty-five degree line represents all points of macroeconomic equilibrium. The intersection of the forty-five degree line and the consumption function shows the relationship between national income and aggregate expenditures. The complete picture includes the rest of the AE (aggregate expenditures) function. None of these has a slope; they are simply additions or subtractions to the intercept.

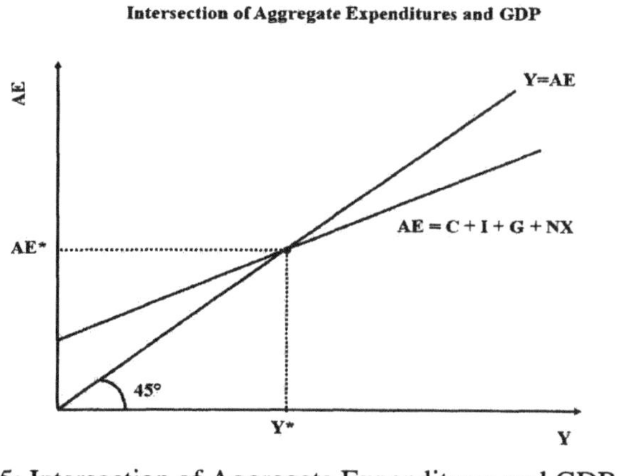

Figure 3.5: Intersection of Aggregate Expenditures and GDP

By definition, macroeconomic equilibrium is where aggregate expenditures equals national income or AE=Y. What happens when income goes down? The

GDP will fall, but since C (consumption) is tied to Y (national income) the AE (aggregate expenditures) will fall as well.

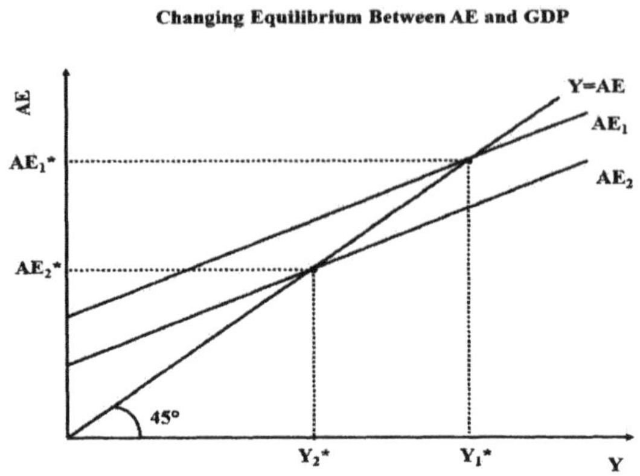

Figure 3.6: Equilibrium Changes as Aggregate Expenditures Changes

In this graph, we see that as the AE curve falls from AE_1 to AE_2 both consumption and income fall to a new lower equilibrium level of AE_2 and Y_2. How big is the effect? The multiplier is used to determine the effect. The multiplier works both forwards and backwards, that is, when AE and Y go up and when AE and Y go down. As explained above, in the case of an economic downturn a $1 decrease will lead to a total GDP loss of $14.08. This is precisely what Keynes was worried about as he wrote during the Great Depression. For Keynes, the waning spirits of investors lowering investment activity was the biggest threat to the economy. Keynes did not worry as much about the reverse, which is why others have modified his theory.

With the Keynesian cross in place, we now turn to supply and demand. The Keynesian relationship holds prices constant. Once prices vary, there is a downward sloping aggregate demand curve that varies by the price level, which is the macroeconomic aggregate of all prices in the economy. This makes the aggregate demand (AD) curve show all equilibrium levels of GDP at different price levels. The aggregate supply (AS) curve shows the amount of GDP supplied at various price levels. The short-run macroeconomic equilibrium is shown below.

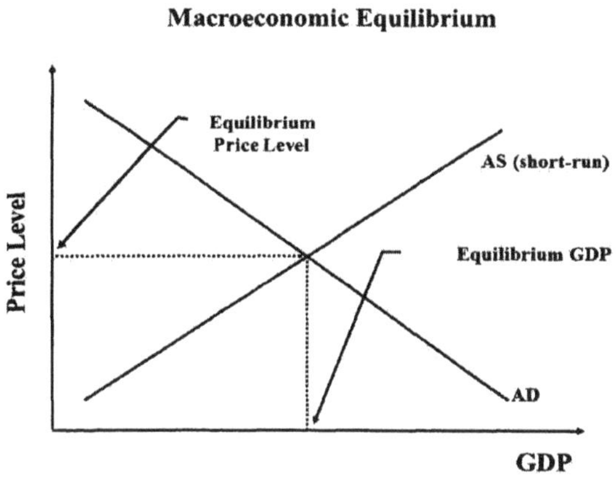

Figure 3.7: Macroeconomic Equilibrium

What about the long-run? It turns out that the macroeconomic system is constrained by the capacity of an economy. That is, there is only so much capital and so much labor at a given point in time, which means that only certain amounts of goods can be produced regardless of the price level. This is pictured as the vertical supply curve in the graph below. Just as water always finds level, a macroeconomic system is constrained by its capacity and that level.

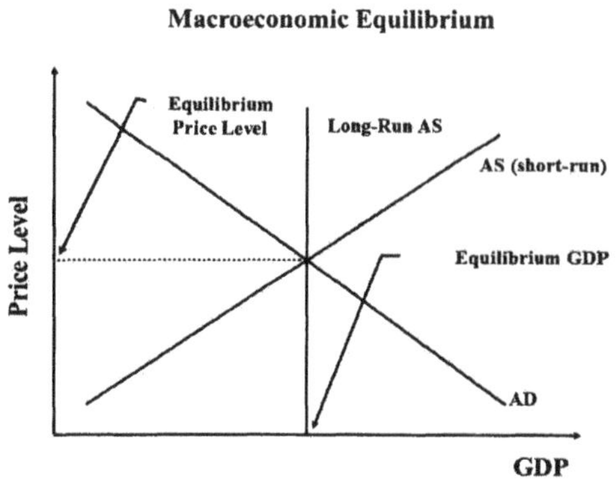

Figure 3.8: Macroeconomic Equilibrium with Long-Run AS

This graph shows that the true macroeconomic equilibrium is where all three curves cross.

Macroeconomic Systems — A Recession Example

To see the interaction between aggregate demand, short-run aggregate supply, and long-run aggregate supply, we will use a typical recession as an example (shown below). Say, consumption falls, which could be for any number of reasons. The fall in consumption causes the AD curve to shift in from AD_1 to AD_2. Thus the intersection of the aggregate demand and short-run aggregate supply curves moves from point 1 to point 2. This means the price level is falling, resulting in lower inflationary pressures, higher unemployment, and a falling GDP level.

What should be done in terms of macroeconomic policy at this point? The classical capital-based and Keynesian solutions diverge here. If we do nothing, as a classical economist would suggest, then all prices fall, including the price of labor (wages). This means that labor is cheaper. Labor is an input cost to a supplier. Since a change in input costs shifts the supply curve, a lower input cost of labor will increase supply and shift the supply curve out. Therefore, if we do nothing the AS curve will eventually shift out from AS_1 to AS_2. The result will be a lower price at the original level of GDP before the recession, a movement from point 2 to 3.

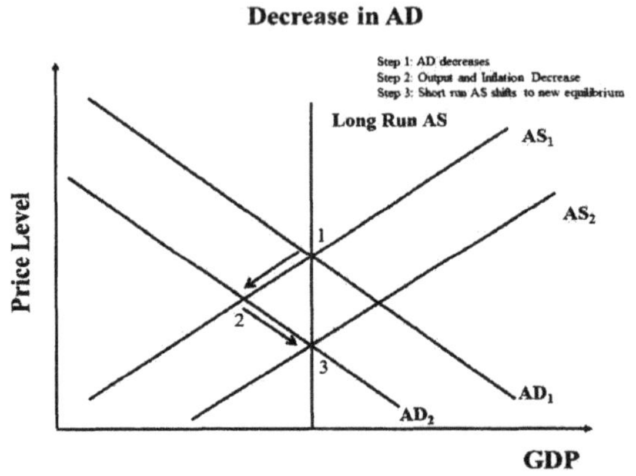

Figure 3.9: Effect of a Decrease in Aggregate Demand

A Keynesian economist would argue, though, that intervention is needed, that we should not let the price level drop and GDP drop, just waiting for them to move back. Remember that Keynes wrote during the Great Depression. Therefore, he was very worried about a reverse multiplier effect. Unfortunately, Keynes did not worry about the inflationary pressures of the multiplier going forward. A Keynesian solution would be to increase G so as to offset the fall in C. Remember that due to the multiplier effect, the government would not have to spend the total amount of the reduction in C, only some fraction of it. So the

Keynesian solution would be to implement a policy so that the economy goes from point 1 to point 2 and then back to point 1. There is a clear trade-off here between time and inflation. Keynes did not worry much about inflation. The opportunity cost is that with a Keynesian solution we might get back to our equilibrium GDP sooner, but at the cost of re-inflating prices.

Before further comparing Keynesian and classical solutions to the recession problem, an examination of what long-run economic growth looks like in the AD/AS framework is required.

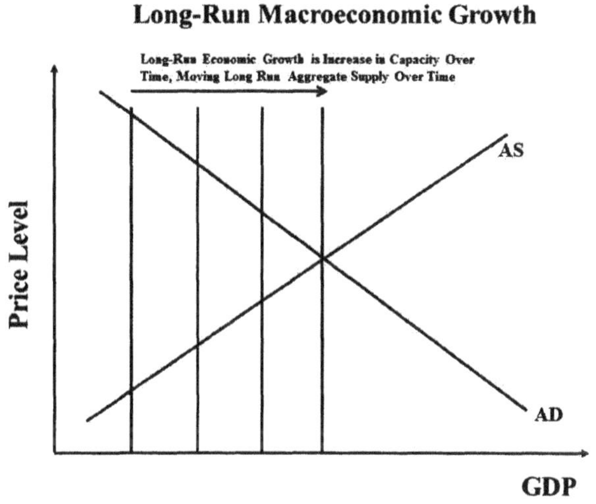

Figure 3.10: Long-Run Economic Growth

This graph shows that long-run economic growth involves continually expanding productive capacity, or long-run aggregate supply. This is the only way to achieve permanence of higher national income. Based on this fact, capital based macroeconomics sees the linear GDP equation as too simplistic. In the short-run, it is true that because Y = C + I + G + NX, increasing government spending (G) could bring national income (Y or GDP) back up to the pre-recession level. This short-run view, however, does not consider the long-run trade-off of such a policy on savings on the one hand, and on investment on the other hand. Nor does the short-run view consider the time that it takes to develop what is necessary to expand productive capacity (and so increase long-run aggregate supply), such as new technology and more infrastructure.

In order to factor in long-run aggregate supply, a production possibilities frontier is necessary. Economists use a production possibilities frontier (PPF) to show all efficient combinations between any two items. A PPF shows all of the efficient combinations between consumption and investment today. Any point along the curve is an efficient combination of consumption and investment today. Any point within the frontier is inefficient, as it indicates that the two resources are not being utilized to their fullest capacity. Also, it is impossible today to achieve any point to the right of the frontier, due to capacity constraints.

Capital based macroeconomics points out that positive net investment is required to have long-run economic growth, to move the long-run AS curve to the right. To have positive net investment, enough investment money must be spent to replace capital no longer useful for production (e.g., worn out equipment) in a given year, plus, add more to the means of production (more capital). Here is a scenario in which a point on the PPF allows for positive net investment.[7]

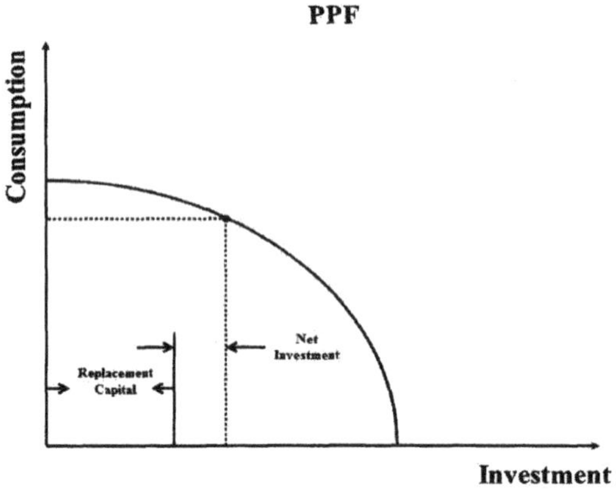

Figure 3.11: PPF of Consumption and Investment[8]

There is, of course, a trade-off here, as economics is, after all, the study of the allocation of scarce resources. The trade-off is that the more we choose to invest today the lower our GDP will be in the current period. Essentially, this is trading income today for a greater income tomorrow. The two different scenarios are pictured below. The equilibrium GDP of an economy with a low savings rate, or investment, will grow at a slower rate than one that saves at a higher rate.

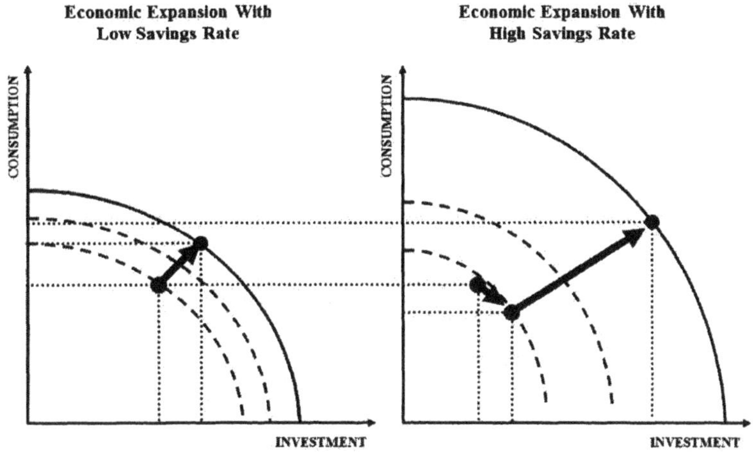

Figure 3.12: Changes in PPF Due to Changes is Saving[9]

The point just made implies that savings equals investment. How is that so? To see why this is the case, further math with the GDP equation is required. Recall:

$$Y = C + I + G + NX$$

so

$$I = Y - C - G$$

Now, there are two types of saving in a macro economy, public and private. The "public" in "public savings" means "government." The equation for public savings is:

$$S_{pub} = T - G - TR$$

Here, T is taxes, or the government's revenue. G is government spending. TR is transfer payments, such as welfare, government funded healthcare, etc. Private savings is as follows:

$$S_{pri} = Y + TR - C - T$$

TR is the government's transfer payments to individuals, which increases their private savings, thus factoring positively into the equation for private savings. T is taxes and is thus negative, because individuals pay taxes. C is consumption spending and Y is national income or GDP.

Total savings (S) is the combination of public savings (S_{pub}) and private savings (S_{pri}), so that the equation for total savings is:

$$S = T - G - TR + Y + TR - C - T$$

Consolidating terms leaves us with:

$$S = Y - C - G$$

Now let us substitute for Y in the above equation with GDP ($Y = C + I + G + NX$). Therefore:

$$S = C + I + G + NX - C - G$$

or

$$S = I + NX$$

When net exports are \$0, then savings equals investment (if $NX = \$0$ then $S = I$). While it is usually not the case that NX=\$0, we have seen that NX is a small portion of the United States' economy, currently. Therefore, savings is very close to being equivalent to investment, currently.

Savings is transferred to investment through financial services markets via the interest rate, which is the cost of borrowing and the reward for saving. The graphs below (under the PPF for consumption and investment) plot the curves for the money supply (savings, functioning as a supply curve) and the demand for the money (investment, functioning as a demand curve), at different interest rates. The x-axis is the amount of money (either in supply or in demand), which is synonymous with the x-axis for the number of goods in a typical supply and demand graph. The y-axis is the interest rate, which is synonymous with the y-axis for price in a supply and demand graph.

In these graphs we see that as savings, or the money supply, increases there is more money to borrow, and so the savings (money supply) curve shifts out. This causes the equilibrium interest rate to fall, just as prices fall when there is a supply increase. As interest rates fall, the quantity demanded of borrowed money (investment or demand) increases, due to the law of demand. Notice the difference between the slower growing long-run economy on the left and the faster growing long-run economy on the right.

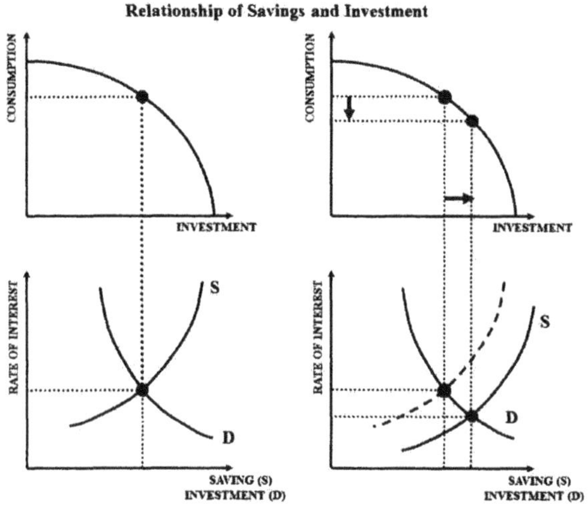

Figure 3.13: Relationship of Savings and Investment[10]

Also important is that capital based macroeconomics does not see the national aggregates as necessarily being linear. That is, they are not necessarily independent of one another, as the additive form would suggest. This implies that there may be more going on here, and indeed there is. While we will not cover other models in depth, it suffices to say that this is a complex topic with many nuances, and that economists will disagree about assumptions.

One thing to note, however, is that there seems to be a correlation between the present and the past, in macroeconomic data. This is evident in the following data. This correlation means that what happens today impacts tomorrow, and what happens tomorrow impacts two days from now, etc. No macroeconomics camp would disagree that this strong correlation between past and present macroeconomic data exists, but there are different assumptions as to why it exists.

In view of all of this, capital based macroeconomics says that investment is very important because of the time it takes to develop the stages of production. The key assumption, of capital based macroeconomics, is that the stages of production are disaggregated over time. In other words, it takes time to alter production patterns in an economy. This is different from the assumptions we have made earlier, where output is assumed to change "automatically."

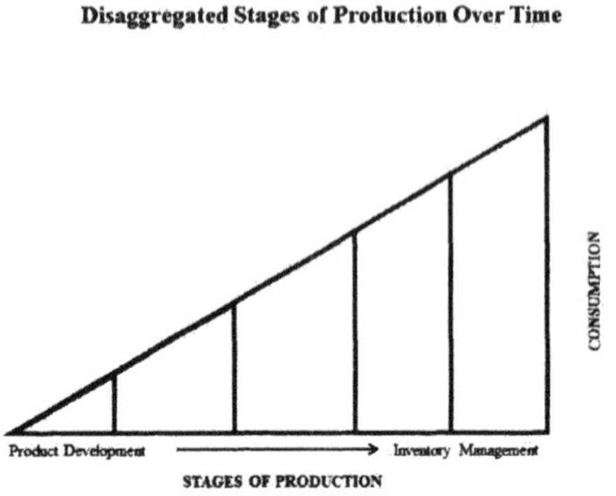

Figure 3.14: Stages of Production Over Time[11]

To get from a product development stage (research and development, or R & D), to the production stage, to finally selling a good, may take more than a year. Also, capital based macroeconomics will argue that as the economy grows, so does the amount of specialization, which increases the number of production stages.

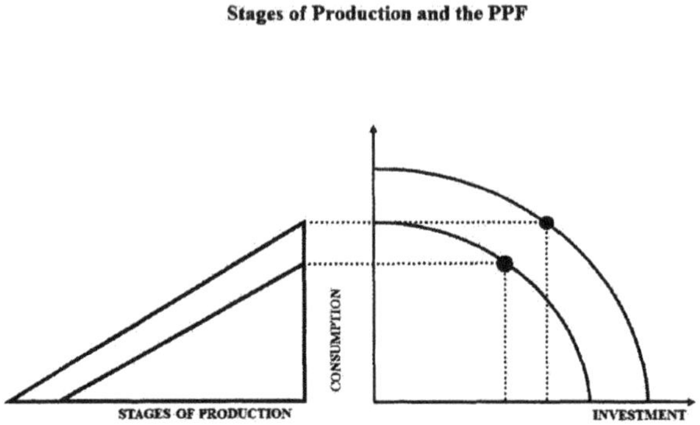

Figure 3.15: Connection Between Stages of Production and the PPF[12]

As we see above, at the end of the production cycle are final sales, which result in consumption for a given time period. In addition, since what is not consumed is invested by default, the rest is investment on the PPF. What if we increase investment? Capital based macroeconomics suggests that increasing investment causes greater long-run growth. Increased investment immediately causes a drop in GDP for that initial year. Yet, it expands the stages of production and, as the economy expands over time, the PPF shifts out farther and faster, as seen below.

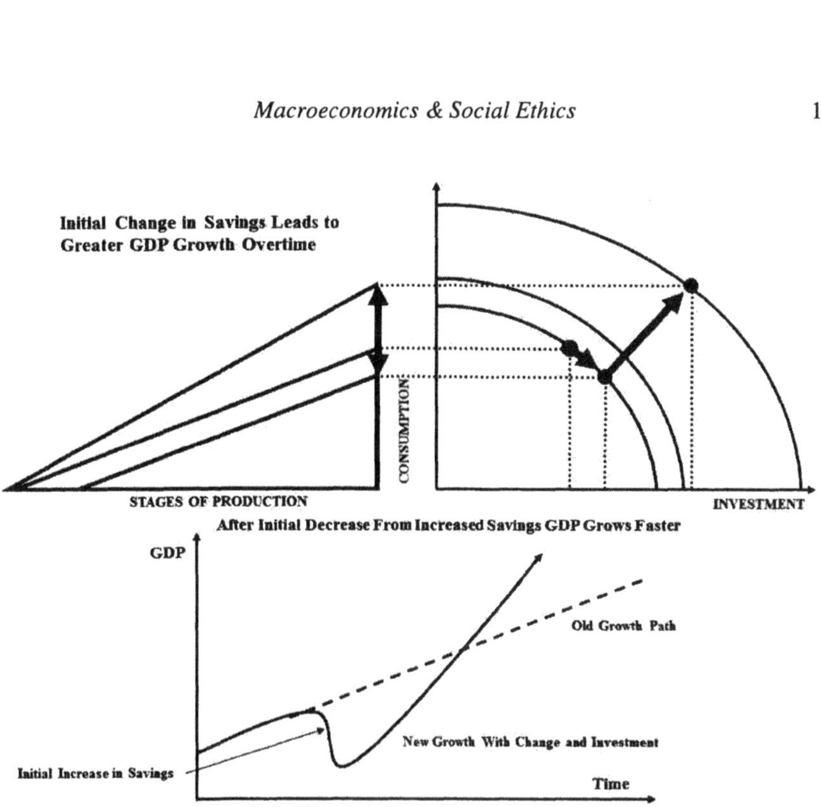

Figure 3.16: How Increased Saving Increases GDP Over Time[13]

Note in the graph, of GDP over time, how this changes the economy's trajectory of growth from the dashed to the solid line. Greater long-run GDP is more real income for all in the long-run.

It may be tempting to survey the recession example and the possible courses of action in purely factual, indicative, terms that are not value-laden. Yet, the question of whether to implement a Keynesian or capital-based solution is value-oriented. As such, it involves axiological limit questions. Not only is the Keynesian solution an action, but the capital-based solution of doing nothing is an action as well. Remember from our earlier discussions how some argue that *all* human actions are subject to moral evaluation, even the most seemingly objective and amoral. This is precisely because humans always act rationally and freely, with a purpose aimed at a specific goal that is valued above the alternatives of other courses of action.

We can ask, then, if a Keynesian or a capital-based solution is better or right. What *should* we do in a recession? How one answers a host of limit questions, and one's normative ethical system, dictate one's answer to what *should* be done in a recession.

We noted above that the core concept of utility, used by economists to measure welfare, comes from the consequentialist normative ethical theory of utilitarianism. Utilitarianism values pleasure and/or happiness, and the best course of action in any situation is whatever causes the greatest happiness for the greatest number. Most economists work on this utilitarian assumption, but disagree over which action will produce the greatest happiness for the greatest number. Many non-specialists in economics agree that a higher GDP is better than a lower one.

The recession example shows that there are trade-offs for each solution, and these involve a time or temporal factor. A Keynesian solution will probably increase the GDP quicker, bringing greater happiness to more people sooner, but at the expense of inflation and long-term growth. It is a short-run solution. A capital-based solution will probably result in a slower recovery of the GDP, and so mean less happiness to more people now, but greater long-run GDP and less long-run inflation. This means greater happiness for more in the future. It is a long-run solution. A strict utilitarian calculus might try to quantify these happiness trade-offs.

If the long-run utility, or happiness, were somehow known with certainty to be better, then, not only a utilitarian, but even hedonistic and ethical egoist theories, would dictate the long-run solution. We would have to know with certainty, or very high probability, that the pain now is worth the payoff in greater happiness later. Again, hedonism and ethical egoism are not merely "immediate satisfaction" theories, but allow for pain now for greater net happiness in the future.

Other normative ethical theories do not prioritize happiness, and some do not hold that consequences should factor into the determination of the right course of action. Purely rule-based *a priori* systems, like Kant's deontological ethics and Divine Command Theory, avoid or even criticize a consideration of consequences in determining the rightness of actions. Using such rule-based theories, one could argue that we have an obligation to help those hurting due to the recession and so must do something now. This obligation could be based on supposed universal human rights, or even a religious claim to the image of God in human beings.

Navigating the numerous answers to the limit questions about values and normative ethical theories applicable to the recession question might seem daunting. Indeed, it is formidable when one has a sense of the number and complexity of ethical questions involved. Yet, these questions are only half of what must be considered in analyzing the ethics of macroeconomic policy.

In addition to limit questions about values and different normative ethical theories, we must also consider social values and social ethics. We have not covered these yet, but questions of justice, freedom, and equality emerge in societies and so bear on the question of what *should* be done in a recession. Further, limit questions about the nature and purpose of human societies bear on ethical questions about macroeconomic decisions. These complex sets of questions and their different possible answers are surveyed later in this chapter and in the next chapter.

Macroeconomics: The Business Cycle

Regardless of normative macroeconomic policies, there will always be economic booms and busts, or increases and decreases in a nation's income or GDP. The inevitable alternation between a higher and a lower GDP is called the *business cycle* in economics. The business cycle alternates between booms and busts because the players in the economy are primarily individual people and groups of people, not the government. Human nature can often be too enthusiastic or too pessimistic. This causes the four stages of a business cycle.

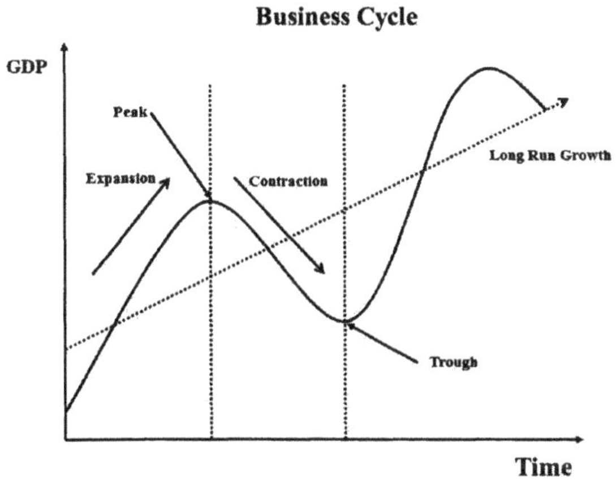

Figure 3.17: Representation of the Business Cycle

This graph, charting GDP across time, shows that any business cycle has four components: an *expansion*, a *peak*, a *contraction* and a *trough*. Long-run economic growth is the general trend of GDP, which is depicted linearly here for simplicity's sake. Private agents in the market (individuals and businesses), and the government as a public agent, can affect the business cycle.

In surveying limit questions in general, we examined those about humans, including those arising from our uniqueness among animals. One of many distinctive features of humans is their ability, through intelligence and reason, to gain knowledge of nature's workings so as to transcend nature and control it. Technology based on scientific knowledge is an example of this.

Since human experience seems to involve an ineradicable axiological dimension, questions of ethics often arise when considering their ability to control nature. The indicative fact is that humans are able to do so in a given instance, for example, clone human beings or turn a natural ecosystem into a city. However, ethical questions arise as to whether or not we *should* clone human beings or convert an ecosystem into a city. Our ability to transcend and alter natural systems, to obtain desired effects, applies to economic systems as well. Thus, ethical questions arise about how we should use our knowledge of how scarce resources are allocated.

The question remains as to how successful modifications of the complex natural systems, embodying humanity's propensity to exchange, will be. Successful technology relies on the completeness of our scientific knowledge of the natural realm controlled. In many physical sciences, the gap between our knowledge of nature and our power to change it is evident. In theory, a brain transplant is possible but we do not have the knowledge, and hence ability, to do one successfully. We do not have the knowledge and power to move the planets or the sun.

The question, of applying economic knowledge to manipulate the natural processes of human exchange, is whether we know enough, and hence have the ability to attain the changes we desire. Are our attempts to control economic activity analogous to building a canal or to moving the sun? If the latter, and even if we judge such economic change to be better from a values perspective, we either must accept our current inability to effect the change we want, or we will engage on a quixotic attempt to move the sun, with a failure marked by numerous unintended and adverse consequences.

The graph below indicates the business cycles of the United States since 1854. It is important to gain a historical perspective. While many complain about our most recent recession, it was by no means our worst. Many are also unaware that the Great Depression was by no means our worst. The worst recession in U. S. history was from October 1873 to March 1879, involving a sixty-five month long contraction. It is interesting to ask why historical comparisons of recent recessions do not include the period from 1873 to 1879.

Table 3.2[14]

US Business Cycles					
Reference Dates		Duration in Months			
Peak	Trough	Contraction	Expansion	Cycle	
		Peak to Trough	Previous Trough to This Peak	Trough From Previous Trough	Peak From Previous Peak
	Dec 1854				
Jun 1857	Dec 1858	18	30	48	
Oct 1860	Jun 1861	8	22	30	40
Apr 1865	Dec 1867	32	46	78	54
Jun 1869	Dec 1870	18	18	36	50
Oct 1873	Mar 1879	65	34	99	52
Mar 1882	May 1885	38	36	74	101

Mar 1887	Apr 1888	13	22	35	60
Jul 1890	May 1891	10	27	37	40
Jan 1893	Jun 1894	17	20	37	30
Dec 1895	Jun 1897	18	18	36	35
Jun 1899	Dec 1900	18	24	42	42
Sep 1902	Aug 1904	23	21	44	39
May 1907	Jun 1908	13	33	46	56
Jan 1910	Jan 1912	24	19	43	32
Jan 1913	Dec 1914	23	12	35	36
Aug 1918	Mar 1919	7	44	51	67
Jan 1920	Jul 1921	18	10	28	17
May 1923	Jul 1924	14	22	36	40
Oct 1926	Nov 1927	13	27	40	41
Aug 1929	Mar 1933	43	21	64	34
May 1937	Jun 1938	13	50	63	93
Feb 1945	Oct 1945	8	80	88	93
Nov 1948	Oct 1949	11	37	48	45
Jul 1953	May 1954	10	45	55	56
Aug 1957	Apr 1958	8	39	47	49
Apr 1960	Feb 1961	10	24	34	32
Dec 1969	Nov 1970	11	106	117	116
Nov 1973	Mar 1975	16	36	52	47
Jan 1980	Jul 1980	6	58	64	74
Jul 1981	Nov 1982	16	12	28	18
Jul 1990	Mar 1991	8	92	100	108
Mar 2001	Nov 2001	8	120	128	128
Dec 2007	Jun 2009	18	73	91	81
	Average	16	42	56	55

This data indicates that, overall, the average length of a contraction is sixteen months and the average expansion is forty-two months. This means that the most recent recession in the United States was only longer than the entire average by only two months.

Some economists would not compare the more recent recession to the long-run average because of significant policy changes in how the government interacts with the economy after the Great Depression. This is a valid point. However, there is also the consideration that all business cycles are different, and so there can be no perfect comparison between different business cycles. All of the fundamental economic variables differ at different periods in time.

We have surveyed some of the fundamental macroeconomic theories in economics. Since macroeconomics is dealing with aggregates it is a very challenging problem. We can start to see that different assumptions as to the underlying macroeconomic structure lead to differences in conclusions. Also as we saw we have seen multiple actions in macroeconomic systems are possible. One such choice would be to either leave the economy alone and let it readjust or intervene to try and end a recession. The choice between the alternatives involves trade-offs as we have seen such as: higher current consumption vs. slower long-run economic growth, those are the positive economic facts. However, different approaches to macroeconomic policy involve many ethical questions, including the limit questions of social ethics, and of social and political philosophy which now involves normative economics. To these we now turn.

INTRODUCTION TO SOCIAL VALUES

Humanity's social nature raises limit questions about social values. When we combine ethics and the *social science* of economics, we must consider *social values.* Many values and virtues discussed in normative ethics apply to individuals. The pursuit of physical pleasure—which a specific normative ethical theory may judge to be either right or wrong—can be an individual act. Individuals exhibit virtues like prudence, temperance, and courage. Some of these values and virtues can also be exercised and exhibited in a relationship between two or more people.

Other values and virtues, though, *require a social context* of at least two or more people, and are thus *inherently social values.* This means some values can only be values in the context of groups of individuals, or in social contexts. For instance, there are different definitions of "justice," as we shall see, but many of these definitions imply that justice is inherently social. If we define justice as "giving all people their due based on how they help or harm society," this definition includes "all people" and "society," and so implies more than one person, or a social group. "Equality" likewise has multiple possible definitions. Yet, it always implies two or more things that either *are* (indicative, or descriptive value) or *should be* (imperative, normative value) "equal" in some way. This is true no matter how, specifically, we define equality. When speaking of people and equality we are presupposing two or more people, and hence a social unit. "Liberty" or "freedom" in the political sense, as opposed to the metaphysical sense (more will follow about this distinction), involves the question of how much individual freedom we should or must promote and forfeit, when humans live together in social groups. If taken as a value, a nation's income is determined by all agents in the national economy, as we have seen. Thus, it is a social value.

Everything we have said about values in general applies to social values. Social values involve descriptive value judgments about the ways things are (indicative, factual), such as this social state of affairs "*is* good or bad," or "*is* better or worse." Social values also involve normative value judgments about how societies ought to be (imperative, prescriptive), such as society "*should be* this way," or "*should not be* that way." As we can contemplate the connection, if any, between what is and what ought to be, we can contemplate the connection, if any, between the facts of positive economics and the normative value judgments of economic policies.

The potential distinction between moral and non-moral values also applies to social values. If someone says: "The American League All-Star baseball team is *better* than the National League All-Star baseball team," then she is making a descriptive value judgment about the American League All-Star team's ability to play baseball successfully compared to the National League All-Star team's ability to play baseball successfully. Some argue that this is not a moral value judgment, but a non-moral value judgment. By contrast, if someone says: "A society with a welfare safety net is *better* than a society without a welfare safety net," they are making an implied or explicit moral value judgment. They are judging it morally better for a society to provide for those who, for whatever reason, cannot take care of themselves.

The possible connection between the purposes, or goals, for a being and value judgments about that being also applies to social values. One might say that a government's purpose is "to provide for the well-being of its citizens." Of course this claim needs unpacking, and more explanation is required. Yet it expresses a belief about the purpose or goal of governments that might be a touchstone for moral value judgments about governments. If so, then we might morally impugn a totalitarian regime where the leaders seek their own personal gain at the expense of their citizens' well-being. For instance, critics of the United States' giving financial aid to third world and developing countries argue that the aid never reaches the people, but is stolen by leaders for their personal benefit. They judge this to be wrong or immoral on the assumption that the state's purpose is to provide for the well-being of its people.

Talk of the purposes of societies, states, and governments raises another set of limit questions intimately bound up with discussions of social values. What, exactly, are "societies," "states," and "governments?" What is the purpose for their existence? Are societies merely collections of discrete individuals, who take priority? Or is a society just as real, or even more real, than individuals, so that individuals are shaped and in some ways determined by their society? These are questions of social and political philosophy that we must consider in thinking about social ethics and economics. We must also consider whether the individual agents in an economy, individual people and groups like businesses, or the economy taken as an organic whole takes priority in applying social ethics to economics and making normative economic value judgments.

There are also different views of what the best form of leadership or governance of social groups and states is. Is the best form of government the government that governs least? Is a pure democracy or a representative democracy the best form of government? Is rule by some elite, who are best qualified to govern, better than a democracy? Should we have an oligarchy, then, or perhaps even a monarchy? These kinds of questions are germane to discussions of ethics in the context of the social activity that we call economic, and hence demand careful consideration.

These social and political questions are philosophical questions because they are limit questions. They arise at the limits of other areas of human inquiry, cannot be answered by the methods of those disciplines, and those engaging in those disciplines assume answers to them and act on those answers. Yet, social and political philosophical questions are valid, important, and immediately relevant to discussions of ethics and economics. Once again, all of the limit questions of philosophy are intimately connected to one another. Discussions of the nature and purpose of societies also imply another consideration: perhaps social values are different from individual values. We must consider this point, too, in this complex discussion.

Normative ethical theories intend to provide systematic ways of determining right and wrong. One could apply a deontological normative ethical theory to argue that "the state should always provide for the well-being of its citizens," based on Kant's two formulations of the Categorical Imperative. The opposite imperative, "the state should not always provide for the well-being of its citizens," arguably cannot be universalized since doing so destroys the very existence of the state with its citizens. One could use the Categorical Imperative to impugn totalitarian regimes for exploiting their citizens, because they treat their citizens as means instead of ends. Similar analyses could be made on utilitarian grounds, so as to argue for maximal happiness or pleasure, or using divine command theory, based on the claim that God has issued the command that "the state should always provide for the well-being of its citizens."

Because social and political philosophy is important for social ethics in general and the intersection of ethics and economics in particular, we now visit some questions about the nature and purpose of societies, as well as questions concerning the best form of leadership in societies.

What is a "Society?"

In considering social groupings the question immediately arises: What is a "society?" This is a question about being as well, and is thus related to the limit questions addressed by metaphysics and ontology. Why? Similar to things like numbers, there is debate over whether or not we can experience societies with our five senses. When asked to identify a social grouping or society, all we really can see are individual people. They might live in close proximity and interact in various ways, but we only "see" individual people. When we say that "North Korea does not like its government," we are really talking about the attitudes of individual people living in North Korea. We cannot point to "North

Korea" as a whole. We cannot point to a society or social group, just like we cannot point to the ideas of the number two and a perfect circle.

Yet, we think and speak of societies as if they were real, do things, and have effects. Societies seem to make a difference in reality. Not only do societies act and make a difference, but we think and speak of them as *influencing* and *shaping* their constituent individuals. Group morale and "mob mentality" can affect a group's members. If a riot breaks out in a crowd, some of the individuals in the group may not at first be inclined to join the riot. Later, though, the "mob spirit" overcomes them and their attitude changes. We speak of "American" values and vices, like freedom, democracy, materialism and consumerism, inculcated in American citizens as they are born and raised in America. Would you not be a very different person if you were born and raised in China, or in an aboriginal Australian tribe? Further, the many individual members of a society come and go as they are born, live, and die, but the society remains. When all current citizens of the U. S. A. are no longer living, will not American society continue to exist?

Such considerations raise the question of the ontological status of a society. Is it real? Is it just an idea in our heads? Did humans construct the idea of society, or does it have independent existence in reality? Is a society merely a collection of individuals? Or, is a society a real thing greater than its individual members, and having effects on reality, including effects on its individual members? These are ontological questions because they involve questions about the relationships between parts and wholes. Are the many parts of something prior to, and determinative of, the whole thing? Or, is the one whole actually something greater than the sum of the parts, with an existence and life of its own? Here, we examine two theories about the nature of societies: one that prioritizes individuals and one that prioritizes the whole society.

The Priority of the Many Individuals in a Society: Social Contract Theory

The modern period of western history, the last five centuries or so representing the epochal shifts away from the medieval period, has been marked by an increased focus on the individual. This has been for a variety of reasons. This increased attention to the individual has given rise to an important theory about the nature of societies, *social contract theory*. There are different formulations of social contract theory but they share important common denominators.

Metaphysically, social contract theory prioritizes the independent individuals comprising a society as primary and real, giving the society a secondary and dependent status. Social contract theory says that many individuals create a society in order to experience certain benefits they would not have if they remained independent. Very important for discussions of economics, this formation of a society by a group of individuals involves trade-offs. The individuals forgo certain freedoms, rights, or privileges they would have individually, in order to obtain the benefits of the society. The individuals have judged the trade-off of what they gain by forming the society as better than what they would have by living and acting alone.

What would your life be like if you lived all by yourself? There are many things that you would not have that you do have, now, because you are a member of a society. You would have to provide your own food, shelter, healthcare, self-defense, and basically anything else that you wanted. If you wanted a technological device you would have to make it from scratch using only the resources available to you in nature. Social contract theorists frequently refer to the state of the individual, not existing in society, as a *state of nature*. Would you be able to make a computer, iPod, car, airplane, lawn mower, or any other thing you use on a daily basis, all by yourself? If you happened upon a cell phone, maybe someone else's who lost it, what would you do when it broke? Could you fix it yourself? If you took ill, you would have to nurse yourself back to health. What if you needed medicine, like an antibiotic? If you needed heart surgery in order to survive, what would you do? Because you live in a society, though, you do not need to worry about these things. You benefit in innumerable ways from the talents and work of others. Many other examples of benefits that you have from living in society could be adduced.

All forms of social contract theory say that humans form and live in societies for mutual benefits they would not otherwise have. Different social contract theorists point to and stress different benefits, but the overall idea is basically the same. Thomas Hobbes (AD 1588 – 1697) was a psychological egoist of a generally pessimistic temper who lived during the tumultuous time of the English Civil War. He argued that people living in the state of nature would be in a very unsafe, violent, unhappy, utterly chaotic state of perpetual fear, at war with nature and with other human beings, and without benefiting from the talents and work of others:

> Whatsoever therefore is consequent to a time of war, where every man is enemy to every man, the same consequent to the time wherein men live without other security than what their own strength and their own invention shall furnish them withal. In such condition there is no place for industry, because the fruit thereof is uncertain: and consequently no culture of the earth; no navigation, nor use of the commodities that may be imported by sea; no commodious building; no instruments of moving and removing such things as require much force; no knowledge of the face of the earth; no account of time; no arts; no letters; no society; and which is worst of all, continual fear, and danger of violent death; and the life of man, solitary, poor, nasty, brutish, and short. [15]

For Hobbes, benefiting from the shared genius and industry of other people is a chief motivation for the formation of societies, but perhaps even more so are security and less fear the primary motivations. For reasons explained later, Hobbes believed that the social contract is made by people abdicating their individual freedoms to one, powerful, person (the monarch) in exchange for the benefits of peace, protection, law and order. Critics have claimed that Hobbes' justification of a monarchy with social contract theory was in part motivated by England's return to a monarchy after the English Civil War and Oliver Cromwell's ill-fated Commonwealth.

John Locke (AD 1632 – 1704) also wrote in a rocky political period in early modern England, this time during the "glorious revolution" against King James II in 1688. Speaking as Hobbes did of individuals as first existing in a state of nature, Locke was more optimistic about the state of nature than Hobbes. Locke believed that individuals apart from societies would, generally, show peace and goodwill to one other, and help one another when time, place and opportunity afforded them interaction. He believed in a "proto-society" or natural interaction of humans in the state of nature before the formal societies that arise only with the social contract.

Living in the Age of Reason or the Enlightenment, Locke stressed the rational faculties of humans in distinction from other animals. These are related to the limit questions of philosophical anthropology, including the fact that although we are very much a part of nature we can transcend nature in significant ways. Our rational faculties include memory and anticipation of the future, apparently to a greater degree than even the most intelligent of other animals. We can think about trade-offs, the long-term instead of the short-term, and long-run benefits we presently do not see or possess. We can control our animal desires and instincts with our reason. Thus Locke reasoned that although the state of nature is not as bad as Hobbes claimed, we reason about the many benefits that living and working in societies would afford, and we make the rational choice to form societies instead of remaining in the state of nature.

Locke added to social contract theory an even greater emphasis on, and discussion of, agreements or contracts, written laws, and processes of legally arbitrating disputes. He employed the Christian theological concept of covenant (*foedus* in Latin) to discuss both the contractual nature of society in general and of contracts between specific parties. Even though individuals in the state of nature could punish injustices, it is more reasonable to have indifferent third parties arbitrate disputes and mete out justice than the self-interested parties in the dispute.

There have been many other forms of social contract theory since Hobbes and Locke; like John Rawls' notable recent work on social and political philosophy and ethics, *A Theory of Justice*.[16] Despite differences in detail, the basic tenet of social contract theories is that humans who are by nature individuals, with a radical freedom inhibited only by the constraints of a nature, trade-off some of their freedoms to gain the benefits of living together in a society. Those in societies cannot, for example, take others' property, harm and kill others, etc., to the extent that they could do so living in nature apart from society. Society imposes restraints on individual freedoms, but this is seen as the opportunity cost for obtaining security, peace, and the benefits other people's talents and work. Individuals enter into at least an informal contract with others to forgo certain freedoms and make certain sacrifices in exchange for certain benefits.

For social contract theorists, the coming together of many individuals to form an agreement is the essence of society. The intangible nature of the agreement makes society, in this view, an arrangement less ontologically real than the individuals who make up the society. The individuals are prior to the contract. If and when they decide to abandon the contract, for whatever reason, the social agreement ends but the individuals continue to exist. The many parts are primary and the one group is secondary. For social contract theorists, society is very much like an artificial structure composed of the many individuals, who alone are real.

Social contract theorists do not believe that a formal historical contract was actually made by individuals in a state of nature. The idea of a contract is an analogy or model that best explains the origin and purpose of societies. And of course, social contract theorists do not claim that every person in a given society has consciously and formally agreed to abide by the social contract. Rather, the argument is that rational individuals, born into and raised in societies, realize the benefits of living in society and so have, at least unconsciously and implicitly, agreed to abide by the social contract.

Advocates of social contract theory commend it as the best explanation of the origin and nature of human societies, for several reasons. First, it explains how societies arise as distinctly human institutions due to the uniqueness of humans in nature as both rational and social. Earlier, we mentioned the general values question of the motivation for being good. So, second, social contract theorists urge that the opportunity costs and the trade-offs made for the social contract are strong motivators for obeying both society's formal laws and informal mores. Rational people freely choose to trade certain natural freedoms for social benefits that they deem more worthy. Thus "keeping the contract" is the most rational thing to do. Anything else would be irrational and inconsistent, given the choice people have made to form, live, and work in society.

Third, social contract theorists stress how social contract theory is more consonant with the modern ideal of a liberal (free) democracy.[17] Hobbes justified a monarchy with his social contract theory, but others, including Locke, have argued that some form of democracy is the best form of government. Social contract theory stresses the original independence, freedom, and equal importance of the individuals who come together to form the society. Thus, social contract theory has an affinity with democratic forms of government.

Classical Economics and Social Contract Theory

The modern science of economics developed during the early modern period in tandem with the emergence of social contract theory. Individuality, freedom, and democracy became important values in the early modern period, influencing not only social and political philosophers but also the fathers of modern economics. Thus, modern economics shares some key assumptions with social contract theory. Viewing societal formation as analogous to a contract, and involving a cost-benefit analysis of the trade-offs of living and not living in society, has parallels in classical and neoclassical economics. The idea of a free individual making a rational choice is common to both. Both prioritize the individual over the group. The idea that individuals are equal in important ways is common to both. Both rely on the idea of benefiting from the talent and work of others. The belief that the state's primary goal is to enforce the social contract is common to both.

In his *An Inquiry into the Nature and Causes of the Wealth of Nations*, one of the fathers of modern economics, Adam Smith (AD 1723 – 1790), describes economic activity in ways that look like a page out of Hobbes or Locke:

> It is not from the benevolence of the butcher, the brewer, or the baker, that we expect our dinner, but from their regard to their own interest. We address ourselves, not to their humanity but to their self-love, and never talk to them of our own necessities but of their advantages. . . . As it is this disposition which forms that difference of talents, so remarkable among men of different professions, so it is this same disposition which renders that difference useful. Many tribes of animals acknowledged to be all of the same species derive from nature a much more remarkable distinction of genius, than what, antecedent to custom and education, appears to take place among men. By nature a philosopher is not in genius and disposition half so different from a street porter, as a mastiff is from a greyhound, or a greyhound from a spaniel, or this last from a shepherd's dog. Those different tribes of animals, however, though all of the same species, are of scarce any use to one another. The strength of the mastiff is not, in the least, supported either by the swiftness of the greyhound, or by the sagacity of the spaniel, or by the docility of the shepherd's dog. The effects of those different geniuses and talents, for want of the power or disposition to barter and exchange, cannot be brought into a common stock, and do not in the least contribute to the better accommodation and conveniency of the species. Each animal is still obliged to support and defend itself, separately and independently, and derives no sort of advantage from that variety of talents with which nature has distinguished its fellows. Among men, on the contrary, the most dissimilar geniuses are of use to one another; the different produces of their respective talents, by the general disposition to truck, barter, and exchange, being brought, as it were, into a common stock, where every man may purchase whatever part of the produce of other men's talents he has occasion for.[18]

Thus some key assumptions about the nature and purpose of economic activity in classical economics parallel key assumptions about the nature and purposes of human societies in social contract theory. There are other ways of understanding the nature and purposes of human societies, though, with different assumptions. These have implications for economics as well. We now turn to one such an alternative.

The Priority of the One Society over the Individuals: Holistic and Organic Theories of Society

We have seen how certain philosophical assumptions of the early modern period, like the priority of the individual, influenced social contract theory. The view that individuals are what are most real is related to some philosophical assumptions informing early modern science as well. As we have repeatedly stressed, all limit questions and the answers we give to them are related to each other and imply one another. How we view being and reality in general is of a piece with how we view the nature of societies as entities. Whether we think physical matter is all that there is, or we believe that there are also non-physical, mental, or spiritual entities, has implications for how we view beings in general, and societies as types of beings in particular.

Early modern science looked to the physical world for explanations, and less to spiritual and mental explanations. We noted how, when one looks at a society, one ultimately sees only the individuals composing it. Society itself is intangible. If visibility and tangibility determine what is real, then only individuals ultimately exist and society is merely a mental construct.

Modern scientific method also isolated and analyzed nature into its component parts. A quest began for the most fundamental material entities out of which everything else is made. The view that reality is ultimately composed of atoms or subatomic particles reduces large-scale seemingly independent things to collections and configurations of many smaller parts. Social contract theory has affinities with atomistic and reductionist theories, which try to explain things in terms of their component parts. Scientists are now questioning atomism and reductionism.[19]

The scientific method also partitions the scientist as observer from the thing observed, as discrete entities. Modern philosophy, pre-occupied with the philosophy of knowledge (epistemology), was also entangled in discussions about the observing subject and the observed object. So the distinction between the subject and object in modern philosophy and modern science contributed to the focus on plurality and individuation. Epistemology in modern philosophy located reason in the individual thinking subject, while seeing the external observed world as non-mental, inert, matter.

Beginning in the late 1700s and early 1800s, however, new ways of thinking arose that criticized these assumptions of the early modern period and the Enlightenment. These changes affected all areas of philosophy's limit questions: metaphysics, epistemology, and axiology. In these movements, the pendulum swung from the many discrete individuals or parts to the one whole. This had enormous implications for social and political philosophy as well.

The broad schools of Romanticism and German Idealism represent these trends. Both criticized the reductionism that tries to explain things by breaking them down to their most basic parts. They argued, instead, that the "whole is greater than the sum of the parts," and that the parts are influenced and determined by the whole. In lieu of viewing the world as a collection of many discrete particles in motion, they stressed nature's organic whole. This included the world's mental and spiritual dimensions, which they did not limit to the human mind. Some even used provocative analogies of dissection and dismemberment when criticizing the prevalent atomistic and reductionist tendencies. For the Romantics and the German Idealists, the many, finite, small, individuals are really just partial manifestations of the one larger and complete whole.

A key transitional figure and a father of Romanticism was Jean-Jacques Rousseau (AD 1712 – 1778). He was influenced by and accepted the social contract theory of society popular in his day. Yet, Rousseau took the radical step of arguing that humans in the state of nature were basically good and quite happy. He claimed societies are unnatural and artificial, and so corrupt, distort, and oppress human nature. In a famous work, *Émile* (1762)[20], he presents in fictional form his thesis that the educational structures of society corrupt the naturally inborn good in children.

German Idealists like Johann Gottlieb Fichte (AD 1762 – 1814), G. W. F. Hegel (AD 1770 – 1831) and Friedrich Wilhelm Joseph von Schelling (AD 1775 – 1854) were *idealists* because they stressed the reality of the mental and spiritual. In fact, they saw the ideal and mental as the most fundamental and most real things, so that "physical" reality is a manifestation of ideas. For these idealists, rationality and mentality are inherent in all reality, not just in individual thinking human subjects. The individual person with her reason is merely a part of a larger process of rationality that heavily determines her thinking and reasoning. There are collective human processes of reason, morality, art and religion expressed in societies and cultures, which are larger and more powerful than individuals. They denied the early modern chasm between the knowing subject and the known non-mental physical object. If something is knowable, then it is inherently rational. Every act of knowing involves cognitive content and interpretation, which inform and determine what is known. There are no raw, uninterpreted, brute facts. Facts about things are laden with ideas and theory, so that things are inherently rational. Hegel said, "*What is rational is actual, and what is actual is rational.*"[21] There is an intrinsic unity greater than the distinction between knower and known. Perhaps, then, there is more to reality than what we can perceive with our five senses.

Are there non-physical things, equally as real as physical things? This is a metaphysical question, but is relevant to the question of whether societies are just as real as the individuals within them. Numbers seem real even though they are ideas, not physical entities. What about "forces" in science? Is gravity real, even though we cannot see or touch it? We experience the effects of gravity, but we never perceive gravity directly with our five senses. What about the English language? How can we "see" the English language? We can look at words on a page, or listen to people conversing in English, but we still do not see or hear the "English language" itself. Yet we speak of the English language as if it were real and of consequence. Similarly, we cannot perceive the "rules" governing English grammar, but we believe that they exist and are real.

Focusing on wholeness and unity over distinction and plurality, the German Idealists also argued that the parts of anything derive their basic identity and meaning only with reference to the whole. Any distinct thing that at first seems independent of everything else actually has its identity only with reference, and in relationship, to everything else and to the whole. How do you identify yourself? Perhaps you would say that you are woman of a certain ethnicity, in college, an American, a fan of a particular sports team, and a member of specific social club. All of these aspects of your individual identity depend on larger groups or wholes: women in general, school, an ethnic group, America, a particular city and sports team, and specific social club.

These wholes determining their parts are often immaterial. We do not see "America," or "Mexican ethnicity," but only individual Americans and ethnic Mexicans. These immaterial wholes also have effects on the world and on their members. The "English language" and its immaterial rules of grammar restrain individual English speakers from saying: "I is a doctor" and "He are going to the bathrooms." Immaterial wholes determining their parts are also different from their parts and not reducible to their parts alone. Individual Mexicans come and go, but the Mexican ethnicity endures. Individual speakers of the English language come and go but the English language endures, regardless of individual English speakers at any given time.

Another argument for the belief that wholes are real things despite being composed of parts is that wholes possess properties that their parts do not have. Philosophers and scientists call these *emergent properties*. They are new properties not possessed by individual parts, emerging only at the level of the whole. We know that animals are composed of small living cells. A dog has properties that seem to give it existence and activity at the level of being a dog. These do not exist on the level of its component cells. Dogs have fur, are mammals, bark, eat meat, wag their tails, growl, bite, have a degree of consciousness, and fetch balls. The individual cells composing dogs have none of these traits and can do none of these things. A whole dog has a reality, activity, history and consciousness different from its cells. We say "The United States elected Barack Obama as president," when in fact not every individual citizen of the United States voted for Obama. The society as a whole elected the president, but not every individual member of the society elected him.

Logicians call attributing traits of a whole that are not traits of parts the *fallacy of composition*, and attributing traits of a part that are not parts of the whole the *fallacy of division*.[22] Ethically, Keynes criticized advocates of capitalism for committing the fallacy of composition when they assume that the good of individuals is also the good of society as a whole.[23]

Likewise, it is also possible that societies have a life, history, and consciousness apart from their members. Like organic cells, individual members of society come and go, but the whole society remains across time. Based on these considerations, some conclude that societies are better understood with the analogy of living organisms than that of a contract: "For the state is not the abstract confronting the citizens; they are parts of it, like members of an organic body, where no member is end and none is means."[24]

Those who say societies are real despite their intangibility appeal to all of these points to say, contra social contract theory, that societies are not mere abstractions without an objective reality apart from their members. This position of *organicism* says societies are more than what social contract theorists hold. They are real, exist, and act as real complex wholes with their own properties and effects, despite their intangibility compared to their societal members.

They also point to the findings of sociology and psychology that indicate groups, small or large, seem to take on a life of their own and influence their individual members. Groups can even force conformity on their members, thus changing their behavior. Again, not all people in a riot necessarily start out with the mob mentality, but the group as a whole can influence them to assume its attitude. Similarly, individuals' beliefs, ways of thinking, attitudes, feelings and values are heavily informed by the groups and societies that they are a part of.

Societies have written and unwritten customs, traditions, standards and rules, all of which affect and are embodied in the societies' members. In fact, most people do not determine their own worldviews and their own answers to the limit questions. Rather, they obtain their worldviews and their answers to limit questions from social groups like their families, friends, cultures, nations, educational systems, and religious communities.

And just as we can speak of individual values and actions that are subject to moral assessment in terms of goodness or badness, we can speak of social values and activities that are subject to moral assessment. Hegel argued that social units take on a level of thinking, rationality, and values different from, but just as real as (perhaps even more real than), those of their individual members. Societally, these are expressed in ethics, politics, laws, and culture. He criticized early modern and Enlightenment philosophers for taking the individual as isolated and private, thinking the individual generates her values and actions in a vacuum, independently of others. He analyzed in detail a number of normative ethical systems that assume the lone human moral agent, with special attention to those of the early modern period. He concluded that those individualist systems and their theorists are entirely dependent on concepts and values meaningful only in social contexts and in terms of ethical communities.

Organicists argue that because every individual is born into a community, the individuals' thinking and values are given to them by their social groups. Much of an individual's identity results from a complex process of socialization. As the German Idealists unified subject and object, reason and material reality, Hegel saw the difference between individual and social morality as more of a distinction of reason, made in the mind, than a real difference. He says: "The state is the actuality of the ethical Idea."[25]

There are critiques of this organic and holistic view of the state. First, those prioritizing the many individuals over the one society, like social contract theorists, point out that the group, society, or state as a whole cannot exist without the many individuals. Organicists respond that just as the whole depends on the parts, the parts depend on the whole for their own individual existence and activity. An animal's individual organs would not last long if removed from the organism as a whole. Even the cells quickly die when they are cut off from the whole living organism. Organicists also respond that human beings as *human* are inherently social, so all that makes them uniquely human, such as language, reason, ethics, culture, art, and shared science and technology, are social realities. These social realities determine and shape individuals to be precisely the human beings that they are. The phenomena of feral children, epitomized in the Tarzan figure, prove the necessity of society for humans to be fully human.

Another criticism of organicism is that its focus on the whole state or society over the individual members removes individuality and begets an oppressive totalitarianism. Critics indicate that this is evident in the glorification of the communist state in the philosophy of Karl Marx, a follower of Hegel. The state can limit the individual's freedom, and even swallow it up. These critics see a connection between organicism and determinism. They say that restriction of individual liberties is necessary in socialism and communism (about which more is said later), and is a manifestation of this totalitarian tendency.

Organicists respond that, if humans by nature live in societies, then they must have self-imposed limitations on their freedoms in order to all get along, live together, and accomplish common tasks and goals. Even social contract theorists admit this and make it central to their theory.

Organicists also respond to the criticism of restricting individual liberty by advocating paternalism over democracy (to be discussed soon). Just as children need the oversight, protection, wisdom, and care of their parents, individual human beings need the guidance and protection of a greater, wiser, and more powerful authority than themselves. As is often the case with children, restriction of individual liberty can be more valuable than not restricting it, paternalists argue. The question of whether paternalism or democracy is the better form of government is, then, intimately bound up with the relative worth of liberty or freedom as a social value.

Economics and the Holistic, Organic, Theory of Societies

As explained, modern economics, as it emerged in its classical period, was informed by modern individualism and the social contract theory dominant at the time. These tendencies persist in neoclassical economics, which stresses maximally free individuals pursuing transactions in their own best interests in markets. Organic, holistic theories of societies can be strong correctives to these assumptions. If humans are not as individual and independent as social contract theory and modern individualism assume, and if their beliefs, tastes, preferences, desires, will, abilities and values are dependent on larger social groupings, then these facts have implications for the intersection of economics and ethics.

For example, some contend that Adam Smith's view of individuals pursuing their own self-interest in markets leads to what they call an "a-moralization" of economics. They claim that, for Smith, market is a "morally neutral" zone free from value judgments. Smith presupposed psychological egoism. He assumed, rightly or wrongly, that everyone, in fact, always acts out of self-interest.[26] This leaves little room for a genuine consideration of the interests of others, some reason, apart from how others' interests impact one's own self-interest. In this case, the only value pursued as an end itself is individual self-interest. Because self-interest is ultimately the only value pursued in markets, some claim Smith's view leads to seeing markets, which are intrinsically social, as amoral. Markets on Smith's analysis, they say, do not involve the pursuit of social value.

Although Smith was arguably a psychological egoist, he did believe that when all pursue their self-interest in free markets, such self-interested actions provide the greatest welfare to all others in society. Self-interest is a value, and the greatest welfare of society as a whole is a social value. Therefore, even if Smith was a psychological egoist, it is plausible that he did not view markets as amoral.

Some argue that, nonetheless, because people are intrinsically social and identify to some degree with the larger society as a whole, the interests of others also play a role in their deliberations in markets. Anthropomorphically speaking, an organism's nervous system is very interested in the well-being of the whole organism, and hence in the well-being of the organism's other parts, in addition to its own interests. Some argue, then, that organicism implies a mutual assistance and genuine concern beyond mere individual self-interest. This is true regardless of assumptions of psychological egoism or psychological altruism. In the latter case it may even lead to a form of ethical altruism in markets.[27]

These considerations are also related to the ethical question, discussed earlier, about whether *all*, not just some, human actions are moral. If so, then economic activity is not amoral but is intrinsically moral activity.

GOVERNMENTS, ECONOMICS AND ETHICS

The question of the nature of society is bound up with questions of good and correct forms of governmental authority. Governments have taken an array of form in history, and in our world today there are a variety of forms of government. Whether authority in a society is distributed among the members, centralized in a smaller group, or subsists in just one individual, all societies have, of necessity, some governing body or authority structure. The question of the best form of government is a values question. Judgments that some forms of government are good or bad, are better or worse, are values judgments. Hence, the question of good government or the best form of government is one of the limit questions dealt with in axiology.

Thus, what an individual or group considers the best or correct form of government is dependent on answers they have for limit questions about values. We have seen that questions about values are numerous and complicated. What one deems the best or correct form of government is also tied to limit questions of social and political philosophy, and their answers. Additionally, what one judges the best or correct governmental form to be is connected to the phenomenon of economic activity, a central part—some would argue *the* central part—of inherently social human activity. Finally, because all limit questions and the answers we give them are related to each other, our questions and answers about the best form of government are related, to various degrees, to all other limit questions and the answers we give them.

Here, we make an important point often overlooked to various degrees in discussions of economic and ethics. Treatments of ethics and economics can blur the distinction between questions of social and political philosophy on the one hand, and the science of economics on the other. *Value judgments about the nature and purpose of human societies and their governments are related to, but not identical with, value judgments applied to the facts of economic activity.* This is worth repeating: *Discussions about what human society is and its purpose, and what government is and its purpose, are* not *the same as discussions about economic activity.* Although they are intimately related, these two types of questions are not identical.

To be sure, economic activity is intricately related to societies and their governments in complicated, and sometimes difficult to sort out, ways. Our working definition of economics is the "study of the allocation of scarce resources." Questions economist ask about this human activity are technically different from questions about what a society is (e.g., contract or organism), what a society's purpose is, and what the best form of governance in societies is. Also, positive economics, as a discipline, has many firm and agreed upon conclusions about the facts of how humans allocate scarce resources, just as any other modern science has firm and agreed upon conclusions about the facts regarding its objects of study. These facts differ, to at least some degree, from normative value judgments about those facts.

Many positive economic facts have been verified using the empirical method and cannot be changed, just as the facts of the natural sciences, like the electrical charge of a proton or the law of gravity, cannot be changed. Because they are limit questions and thus in the purview of philosophy (and religion), social and political philosophical questions must be addressed by methods other than the empirical methods of science. This does not mean that they are not valid questions, or that there are no viable answers to them. The nature of the methods for answering the limit questions necessitates disagreement and dispute regarding their answers, however.

When values discussions are brought to bear on economic activity, the intersection of ethics and social and political philosophy can be surreptitiously treated as if it were the intersection of ethics and economics. Because economics on the one hand and social and political philosophy on the other hand are different entities, discussions of the intersection of ethics with each entail two related, but different, discussions. The uncertainty and ostensible flexibility of answers to the limit questions of social and political philosophy can be wrongly transferred to economic facts as if they were uncertain, flexible and open to dispute. This is an error that we want to avoid in our discussion of ethics and economics.

Economists disagree on assumptions of how to measure economic activity, but their understanding of basic economic theory is the same.

At the intersection of economics, social and political theory, and ethics, the three are thoroughly intertwined. Discussions of how government *should* be structured due to ethical considerations can be predicated on judgments about how resources *should* be allocated. In economics, as in other sciences, our ability to transcend and control nature generates questions about whether or not, and if so, then, how, we should alter the facts about how scarce resources are allocated.

We must always keep in mind that economics deals with certain settled facts about the natural, and in some cases unavoidable, ways we trade. Modern technology raises ethical questions regarding whether, and how, humans should alter nature, but these are informed by inalterable facts of science. So, too, discussions concerning whether, and how, humans and governments should alter economic activity are informed by certain inalterable facts of the science of economics. Some inextricable economic laws impose limitations and unavoidable trade-offs if we do alter economic activity.

Questions regarding whether it is moral to clone human beings, extend human life in certain ways, terminate life at a certain point with certain means, or alter the environment, must, in order to be taken seriously, reckon with scientific facts. Questions of whether we *should* alter market activity, and how we should do so, involve *normative economics*, and questions of governmental policies and their applications to natural market systems involve normative value questions. As with other questions about our ability to alter natural systems, discussions concerning whether, and how, we should alter economic activity must reckon with the facts of economics as a science. Positive economics comprises a large share of economics as a discipline. As the "study of the allocation of scarce resources," economics largely deals with the *descriptive*, *indicative* facts about how humans naturally allocate scarce resources, with the "is." This is one reason for the extensive discussions of economics in this volume. Normative economics about policies is *normative* and *imperative*, dealing with the "ought."

We can alter the way water naturally flows by damming or redirecting a river, but we cannot change the laws of physics by which water flows. Likewise, we can change natural market activities but not the basic laws of economic activity. We might not like these immutable economic laws, but this does not change their reality and inalterability. Some normative economic discussions treat economic activity as if it were wholly a human contrivance, easily altered. On the contrary, certain aspects of economic activity and its fundamental laws are as given and unalterable as the physical laws of nature. We might not like gravity, but we cannot "wish it away." We can use other physical laws to alter and curtail its effects, as in aerodynamics and flight, but we cannot remove gravity and its effects. And altering gravity's effects always involves trade-offs with consequences, such as expending large amounts of energy necessary to make an airplane fly.

Governments can make trading a particular good illegal, but market activity for that good still naturally and ineluctably occurs, but with higher stakes. The U. S. A. prohibited buying and selling alcohol during Prohibition in the 1920s, but a massive underground black market for alcoholic beverages developed. This also greatly increased crime associated with this market.

We have seen that economic laws dictate that interference in a market almost always introduces some degree of inefficiency and deadweight loss (as defined and measured by positive economics). Conversely, non-interference results in greater disparities in income and wealth. Historical data shows a direct correlation of longer life expectancy and higher standards of living for all in a society on the one hand, with less interference in markets on the other hand. Altering natural activity has numerous, often unintended, consequences. These are but a few of the settled and agreed upon economic facts that must we must consider as we treat the complicated intersection of economics, social and political theory, and ethics.

Thus, discussions of the best form of government must include a consideration of the relationships between governments and natural societal economic activity. Before examining some arrangements that many modern people would argue are a good, or the best form of, government, we here briefly summarize the primary options for governmental structure. Each of these has its advocates and detractors. They predicate their value judgments on other reasons in addition to the ways that these forms of government interact with a society's economic activity.

Historically, there have been many of forms of government in societies. Each has benefits as well as deficiencies, or its opportunity costs. If there is a connection between the purpose for a particular type of being and value judgments, then the question of a government's purpose is related to the question of the best form of government. A frequent assumption is that the proper role of government is to benefit the people, to promote their common good. This means that, whatever form it takes, a government must serve its citizens individually and collectively. Yet, what this means specifically, and which precise goods are promoted, are different in each case. Each form promotes some goods at the expense of others, and hence always involves trade-offs.

Democracies

A form of government, advocated since antiquity and with great popularity in the modern period, is democracy. There are different types of democracy on a spectrum from pure democracies to representative democracies. In pure democracies every citizen participates in governance. In representative democracies elected officials govern. Democracy values an individual's freedom to choose what they think is best for society as a whole, as well as for themselves. Judgments about what is best for one's self and society are value judgments. Democracy also assumes the general competency of individual citizens to make such value judgments. In many cases these assumptions and values are based on supposed natural or divinely given rights. Hence, they are dependent on some type of natural law and/or divine command theories of normative ethics.

In *Two Treatises on Government* (AD 1690), John Locke argued for a form of democracy based on his social contract theory of societies. He argues for God-given moral laws and natural rights as natural as scientific laws. Neither society nor government is the source of these moral laws and natural rights, but rather nature secondarily, and God primarily. This means that the government cannot abdicate natural moral principles nor take away natural human rights.

A cardinal natural moral principle for Locke is that, "no one ought to harm another in his life, health, liberty, or possessions."[28] Economically, Locke had a labor theory of property, which was popular in the early modern period. His labor theory of property holds that whatever natural resources can be found in nature, earth, water, air, etc., are the common property of all people. However, if a person mixes her labor with a natural resource to produce a product, like using the wood of a tree to build house or iron to make a tool, then the product becomes her private property.

Locke based his democratic form of government on his social contract theory. In exchange for certain benefits, individuals come together in a contract, transferring some of their natural individual powers and freedoms to a governing body. He advocated a written contract in the form of a constitution ratified by vote. This could take a variety of forms, from constitutional monarchy to representative democracy. Central to his theory, however, is that the ultimate power lies with people, the many individuals in the society. Also, the government's authority should be limited to what is in the best interests of the society and the common good of the people.

Locke also argued that the government should be divided into separate branches that limit each other's powers. He spoke of a legislative branch enacting laws, an executive branch executing the laws and governance, and a federative branch overseeing the relationships between the state and other states. Others, building on Locke, like Charles Montesquieu (AD 1689 – 1755), added a judiciary branch to adjudicate legal disputes and prosecute violations of law.

Locke highly valued all individuals' having the freedom of their own say in their society's government. Liberty or freedom is arguably the most important social value for Locke. As we might conclude from our discussion thus far, there is an inverse correlation between individual liberty and the scope and power of government. The strong value of individual liberty relegates the government to minimalist functions in Locke's political theory.

Again, Locke presupposed a strong degree of competence of individuals to make value judgments as to what is best for themselves and society. Locke lived during the Enlightenment. As an outgrowth of the early modern period, this "Age of Reason" placed strong confidence in reason as a faculty universal to all human beings. Locke also assumed the Deism of the Enlightenment. Deism held a metaphysical belief in an ultimate reality similar to the personal monotheistic God of the Judeo-Christian religions, but with important differences. For Locke, the Creator had established certain moral principles and natural rights, and human reason could discern these principles and rights in the natural world, which the Creator had made.

Locke's posited best form of government bears striking similarities to the United States' government. The founding fathers of the U. S. A., and the documents they wrote, heavily relied on Locke's political philosophy. In the *Declaration of Independence* we read:

> We hold these truths to be self-evident, that all men are created equal, that they are endowed by their Creator with certain unalienable rights, that among these are life, liberty and the pursuit of happiness. That to secure these rights, governments are instituted among men, deriving their just powers from the consent of the governed.

The idea of self-evident moral principles and natural rights ultimately derived from God, such as "life, liberty and the pursuit of happiness," is a page out of Locke. This understanding of the role of government, how it should be formed, and its limitations are from Locke. The *Constitution of the United States of America's* three branches of government: executive, legislative, and judicial, are based on Locke and Montesquieu.

Even the justification of the American Revolution, based upon "no taxation without representation," is derived from Locke. Locke provided the theoretical basis for the American Revolution against Britain when he said: "Here, it is like, the common question will be made: 'Who shall be judge, whether the prince or legislative act contrary to their trust?' . . . To this I shall reply: 'The people shall be judge'."[29] That is, the people judge when the governing body, be it king, parliament, or other, has broken its social contract and gravely failed in its duties. Because the government was formed by the people and for the people, the people can and should replace it in such cases.

The combination of the primacy of individual liberty, as the most important social value, along with some form of democratic government presupposing social contract theory of society, gave birth to *liberal democracy* in the modern world. "Liberal" here can be confusing since we usually associate "liberal" with certain political agendas in America today, in contrast to opposing "conservative" agendas. The "liberal" in liberal democracy is older than the liberal vs. conservative divide in contemporary America, and does not connote a particular political agenda. "Liberal" here simply stands for the word "liberty," indicating that individual freedom or liberty is the prized social value. "Democracy" specifies the form of government. Liberal democracy is thus the basic structure of the social and political system of the Unites States of America, regardless of one's position in partisan political debates, in America today. It has also, recently, been the structure of governments allied with the U. S. A. and the "free world" during the Cold War.

Paternalism

Assumptions, about the importance of individual liberties and individuals' competencies to judge what is best for themselves and society, though cherished modern and American values, have not gone unchallenged. Alternative forms of government by a competent but elite few, or even by one person in monarchy, still have their advocates. These alternatives take a variety of forms, but there are fundamental common features to them all.

Consider an eight year-old child who wants to only eat candy and desserts, to stay up late into the night, to play on train tracks and highways, to toy with fire, and to avoid unpleasant tasks like going to school and doing homework. Most would agree that such an eight year-old's value judgments are flawed, and that adults know what is really best for the child. The child's parents make differing value judgments as to what is best for the child. They do not believe the child is fully competent to make value judgments about what is in his or her best interest. The child's parents place strictures on his or her freedoms to attain the goals and values that the parents, with greater knowledge and wisdom, deem best. The child *will* eat three healthy meals a day, go to bed at a proper time, play only in safe places, and not play with fire. The child *will* go to school and do his or her homework. The parents override the individual liberty of the child for the child's benefit.

Many adults have had the experience of looking back on earlier decisions, perhaps made only a year or months ago, and regretting those decisions in view of later knowledge and experience. Hence, in the view of some, many mature adults do not have the knowledge and wisdom to know what is in their own best interest and in society's best interests. Many adults frequently have inordinate desires and preferences. Certain other adults do, however, know what is best for themselves, others, and society. Based on the parent–child analogy, those who advocate such a position are called *paternalists*, from the Latin *Pater*, which means "father."

As we have seen, advocates of democracy, like Locke, assume that individual adults exercise their reason well as they make value judgments about what is in their own best interest and in society's best interests. They assume that individuals in a society act rationally and responsibly. Paternalists question this assumption. The assumption that most individuals can assess means and ends rationally, and can with their reason transcend short-term goals and pleasures in view of greater long-term interests, may be incorrect. Some, of course, do, but many do not. Think of all of the failed New Year's resolutions, and the times people choose and later regret a short-term lesser pleasure over a greater long-term benefit. That many people violate laws in place to benefit themselves and others, such as speeding, gives the lie to the assumption that individuals in a society always act rationally and responsibly, say paternalists.

Whether or not this assumption, about individuals' rational abilities is correct, is essential to economics and ethics, because neoclassical economics assumes that individuals in markets are rational. Similarly, the question, of whether individuals have satisfactory knowledge and preferences to act in their own and in society's best interest, has implications for the neoclassical economic assumption that individuals in a market are the best judges of what is really best for themselves and society as a whole. This is related to the possible ethical distinction, discussed above, between what is in fact good and what is only perceived to be good, the distinction between real and apparent goods.

We have noted the affinities of democracy with social contract theory. In contrast, there are affinities between paternalism and the organic, holistic, view of societies. Hegel argued for an emergent reason in the state, which is even more rational than that of the individual. Paternalists similarly argue that there is a greater, more reliable, reason in the state and governing bodies than the reason of individuals who comprise the state.

Advocates of democracy, like Locke, champion individual freedom or liberty as a very important or even the most important social value. Paternalists question this assumption as well. The U. S. A. was founded on the principle that freedom is a value on par with life and happiness, and the word "liberty" appears on all U. S. A. currency.

Paternalists and others, who do not see freedom as such an important social value, question what is meant by "liberty." Parties on both sides admit that the value in question is social or political, not metaphysical, freedom. Metaphysical freedom means that not all human actions are determined in an unbreakable chain of cause and effect, due to the laws of nature, God's decree, or something else. Another important limit question is precisely the question of metaphysical freedom: Do humans have metaphysical freedom? Are human choices really determined despite contrary appearances and beliefs? Or, are our choices free or uncaused in some way? If so, then what does "free will" mean? Social or political freedom involves questions of whether or not humans really do have, and/or should have, maximal freedom in their social relationships and in the political sphere. One could hold to metaphysical determinism but still debate the reality and merits of striving for the widest latitude in the range of choices people have, socially and in the political realm, even if those choices are ultimately determined by prior causes.

Paternalists and others, who do not value freedom as the most important social value, say that the idea of social and political freedom sounds very good and nice, but is really nebulous and unclear upon closer examination. What, exactly, do we mean by "freedom" or "liberty?" Do we mean freedom to do absolutely anything we want, like take others' property, physically harm others, do things that only affect ourselves but do not impose harm on others (so called victimless crimes like taking drugs and prostitution), drive as fast as we want, marry multiple persons, say things that offend other people, etc.?

It seems that all societies have limits imposed on individual freedoms so that in no society, except perhaps an anarchy, do people have unlimited freedoms. We have seen that even social contract theorists, who often value individual freedom highly, make the self-imposed limitation of individual freedoms, for the greater benefits of society, a central part of their theory.

Building on his early modern predecessors, the nineteenth-century British philosopher, John Stuart Mill (AD 1806 – 1873), claimed that in a free society, "The only purpose for which power can be rightfully exercised over any member of a civilized community against his will is to prevent harm to others."[30] This is called *Mill's harm principle.* Most Americans and many modern people would agree with Mill's harm principle.

Critics, however, say that when pressed, advocates of the harm principle cannot explain what "harm" in the harm principle really means. The question arises as to what, specifically, constitutes "harm?" Is it merely physical bodily harm? Is it mental, psychological or emotional harm? Can we harm a person by harming another person or object, with whom or with which that person is intimately associated? Is harm to one's property harm to the individual, in Mill's sense?

Limiting harm to physical or material harm, as many interpreters believe Mill intended, seems to be too narrow of a definition. If harm means only bodily harm, then taking another's property, putting them in prison, tying them to a bed, sedating them with drugs, or limiting their actions in other ways, without physically harming them, would not violate the harm principle. If we extend harm to mean taking their private property, then many of these things still do not harm them. We could still say things that offend them, psychologically or emotionally "abusing" them. We could say racial slurs, make sexist remarks, or criticize their religion as stupid.

If we extend the definition of harm to include mental and emotional harm, then being snubbed by a co-worker would make the co-worker culpable. When I receive a gift for my birthday that I do not like, the giver would be liable. When the supermarket clerk is rude or takes too long, stretching my patience, then the clerk would be guilty. When friends tell me my new haircut looks horrible, or that I have terrible taste in clothing, they would violate the harm principle.

If only some mental and emotional harm violates the harm principle then the question arises as to where we draw the line. People are always "hurting" each other psychologically and emotionally, along a spectrum of degrees. What constitutes "real" or "serious" psychological and emotional harm, as opposed to "minimal" or "trivial" mental and emotional harm?

The question of defining harm is also related to the question of judging when harm has been inflicted. Here the problems of bias, self-interest, and perspectives enter. One might claim being harmed, but the person allegedly inflicting the harm may think they have not inflicted harm. If we allow ostensibly harmed people to judge what constitutes harm, then there would be an ever-growing, unmanageable litany of grievances to be prosecuted. If we allow the one accused of inflicting harm to be the judge, then we would have very few, if any, instances of harm to deal with. Even the cherished value of majority rule in democracy would be suspect here. If we, in good democratic fashion, allow the majority to define and judge harm, then they might try to inflict harm on the minority and judge it to not really be harm.

Paternalists and others, who do not see freedom as the greatest social value, also raise inconsistencies with and practical problems in implementing the harm principle. As social contract theory, which values individual freedom highly, admits, in order for humans to successfully live together there must be some form of limitation on individual liberties. Otherwise, the insecurity of the social situation would lead people to abandon the society.

Also, in practice, it seems that in modern liberal democracies, like the U. S. A., there are many instances where it is assumed that someone, other than the individual, knows what is best for the individual and society. From its incipience, the U. S. A. has frequently placed strictures on individual liberties. Take the case of so-called "victimless crimes." To this day, in most places in America, it is illegal to take certain drugs like marijuana, cocaine and heroin, and prostitution is illegal. In many places seatbelts and motorcycle helmets are required. Those favoring legislation against these activities claim they are harmful to the individual or society, and therefore should be outlawed. This allegation assumes that someone other than the individual who wants to engage in such activities knows better than the individual. This goes against the assumption of liberal democracy, that individuals are the best judges of what is best for themselves and society.

Some also argue that there are no "victimless crimes." Prostitution can affect not only the prostitute and the solicitor, but also others with whom both are related. The solicitor's spouse, significant other, or future partner, could be affected. Taking drugs may seem private, affecting only users, but family members, friends, and society have to deal with adverse health, financial, and other effects. Job performance could slacken. Someone in an altered state of consciousness could unintentionally harm himself or others. If a motorcyclist is permanently handicapped due to not wearing a helmet, his family, friends, and workplace are affected. He might need financial support from others and/or the government. Paternalism has affinities with views of society that see humans as inherently social, while social contract theory sees humans as primarily as individuals, and social only secondarily.

Thus, paternalists and advocates of organic and holistic views societies urge that humans are inherently social. They say people are in complex, inseparable relationships with others, so that all individual actions have effects on others and society as a whole. Are social contract theorists and those in favor of liberal democracies but who still advocate such laws against so-called victimless crimes, then, really admitting what their opponents have been saying all along?

Ethical considerations based on consequentialism also play a role here. The assumption is that certain actions have negative effects on society, and so there must be restrictions on individuals' liberties to engage in them. Prostitution spreads sexually transmitted diseases, and drug trafficking leads to crime, ill-health and death, they argue.

Another consequentialist consideration, though, is that legalizing these activities can result in changes that remove these adverse effects. Legalizing prostitution could involve health and safety check-ups, which could curb the spread of sexually-transmitted diseases. Legalization of drugs could drastically lower the price, and so probably drastically reduce, if not eliminate, the crime associated with illegal drugs. Rarely does anyone shoot another person over a pack of cigarettes or a pack of gum. Individuals free to purchase and use "hard" drugs could choose not to do so, as they weigh the health and personal trade-offs and opportunity costs.

There are also seemingly harmless activities an individual might choose, like expressing beliefs and opinions, which could be judged as irrevocably detrimental to society as a whole. Hiring or firing someone, because of their gender, race, or age, is not allowed. As this is being written, a book touting itself as a handbook for pedophiles has been recently censored and banned.

Religious ethical theories, like divine command theory, also can play a role in the restriction of individual liberties, even in modern "secular" liberal democracies. Taking drugs, prostitution, expressing perverse views about the sexual corruption of youth, etc., have been prohibited based on a version of divine command theory. In some counties in the U. S. A., to this day, sale of alcohol is prohibited, and there are still "blue laws" banning commercial activity on Sundays in order to keep the Christian Sunday Sabbath. Such appeals to a form of divine command theory are liable to the criticisms of divine command theory discussed earlier. They also, again, assume that someone other than the individual knows what is best, but in this case, that someone is God rather than the state, government, or society as a whole.

Paternalists and others who do not make individual freedom the greatest social value also point to additional inconsistencies in attempts to maximize individual freedom in society. Often, individual liberties are mutually exclusive, thus coming into conflict. My freedom of speech to say something that offends you might come into conflict with your freedom to silence me by force.

Another issue with making individual freedom the highest social value, particularly as it is enshrined in modern liberal democracy, is the problem of individuals disagreeing on what is best. People frequently disagree, sometimes heatedly. With many individuals freely expressing their opinions about what is best, their desires, and their wants, there will be disagreement and discord. Economically, there is an opportunity cost for individual freedom and participation in government: the time and energy required to sort through disagreements and come to a final decision. If this is problematic on the very small scale of groups like committees and teams, then the problem escalates on the larger scale of governments. Naysayers thus advocate a centralized power that makes all of the decisions, and find the trade-off of sacrificing individual freedom and participation in government necessary for greater efficiency in the decision-making process.

Another problem in the extreme is revolution and/or anarchy, an inherent possibility built into Locke's theory of democracy. Hobbes was another early modern social contract theorist, probably the first. Yet, his view of the best government is different from Locke's liberal democracy. We saw that, compared to Locke, Hobbes had a pessimistic view of the state of nature before the social contract, and an equally pessimistic view of human nature. A radical psychological egoist, Hobbes does not believe that humans have an in-built empathy for other members of the human race. For Hobbes, the selfishness, conflicts, chaos, and difficulties of survival in the state of nature, would carry over into the social contract scenario, were it not for a powerful authority to curb these things and insure survival. Even the labor theory of property, also advocated later by Locke, is questionable to Hobbes, who thinks that even in society there will be disputes over private property. Thus, a third party is necessary to define property rights. In order to get along and survive communally, all individuals must sacrifice their natural freedom and individual liberties to some third party, according to Hobbes. This party must be powerful enough to force the individuals to keep their social obligations, which otherwise would be impossible:

> Therefore, before the names of just and unjust can have place, there must be some coercive power to compel men equally to the performance of their covenants, by the terror of some punishment greater than the benefit they expect by the breach of their covenant; and to make good that propriety which by mutual contract men acquire in recompense of the universal right they abandon.[31]

Hobbes calls this third party an "artificial man," as it is in contrast to the natural state of humans, and hence artificial.[32] He also calls it a "great Leviathan" (the title of his 1651 book), based on the fearful and powerful creature of uncertain meaning mentioned in the Hebrew Bible.[33]

For Hobbes, the social contract is not between the individuals in society. Rather, it is between every individual and Leviathan. In order to survive, live, and act together in a harmony impossible in the state of nature, all individuals voluntarily give up their natural freedoms and rights, "sacrificing" them to the Leviathan and giving it absolute power. For Hobbes, individuals give up *all* of their natural freedoms and rights, and the new "artificial man" gives new freedoms and rights, in the form of law. This Leviathan then enforces the laws with all of the awesome and fearful force of the biblical Leviathan.

The criticisms of totalitarianism and tyranny immediately arise. Hobbes anticipated this objection and addressed it. He argued that tyranny is better than anarchy, and since, in his view, something like Locke's later liberal democracy would result in disorder, tyranny is the "least of all evils." He saw this trade-off but was willing to accept it. This is a sort of "greater good" argument. We must tolerate something undesirable, like a trip to the dentist or exercising, for a greater goal, the desire of which outweighs the undesirability of what must be tolerated. In his organic, holistic, theory of the nature of society, Hegel made a related greater good argument, that some sacrifice of the individual parts of society is sometimes necessary for the greater good of the state, as an organic whole. This is akin to pulling out a bad tooth or removing an appendix.

Hobbes also responds that since individuals abdicate their freedoms and rights in the state of nature, by contracting with Leviathan, the new artificial man is the source of all law and justice. This means, for Hobbes, that the Leviathan is above the law. The Leviathan cannot act justly or unjustly since it determines what is just and unjust.

Hobbes allows the form of Leviathan to be a monarchy or representative assembly but favored monarchy at a time when the English civil war and Cromwell's Puritan commonwealth were ending, and England was returning to a monarchy. He argues for a monarchy, using the point already made about dividing power among individuals or groups: there will be disagreement and strife between multiple power holders. He argued that the English civil war resulted directly from the division of power among the King, the House of Lords, and the House of Commons.

In contrasting Hobbes' and Locke's political philosophies, we see both the interconnected nature of all limit questions and the important distinctions between limit questions, regarding the nature of society and social values as a species of ethics. Both Hobbes and Locke saw the basic nature of society as contractual. The many unrelated individuals in a state of nature are primary, coming together on the analogy of a contract, in which they trade-off some natural freedoms for certain benefits. Different philosophical anthropological understandings of the nature of humans as individuals, psychological egoist (Hobbes) or psychological altruist (Locke), led them to view the state of nature and the reasons for the formation of the social contract, differently.

In terms of social values, Locke championed individual liberty, which he included in his democratic form of the social contract. Hobbes thought that the opportunity cost of sacrificing individual freedoms was the best trade-off for humans in order to survive and remove the fears and anxieties of the state of nature, which he called a "state of war." Their differences on the view of liberty as a social value led to different prescriptions for the best form of government. Locke advocated a representative liberal democracy with a distribution of powers, but Hobbes argued for centralized power, ideally, in just one person, in a form of paternalism.

Economic activity always exists regardless of society's nature and form of government, and the government always has a relationship to this economic activity. Social and political philosophical questions regarding the nature and purpose of society and of the best form of government are limit questions, bound up with but distinct from limit questions about values. How one answers these questions leads to different conclusions about the best form of government and the best relationship of government to market activities. Any society necessarily involves some governmental regulation of and involvement in markets, but how much is best depends on one's answers to these limit questions.

Liberal democracy in Locke's form of social contract theory assumes humans are primarily individuals, and that they alone know what is best for them and society. Neoclassical economics makes these assumptions. If a consequentialist utility maximization is the greatest value, then it follows that individual liberty is the prime social value. Minimalist governmental interaction in market activities is necessary to promote individual liberties, so governments should only set property rights, define laws, and enforce contracts.

Organicist theories of society assume that individuals are inherently social, constituted by their relationships to all others and to society as whole. Paternalism, which has affinities with organicism, assumes that many do not know what is best for themselves and society: individuals often seek an apparent as opposed to a real good. Even if a consequentialist maximization of utility is the ethical norm, a big centralized government heavily involved in market activities, as in socialism or Marxism, is necessary in this view. The utility of one is the utility of all in the organic, holistic view of society. These assumptions justify greater governmental involvement in market activities through taxation, wealth redistribution, and government safety nets, in order to provide a more equal amount of goods and services to all. Greater restriction of individual liberties is necessary, but may be justified if coupled with the paternalist assumption that many individuals do not know what is best for them and for society as a whole.

SUMMARY

So far in our discussion of social ethics, social and political philosophy, and economics, we have summarized questions about the nature of societies and the best form of government. We have also seen that questions about social values like liberty, equality, and justice, arise at the complex intersection of social and political philosophy, ethics, and economics. We have also seen that a social value, like freedom, is valued more or less depending on other considerations. Those favoring democracy, and those favoring some form of paternalism, place different degrees of value on freedom. Discussions of social and political philosophy, social values and economics will, of necessity, involve a prioritization of social values. Even once the difficult task of gaining clarity and precision about what, exactly, social values like liberty, equality, and justice mean, there is the further consideration that social values can and do conflict, so that one must be given priority over another.

Therefore, in the next chapter we consider three important social values: liberty, equality and freedom. We will see that there are different understandings of what each of these values entails, they can and do come into conflict, and therefore they must be prioritized. We will examine some of the arguments in favor of prioritizing and not prioritizing each one.

NOTES

1. "U. S. Department of Commerce. Bureau of Economic Analysis," U. S. Bureau of Economic Analysis (BEA), http://www.bea.gov/national/nipaweb/selecttable.asp? (accessed January 10, 2011).

2. "U.S. Bureau of Economic Analysis (BEA)," U. S. Bureau of Economic Analysis (BEA), http://www.bea.gov/iTable/iTable.cfm?ReqID=9&step=1 (accessed January 10, 2011).

3. Ibid.

4. The Keynesian cross is named is named after John Maynard Kenyes (AD 1883 – 1946), one of the founders of modern macroeconomics.

5. "U.S. Bureau of Economic Analysis (BEA)," U. S. Bureau of Economic Analysis

6. A note to economists: The constant is negative, which does not make sense from an autonomous consumption standpoint, but this exposition is simplified so as to not confuse non-specialists in economics with a more rigorous discussion of the standard error of the constant.

7. Adapted From: Garrison, Roger. *Time and Money: The Macroeconomics of Capital Structure*. London: Routledge, 2001. Ludwig Von Mises Institute Presentations (http://www.mises.org)

8. Ibid.

9. Ibid.

10. Ibid.

11. Ibid.

12. Ibid.

13. Ibid.

14. "U.S. Business Cycle Expansions and Contractions," The National Bureau of Economic Research, http://www.nber.org/cycles/cyclesmain.html (accessed January 11, 2011).

15. Thomas Hobbes, *Leviathan*, ed. J. C. A. Gaskin (Oxford: Oxford University Press, 1998), 84.

16. John Rawls, *A Theory of Justice* (Cambridge, MA: Belknap Press of Harvard University Press, 1971).

17. "Liberal" in the term "liberal democracy" refers to the social value of liberty or freedom, not to current liberal, as opposed to conservative, political agendas in contemporary politics.

18. Adam Smith, *An Inquiry into the Nature and Causes of the Wealth of Nations: A Selected Edition*, ed. Kathryn Sutherland (New York, NY: Oxford University Press, 2008), 22, 24 – 25.

19. Experimental findings in quantum physics, such as the invalidation of Bell's Inequalities, have led theoretical physicists to question the older physical assumptions of locality and separability, which have grounded atomism and reductionism. See, for instance: D. J. Bohm and B. J. Hiley, "On the Intuitive Understanding of Nonlocality as Implied by Quantum Theory," *Foundations of Physics* (1975), no. 5(1): 93 – 109; David Bohm, *Wholeness and the Implicate Order* (London: Routledge, 1980); Paul Teller, "Relativity, Relational Holism, and the Bell Inequalities," In *Philosophical Consequences of Quantum Theory*, ed. J. T. Cushing and E. McMullin, 208 – 23 (Notre Dame: University of Notre Dame Press, 1989); and Timothy E. Eastman and Hank Keeton, eds., *Physics and Whitehead: Quantum, Process, and Experience* (Albany, NY: SUNY Press, 2003).

20. Jean-Jacques Rousseau, *Emilius and Sophia: or, A New System of Education* (London: T. Becket and P.A. de Hondt, 1762).

21. G. W. F. Hegel, *Outlines of the Philosophy of Right*, ed. Stephen Houlgate, trans. T. M. Knox (New York, NY: Oxford University Press, 2008), 14 (Italics in original). Here "actual" means "to be real" and "to have existence."

22. The informal logical fallacies of composition and division inform Arrow's Impossibility Theorem, discussed in the first chapter.

23. John Maynard Keynes, *The End of Laissez-Faire* (London: L. & Virginia Woolf, 1926).

24. G. W. F. Hegel, *The Philosophy of History:* A General Introduction to the Philosophy of History, trans. Robert S. Hartman (Indianapolis, IN: The Bobbs-Merrill Company, Inc., 1953), 52.

25. G. W. F. Hegel, *Elements of the Philosophy of Right*, ed. Allen W. Wood, trans. H. B. Nisbet (Cambridge: Cambridge University Press, 1991), 275.

26. Some argue that Smith's *Theory of Moral Sentiments* (AD 1759) tells against the claim that Smith was a psychological egoist. In this work he argues that humans have an innate benevolence and a capacity for sympathy with others, which grounds his theory of morality. Upon closer analysis, however, in this work Smith holds that moral passions arise from pleasure derived at in seeing certain states of affairs. This is similar to Hume's theory of morality predicated upon subjective states of pleasure and displeasure, which allows for translating value judgments into indicative statements (see the discussion in of Hume in the preceding chapter). Smith speculates that the pleasure giving rise to moral sentiments derives from a process of sympathy and imaginative *mimesis* with others, as we imagine ourselves to be in situations we see others in and which we would enjoy, and as we see others treated as we would like to be treated. Thus:

> How selfish so ever man may be supposed, there are evidently some principles in his nature, which interest him in the fortunes of others, and render their happiness necessary to him, though he derives nothing from it, except the pleasure of seeing it. Of this kind is pity or compassion, the emotion we feel for the misery of others, when we either see it, or are made to conceive it in a very lively manner. That we often derive sorrow from the sorrows of others, is a matter of fact too obvious to require any instances to prove it; for this sentiment, like all the other original passions of human nature, is by no means confined to the virtuous or the humane, though they perhaps may feel it with the most exquisite sensibility. The greatest ruffian, the most hardened violator of the laws of society, is not altogether without it.
>
> As we have no immediate experience of what other men feel, we can form no idea of the manner in which they are affected, but by conceiving what we ourselves should feel in the like situation. Though our brother is on the rack, as long as we ourselves are at our ease, our senses will never inform us of what he suffers. They never did, and never can, carry us beyond our own person, and it is by the imagination only that we can form any conception of what are his sensations. Neither can that faculty help us to this any other way, than by representing to us what would be our own, if we were in his case. It is the impressions of our own senses only, not those of his, which our imaginations copy. By the imagination, we place ourselves in his situation (Adam Smith, *Theory of Moral Sentiments*, ed. Robert M. Baird and Stuart E. Rosenbaum [Amherst, NY: Prometheus Books, 2000], 3 – 4).

Later in the work, Smith also explicitly makes the claim that pure, unadulterated, self-interest in economic activity produces benefit for all, laying the foundation for the later theory of the "invisible hand" of *The Wealth of Nations*:

> [A]nd in spite of their natural selfishness and rapacity, though they mean only their own conveniency, though the sole end which they propose from the labours of all the thousands whom they employ be the gratification of their own vain and insatiable desires, they divide with the poor the produce of all their improvements. They are led by an invisible hand to make nearly the same distribution of the necessaries of life, which would have been made, had the earth been divided into equal portions among all its inhabitants, and thus without in-

tending it, without knowing it, advance the interest of the society (Smith, *Theory of Moral Sentiments*, 264 – 65).

27. Luigino Bruni, and Robert Sugden, "Fraternity: Why the Market Need Not Be a Morally Free Zone," *Economics and Philosophy* 24 (2008): 35 – 64.

28. John Locke, *Two Treatises of Government and A Letter Concerning Toleration*, ed. Ian Shapiro (New Haven, CT: Yale University Press, 2003), 102.

29. Locke, *Two Treatises of Government and A Letter Concerning Toleration*, 208.

30. John Stuart Mill, *On Liberty* (London: John W. Parker and Son, 1859), 22.

31. Hobbes, *Leviathan*, 95 – 96.

32. Hobbes, *Leviathan*, 7.

33. Job 3:8, 41:1, 41:12; Psalms 74:14, 104:26; Isaiah 27:1.

CHAPTER 4: SPECIFIC ISSUES IN MACROECONOMICS & SOCIAL ETHICS

THE SOCIAL VALUE OF LIBERTY OR FREEDOM

In our discussion of the best form of government, we have already broached the social value of freedom or liberty. People living and working in social groups must forgo certain liberties they would have, living and working as independent and unrelated individuals. The word "liberty" comes from the Latin *libertas*, meaning, "freedom." As is often the case, etymology does not, here, give us a clear idea of what this means. The social value of liberty is variously defined, but typically includes the ideas of: (1) a maximum number of possibilities to choose from, and (2) the lack of external restraints prohibiting a choice of one or more of those possibilities, so that the individual can actually choose any of the possibilities. Thus, a society highly valuing liberty is structured so that individuals have a maximum number of choices and can freely choose them without external restraints or prohibitions. An inverse corollary of this is a minimum of laws and regulations since these restrain the amount of, and ability to make, choices. This structure directly affects economic activity in that society.

In our discussion of paternalism, we saw some of the chief criticisms of the claim that liberty is the most important social value. We will not reiterate those here, but will, instead, examine some of the arguments for the claim that liberty is the greatest social value. A common line of reasoning is similar to the argument for why pleasure or happiness is the greatest value in general. We saw that hedonists, ethical egoists, and utilitarians argue that pleasure or happiness is the greatest value, because either: (1) every other value is merely a means to the ends of happiness or pleasure, or (2) other values are really identical with happiness or pleasure. This line of reasoning assumes that what *is* the case, namely, what actually is our most important value, *should be* our most important value.

Those arguing for liberty as the greatest social value also often say that: (1) every other social value is merely a means to the end of liberty; (2) every other social value is really identical with freedom; and (3) when faced with a mutually exclusive decision between freedom and another social value, people always choose liberty over the other value.

Regarding the third, consider the social value of justice, about which we will say more later. One understanding of justice is retributive justice, involving merit and demerit. One should receive benefit or good to the extent that she does good for society, and she should be penalized or receive bad to the degree that she does bad for society. Inflicting legal penalties for crimes and receiving a reward for a heroic act are examples of justice, understood as retributive justice.

Some argue that retributive justice is merely a means to the end of freedom. The real goal of punishing criminals, they say, is to prevent them from inhibiting the liberties of others. Order, peace, and security are designed to promote maximal freedom for citizens. When people do not feel safe enough to go through the "bad" part of town at night, they really are not free to do so. That choice is not open to them. More choices mean more freedom on our definition of liberty. We mete out retributive justice by punishing criminals, then, in order to maximize peace, security, and safety, which is itself a means to the end of greater liberty. Of course, incarcerated criminals value their individual freedom, too, and so would rather not go to jail, but stay free. Conversely, we reward the hero who rescues one in danger, from physical harm or rape for instance, because doing so promotes the victim's liberty. Rape is an obvious violation of individual freedom, and physical harm inhibits a people's freedom by limiting what they can choose to do physically, like run or use their arm, for example.

What about liberty, compared to the social value of equality? If we are talking about equality of situation or condition, advocates of liberty cite examples where people prefer having the freedom to succeed or fail than being forced to remain at an equal level with others. If we really valued equality of condition over liberty, for example, then we would outlaw competitive sports, because every game results in an inequality between winners and losers.

Economically, advocates of liberty argue that not only citizens of countries with free market economies, but also those in countries controlling the economy to provide greater equality of condition, value the freedom to increase their wealth, more than having the same private property and income as everyone else. Ways to improve one's individual situation exist and are abundantly used in socialist and communist societies, in black markets, for example.

Equality can also mean equality of opportunity. Those, saying freedom is the greatest social value, argue that equality of opportunity promotes the maximum number of choices for the greatest number of people. When African-Americans in the U. S. A. were denied jobs and public facilities on the basis of their race, this was a limitation on their individual freedom. They were not free to stay at certain hotels, use certain restaurants, or apply for certain jobs. Equality of opportunity thus seems like a means to the ends of promoting maximal individual liberties.

Some argue that the whole goal of economic activity is to increase individual freedom. Markets presuppose the freedom to buy, sell, and trade. Further, they argue that we value wealth, because it is a means to freedom. People accumulate private property and wealth, because more "buying power" results in more choices in a free market. More wealth provides more choices. More wealth means more choices about the type of clothes one can wear, what kind of car one can drive, how often and where one can go out to eat, and how frequently and where one can go on vacation. Those with less wealth thus have fewer choices and therefore less freedom. The disparity is not only in material goods, but also in freedom. Wealthier people have more freedom than the less wealthy. In this argument, material possessions and money are merely means to the end of liberty, and economic activity both presupposes and promotes liberty as its source and goal. The degree to which liberty is valued will affect normative economic policies. Social groups that highly value liberty will place fewer restrictions on market activities.

There are other views, however, which argue that liberty is not, or should not, be the highest social value. We discussed common criticisms of elevating liberty to the apex of social values in the section on paternalism, in the previous chapter. Important, for any discussion of liberty, is the fact that all social groupings, by nature, must restrict at least some individual liberties people would have were they to exist and act individually in nature, as discussed earlier.

Also, arguments, in favor of liberty as the greatest social value, move from *is* to *ought*, from the way that things are (indicative) to the way things should be (imperative). They claim that people actually do (indicative) value liberty over every other social value, and, from this, conclude that this is right, that liberty *should* be (imperative, normative) the highest social value. This move from *is* to *ought* is liable to the critique of deriving values from facts, discussed earlier.

Finally, not only are there criticisms of elevating liberty to the highest social value, and criticisms of moving from the (arguable) fact that humans prefer liberty over all other social values, to the conclusion that they should value liberty the highest. There are also positive arguments put forth that other social values, not liberty, are, or should, be most important.

THE SOCIAL VALUE OF EQUALITY

As with other social values, there are different definitions of equality. Saying that all people are, or should be, equal sounds good, but what precisely do we mean by "equal?" Do we mean that all people are, or should be, the same in every way? Or do we mean that all have the same amount of private property and income? Do we mean the same possessions, amount of wealth, type of housing, education and healthcare? Does equality mean, removing all comparative distinctions of class, rank, status, prestige, and authority? Or do we mean that all have the same opportunity to succeed or fail? Do we mean that everyone starts at the "same place," so that whatever they achieve is due to their own ingenuity, will, effort, and hard work?

First, we can speak of equality as a natural or "God-given" equality of people, by virtue of their being humans. We have already mentioned how the *Declaration of Independence of the United State of America* speaks of the fundamental right to liberty, which all human beings have:

> We hold these truths to be self-evident, that all men are created equal, that they are endowed by their Creator with certain unalienable rights, that among these are life, liberty and the pursuit of happiness.

Thomas Jefferson, here, grounds the right to liberty on the claim that all humans are created "equal" by their Creator. What does this mean? We have been saying that all limit questions are related and tied to each another. The question of equality, here, is on one level an ontological question, or question about being. This is because, on the one hand, human beings are very different in many different ways, but also very similar or at least similar enough to be classified as the type of being we call, "human."

Jefferson probably did not mean that every human is equal in size, shape, skin color, eye color, physical abilities, mental faculties, geographical location, etc. What did he mean? He is probably expressing a view many have held throughout history: by virtue of being a *human* being all people have certain natural rights, or *equality of rights*. The topic of "rights" is important in any discussion of the intersection of social and political philosophy, economics, and ethics, and is related to social values.

Second, equality can mean the starting point in any endeavor. If, during an Olympic track race, we let one runner begin ten yards ahead of the rest, then there would be an inequality of staring point. If we began a baseball game with giving one team one run, there would be an inequality of staring place. By making all runners start behind the same starting line and both baseball teams begin with the same runs (usually zero, but we could let each team start with one, two, or three runs each), we are insuring equality of starting position.

In discussions of social endeavors, equality in starting points is called *equality of opportunity*. Equal opportunity laws are based on the idea of equality of opportunity to succeed or fail in social endeavors, and these are often reducible to economic endeavors: equal opportunity to secure a job or be in the market for a certain type of good. Equality of opportunity has become an important social value in modern times. Until fairly recently, gender, ethnicity, class, and religion have barred individuals from equal participation in various marketplace activities in many places in the world. Arguments, in favor of some type of equality of opportunity, usually rely on the claim that an equal starting point is just of fair. We will visit the social value of justice shortly.

Equality of opportunity is an important social value for most modern people. Although discussions about the pros and cons of emphasizing this value, how it should be promoted, and its relationship to other social values are very important, it is typically not a contender for the greatest social value. Indeed, we have seen how some argue that equality of opportunity is just one of the many means to the end of promoting the social value of liberty or freedom.

What is really at issue in most discussions of the equality, as a social value, is *equality of condition*. This means that all of society's members have equality in material well-being in some or all forms. This includes things like equality of private property or possessions, disposable income, living conditions, education, and healthcare. Those who highly value equality of condition, or claim it is the most important social value, are sometimes called *egalitarians*.

From the arguments in favor of liberty over equality of condition, we saw a potential conflict between these two social values. This conflict is evident on much many levels. If at Thanksgiving I exercise my freedom to take a second helping of sweet potatoes, when there is not enough for everyone to have a second helping, then I introduce an inequality, albeit a trivial one. But say we value equality of condition above freedom. Someone, or the group, could impose a restriction on my freedom to take a second helping of sweet potatoes. Perhaps they would even divide the remaining sweet potatoes, really only enough for one helping, into equal micro-units and give everyone a spoonful more of sweet potatoes.

On a larger level, striving for maximal individual liberty in social contexts and markets will most likely result in disparities of condition between individuals. If a worker exercises her freedom to work more industriously than others, then she may end up with more material goods or scarce resources, economically speaking. This means that the extra goods she has earned cannot go to the others, since they are no longer available. In certain understandings of justice—about which more will follow—this would also be just or fair. An inequality of condition of economic disparity results, though. Conversely, we could limit the amount of work that she could freely choose to do, so that she earns only a limited amount of material goods, and more are left for others. This is what market regulations, in effect, do. In certain views of justice, this would be just, or fair. This limits freedom, or liberty, however.

Similarly, if we value equality over freedom then we might redistribute the material goods of the wealthier to those who have less. Assuming that more wealth means more freedom, this would bring greater equality of condition and slightly more freedom for those who had less, but it would diminish the freedom of those from whom the wealth is taken away. This is what higher taxes, in effect, do. In certain views of justice this would be just, or fair. Yet, we limit freedom, or liberty, to make way for equity and justice, so conceived. Other views of justice, though, would see this as unjust, or unfair.

Thus, at the heart of many debates, over the best form of government and the ways governments should or should not be involved in market activities, is a mutually exclusive choice between equality of condition and liberty. Free market capitalist arrangements, with little government involvement in markets, typically value individual liberty over equality of condition. Socialist and communist arrangements, with more government involvement, typically value equality of condition, in at least some cases, more highly than individual liberty. We will later examine the cases for which relationship between governments and economies is best. Here we visit some of the arguments for and against promoting equality of condition in general. These are relevant, though, to considering the best form of governmental interaction with economies.

Which arguments are advanced by those who highly value equality of condition? Many are consequentialist, or *a posteriori*, ethical arguments. They compare and contrast the consequences of equality of condition and inequality of condition, respectively. Key is the claim that many personal and societal ills result from inequality of condition, but that equality of condition lessens or eliminates these ills. Crime is often related to people not having what they need, so perhaps more equality of condition would result in less crime. Equality of condition can also remedy unemployment and homelessness. Equality of condition can decrease competition, which many see as bad—although there are arguments for competition as better for all. Further, competition leads to conflicts between individuals, groups, companies, classes, and races. These conflicts result in many casualties that could be avoided, if there were more equality of condition.

On the individual level, there is more anxiety and fear when there is inequality of condition. People are worried about having enough money, keeping their jobs and houses, selling enough in the marketplace in order to survive, getting so sick that they cannot afford the cost of being cured, etc. If everyone in society were provided with their physical necessities, then there would be less fear and psychological anxiety.

Positively, some argue that because all would contribute to society through work in societies aiming at greater equality of condition, each person would have to work less. When there is inequality of condition some have so much wealth that they need not work, or work very little compared to their ability to contribute to society. Some, for other reasons, do not contribute as much as they could to society, such as royalty, and beneficiaries of the wealthy. Assuming certain answers to other limit questions, some argue that religious leaders and religious communities do not really contribute to society. If these large groups entered the workforce, then the same level of productivity could be achieved with less work per individual. Having to work less is not only a good and beneficial consequence in and of itself, but greater leisure time to do what one enjoys, or for personal development, is an important potential consequence.

Some arguments in favor of equality of condition are based on rule-based, or *a priori*, systems of ethics. These arguments are bound up with justice as a social value and discussions of rights, and are often coupled with religious arguments. Some use divine command theory to say that God has commanded that we provide for others' material necessities, in the sense of being "our brother's keeper," or that God commands some form of an equal distribution of material goods among humans. Some argue that people, simply by being human beings, have an inherent dignity demanding fundamental rights, by nature and/or by virtue of being created in the image of God, which include entitlement to certain material necessities.

If this is the case, then it is the case regardless of the consequences. The laws of economics are such that government involvement in markets, as in taxation and wealth redistribution, almost always results in market inefficiency, as defined by positive economics. Those using rule-based ethics to espouse equality of condition claim that an *a priori* rule, divine command, or basic human right still dictates that we promote greater equality of condition, regardless of adverse consequences for the market or the overall well-being of society in terms of inefficiency.

Another line of reasoning for equality of condition is based on certain answers to a limit question of metaphysics and philosophical anthropology, the question of *metaphysical freedom.* Again, all limit questions are interrelated. The metaphysical limit question about free will and determinism is related to the relationship and prioritization of the social values of liberty, equality of opportunity, equality of condition, and justice.

We have already mentioned metaphysical freedom in distinction from political freedom. The limit question of metaphysical freedom regards whether or not the laws of cause and effect ultimately determine the choices we make. A commonsense intuition of many is that they really have a freedom from prior determining causes, so that, when they make choices, they really can choose different possibilities. The question of metaphysical freedom asks if this intuition is correct.

The intuition is questionable, because we know that everything in nature operates according to causal laws.[1] We can explain any effect in nature by prior causes. We can ask, then, if our choices are really determined by prior causes, regardless of how we feel about our choices or perceive them. If our choices are really determined by prior causes, then, even if we feel that we have multiple choices and can choose any of them, the choice we make is really determined by prior causes. This means that we were not really free to choose contrary options, even if we feel that we do have this ability. If there is determination of our choices by prior causes, we either must define free will in terms other than our commonsense intuition that it is a "power of contrary choice," or we must deny that we have free will.[2]

The metaphysical debate over free will and determinism has implications for personal responsibility and, hence, ethics. Central to many conceptions of moral praise and blame is the belief that individuals have control over their choices. If a mischievous student pulls the school fire alarm, we usually blame him based on the assumption that he could have done otherwise. But what if the school bully takes his hand and forcibly uses it to pull the fire alarm, or if the bully threatens to beat him up if he doesn't pull the fire alarm? Then individual responsibility might be lessened or eliminated, because he had no choice.

If our choices are really determined by prior causes, regardless of how free and in control of our choices we feel, then it seems that an important requisite for personal responsibility, and hence for praise and blame, is removed. If all of our choices are really determined, then we are not as responsible for our choices and actions as we would be if we really had the power of contrary choice. Thus the question of metaphysical free will or determinism has implications for ethics in general. It also bears on the intersection of government, economics, and social values.

As we will see, there are different understandings of the social value of justice and which specific understanding should take precedence. Some views of how governments should be organized and involved in markets—like free market capitalism, libertarianism, and other minimalist theories of government—view merit-based justice as the most important form of justice. Merit-based justice is the meting out of rewards and punishments, based on one's contributions to society. These same theories also highly value the social value of individual liberty. They stress the *willing* part of the theoretical assumptions of economic theory regarding participants, in markets, who determine the supply and demand curves. Market agents are "*willing* and able."

Merit and demerit usually imply responsibility. One "gets what one deserves," based on one's contributions and lack of contributions, which are assumed to be freely chosen. In stressing individual contributions and freedom as constitutive of what an individual justly gets, these theories of government assume the individual's personal responsibility, and, hence, real freedom.

Other normative theories, of how governments should be involved in economies, question the *able* half of the theoretical assumptions economists make, about participants in markets who determine the supply and demand curves. Market agents are "willing and *able*." Notions of responsibility assume the ability to do what is required. While you might pity me if I cannot play golf like Tiger Woods, you would not *blame* me. Merit and demerit assume responsibility, which assumes ability. Theories of government advocating a more active governmental role in providing equality of condition, like socialism and communism, claim that some people are unable to contribute as much as others for various reasons—class, background, upbringing, education, race, gender, physical or mental condition, etc.—and therefore cannot be held as responsible as others. Therefore, rewarding and punishing them as we do other, more able, participants is unfair or unjust. Advocates of these systems believe that the government should redistribute income through taxation and welfare, to provide certain goods and services, and regulate markets, as with minimum wage laws and rent ceilings, to help those judged less able or unable.

In terms of the metaphysical question of the free will and determinism, one side in this debate assumes that individuals are not entirely determined by prior causes and circumstances, have some sort of free will, and are thus responsible for their actions in society and in markets. If individuals would just freely take the initiative and contribute, then they would have more. The other side assumes that prior causes and circumstances do determine one's ability to contribute to society. To the degree that causal determinism trumps free will, there is a decrease in personal responsibility. It is unfair to reward and punish people who are not in control of their ability, and thus not in control of their decisions. In fact, the view of prison systems as "correctional facilities," instead of purely punitive facilities, assumes that criminals act the way they do because of a sort of causal determinism, and that the system can "correct" them so as to make them behave properly. Changing the causes of their behavior will change their behavior.

In economics, the supply and demand curves for a market are based on the hypothetical individual who is *willing and able* to participate in market activities. Here, we see an acknowledgement of individual freedom and hence personal responsibility, and an equal acknowledgement of ability or inability, and hence lack of responsibility. Normatively, though, either freedom and willingness, or determinism and ability/inability, receives greater emphasis. One's answer to the metaphysical question of free will and determinism determines where one falls regarding the hypothetical market agent. This, then, informs one's view of justice in the marketplace, and how governments should or should not be involved in economic activities.

One's answer to the limit question of free will and determinism also affects how one prioritizes the social values of liberty, equality of condition, and equality of opportunity. This is also because the free will vs. determinism debate has implications for personal responsibility.

Belief in free will can lead to promoting individual liberty as a social value so that individuals can exercise their freedom in society and the marketplace. This, also, can lead to saying that, regardless of prior causes affecting them, people have a natural equality of opportunity. Because all have free will, all can exercise their freedom to succeed or fail in society and the marketplace, regardless of their backgrounds, upbringing, education, class, race, gender, etc. A robust view of free will thus places all at the same starting place, as all by nature possess the freedom to succeed or fail. A robust view of free will can also lead to downplaying equality of condition, because the condition that people are in is heavily dependent on the exercise of their free wills, and hence is their own personal responsibility.

Conversely, a strong belief in metaphysical determinism can lead to deemphasizing the social value of liberty. Stressing determinism can lead to the conclusion that individuals in society are not at equal starting points. This means that they do not naturally have the same equality of opportunity. Perhaps, then, society and the government should change the natural order of things to insure greater equality of opportunity. Similarly, because determinists deny free will, they believe that one's condition in society is not their personal responsibility. This can lead to emphasizing equality of condition more than liberty, as a social value. Liberty presupposes freedom, which, if absent, undercuts valuing liberty. Why promote individual liberties if free will is an illusion? Thus, assuming metaphysical determinism can easily lead to another argument for prioritizing the social value of equality of condition.

As with other social values, there are also arguments against prioritizing equality of condition. We have seen how a robust view of free will over determinism goes hand in hand with a strong emphasis on personal responsibility, in social and economic contexts. Some views of justice see justice as primarily merit-based, a person justly receiving rewards and punishments or economic benefits and burdens, based on their contributions or lack thereof to societies and markets. This means that individuals have only what they have freely chosen and worked for. Since there are differences in effort and contribution among different members of society, there are fair differences in the distribution of rewards and benefits. Equality of condition, in this line of reasoning, is unfair or unjust to those who have worked harder and have made greater contributions.

Champions of equality of condition respond to this by saying that, in economies with strong centralized governments and heavily involved markets, as in socialism and communism, everyone, at least in theory, works and thus contributes to society and the marketplace. They also argue that no one type of contribution is more valuable than another. A janitor or trash collector is just as important as a doctor, lawyer, or president of a large corporation. This response is also related to the organic or holistic view of societies. In living organisms each component part, every system and every organ, is equally valuable for the proper functioning of the whole.

Those against prioritizing equality of condition, as the greatest social value, respond to this line of reasoning by arguing that some jobs are really more valuable to society than others. Doctors promote human health and save lives, which seems more valuable than custodial and waste removal jobs, they claim. We will see (when we discuss justice and the arguments in favor of free markets and capitalist systems) that they also argue that the neutral and unbiased market mechanism is the best judge of which contributions are more valuable than others. No one individual or group of individuals, like governmental central planners, is capable of making such judgments. Free markets consistently "judge" the relative values of different jobs, by naturally rewarding those who contribute more. Coupled with a merit-based view of justice, these points can be made against highly valuing equality of condition. In fact, inequality in distribution of benefits is just, in such reasoning. The neutral market rewards the value of each job to society, with commensurate rewards.

Another argument against making equality of condition the most important social value is that, to do so, the government must be more involved in markets. This results in market inefficiency, as defined by positive economics. We saw in our discussion of supply, demand, and utility in economics, that the natural equilibrium point in a market results in maximum utility or welfare. Free markets do not naturally distribute resources so as to promote equality of condition. To achieve equality of condition, constant interference in the market is necessary to redistribute wealth. The laws of economics are such that interference in markets, through taxation and regulation, almost always results in deadweight loss. There is an unavoidable loss of market efficiency, and hence of utility.

In this way, free market advocates, of as little interference as possible in markets, argue their position with a consequentialist moral argument. A utilitarian argument, for example, might equate what economists call utility or welfare with happiness or pleasure. It could say that since free market activity, which naturally results in inequalities of distribution in resources and benefits, *overall* produces maximum utility (happiness or pleasure) for society as a whole. As discussed earlier, the goal or consequence aimed for in utilitarian normative ethics is maximal pleasure or happiness, the "greatest net happiness for the greatest number." This means that the opportunity cost of inefficiency, which lessens a society's net utility in order to achieve greater equality of condition, is not worth it.[3]

Some advocates of equality of condition judge that the value of equality of condition in society is greater than the opportunity cost of decreased efficiency and overall welfare, and accept this trade-off. It is important, however, that they are cognizant of the opportunity cost and the trade-off involved. Aiming for equality of condition is also justifiable with a consequentialist ethical argument, including a modified form of utilitarianism. Again, utilitarianism, originally formulated by Bentham and modified by Mill, made pleasure or happiness the greatest value. They argue that equality of condition increases the greatest net happiness for the greatest number in ways other than strict utility, as defined by positive economics. This affects the utilitarian calculus used to determine the right course of action. This could very well lead to sacrificing maximum market efficiency, and hence the maximal positive economic utility and welfare generated by free markets, in order to achieve greater equality of condition.

Some egalitarians argue that humans have inalienable rights, including necessities for survival and flourishing, like adequate food, shelter, living conditions, healthcare, education, etc. If honoring these rights is a valued consequence alongside of happiness and pleasure, then the utilitarian calculus, used to determine the right relationship between the government and markets, could lead to concluding that the opportunity cost of reduced efficiency and net utility is worth the trade-off for the consequence that these basic human rights are honored.

Another argument, against making equality of condition the most important social value, is that equality of condition robs people of their individuality, which they highly value. In some theories of human identity in philosophical anthropology, like existentialism, individuals "create" themselves and their individual identities through their free and responsible choices. To the degree that a socio-political system aims for greater equality of condition, it must limit the free choices individuals can make in that society, which, therefore, derogates their individual identities. A similar argument is that people identify themselves with their private property, so that the degree to which all have an equal quantity and quality of private property—the same housing, the same clothes, the same food, the same car, the same "toys", etc.— they are robbed of their individuality.

Egalitarians have several rejoinders to this. First, the question of individual identity is a metaphysical question, about being, and is related to the metaphysical question of free will and determinism discussed above. Existentialism, to which this objection is related, assumes that there is no given human "nature" or "essence" common to all people. Rather, all people create their individual identities through their free and responsible choices.

Another ontological view is that all people share a basic human nature or essence. Lacking certain material necessities, for instance, might "dehumanize" a person. This can be linked to appeals to human rights. Some argue that for all people to be truly human, they must have certain basic things, like adequate nourishment, food, shelter, clothing, living conditions, healthcare and education. Letting an unregulated market naturally distribute scarce resources causes radical inequalities, so that some, the "very poor," do not have these necessities. This robs them of their human nature. On this essence-based view of human nature, then, in order to promote the full humanity of individuals in society, we must strive for a certain degree of equality of material condition.

Another egalitarian response is that, although it might presently be the case (indicative, "fact," is") that people find their individual identities in their material possessions, the way things are might not be the way things should be (imperative, normative, "ought"). The real identity of a human being involves their individual personality, likings, interests, and hobbies, not their private property. Later, we will see that one of the criticisms of capitalist systems is that they promote the wrong values, like materialism. Egalitarians argue, then, that equality of material condition does not rob individuals of their real identities since their real identities do not lie in their material possessions. So what if we all have the same clothes, car, house, toys, etc.? One's identity lies in things other than what she has. Advocates of equality of condition also argue that, in highly competitive unregulated markets, people can get so caught up in competition that much of their time is occupied in trying to survive. They thus have precious little leisure time to develop the individual personality traits that really define who they are as individuals.

Related to the criticism, that equality of condition robs people of their identities, is the claim that restricting the individual liberties required to attain equality of condition does not do justice to individual preferences. Being "*willing* and able" to choose according to individual preference is essential in markets, in positive economic theory. What people want differs from person to person, but free choice based on preferences is essential to all market activity. Highly regulated markets diminish people's ability to choose according to their preferences. As a result, ancillary markets naturally emerge alongside officially sanctioned markets, so that individuals can more freely trade according to their preferences. This naturally results in an inequality of condition but the fact that people still seek this free market activity, even if illicit, proves that they value freedom to choose according to their preferences over equality of condition.

Say that Bob and Joe live in a communist society with central economic planning by the government. Every citizen gets an allotted amount of sardines and an allotted amount of canned meat, like *Spam*. Since everyone gets the same amount of both, there is equality of condition. Bob and Joe both have the same amount of sardines and *Spam*. Yet, Bob likes *Spam* and not sardines, while Joe likes sardines but not *Spam*. So Bob and Joe trade with each other so that Bob gets Joe's *Spam* and Joe gets Bob's sardines. This ancillary market naturally emerges so that individuals can trade according to their preferences. We see this in almost any case of regulation, as when some goods and services are illegal. There are black markets for illegal drugs, and there were underground abortions in the U. S. A. long before abortion was legalized.

Those opposed to prioritizing equality of condition thus argue that while we may say we value equality of condition, in reality we value the social value of freedom to choose according to our preferences. The natural result is an inequality in distribution of goods and services: Bob has all the *Spam* and Joe has all of the sardines. But the freedom to choose according to individual preferences is what people *really* value, not equality of condition. Those opposed to prioritizing equality of condition also argue that the black market activity, resulting from market regulations used to promote equality of condition, leads to more social ills because these markets are illegal. The illegal drug trade results in much violence and death, and underground abortion causes sanitation and health problems for women seeking abortions on the black market.

Egalitarians have rejoinders to this as well. Valuing individual liberty to choose according to preferences assumes that individuals know what is best for them. Recall the possible distinction between a *real* good or value and an *apparent* good or value. Egalitarians say those championing individual liberty to choose according to one's preferences assume that what people value is *really* good and valuable for them, not merely *apparently* good and valuable for them. Egalitarians say that while some may prefer illegal drugs and aborting their children, their preferences are wrong. They wrongly value these things, but really should not value them.

This response recalls the debate over the best form of government. Democracy, which values individual freedoms, assumes people know what is best for themselves and society. Paternalism assumes that individuals often make the wrong value judgments about what is best for themselves and society, so, others know better and should make these judgments for them.

Advocates of equality of condition add to this, again, that societies can inculcate the wrong values, like materialism. Individuals are influenced to think, wrongly, that if they have more private property, or certain kinds of private property, like designer clothes and sports cars, then they are better than others. These wrong values influence individual preferences. People choose based on ill-informed preferences, which must be corrected by those who "know better."

Another argument against equality of condition is that it removes the motivation to contribute to society and markets because the government provides for those in need. We see this criticism when people say that individuals who are really able to work and contribute to society "abuse the system" by claiming disability or welfare when they really do not need it. A socio-political system, which sees justice as merit-based, promotes competition and production. However, the degree to which individuals are guaranteed resources and benefits, without having to compete and produce, reduces both quality and production, and thus the overall welfare of society as a whole. Those making this argument also point to the way, historically, socialist and communist societies have had a low gross domestic product, gross inefficiency, poorer quality of goods and services compared to free market societies, and, in many cases, have utterly failed.

Responses to these points, by advocates of equality of condition, have varied. One response is that the ways socialist and communist societies with lower productivity, lower quality of goods, and economic failure have been structured, were wrong. Just because the ones that have existed have had these problems does not necessarily mean that all such systems aiming at equality of condition are destined to fail. A better social-political system will be found, eventually. This should include, they say, greater government enforcement of work and making citizens do their part.

A final criticism of egalitarianism is the question of whether it is even possible to attain a relatively equal distribution of material goods, income, healthcare, education, status, rank, position, etc., given the scarcity of resources and given the way the world works due to finite metaphysical limitations. Some recalcitrant facts, agreed upon in positive economics regarding the allocation of scarce resources, can be used to cast doubt on this possibility. A related criticism applies to equality of opportunity. We can question whether getting everyone to the same "starting point" on a "level playing field" is ever really possible, given natural limitations and insurmountable metaphysical differences between different human beings.

THE SOCIAL VALUE OF JUSTICE

In our survey of liberty and equality as social values, we have already referred to the social value of justice. "Justice" is a common term used in a variety of ethical, political and economic discussions. Quoting the journalist, Henry Louis Mencken, Pope Paul VI said: "If you want peace, work for justice."[4] Justice is a *value* because it is something that practically all people agree is good and important, and something toward which communities, states, and other social groupings should strive. Justice is a *social* value because it involves a state of affairs between multiple human beings. It is arguably a necessary condition for human societies.

An ancient Greek creation myth explains the origins of justice this way: After creation, the gods equipped living things in the world with characteristics necessary for their survival and self-preservation. Humans were different from the other animals, however. They were physically weaker and intellectually superior, but their physical weakness jeopardized their survival in the natural world. Therefore, Zeus, the king of the gods, sent Hermes, the messenger of the gods, to give humans a sense of justice so that they could exist in community together, collectively face the natural world, survive in it, and even master it.

We have already seen how different understandings of justice can confirm or compete with the social values of liberty and equality. And just as it is easy to broadly appeal to "freedom" and "equality" without being clear as to what is meant, it is easy to speak of "justice" so as to evoke spirited emotive responses without being clear as to what is specifically meant by "justice." Probably, most people would say that society should be "just" and should combat "injustices." This sounds nice, but such platitudes are useless without clarity as to what is meant by justice and injustice. We have seen that liberty and equality are complicated ideas with multiple nuanced meanings. This is even more so with the social value of justice. And, as with liberty and equality, disagreements arise about justice because people mean different things when they talk about justice. Justice is one of the most complicated and controverted ideas in social ethics.

Our English word "justice" comes from the Latin word *iustitia* (the letter "j" was imported from Arabic in the Middle Ages, and is related to the letter "i"). *Iustitia* was used in medieval theology and philosophy to refer to a variety of things: God's covenant faithfulness to God's people of the Bible, the metaphysical status of a being existing "as it is supposed to exist," general morality or goodness, the question of how a person is put right with God (the question of "justification" or *iustificatio*), rewards and punishments based on merits and demerits, fairness in a variety of contexts, and a property of human societies that exist "as they are supposed" to exist.

Long before the Middle Ages, Aristotle had distinguished between different meanings of justice: (i) what is right, not wrong, generally speaking and hence equivalent to what is moral; (ii) a virtue or ontological state of a being that is as it "ought to be" (integrity of being); (iii) the keeping of laws, fairness, and rectification of imbalances caused by wrong actions; and (iv) distribution of rewards and punishment based on merits and demerits.[5]

At the intersection of economics, social and political philosophy, and ethics, questions about justice center on the social dimensions of this value. Yet, even here there are a number of different understandings of what precisely justice is. Before discussing these different definitions of justice, we must make two observations. First, while justice, however it is specifically understood, is a social *value* and hence judged to be good, in some cases we can distinguish between: (i) the goodness of justice itself and (ii) the goodness or badness, rightness or wrongness, of other things associated with the presence or absence of justice.

Say we have a conception of justice as merit-based reward and punishment. Now say that there is a kindergarten classroom and a teacher who has assigned specific rewards and punishments for good and bad behaviors, respectively. She decides that sitting quietly and not talking deserves a reward, while making noise and talking deserves punishment. Now say Johnny is not doing his work but talking, making noise, and teasing Sally. If the teacher gave Johnny a reward and punished Sally in this scenario, we would say that she is acting unjustly, but if she punished Johnny and rewarded Sally, she would be acting justly. We have not yet talked about what the rewards and punishment are, but we can recognize justice and injustice solely on our merit-based understanding of justice, regardless of specific the rewards and punishments.

Now, let's say the teacher is an extremist. The reward for good behavior is candy, soda, and the day off from classroom work. The punishment for bad behavior is to silently sit in the corner for the rest of day. We can judge the goodness or badness of these rewards and punishments, perhaps that they are worse than other types of rewards and punishments because they are too extreme, even though the teacher may be acting perfectly justly in meting out rewards and punishments when she punishes Johnny and rewards Sally. It would still be unjust to put Sally in the corner for being good and to give Johnny candy for being bad.

In punishing Johnny and rewarding Sally, justice is present and is judged to be good by itself. We would not want the teacher to stop rewarding good behavior and punishing bad behavior. We would only want her to change the specific rewards and punishments so that they would be better. Judging specific rewards and punishments to be better and worse compared to other rewards and punishments is a value judgment, but it is different from the value judgment that the mere presence of merit-based justice is good. So, in this scenario, we can distinguish between the value judgment about justice and injustice on the one hand, and the goodness or badness of the rewards and the punishments on the other hand.

There are other cases when administering rewards and punishments can be more intimately bound up with the presence or absence of justice. This example merely shows that in some cases we can distinguish between the presence or absence of justice itself, and the goodness or badness of other things associated with the presence or absence of justice.

There is a second observation we can make before considering different definitions of justice in social contexts. This has to do with why these various definitions of justice are each still classified as justice. It is the question of what the "essence" of justice is, regardless of the particular type of justice we are considering or talking about. The question, of what the many instances of what we call "justice" have in common, is related to, and involves, limit questions of being (ontology), and limit questions of truth and knowledge (epistemology).

Justice as Naturally Appropriate Order

What are the possible meanings of justice as a social value? One is related to the metaphysical meaning of justice as "integrity of being," or as a being existing "as it is supposed to be." Here, justice means that there is a certain harmony, order, and balance in society. When this is disrupted by disharmonious and disorderly actions, the balance and order must be restored. This is an old view of justice present in a wide variety of cultures from the dawn of human history. Many religious taboos and restitutions, like sacrifices to deities, originated from the idea that harmony, order, and balance in society or nature are disrupted by certain actions, so that restitution is necessary to restore the balance. We still speak of "cosmic justice" and of "mother nature bringing balance" today in the wake of a real or perceived disruption of the natural order.

This idea of justice is more familiar to us and more related to economic activity in the idea of restitution for damage or theft of private property. Having to pay personally, or through an insurance policy, for damage to another's car when responsible for an automobile accident is an example. A CEO caught extorting money from the company and subsequently forced to make restitution to the shareholders is another example. Many examples of this conception of justice as restoration and restitution in modern society could be adduced.

The idea here is that it is naturally right (orderly, harmoniously, "the way things should be") for individuals to own private property. When private property is destroyed, damaged, or stolen, disorder, lack of harmony, and lack of integrity are introduced. To maintain justice—restore order, harmony and integrity of the "way things are supposed to be"—the private property, or its equivalent, must be restored. This view of justice as restoring order and balance is sometimes called *corrective justice*, because it corrects a real or perceived disorder and imbalance. Again, corrective justice is related to the metaphysical limit questions about ontology, because it involves assumptions about the way things (beings) and states of affairs (also "things") should be, and again, all limit questions are intrinsically related.

Legal Justice

Another narrower but still important idea of justice is *legal justice*. As the name suggests, legal justice deals with what is considered just or fair in the realm of law. It deals with what is judged to be the right or proper procedure in prosecuting crimes and adjudicating legal disputes. The right to remain silent when arrested, the right to a fair trial by an impartial judge or jury, the right to choose to represent one's self or to have a lawyer, and all the other trappings of what is considered due process of law in modern societies, are examples of legal justice. If a person did not have his Miranda Rights read to him when arrested, or did not have an attorney appointed to him if he wanted one appointed, then legal justice would be violated. If a party in a lawsuit were to bribe the judge or jury for a favorable judgment, legal justice would be violated. Legal justice is still a social value because processes of law occur in social contexts.

Commutative Justice

Another understanding of justice in societies involves the oversight and enforcement of agreements made between individuals and groups of individuals, like corporations. This is called *commutative justice*. It is different from, but related to, legal justice. Commutative justice is more directly relevant to economic activity, because it often involves the setting of rules for trade and their enforcement. In the natural market phenomena, which economists study, individuals and groups engage in trade. Important to this process is that both parties do what the other expects in the transaction. The seller is expected to disclose proper information relevant to the transaction, so that, for instance, false advertising might be prohibited. Likewise, the buyer has certain obligations, the most basic of which is to provide the money or other means of exchange for the good or service provided. When one buys a house and signs a mortgage, she promises to pay back the money she borrowed from the bank, with interest. If she fails to keep the terms of the mortgage agreement then the bank may foreclose. Many examples could be adduced. Thus commutative justice deals with establishing and enforcing the rules for trading in a market.

Positive economic theory assumes commutative justice as a condition of the possibility of quantifying market, supply and demand curve, utility, and welfare maximization analysis. The presumption of the presence of commutative justice, in all cases, is questionable, however. If so, then some ethical considerations regarding economics change. For example, if a mechanic tells a customer that his car needs more work than it really needs, then the buyer engages in a transaction without true knowledge of what he really needs to spend to attain his preference, the fixing of his car. The preference he expresses, through what he is willing and able to pay, is skewed and unnatural, and there is no way to account for this in utility and welfare analysis. Thus, an ethical analysis in economics based, on a consequentialist maximization of utility, can go awry if commutative justice is violated. Those who oppose making utility maximization, through the free markets with minimal regulation, a normative economic principle, point to such—perhaps frequent—violations of commutative justice. False advertising, lying in transactions, the creating of false preferences, etc., can call into question an ethical theory based on utility maximization. This is also an argument for more regulation. Yet, perhaps no amount of regulation can safeguard commutative justice in every single transaction in a market.

The degree to which a government stipulates rules for trade is directly related to different views of how governments should interact with economies. Almost all agree that commutative justice, or fairness in trade, is important, and, so, there should be a minimum degree to which governments should regulate economic activity in markets. Even those who are conservative (minimalist), about the right degree of government involvement in markets, typically agree that those engaging in trade *should* be honest with each other about transactions, *should* not withhold relevant knowledge from other parties, that sellers *should* deliver the goods or services expected by buyers, that buyers *should* deliver the payment or means of exchange for goods or services provided, that contracts *should* be kept and honored, and that parties who do not keep these obligations *should* be penalized. Penalization could be legal, governmental, or delivered by the market itself, but, nonetheless, most share a fundamental belief that violations of commutative justice in markets *should* be punished.

These are commonly held expectations but they are not necessary for trade to occur. Dishonest trading can and does occur. Sellers sometimes don't deliver and buyers sometimes don't pay. Sometimes parties to a contract violate the contract. Sometimes these violations of commutative justice in the marketplace go unpunished. But even the most conservative, regarding government regulation of market activity—as little regulation as possible, believe in these obligations and so have a standard of commutative justice.

Those on the more liberal end of the spectrum, regarding the right degree of government involvement in markets, include these minimalist obligations of commutative justice, but they add others. These extra obligations are usually based on other, larger-scale, considerations than the simple transaction between buyer and seller. This is related to the way propounding greater governmental control over markets is associated with the organic view of societies. Imposing extra obligations on individual transactions is based on the belief that every transaction is interrelated with other aspects of society as a whole.

Consider regulations against charging exorbitant interest. There will always be some willing and able to pay exorbitant interest for a loan. The higher the interest, the fewer the transactions the lender needs to get the same profit. In fact, perhaps lenders would choose to sell fewer loans at higher rates to the fewer willing and able to buy them, because they would have to do less work—make less loan transactions—to make the same amount. Yet, governments regulate interest rates to insure that more people who are not willing and/or not able to pay exorbitant interest are able to get loans, too. This restricts lenders' freedom, but in the interest of another value: more people getting loans.

Judging exorbitant interest to be unjust moves beyond the minimalist demands of commutative justice that obligate parties in individual transactions (honesty, disclosure, and following through on doing what one promises). Judging exorbitant interest to be unjust considers an individual transaction's implications for society as a whole, instead of only considering the many transactions made by the individual parties, considered discretely.

Conservatives advocating minimal governmental involvement in markets claim that less market regulation is better, and for a variety of reasons. One is the focus on the many individuals over the one whole, corresponding to the social contract theory of societies. Again, social contract theory has affinities with the values of conservative political and fiscal philosophy. Another reason is that more regulations inhibit freedom, as a social value. Regulations against exorbitant interest constrain the freedom of sellers who prefer to sell one loan at exorbitant interest, instead of many loans at lesser interest.

Commutative justice also bears on discussions of the details of the fairness of individual transactions. Take the issue of a "just wage." Some judge a specific price of labor (wage) agreed upon by a buyer (employer) and seller (laborer) to be unjust to the laborer, so that it must be higher in order to be just. This assumes that the laborer does not know what is best for her utility maximization, but that the one judging the wage to be unjust does. This is a paternalistic assumption. It also assumes that the laborer's preferences are for an apparent, not a real, good. Others assume that each individual is the best judge of what is best for her, so that, even if others judge the wage to be unjust, it is just by virtue of the fact that the employer and laborer agreed on it. Thus one will answer questions of commutative justice regarding the specifics of individual transactions differently, depending on one's answers to other philosophical anthropological, and social and political, limit questions.

DISTRIBUTIVE JUSTICE

We have seen how justice can be understood as fairness in market activity. Another understanding of justice, as a social value, is *distributive justice*. Distributive justice deals with how benefits and burdens should be distributed among people in groups. Questions of distributive justice are at the heart of the intersection of economics, social and political philosophy, and ethics, because economics is the study of the allocation of scarce resources. There are many ways to distribute the scarce resources. How should scarce resources be distributed? Should everyone get an equal share of the scarce resources, or should some people get more than others? If some should get more, then why should they? What are the criteria for distributing scarce resources?

Consider a lottery. We think it is just or fair that the person whose number is drawn gets the jackpot, and we do not consider it unjust or unfair that others do not get the winnings. In fact, we would consider it unjust if a winning number were drawn and the winnings were divided equally among everyone who bought a ticket. This is because there were agreed upon rules for the lottery and those playing the lottery knew, or were responsible for knowing, those rules. The *rules* were that whoever's number was drawn would get the jackpot. Violating those rules introduces injustice in the distribution of the winnings. The distribution is based on the randomness of the lottery, and all agreed on this distribution beforehand.

Lotteries are simple and very common. Questions arise, though, when the rules are complicated and the situations less common. What should the rules be? Who determines them?

Need-Based Distributive Justice

Consider a charity to help poor families. There is a limited amount of money that can be distributed. If the charity gave the money to a wealthy, upper-class family, we would consider that unjust. This is because the distribution of the charity's money is supposed to be based on *need*. A question arising for need-based distributive justice is what type and level of need dictate distribution? The more people there are who meet the need-based criteria, the less each person in need gets. Should every person or group who meets the need criteria get an equal share of the resources? Or should there be a sliding scale, so that those with more need get more resources?

Merit-Based Distributive Justice

Now consider a scholarship for the best student at a school. If the scholarship were given to a very poor student, say one with a failing grade point average, we would consider that unjust. This is because the scholarship should be distributed according to *merit*. Merit-based distributive justice is very important for discussions of the social value of justice and economics. The merit-based view of distributive justice is common among those advocating little governmental intervention in market—those who advocate liberal democracies, free markets, and capitalism.

They typically argue that through their work in using their gifts and skills (Adam Smith's "individual and unique genius"), individuals contribute to the overall betterment of others in society. One's effort in using one's gifts and skills, thus, betters society as a whole. The degree to which one makes such contributions constitutes a sort of merit for which they should be rewarded. Conversely, those who do not use their natural gifts and acquired skills in benefiting others through trade, and hence not bettering society as a whole, accrue a sort of demerit.

The nature of the free market is that it automatically rewards those who contribute and punishes those who do not. Further, no individual or group has enough knowledge, competence, and freedom from bias to judge the merit or demerit of every individual, in contributing or not contributing to society as a whole. The disinterested, neutral market mechanism metes out rewards and punishments. This is done as innumerable individuals "vote" for which contributions they value most, through buying and selling. In fact, what some individuals or groups intuitively judge as less valuable may be, as seen by the market's impartial judgment, actually more valuable. Many do not think that professional sports stars and movie stars make contributions to society commensurate with the money they make. However, the many individuals, as a whole, in society, have "voted" with their money, and this intuitive judgment is seen to be wrong.

In this view, then, if the government redistributes wealth through taxation, regulations, and welfare programs, it overrides the impartial merit-based distributive justice of the market, and therefore acts unjustly. Such redistribution of wealth, from those who rightly merited it, according to the free market, is analogous to giving the scholarship to the failing student, in the example above. In stronger formulations, this is construed as tantamount to theft.

In this view, inequalities between individuals' natural gifts and skills are necessary and unavoidable. Some are born with better athletic ability than others. Some are naturally better artists than others. Some are naturally better at working with their hands than others. Some are better with critical thinking and numbers than others. Some are better caretakers than others. Typically, people are interested in and enjoy doing activities at which they excel. By developing and using their natural gifts and interests, people contribute more, in those areas, to society than those who are not gifted and skilled in them. By doing so, they merit more than if they tried to contribute in ways in which they are not gifted and skilled, and they are also happier.

Conversely, if some central-planning agency dictates people's occupations, as in some communist governments, then it is probable that some, if not many, would end up contributing to economic activity by doing something they are not gifted at or skilled in. This means that those who are best at certain jobs will not be doing them. This introduces inefficiency into the market and makes people unhappy, as they are doing something in which they are neither gifted nor interested.

Questions arise for a merit-based distributive justice, though. In the system just described, there are certain talents and skills people will value more, and so the market will naturally reward them more than others. Doctors, who save lives, may be valued more than janitorial custodians and thereby accrue more merit and financial rewards. Those better at discovering and implementing new technologies may be valued more than clerks, and so merit more rewards. Critics question whether such unequal valuation and rewarding of people's gifts and talents is fair, or "just," in another sense of the word.

Typically, advocates of merit-based distributive justice respond by saying, "yes, inequalities result but they are natural, necessary, and unavoidable." Rather than living under the illusion that all are equal in every way, we should accept the fact that some are better than others at things that are more valuable to society, and live with this fact.

What constitutes merit, and who decides what constitutes merit? Who judges if a person or group has the merit to receive benefits? In our scholarship example, suppose that the student with the highest GPA is naturally gifted and did not have to put forth much effort to perform well. Another student with a slightly lower GPA had to exercise much effort to do as well as the first student. Maybe the second student should get the scholarship because we consider the effort and personal responsibility of the second student to be meritorious as well. Or maybe not, but who decides this?

The question of ability-to-merit is important for merit-based forms of distributive justice, especially when considering distributive justice in economies and societies. This is because people are naturally endowed with different abilities in different areas. Should only the level of merit achieved be considered, regardless of how it is achieved (natural or freely chosen effort)? Or should freely chosen effort and hard work be considered meritorious, in addition to natural ability-to-merit? This question is related to the metaphysical question of determinism and free will and its attendant questions of personal responsibility, as discussed earlier. It is also related to the assumption in positive economics, that agents in a free market are "willing and *able*" to engage in transactions. What if they are unable?

Similar questions emerge in reversing the scenario and making it one of punishment for demerit. Justice systems largely have the purpose of meting out punishment for demerits. We consider it unjust if a person who did not commit a crime is punished for the crime, but the guilty person goes unpunished. Again, we can ask questions about determinism and freedom. We often hold people less responsible and, thus, impose less punishment when they are caused to commit a crime, by some other factor. This happens when a person is judged psychiatrically unsound and is acquitted of a crime they did commit, while a person of sound mind, who freely committed the same crime, is judged responsible and is therefore punished. We can ask, though, whether persons coming from a dysfunctional background and upbringing, who grow up to become criminals, really made their choices freely, or whether they were, in sense, determined by their background and upbringing. Likewise, if we base the distribution of scarce resources in an economic system on merit and demerit, we can ask whether those who contribute more, and those who contribute less, are personally responsible for their contributions and lack of contributions, or whether prior factors, in some way, determined their contributions and lack of contributions.

Equality-Based Distributive Justice

Consider this scenario. Friends order pizza while watching a football game, and there are three pieces left. How should the three pieces be distributed? Equally? If there are three friends, this is easy, but if there are more or less than three, the slices must be divided. Understanding justice as distributing resources in equal portions to all is very similar to the social value of equality of condition. Distributive justice, understood as distributing resources equally among individuals in a group, is sometimes called *egalitarianism.*

Egalitarian understandings of distributive justice are also important for discussions of justice at the intersection of economics, social and political philosophy, and ethics. An egalitarian understanding of distributive justice is frequently appealed to by those who advocate more governmental involvement with market activity, and naturally leads to the endorsement of taxation, regulations, and the redistribution of wealth, through programs like welfare safety nets.

Many of the arguments, against the social value of equality of condition, are relevant for the claim that distributive justice should be egalitarian. Advocates of egalitarian distributive justice appeal to natural human dignity, worth, or rights to which all human beings are entitled, which similarly are based on natural law or divine command theories. According to this view, inequalities in resources among individuals and the disparities between the "very rich" and the "very poor" are grossly unjust. Although advocates of merit-based distributive justice stress individual freedom and responsibility, the "willing" in "willing and able" market agents, advocates of egalitarian distributive justice stress the "able" in "willing and able" market participants. They claim that it is unjust to punish, with less material resources, those who are unable to contribute as much as others. Some arguments for egalitarian distributive justice are also consequentialist. They urge that many individual and societal ills, like anxiety over having enough to survive and high crime levels, result from an unequal distribution of resources.

Likewise, many criticisms of prioritizing equality of condition apply to egalitarian distributive justice. Critics point to how the level of manipulation of market activities, required for equal distribution, introduces gross inefficiencies. Such involvement requires more regulations, which, in turn, limit individual liberties. It is alleged, that if people are guaranteed to get an equal share of the resources, they lose their motivation for working and contributing to society. And, again, critics typically stress the freedom side of the debate over metaphysical free will and determinism. They claim that people are free to contribute to society through market activities, and if they do not, it is their fault and they should not be given the same reward as those who have freely chosen to put forth the effort. Again, some say, that distributing material resources equally, robs individuals of their individuality, and that people do not really want this, as the natural phenomena of black markets bear witness to.

There is also the problem of individual preferences, central to the explanations of market activities by economists. Consider again our left over pizza example. There are drawbacks to distributing the remaining pieces equally. What if only some are still hungry and want the pizza, but others do not? It might be better to let only those, who want the pizza, have it. This distribution would be based on wants and preferences. Forcing everyone to have an equal share of the remaining pizza violates the preferences of those who do not want more pizza, as well as the preference of those who do want more. It would thus introduce inefficiency in utility maximization. Perhaps distributive justice here should be based on *preferences*.

Yet, as we have also said, there are potential problems with basing the distribution of resources on preferences. What if one of the friends, who wants more pizza, has high cholesterol and has been warned by his doctor to eat more nutritiously lest he have his third heart attack? He really wants more pizza but his friends stay his hand, reminding him of his doctor's admonitions. In the worst case scenario, the friends prohibit him from eating more pizza, even though that is what he really wants. Maybe his preferences are wrong, as what he wants is an apparent, not a real, good. So, perhaps it is wrong to assume that people's preferences are *de facto* right.

Maybe people's preferences can be disordered or wrong. What if what people want is not always what is best for them individually, or for society as a whole? We saw, in our discussion of the relationship of governments to societies, that some theories, like liberal democracy, prioritize individual freedom and preferences. They advocate not interfering with individuals' liberty and letting them choose according to their wants and desires. Other theories, like paternalism, hold that people are not always right in their wants and desires, so someone, or some group, who "knows better" should determine, in some cases, what people get, not individuals themselves.

"Egalitarian" Distributive Justice vs. "Equalitarian" Distributive Justice

Distributive justice involves the question of how benefits and burdens should be distributed—equally, by merit and demerit, or randomly according to chance—and each answer involves other questions. The answers can have an *a priori* character. Once they are settled, they might be applied without consideration of the consequences. Or they can be consequentialist, so that some consequences of the distribution of benefits and burdens determine the right distribution. The consequences may be different for different individuals, and there may be consequences that go beyond the individual, affecting others and society as a whole.

Take for example the consequences of egalitarian distributive justice. Here, every person should receive an equal share of the relatively scarce resources. Say we distribute equal shares of money so that everyone in society has enough money to get the basic necessities of life, like food, clothing, and shelter, with a degree of liberty to choose according to their preferences (what kind of food, shelter, and clothing they will buy). The equal distribution of money is designed to get every person in society what they need to survive, with a relative degree of freedom to choose according to their preferences in these basic necessities.

Now, say that some individuals who receive their equal share of the money are addicted to illegal drugs or other expensive habits, which are not part of their basic necessities. Say, also, that there is a high probability they will use the money for these bad habits instead of providing basic necessities for themselves and their families. We might then change the way we distribute the material goods so as to achieve that goal. We might give those persons actual rations of food, shelter, and clothing instead of money, because we want them to have the basic necessities of life they will probably not get, if we just give them money. Doing this, though, removes the element of relative freedom of choice among material goods. This means that not all people are treated equally in the distribution. Some get the material goods they need and freedom of choice among the goods they prefer, while others do not. Strictly speaking, the distribution is not equal in regard to freedom of choice according to preferences. Yet, this inequality is introduced in order to attain the intended consequence: that all equally receive what they need to survive.

Theorists of justice distinguish between *egalitarian* distributive justice, which is purely equal distribution without consideration of consequences, and *equalitarian* distributive justice, which does consider the consequences of distribution. Because equalitarian theories of justice are more consequentialist than egalitarian theories, they are subject to the pros and cons of all consequentialist ethical theories, discussed earlier.

One such criticism is that no matter how hard we try, the specific consequence aimed at might not be achieved. Achieving the intended consequence is never absolutely certain. In our example, those individuals inclined to spend their money on expensive habits, unrelated to survival, might find another way to do what they are inclined to do. They could sell their rations for cash and use the cash on their expensive habits. In that case, the intended consequence that every individual gets the basic necessities of life is not achieved.

Another criticism of consequentialism is that even when the intended consequences are achieved, there are often negative unintended consequences. It is practically impossible to know beforehand all consequences of a given action. Because of the complexities of economic systems and markets, the number of consequences exponentially increases. Economic policies are often implemented with specific goals in mind, but leaders implementing those policies would not implement them, if they knew all of the negative unintended consequences beforehand.

In order to attain the equalitarian goal, that everyone gets basic necessities, the government must be heavily involved in the markets, redistributing material resources. As we have seen, intervening in natural markets usually changes the natural equilibrium point of the intersection of the supply and demand curves. This introduces some degree of positive economic inefficiency. Economic laws dictate that price regulations, like minimum wage laws and rent ceilings, necessarily produce a supply shortage of the good or service. Although such regulations make goods and services available to some who would be unable to get them without the regulations, the shortage means that more people, overall, are unable to get the good or service. In this way, supply shortages can be the unintended consequences of otherwise well-intentioned economic policies.

"Fairness" and the Social Value of Justice

As is now evident, there are different understandings of the essence of justice. One common denominator, regardless of their specific differences, seems to be a concern for sameness of treatment of similar things in similar circumstances. Regardless of the specific understanding of justice, the common factor between them all seems to be a consistency in treatment. The specific treatment differs between different conceptions of justice, but the assumption remains that instances of a specific type of thing in the same situation *should* be treated similarly.

Regarding limit questions of being, this means the same types of beings in the same circumstances ought to be treated the same way. People disagree over what type of treatment we mean when we speak of justice, but they all seem to agree that similarity in treatment of similar things in similar circumstances is an obligation. The assumption, that "similar things ought to be treated similarly," seems to be at the heart of the idea of fairness underlying different specific conceptions of justice.

As discussed earlier, the question of whether a thing or being is of a specific *type* of being is an ontological question. It deals with the limit question of the classification of beings. Pine trees have different properties from maple trees, which have different properties from oak trees. Different pine trees have different properties—no two pine trees are exactly alike. What, then, makes all pine, maple, and oak trees of the type of beings we call "trees?" This is the question of the classification of the beings we call "tress" generally, and "pine trees" specifically.

This means that disagreements can arise over whether a given being is of the type of being that should be treated a certain way, even when there is agreement over the type of treatment that constitutes justice. Consider the right to vote in nineteenth-century America. All white American males had the right to vote, but females and African-Americans did not. Some argued that this was unjust while others argued that it was just. Both sides agreed on the type of treatment involved: extending the right to vote to a specific group. They agreed that there is a certain group of people in America with certain traits distinct from others who should be allowed to vote. The question was over classification. Should only Americans of a certain age who fall under the classification of "white male" be allowed to vote, or should all people in America of that age, women and African-Americans too, be allowed to vote? How one defined the class of Americans that *should* be given the right to vote (treated the same way) determined whether or not denying the right to vote to women and African-Americans was just/fair or unjust/unfair. To this day, there is a limitation on the class of Americans who can vote in the U. S. A., since there is a voting age. Most would not say it is unjust to forbid a ten year-old American the right to vote.

In summary, although the diverse theories of justice (as a social value), we have considered, have important differences, the common factor uniting them under what we call "justice" seems to be the uniformity and consistency of treatment that we call "fairness."

Procedural Theories of Justice

So far, in our survey of the complexities of distributive justice, we have seen how factors like merit or demerit, equality, and consequences are used to determine the just distribution of benefits and burdens. Another approach focuses exclusively on the procedure used to distribute benefits and burdens. The procedure itself, regardless of specific criteria for distribution and regardless of the consequences, can also dictate justice in distributing benefits and burdens.

Such views of justice are called *procedural theories of justice*. Procedural theories of justice came to the fore with the appearance of and interaction with John Rawls' famous 1971 work *A Theory of Justice*.[6] Rawls' discussion, distinctions, and terminology have largely determined contemporary discourse on procedural justice.

Rawls set out to formulate a theory of justice that adjudicates between the social values of freedom and equality while, at the same time promoting justice as fairness. He formulated and defended an alternative to both merit-based and equality-based theories of distributive justice. As discussed, merit-based theories stress the individual's freedom and ability to engage in market activities, while equality-based theories focus on inability and a determinism that lessens individual freedom in market activities. Also, Rawls includes among benefits to be distributed not only relatively scarce material resources, but also social benefits, rights, and duties in society.

Rawls believes that his pure procedural theory of justice is better than the alternatives. He believes this because every human being has an innate intuitive sense of justice, prior to free economic and political bargaining, and prior to consequentialist considerations of what would be the best outcome for society. This intuitive sense of justice means, for Rawls, that the procedure itself, not consideration of specific outcomes judged to be just or fair and aimed at in the distribution of resources, by itself determines what the fair or just outcome will be.

Because all of the limit questions addressed by philosophy and religion are interrelated, it is impossible to embark on a theory of justice as a social value without addressing, at least with implicitly if not explicitly assumed answers, a host of other limit questions. Thus, in forging his theory of justice, Rawls self-consciously avoids assumptions that ground justice in the natural order of things and / or religious considerations, like God-given rights. He works on the basis of the answers to several limit questions assumed in the secular modern world. These include the social contract theory societies, and the view that human beings in societies, not nature or God, forge their own values, including the social value of justice. Rawls also assumes neither a psychological egoist nor a psychological altruist view of human behavior. He assumes people are rational and self-interested but are willing and able to distribute benefits in society in cooperation with others for their own good and the greater good of society. With other social contract theorists, he believes societies exist because people see the opportunity cost of living, in society with its restrictions on freedom, as worth the trade-off for the greater benefits of a society.

Rawls describes three possible procedures for a group to distribute benefits and burdens—three types of procedural justice. He advocates what he calls *pure procedural justice*, which he illustrates by way of contrast with *perfect procedural justice* and *imperfect procedural justice.*

In *perfect procedural justice* (1) there is a criterion independent of the procedure itself for determining what a fair outcome will be, which can be known separately from and prior to using the actual procedure and (2) it is possible to devise a procedure that will certainly produce the desired outcome. He gives, as an example, the scenario of a group trying to divide a cake into equal pieces, which is considered the fair distribution. To guarantee the desired outcome we could devise the procedure in which one person divides the cake knowing he will get the last piece. This guarantees that he will divide the cake equally.[7]

In *imperfect procedural justice* (1) there is a criterion independent of the procedure itself for determining what a fair outcome will be, which can be known separately from and prior to using the actual procedure, but (2) there is no way of devising a procedure that makes the desired outcome certain. He gives, as an example, the procedure of criminal trials. The desired outcome is a guilty verdict and punishment if, and only if, the defendant really has committed the crime. The procedure includes the process of weighing evidence and trying to determine the truth of the defendant's guilt or innocence. The problem is that it is impossible to create a trial system that always leads certainly and infallibly to the correct verdict. Although the processes of a trial can be designed so as to, probably in most situations, produce the correct verdict of guilt or innocence, there will inevitably be times that a wrong verdict results. Sometimes, in fact, the innocent are judged guilty and those who are really guilty go free.[8]

Rawls contrasts pure procedural justice with perfect and imperfect procedural justice. *Pure procedural justice* differs from perfect and imperfect procedural justice in that (1) there is no criterion, independent of the procedure itself, for determining a fair outcome, separately from and prior to applying the procedure and (2) since only applying the procedure itself determines the fair or just outcome, whenever the procedure is applied, the fair outcome always, by definition and of necessity, results. He gives gambling, as an example. In a game of chance and according to the pre-established rules for bets, the distribution of the winnings at the end is necessarily fair, or just. Any player could win, and no matter who wins, the result is just, or fair. The procedure that the players agree upon beforehand guarantees that the outcome is fair, and only going through the procedure determines what the fair result is.

The distinguishing feature of Rawls' pure procedural justice is that the procedure must be carried out, because there is no independent criterion, apart from and prior to the procedure itself, that determines what the fair, or just, outcome is. It would be absurd for one player, prior to playing the game, to claim that his getting the winnings would be fair, by saying that *if* the procedure is carried out *then* he wins. Rather, the game must actually be played, the procedure actually applied, in order to manifest the fair and just outcome.[9]

Because only pure procedural justice satisfies our intuitive sense of justice prior to bargaining and prior to our judgments about what outcome would be just or fair, it is better than all other theories of distributive justice, including perfect and imperfect procedural justice. Insofar as it is separated from consequences or outcomes, Rawls' proposal is an *a priori*, deontological normative theory of ethics along the lines of Kant's. In fact, he draws heavily on Kant's deontological ethics and Kant's critiques of consequentialism.[10] Rawls takes issue with utilitarian theories of distributive justice, which consider specific outcomes and consequences. He believes that utilitarian assumptions have wrongly guided discussions of distributive justice in economics, with their assumptions of maximizing utility in the last two centuries.[11] The question, then, is what exact procedure results in pure procedural justice?

This brings us to the centerpiece and also the most controversial piece of Rawls' theory. In order to envision a procedure exhibiting pure procedural justice in the distribution of benefits of material benefits, social benefits, rights, and duties in society, he self-consciously proposes an explicitly hypothetical situation called the *original position*. This has affinities with the state of nature, prior to the formation of the social contract, in classical social contract theories, like Hobbes' and Locke's. With classical social theorists, Rawls is adamant that the original contract is hypothetical[12] but does not believe this invalidates the social contract model for understanding the nature, purpose, and structures of societies.

Here, he assumes that the rational, self-interested individuals, still inclined to a degree of social cooperation and thus forming the social contract, are aiming at what he calls a *well-ordered society*. A well-ordered society is one designed to advance the good of its members, to be regulated by a public conception of justice (shared by all individuals in the society), in which all accept, and know the others accept, the same principles of justice, and the basic social institutions do satisfy and are known to satisfy these principles.[13]

Because of the assumption of individual self-interest, there are problems with constructing such a well-ordered society, says Rawls. Individuals naturally choose principles favoring their own interests over those of others. To avoid the differences in principles of justice that would result from each individual and each sub-group seeking their own self-interest, Rawls deliberately constructs the hypothetical scenario of the original position. In this hypothetical original position, the individuals, coming together to form a well-ordered society, choose the principles of justice from behind what he calls a *veil of ignorance*. The veil of ignorance blinds all individuals to all facts, about themselves and their position in society, which would bias their conception of justice. He defines the veil of ignorance in the deliberately hypothetical original position in this way:

> Among the essential features of this situation is that no one knows his place in society, his class position or social status, nor does anyone know his fortune in the distribution of natural assets and abilities, his intelligence, strength and the like. I shall even assume that the parties do not know their conceptions of the good or their special psychological propensities. The principles of justice are chosen behind a veil of ignorance. This ensures that no one is advantaged or disadvantaged in the choice of principles by the outcome of natural chance or the contingency of social circumstances. Since all are similarly situated and no one is able to design principles to favor his particular condition, the principles of justice are the result of a fair agreement or bargain. For given the circumstances of the original position, the symmetry of everyone's relations to each other, this initial situation is fair between individuals as moral persons, that is, as rational beings with their own ends and capable, I shall assume, of a sense of justice. The original position is, one might say, the appropriate initial status quo, and thus the fundamental agreements reached in it are fair. . . . One excludes the knowledge of those contingencies which sets men at odds and allows them to be guided by their prejudices.[14]

The original position and veil of ignorance aim at a hypothetical situation where every person is equal with every other. Rawls says the original situation with its vale of ignorance expresses the idea that the principles of justice are agreed upon on the basis of an initial situation that is fair.

For example, if a person knew that her position in society would involve her being rich, then she might conclude it reasonable that taxation for income redistribution like welfare programs would be unjust, whereas a person who knew he would be poor would probably see taxation and income redistribution as just.[15] The veil of ignorance extends even to ignorance of the psychological factors of each person's psyche. Individuals would not even know if they were risk-averse or risk-loving.[16] The veil of ignorance extends to ignorance of the period in the history of one's society in which the individual lives, its current economic or political situation, and the level of civilization and culture the society has achieved.[17] The goal is a vision of absolute equality, and principles of justice resulting from the original position and veil of ignorance are justified because all individuals would agree upon them in this initial situation of equality.[18] In order to guarantee compliance with the principles of justice agreed upon in the original position, Rawls also assumes the contractors are moral and have an innate sense of justice, such that they can trust each other to understand and act according to whatever principles are finally agreed upon.[19] Rawls argues that because the total equality of the original position bars any outside influence on the formation of the principles of justice, an instance of pure procedural justice results.[20]

The veil of ignorance means that the principles of justice are being forged under a situation of uncertainty. No one knows whether they will be in the best possible position in society or the worst possible position. Drawing on economic theories of the rules of choice under conditions of uncertainty, Rawls believes that those in the original position would use a *maximin rule* for choosing and agreeing on the principles of justice. The *maximin rule* tells those in a position of uncertainty to rank alternatives according to the worst possible outcome for each alternative, and then to choose the alternative in which the worst possible outcome for that alternative is better than the worst possible outcome for all other alternatives.[21]

Because those in the original position do not know if they will be in a good or bad situation in society, they all agree on the alternative in which the worst possible outcome, for those in the worst position in society, is better than all of the other worst possible outcomes, for those in the worst position in society, in the other alternatives. Since they might find themselves in the worst position in society, the individuals will choose the alternative where the worst possible outcome is better for the worst in society, rather than the worst possible outcome for the worst in society in other alternatives. That is, they will choose principles that insure the best situation for the least well off in society, because they might find themselves in that situation.

What principles of justice would those in the original position choose according to this maximin rule? Rawls argues that they would choose two principles for determining how to assign rights and duties, and how to distribute economic and social advantages. These two principles are special cases, of a more general idea, of justice that all agree on. This general idea of justice is that all social values should be distributed equally unless an unequal distribution benefits everyone:

> All social values—liberty and opportunity, income and wealth, and the bases of self-respect—are to be distributed equally unless an unequal distribution of any, or all, of these values is to everyone's advantage.[22]

The first principle of justice, which Rawls believes they would agree on, is the *liberty principle*. The liberty principle is, that everyone has an equal right to the most extensive basic liberties that everyone else has. These basic liberties include the *rights* to vote, to be eligible for public office, and to private property, as well as to *freedom* of speech, of assembly, of conscience, and of thought, and freedom to have private property, from arbitrary arrest, and from seizure of private property.[23]

In a later revised edition responding to critics,[24] he admits that these basic liberties will sometimes conflict, and so some of them must be limited to produce the best possible system of rights that applies equally to all. Because each basic right can be limited, due to conflicts with other rights, none of them is absolute.[25] He also specifies that some freedoms, like the right to own the means of production and freedom of contract, are not basic, and are therefore not covered by the first principle of justice, the liberty principle.[26]

The second principle of justice that Rawls believes those in the original condition and acting according to the maximin rule would agree on, is that social and economic inequalities should be arranged so that they are (a) reasonably expected to be to everyone's advantage, and (b) attached to positions and offices that are open to all.[27]

The first part of this second principle, which Rawls calls the *difference principle*, means that social and economic inequalities are justified only if they improve the lot of the worst off in society. Distribution of wealth and income do not have to be equal so long as the distribution is to the advantage of everyone, including the least well off. Conversely, this also means that, for Rawls, the basic right of every person in society is an equal share in material wealth. One's natural talents, family of origin, and social position into which she is born cannot affect her basic right to have an equal share in social benefits and material wealth. This corresponds to the social value of equality of condition, which we discussed earlier. Rather, inequalities in social benefits and material wealth are only justified when such inequalities will benefit everyone more so than maintaining absolute equality in social benefits and material wealth.[28]

Even though the difference principle specifies that inequalities may be justifiable in some cases, there can never be inequalities in the basic liberties articulated in the first principle. This means that the first principle of justice, the liberty principle, takes precedence over the first part of the second principle of justice, the difference principle. Rawls notes, for instance, the criticism of utilitarianism that it must allow for the slavery of human beings in some cases, and hence the denial of some of their basic freedoms. This is because economic systems with slavery can result in the greatest net happiness for the greatest number of persons, including the slaves, through exponentially increased productivity, even though the opportunity cost is the impingement upon the basic liberties of the slaves.[29]

The second part of this second principle of justice, which Rawls calls *fair equality of opportunity*, means everyone, regardless of their natural skills, family of origin, or social position into which they were born, should have the same opportunities in society. Rawls' fair equality of opportunity is essentially the same as the social value of equality of opportunity.

These are the rudiments of Rawls' theory of justice. As noted, his theory of justice has been the centerpiece of much discussion concerning the intersection of economics and social values for the last forty years. Some concur with much of what Rawls says, but others disagree on various points. This leads to a summary analysis of the pros and cons of Rawls' theory of justice.

Immediately commending Rawls' theory is that it is one of the most robust attempts at reconciling the social values of liberty and equality in a way that is deemed just, or fair. We have seen that social values can conflict, so that one must be sacrificed at the expense of the other.

The first principle of justice, the liberty principle, aims at promoting the social value of freedom, highly valued in modern social contact theories of societies and in modern liberal democracies. That everyone has an equal share in social benefits and material wealth, regardless of inborn talents, family of origin, and social position into which they are born, strongly promotes the social value of equality of condition. By excluding any inequality in social benefits or material condition that does not benefit everyone, the first part of Rawls' second principle, the difference principle, promotes the social value of equality of condition.

The second part of Rawls' second principle, fair equality of opportunity, promotes the social value of equality of opportunity. Thus, the pros and cons of equality of opportunity, discussed earlier, also apply to it. Again, equality of opportunity addresses the problem arising from a strong view of metaphysical determinism, in which prior factors like inborn natural abilities and the social position into which one is born, can hinder freedom. Promoting equality of opportunity tries to give everyone a "level playing field" or the "same starting position," so that no one suffers negative effects due to prior causes for which they are not personally responsible.

Another benefit of Rawls' theory is the pure procedural justice. In pure procedural justice, nothing apart from or prior to the procedure itself determines the fair, or just, outcome. Social contract theory allows Rawls to effectively say that all the individuals coming together in the social contract agree on a just or fair procedure, which means that the outcome of the procedure is *ipso facto* just, or fair. By avoiding the contingencies and uncertainties of consequentialist ethical theories, Rawls' theory shares the strengths of deontological normative theories of ethics, epitomized in the moral philosophy of Kant, from whom Rawls draws also heavily.

At the same time, Rawls' theory of justice is criticized on a various points. Perhaps the most famous libertarian response is that of Robert Nozick.[30] Nozick argues that the social values of liberty and equality are ultimately incompatible, but because it is, in his view, the higher social value, we must opt for liberty. He urges the essential incompatibility between liberty and equality of condition, by arguing that any imposed pattern of equal distribution interferes with individuals' freedom to redistribute wealth based on their needs, wants, and preferences.

Identifying what he sees as a key problem with Rawls' theory, Nozick says that Rawls assumes that the static system of equality of condition determined by all in the beginning (in the original position and behind the veil of ignorance) cannot change. Those in the hypothetical original position may choose Rawls' principles initially but, in the "real time" historical movement of society, people are aware of what they do not know behind the original position's veil of ignorance. They will therefore make different choices, including redistributing wealth and social benefits. In order to maintain the original principles of justice, the government must continually interfere with the many free choices of individuals as they exercise their liberty to redistribute wealth and social benefits, based on what they do really know in the historical movement of society. To maintain the original principles of justice, the government must continually override the freedom of real individuals in the real society.

From the other side, egalitarians, who value equality of condition over liberty, also criticize Rawls. Focusing on the distribution and number of primary social and economic goods that Rawls uses in his understanding of equality of condition, egalitarian critics say that the problem of equality of condition is not limited to equally distributing primary social and economic goods. There is the further problem of how well people can use those goods, once distributed, to achieve the ends for which they were intended. This criticism recalls the distinction between *egalitarian* distributive justice and *equalitarian* distributive justice. Rawls stops with egalitarian distributive justice—everyone receives an equal share. He does not, however, consider the possibility that an original equal distribution of goods can result in different outcomes, based on differences between individuals, so that the goals of social and material equality are not achieved. Regarding the number of primary goods to be distributed equally, in our contemporary climate there is much debate over healthcare. Some criticize Rawls for not including healthcare among the primary goods to be equally distributed.

A prime target for egalitarians, valuing the social value of equality over individual liberties, is the first part of Rawls' second principle, the difference principle. Egalitarians question whether inequalities in social and economic benefits are ever justified at all. Some, who come from socialist or communist perspectives, claim that Rawls' theory is a highly qualified and nuanced defense of liberal democracy and capitalism.[31] They argue that a closer examination, of the two principles that Rawls says people would chose in the original position and behind a veil of justice, reveals the prioritization of liberty over equality of condition, with all of its attendant inequalities, which egalitarians judge to be unjust. The basic liberties everyone should have, according to the first principle of justice, are the liberties cherished by modern liberal democracy with relatively free market economies. They also say that the first part of Rawls' second principle justifies the inequalities of condition legitimated in modern liberal democracies and free market economies. They say Rawls' difference principle merely repeats the capitalist mantra, that inequalities of social and material condition are justified because they maximize production and efficiency, making everyone, including the poorest, better off. This, they say, leads down the slippery slope to the gross inequalities and mass exploitations of capitalism.

That both strong advocates of liberty as a social value, and strong advocates of equality as a social value, criticize Rawls' attempt at their rapprochement, indicate the difficulties of such a reconciliation of liberty and equality, no matter how nuanced and circumspect the attempt.

Similar to the Marxist[32] critique, that Rawls devises his system so as to yield modern liberal democratic and capitalist principles of justice, are those who from other quarters attack the hypothetical original position as artificially fabricated to arrive at the two principles of justice that Rawls arrives at. Some add that Rawls uses the maximin rule precisely with this goal in mind. Others, like Rawls' student Amartya Sen,[33] argue that the two principles, which Rawls derives, need not necessarily result from the original position and that other principles could result.

Other critics claim that the purely procedural derivation of justice, by a group of contracting parties and apart from ontological connections to the real world objectively, makes justice relative. Feminist critics question whether Rawls is justified in assuming that individuals in the original position would not know their sex, and if not, then whether it is possible to avoid all individual biases. They also tie this to, and focus on, the hierarchical and patriarchal structure of the family unit and household as the fundamental societal unit.

In conclusion, Rawls is one of the most important interlocutors in contemporary dialogue at the point of intersection of economics, political philosophy, and social values. Discourse in this area over the past forty years has had to interact with his theory. Rawls' theory has much to commend it, but it is liable to criticisms on a number of points and from different fronts.

ISSUES IN MACROECONOMICS

Having surveyed macroeconomics and political philosophy in chapter three, and having examined social values in this chapter, we now consider some issues in macroeconomics.

Issues in Macroeconomics: Income Per Capita and Family Assistance

As we said in discussing macroeconomics, long-run economic growth is important since it increases the standard of living of all people, whether it is distributed evenly or not. Below we see how the income per capita of the U. S. A. has grown (all of the figures are in year 2005 dollars).

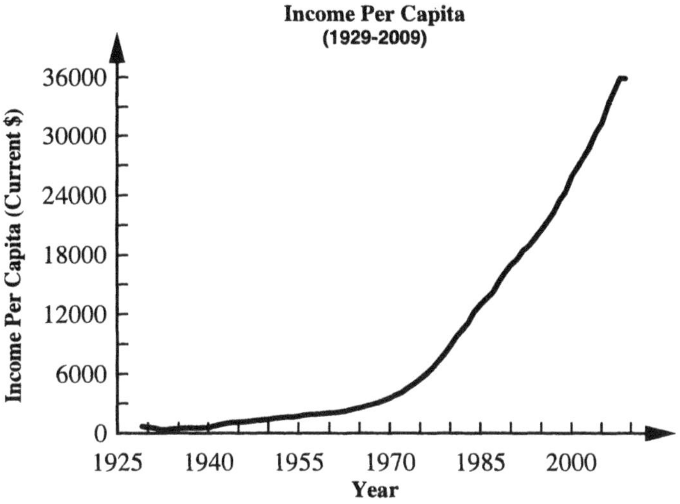

Figure 4.1: Income Per Capita[34]

We see that in the last eighty years the standard of living has increased by eight times what it was in 1929. To an economist, this has important implications, because economists have discovered that countries with higher income per capita tend to have better mortality rates, less disease, and better overall quality of life among the population.

Of course, as a nation's income grows it can also afford to do more things, like provide government financial assistance for some of the population. Below is a graph of the U. S. A.'s government assistance in billions of dollars per year.

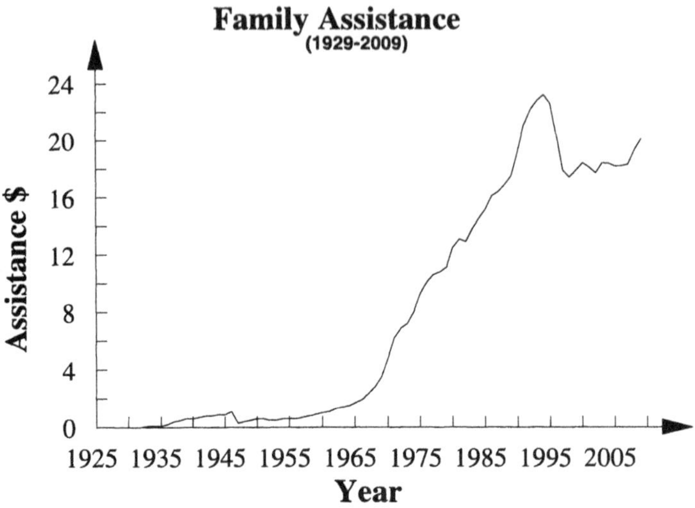

Figure 4.2: Family Assistance[35]

Amount of assistance has increased dramatically since 1965. Also, as we said in chapter three, the poverty rate has fallen. Yet, this increase in government assistance has by no means eliminated poverty, and there is no evidence that spending more would eliminate poverty. Indeed, it probably never would eliminate poverty, due to the increasing marginal cost. We often say in economics, "Pick the low-hanging fruit." What we mean by this is, that since the low-hanging fruit is near the ground, it is very easy to access and hence the cheapest to pick as well. However, once we have removed the low-hanging fruit and want to pick more, we must continually reach higher and higher. We may even have to get a ladder, further increasing our cost to pick the fruit. Eventually the benefit we gain from picking the fruit is outweighed by the cost of doing so, and so it is more beneficial for us to stop. Such is the case with many social issues as well. Indeed, such a point must exist for any policy or program.

We might be tempted to say that income per capita results in increased government assistance, based on the data presented in the following graph.

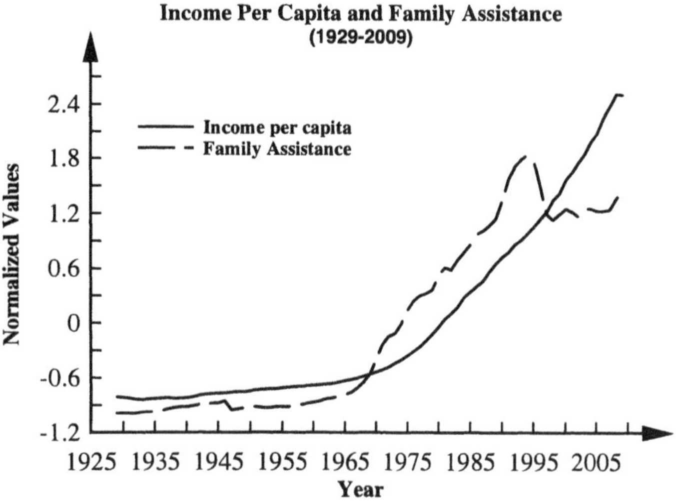

Figure 4.3: Normalized Comparison of Income Per Capita and Family Assistance[36]

From this we might conclude that increased income per capita, or Gross Domestic Product (GDP), results in more government assistance, since the nation's income has grown and it can "afford" to do more. But why should this be? Indeed, if we think about it, the opposite should be true, as income per capita rises we should, in general, see a need for assistance fall (at least during economic expansions, anyway, since unemployment would be falling).[37] So what we see is a picture of continually increasing amounts of aid, while economic theory suggests aid should vary in proportion to other variables, such as the unemployment rate. During economic expansions we would at least expect the amount of family assistance to fall. Although this is a complex problem, and we do not posit that this is the complete solution, it is clear that a strong relationship exists between government assistance and the previous year's level of assistance. In other words, it is more likely that government assistance given in the prior year is somehow causally related to the increase in assistance the next year.

For economists it is difficult to formulate general conclusions on this topic, in this case we are not doing enough analysis to prove or disprove anything. We merely make the points here, however, that since economic systems are very complex it is difficult to arrive at definite answers, and that it can be very easy to draw the wrong conclusions from economic data. Indeed, many economists disagree as to the best way to appropriately model this data in a positive economic sense. This is but one of many examples of how non-economists can misunderstand cause and effect in economic systems, by imposing normative opinions on the data. While all sciences seek to identify cause and effect relationships, acting on wrongly-derived causal relationships can be problematic, even disastrous.

This relatively simple example shows why, in economic discussions, we must not confuse positive economic data with normative economic opinions. We must be careful to not draw hasty conclusions about causes and effects from what may appear to be correlations in complex economic systems. We need to use both economic theory and data in tandem with one another. In normative economics, attaining the goal valued as good or right, regardless of the normative ethical system used and regardless of which social value is prioritized, depends on employing the appropriate means to that end goal. Mistaken conclusions, about cause and effect relationships, result in using the wrong means to attain the end value pursued.

Issues in Macroeconomics: Inflation and Gross Domestic Product:

We have seen how there is a trade-off between governmental action and other economic variables. One such trade-off involves the interaction between government spending, tax reduction, and inflation. We saw, when considering the macroeconomic equilibrium of the national aggregate supply (AS) and national aggregate demand (AD) curves, that if the AD curve shifts out (aggregate demand increases) then the price level will rise:

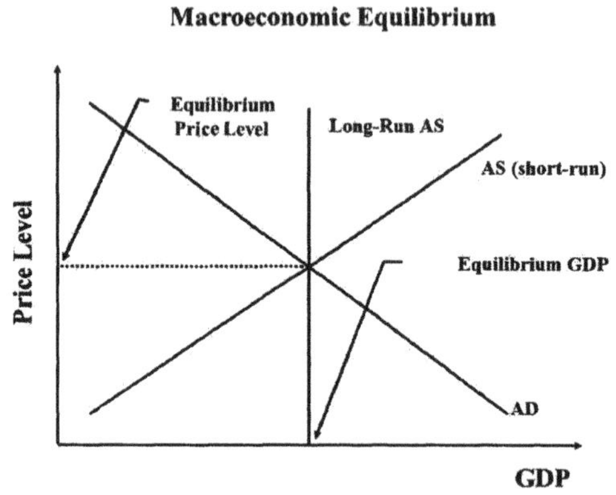

Figure 4.4: Long-Run Macroeconomic Equilibrium

The graph below charts the consumer price index (CPI), which is the average of the prices of goods and services purchased by the typical urban family of four. The CPI uses a "basket of goods and services" that a typical family of four would buy in a year. This, of course, is not true of every family, so it is a far from perfect measure of inflation. It is impossible to include every family's expenses, so the "basket of goods and services" is adopted as a common measurement. Inflation is measured by the percentage of change in the CPI from one year to the next.

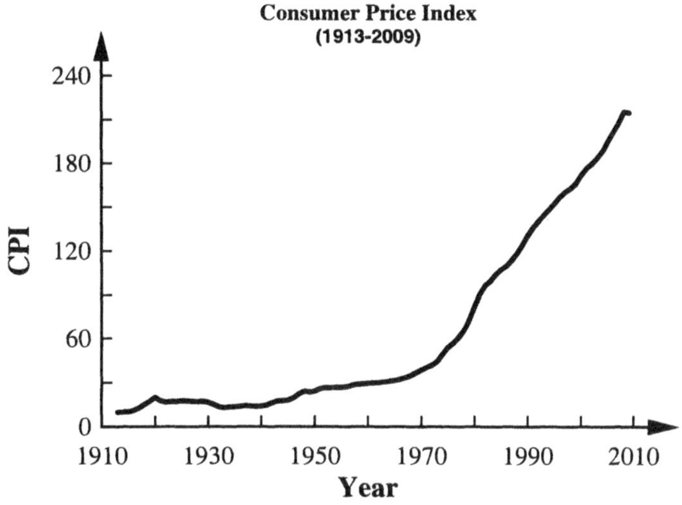

Figure 4.5: Consumer Price Index — Annual Average[38]

Notice the dramatic change in the index since 1970. While it is difficult to prove direct causality, it is clear that there is a correlation of increased inflation with increased levels of income and assistance. Whatever the cause it is clear that something drastic happened, for which there are different possible explanations.

If we think about macroeconomic theory, this result may be from government policy designed to increase aggregate demand. Such policies have the opportunity cost of inflation, as the macroeconomic model described in chapter three suggests. Recall that in the recession example of chapter three, government intervention can affect the aggregate demand curve through government spending (G), or through a stimulus to increase consumption (C). This has the short-run effect of increasing a GDP that has lessened. In the long-run, however, it is possible that long-run aggregate supply may not increase as quickly. When there are more dollars in the system but supply does not concomitantly increase, the value of the dollar decreases, which is inflation.

Sometimes, we might judge the trade-off of a short-run increase in GDP to be worth the opportunity cost of inflation. Some might say that during the Great Depression, when the inflation rate went from a negative percentage to zero, such inflation was a reasonable opportunity cost. Yet, when inflation is already positive, we might care more about the opportunity cost of more inflation. The figure below shows the inflation rate from 1914 to 2009.

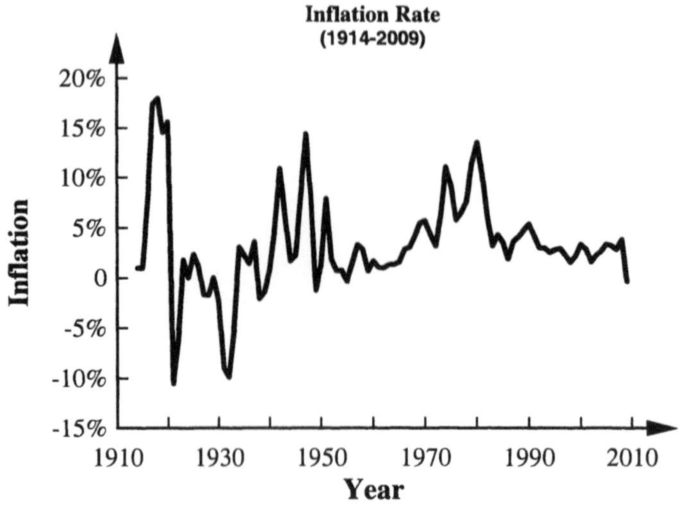

Figure 4.6: Inflation Rate[39]

We might also ask what individuals are, or should be, concerned about. In general, most economists think that individuals should be concerned with purchasing power. If the price of everything in the economy doubled overnight, but one's income also doubled, they would not care about the price increase. They could still afford the same amount of goods and services as before the increase. This shows an important link between economic growth and inflation: If we modify the economy, then, GDP must grow faster than the inflation we have caused, otherwise everyone is worse off.

Below, we can see that, for the most part, since 1930 the change in GDP has been larger than the increase in inflation. Notice, however, that in our last recession, inflation has increased slightly more than the increase in GDP.

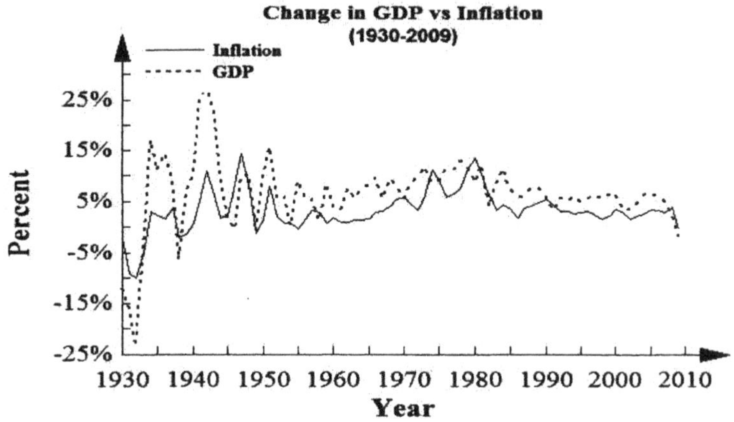

Figure 4.7: GDP and Inflation Over Time[40]

Government policies may be introduced in order to promote a social value, like a type of justice or equality, but we must realize the trade-offs. The opportunity cost of promoting a social value, through government action, might mean an increase in inflation more than an increase in GDP. This, in turn, means less purchasing power for everyone. Also, as said above, some equate the social value of liberty with purchasing power. A consequentialist theory must incorporate both of these considerations. A utilitarian calculus, of the greatest happiness for the greatest number of people, must include both the social value being promoted by the government action, and the potential decrease in purchasing power, which might also be detrimental to the social value of liberty.

A deontological or rule-based normative ethical theory, like divine command theory, Kantian ethics, or a theory of rights, might hold that consequences do not matter and so the social value being promoted takes priority. It might also urge that the correlation between government policy and inflation does not imply causation. It might also argue that we cannot be certain of all of the consequences of a given governmental policy, and so the *a priori* rule must be applied or the supposed rights honored. It might say that GDP could very well increase faster than inflation and such contingencies, as GDP not keeping pace with inflation, cannot preclude the application of the rule.

Issues in Macroeconomics: Government Regulation of Markets

Some believe that market regulation helps a society, while others believe it hurts society. These opposite judgments flow from different answers to a host of limit questions dealing with societies and values. Government regulations are implemented for a number of values-related reasons, like promoting the social value of equality of condition or a certain distribution of benefits and burdens, based on a specific theory of distributive justice. Sometimes they are implemented on the view that certain material benefits like food, adequate living conditions, gainful employment, healthcare, and education are inherent human rights.

In the allocation of scarce resources, there are always trade-offs to consider. Economically, many would agree, though, that an increase in GDP is good for the nation's economy. See below for the percentage of change in regulation spending and the percentage change in GDP, plotted together.

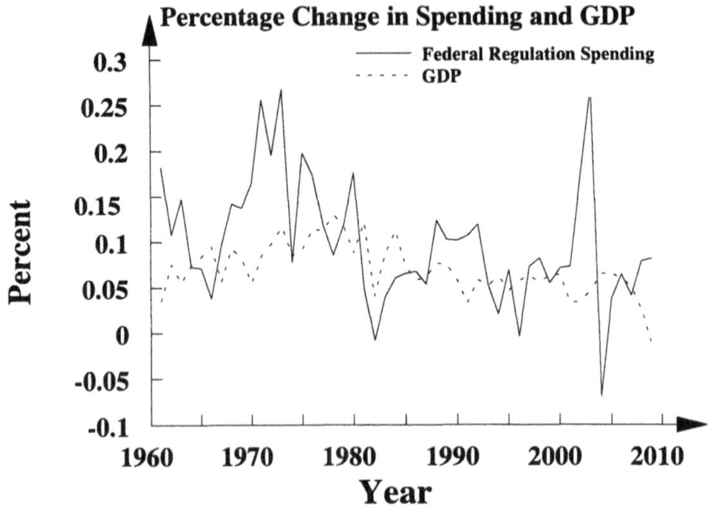

Figure 4.8: Spending and GDP Over Time[41]

This graph reveals no apparent relationship between GDP and the amount of government regulations. Hence, we have the problem of no apparent empirical answer to the question of the relationship between GDP and government regulation. This is the where economic theory becomes important. Economists need to use both economic theory and economic data, together, to model and answer different questions, such as this one.

Here is one possible answer, derived from an application of economic theory to the data. Although we might use some other formulation, we can construe the relationship this way: regulations cost firms money to comply. This increases input costs in the supply curve. Increased input costs shift the supply curve left, or in. If demand remains the same, a higher equilibrium price and a lower equilibrium quantity result. If prices are higher and quantity is lower, then GDP decreases. This reasoning, based on economic theory, leads many to say that regulations can cause lower GDP.

Others suggest that a regulation may lower uncertainty, causing consumers to change their preferences, and so cause the demand curve to shift right, or out.

The demand curve shifting out at the same time that the supply curve shifts in causes the equilibrium price to increase, and the equilibrium quantity to be uncertain. Equilibrium quantity will depend on which curve shifts more. If the equilibrium quantity does increase, then GDP increases as well. Notice, in both cases, the same economic theory is used, but with different assumptions. One answer assumes that regulations will increase in supply costs, shifting the supply curve in. The other answer assumes that regulations lower consumer uncertainty, shifting the demand curve out. It is essential to realize the importance of correct assumptions in predicting the effect of government regulations on GDP.

Again, government regulations are often implemented with certain ethical values in mind. Another consideration is the ethical import of higher or lower GDP. Previously, we saw the causal relationship between GDP and income per capita. If income per capita is higher than inflation, then individuals have more spending power. Any consequentialist normative ethical theory must consider the increased income per capita as a result of any policy increasing GDP, and, conversely, the decreased income per capita of any policy, decreasing GDP.

Also, if more spending power means more freedom, then we must consider that increased GDP promotes the social value of freedom, but decreased GDP is detrimental to this social value. Further, we noted above, on income per capita and government assistance, that higher income per capita is correlated with a higher standard of living and an overall better quality of living for all in society. If higher GDP means higher income per capita, and higher income per capita means a better life for all members of society, then this consequence must be factored into a consequentialist analysis of any proposed government policy.

If it is true that government policies do increase GDP by increasing consumer confidence and thus shift the demand curve out, increased prices are another consideration. This is inflation, and inflation decreases purchasing power even if there is a higher income per capita. This could offset the effects of increased income per capita on spending power and freedom.

Another consideration is that, although we do not see a causal connection between GDP and government regulation, we saw, in the previous chapter, how government spending almost always causes deadweight loss. So, if regulations are not increasing GDP, then they can only be causing loss to society as a whole. Some might say, then, that we should only enact a regulation if it increases GDP beyond the deadweight loss that it causes.

Any consequentialist normative ethical theory used to judge the morality of a government policy must consider all of these definite and potential consequences. There are many real and potential consequences to consider, some of which are uncertain, depending on the assumptions used. The economic theory, itself, is the same and grounded in natural systems. The same theory leads us to conclude that a government policy will shift the supply curve in or out, depending on the assumptions. The same theory also tells us that government policy will definitely result in increased prices, but also result in increased or decreased output quantity, and thus increased or decreased GDP, depending on the assumptions used.

A strictly *a priori* rule-based theory of ethics would not consider the consequences of the government policy. Kantian deontological ethics and divine command theory would say that the right thing must be done, regardless of the consequences. Many normative ethical theories that stress *a priori* rules and/or rights still consider at least some consequences of an action, like the honoring of rights, and are thus consequentialist. They, too, would consider, at least to some degree, the consequences for GDP of implementing a government policy.

Issues in Macroeconomics: GDP and Unemployment

Another macroeconomic relationship to consider is the one between GDP and unemployment. Below is a graph of the change in GDP and the unemployment rate. Economic theory suggests that lower unemployment should lead to a higher GDP. In this case, the data validates what the theory predicts: GDP does go up as unemployment decreases.

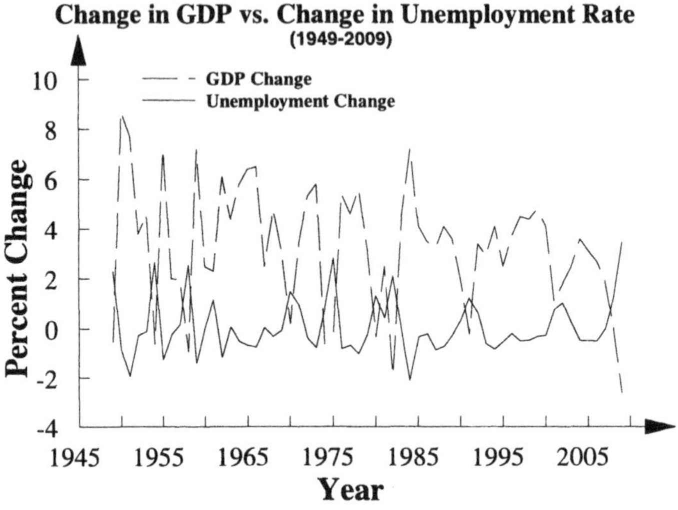

Figure 4.9: GDP and Unemployment Rate Over Time[42]

What is debatable is whether the government should do something to lower unemployment and if so, then, how the government should do it. There are trade-offs and opportunity costs, and one's values and normative ethical theory will determine the trade-offs that one is willing to make.

A Keynesian macroeconomic solution would be for the government to increase spending, through governmentally-funded projects or stimulus packages, to create jobs now. This decreases the unemployment rate in the short-run. A capital-based macroeconomist would say that government spending crowds out private investment, by raising the interest rate. This means that there may be a temporary boost today, in employment, but the economy will not grow as fast in the future. The result is a lower, but not as drastically low, unemployment in the future, in the long-run. A capital-based approach would advocate not increasing government spending but rather inducing more savings, which leads to more investment. Eventually, the employment rate will return to higher levels as a natural result of market mechanisms. In an analysis of our most recent stimulus package, Harald Uhlig argues ". . . that short-run fiscal multipliers may be dramatically misleading." He finds that while the initial effect of government spending stimulates output, over a longer period of time, the trend of GDP is different. In a long-run horizon, $3.40 of GDP is lost for every dollar of increased government spending.[43] All agree that, considered in isolation, a lower unemployment rate is better than a higher unemployment rate. The problem is that unemployment cannot be considered in isolation from other factors. There are always trade-offs in policy actions. There is a necessary value to the economy of having some unemployment, but the trade-off regards when and how much. Again, the theory is identical, but different values dictate whether short-run or long-run employment rates are more important, in conjunction with the other benefits of economic growth. In terms of distributive justice, should the burden of unemployment be borne by more people, now, or fewer people, now, but by more people, on average, in the long-term?

Issues in Macroeconomics: Income Inequality

A macroeconomic issue commonly discussed, by specialists and non-specialists alike, is income inequality. Most economic measures of income inequality and poverty are difficult, because there are numerous factors to consider. Economists measure income by quintiles, or fifths. This is an ordering of every individual in the population according to their income, and then dividing the entire group into five groups. Once all individuals are lined up by income, economists consider the cumulative sum of the distribution. This is perhaps best seen by example. Assume we have only five people in an economy so that the population is easily divisible into fifths.

Table 4.1: Example of Incomes by Quintile

Person	Quintile	Income	Cumulative Income	Cumulative percent of Population	Cumulative percent of Income
Jim	1	$ 20,000	$ 20,000	20%	10%
Jane	2	$ 30,000	$ 50,000	40%	25%
Joe	3	$ 40,000	$ 90,000	60%	45%

Jack	4	$ 50,000	$ 140,000	80%	70%
Jerry	5	$ 60,000	$ 200,000	100%	100%
Total		$ 200,000			

This table lists the five individuals in the economy from lowest to highest income. The "income" column lists each person's income, and the total of the individual incomes is $200,000. The "cumulative income" column displays the cumulative total of each person's income, starting with the lowest income at the top and adding each higher income successively and in order. Jim's income + Jane's income is $50,000, listed in Jane's row. The "cumulative percent population" column indicates which percentage of the total population the cumulative income constitutes. Jim and Jane constitute two out of five people in the population, or forty percent of the total population. The "cumulative percent of income" column indicates the cumulative percent of the total income. Jim and Jane's cumulative income of $50,000 is twenty-five percent of the total income of $200,000.

The cumulative distributions of the percent of the population and percent of income are used to generate the *Lorenz Curve*, graphed below. The two axes go from zero to one, or zero percent to one hundred percent, because they chart percentages.

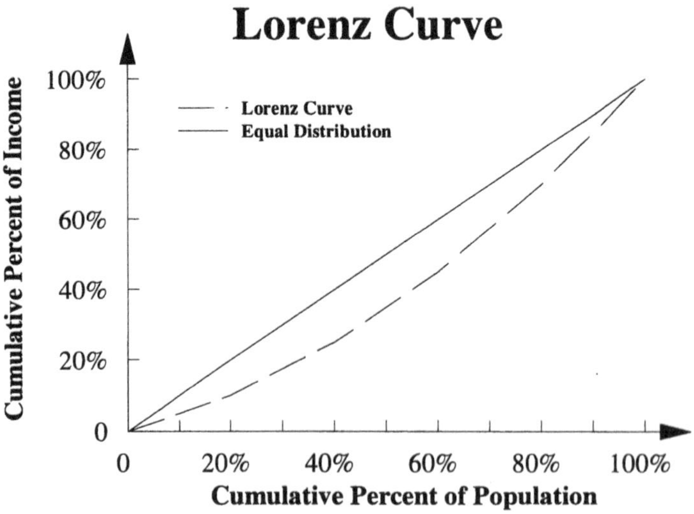

Figure 4.10: Lorenz Curve

The Lorenz Curve plots the last two columns of data from the table, "cumulative percent of the population" on the x-axis and "cumulative percent of income" on the y-axis. The Lorenz Curve is the dashed line, and the solid line is called the *equal distribution line*. The equal distribution line is only for reference and shows the case of everyone in the population having an equal income.

Economists do not use the equal distribution line as a policy goal, but as a reference point. One might assume that the equal distribution line should be the value or goal pursued in a normative economic policy. However, economists are dealing with and charting only the facts. How one defines good and bad outcomes, that is, the precise goal being sought, dictates whether absolutely equal income distribution is a good or bad thing.

How one answers limit questions about values, the normative ethical system one uses, and the social values one prioritizes may very well set equal income as the right goal. Prioritizing the social value of equality of condition or seeing distributive justice as the absolutely equal distribution of burdens and benefits, in a society, could lead one to judge equality of income distribution to be the best or right situation. The laws of economics dictate that the diminishment of other social values, such as freedom or liberty, is the necessary opportunity cost for attaining such a goal. Some, but not all, might be willing to make this trade-off.

Thus, equality of income distribution, as a good and a value to be sought, does not necessarily follow from everyone's answers to the limit questions about ethics and social values. Others, who value the social value of liberty, equality of opportunity, or distributive justice, according to merit and demerit, might judge equality of income distribution to be bad and negative. What these various social values can mean, how they come into conflict with one another, and the pros and cons for emphasizing each one over the others, were discussed previously. Hence, claiming that an equal distribution is a good or right outcome depends on answers to many questions. Economists, from a wide spectrum of policy assumptions, agree that absolute equality of income is not good for an economy. It is important to avoid the mistake of assuming that equal income distribution is automatically and necessarily the best situation.

In order to quantify the change in the Lorenz Curve's shape at different times and to compare the income inequalities of different countries, economists look at the ratio of the areas under the equal distribution line, called the *Gini coefficient*. The areas to calculate it are depicted below.

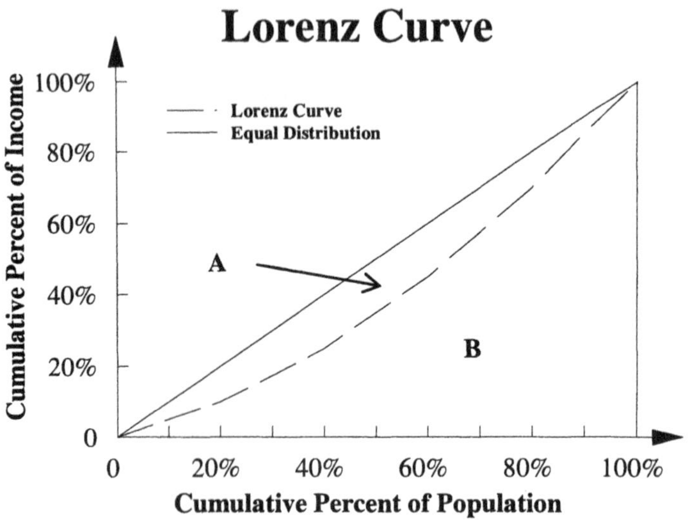

Figure 4.11: Parts of Lorenz Curve

The Gini coefficient is just the ratio of the area A to the area of A + B, or gini = A/(A+B). In this graph, of our simple example, the Gini coefficient is .208.

Some interesting research has been done on both people's perceptions of, and the realities of, equity and fairness in distribution. Prioritizing a form of equality of condition, some prescribe a greater degree of, or absolute equality of, income equality as good and desirable. However, mathematically it has been proven that the only way to attain equal income distribution is a competitive market.[44] This is because if equal distribution is imposed by an external agent, like the government, and individuals subsequently trade, then the distribution is unequal again. Therefore, it would require constant external intervention to keep it equal.

Why would the income distribution change after income equality was imposed? It would change because individuals wanted something, and so they traded. Recall how those, who prioritize liberty as a social value, argue that, no matter what they say, people really value their freedom. Freedom to exchange for mutual benefits, which is the essence of any natural economic market, is an example of this. However, diminished equality of condition is the opportunity cost for such freedom to engage in exchange. It is an economic fact that equal income distribution usually implies the corollary that freedom of choice is lost, and vice versa. There is no simple and easy answer to equity, either from a positive economic or normative ethics standpoint.

The debate over free markets vs. command and control economies is, in part, fueled by beliefs about the degree to which equality of condition should be valued. We will visit this debate in more detail in chapter five. To be clear, no economy is truly a free market, as all current governments engaged in some form of command and control. This is why economists call modern economies, including the current economy of the U. S. A., *modern mixed economies*. Economists have found that markets with a more free-market structure are more efficient, in terms of positive economic efficiency, and excluding issues of public goods and externalities, which will shortly be discussed. Yet, there are still many individuals who argue that a command and control system is preferable. Usually, their claim is based on highly valuing equality of condition and on the vision that some arbiter could distribute goods in what is judged to be a more equitable fashion. Economists and philosophers have done much research on this topic. Nozick[45] and Varian[46] offer examples of the problems with equity in distribution.

The first problem is the identification of what "fairness" means, precisely. We have seen that there are multiple definitions of equity, justice, and fairness. Bart Wilson[47] has investigated the term "fairness" from an economic standpoint, as well as incorporated research from the semantic primitives of the word. Many intuitively think of fairness as equal division, which is one understanding we have visited, but this is not the root of the word. Historically, the word "fairness" stems for someone being honest or reputable. As an example, someone who has lied has been unfair.

However, most people today use the word "fair" as some type of proxy for equity. The problem is that such a use of "fairness" in economics leads to declinational problems, because fairness to one may not be perceived as fairness to another. Different individuals' visions of fairness are akin to different ideas of "monsters." If we ask two people to picture a monster, their mental ideas may have some similar qualities, but once depicted visually, each individual's vision is portrayed two very different results are seen.

Bart Wilson has witnessed this in his research,[48] via what economists call an *ultimatum game*. The game works as follows: Two individuals play the game with each other. One individual makes an offer and the other can either accept or reject the offer. If the second individual accepts the offer, they both keep their share. If the second individual rejects the offer, then they both get nothing.

Assume the first person has a choice about how to allocate $10, divisible in $1 units. An economist working on positive economic principles would say that the if the proposer offers the second person only $1, then the second person should accept that amount, because they both started the experiment with no money and $1 > $0. Yet, the modal response that Wilson has found is $5 to both. The most common response for why participants divided the $10 this way is that they considered $5 to each the "fair" distribution. However, Wilson has also found that if the proposer is given some qualification, which both parties know, for instance, education, professional status, etc., then the parties receiving the proposals are willing to accept offers that are not equal. This is analogous to saying that people do not mind paying more for a medical doctor because they had to go through rigorous training. So we have an example that fairness is not always construed as equal distribution, and that different considerations lead to different understanding of fairness. If we move from the idea of fairness to equality, again, we may have the same issue of definition.

Earlier we considered the different possible understandings of distributive justice, or just distribution of benefits and burdens. In Nozick's analysis, the question of distributive justice arises when individuals feel that the initial allocation of resources involved some sort of mistake leading to an "unfair" distribution, and that we now need must reallocate, redo what was already done, because it was done poorly.[49] A problem for distributive justice, says Nozick, because the initial distribution of resources is the result of innumerable decisions of individuals.

As Varian noted in the form of a mathematical proof, any government allocation necessarily results in an equitable distribution.[50] Varian use thought experiment. Imagine that there is an initial distribution of resources, which everyone in society agrees upon as fair or just. Now, after a while, someone in the economy wishes to trade with another. Once the trade is made, the distribution that was initially considered fair no longer exists. Is the new distribution, now, after the trade, no longer fair or just? The parties involved wanted to trade of their own free wills, and they, as individuals, most likely view the outcome of their private trade as fair or just.

This is where government reallocation can fail to produce a fair or just distribution. In Varian's thought experiment, on the one hand, if the initially agreed upon distribution is fair or just and we want to maintain it, then the government must intervene, again, in order to reallocate the resources to their original distribution. On the other hand, should not the new distribution, after the private trade, be considered fair as well, since both parties involved wanted to trade? Through this example Varian proved that only a free market could arrive at a distribution in which all individuals, in "real time," would consider fair or just.

Nozick builds upon on Varian's point by looking at the acquisition of previously unheld property. Those who believe in entitlements are usually concerned about the justice in the original acquisition of holdings as well as in the transfer of holdings. If the world were wholly just, the following definition would exhaustively cover the subject of justice in holdings:[51]

> A person who acquires a holding in accordance with the principle of justice in acquisition is entitled to that holding.
>
> A person who acquires a holding in accordance with the principle of justice in transfer, is entitled to the holding.
>
> No one is entitled to a holding except by (repeated) applications of (1) and (2).

Also, it follows that a distribution is just if it arises from another just distribution. Now, what happens if something unjust happens to change the distribution, such as by stealing? This, of course, would cause an unjust distribution, and raises the problem of how to rectify the distribution for past injustices.

At root in discussions distributive justice and reallocation for fair distributions is the difference between a historical distribution (entitlement) and the current time slice distribution, which is the familiar positive economic concept of welfare that we have discussed. This causes a problem now, in the current time slice, with redistribution in the form of taking from descendants of those who have received an "unjust" distribution on account of past injustices of their ancestors. To do so would also be an injustice. It is impossible to unwind the size of the effect from the past indiscretion.

To most practitioners in this area, principles of distributive justice are patterned in ways, such as: to each according to merit, to each according needs, to each according to marginal product, etc., as discussed above, regarding different possible ways to "justly" distribute benefits and burdens. However, those who want to change the historical distribution now have no such pattern to follow. The problem with changing the historical distribution is that there is no pattern to quantify the new distribution. On such an analysis, the only thing that a society accomplishes in redistribution is transferring harm from one party to another, in the current time slice. This violates the principles of justice in holdings itself.

To further compound the problem, non-economists commonly make the mistake of tacitly assuming that those who have more are prospering, now, at the expense of others who have less, relative to them, now. Economists see this as fallacious because, as economies grow, the "economic pie" is constantly growing larger, allowing all to have a larger slice. In our discussion of macroeconomics we saw that, with long-run economic growth, the income and wealth disparities between those in the current time slice in any economy are exponentially less than the disparities in wealth and income between *all* in a society at some point in the past compared to *all* in a society in the present, assuming long-run macroeconomic growth.

What is frustrating to many is that some never seem to get a bigger piece of the "economic pie" in the present. Those who do not get a bigger slice usually cannot, because their productivity is low, and often for other reasons: education, upbringing, economic opportunities, social class, ethnicity, gender, etc. This brings us back, again, to the ethical dilemma of whether or not we should redistribute some who currently have a larger slice of the "economic pie" those who currently have less. All modern mixed economies do this to various degrees currently, through some form of taxation and attempts at wealth redistribution. However, Varian's point about the mathematical impossibility of attaining equity and fairness due to the differences between individuals—which are the reasons for trade in the first place—tells against the efficacy of taxation and redistribution tactics. The fact that different individuals really do assign different values to different distributions, regardless of the philosophical question about the accuracy of their judgments, means that there it is impossible to find a distributive justice solution that will satisfy the equity and fairness values of all individuals. In so far as such reallocation violated individuals' preferences and values concerning equity and justice, and hence imposes harm on individuals in the positive economic sense of utility and welfare analysis, reallocation solutions to the distributive justice problem are themselves liable to charges of unfairness and injustice.

There is also the question of the actual success of such reallocation solutions in terms of achieving the goal of getting more people a bigger slice of the "economic pie." An examination of the data on recent wealth transfers is telling in this regard. Here are some recent figures that include cash transfers. *Cash transfer* is income tax that is transferred from one group to another, such as government taxes redistributed in a welfare program, like government unemployment, family assistance, disability, and healthcare payments.

Table 4.2: Taxes Paid by Income Group[52]

Share of Income Taxes Paid by Income Group (in percent)				
Income (Year)	1980	1990	2000	2008
Top 1percent	19.1	25.1	37.4	38
Top 5percent	36.8	43.6	56.5	58.7
Top 25percent	73	77	84	86.3
Bottom	7.1	5.8	3.9	2.7

Table 4.3: Share of Income by Quintile[53]

Percentage Share of Money Income by Quintile, Including Cash Transfers					
Year	Quintile 1	Quintile 2	Quintile 3	Quintile 4	Quintile 5
1980	4.2	10.2	16.8	24.7	44.1
1985	3.9	9.8	16.2	24.4	45.6
1990	3.8	9.6	15.9	24.0	46.6
1995	3.7	9.1	15.2	23.3	48.7
2000	3.6	8.9	14.8	23.0	49.8
2008	3.4	8.6	14.7	23.3	50.0

This data shows that the top income earners have been taxed more over the last few decades. We would thus expect cash transfers to have caused the share of income by quintile to go up, but this has not happened. With taxation and income redistribution, most quintiles have actually gone down, with a marginal increase in the fifth. The fifth quintile includes the highest earners. This means that taxing those with the highest incomes and redistributing their wealth has not resulted in higher incomes for those with lower incomes, the lower four quintiles. Instead, concomitant with taxation of the highest earners, there has been a decrease in income for all quintiles below the fourth, and even minor increases of income among the highest earners.

This data suggests that redistribution of income does not solve income inequity problems. This is the opposite of what many non-economists assume. This demonstrates one of many examples of how the consequences of economic policies are frequently different, even the opposite, of what policy enactors and supporters of the policy might expect. An *a priori* normative ethical system, deontological, divine command, or rights based, could use this as an example of how consequences should not and cannot factor into a consideration of the morality of a given action. This could be taken as a case supporting Kant's arguments against consequentialism.

Nonetheless, those embracing a form of consequentialism, despite its liabilities, must take into account *real* as opposed to *anticipated* consequences. The fact, that taxing the highest earners and redistributing their wealth has not produced the anticipated results and, in fact, has seen a corresponding actual minor reversal of what the policy implementers intended, is a fact that must be included in consequentialist considerations of right and wrong policy. The problem is that there are many factors interplaying here. For example, income is measured by households, but there has been an increase of two-income households. While it is difficult to determine all of the causes underlying such phenomena, it should be clear that there is no simple solution to income inequality.

Even if greater equality of condition is the chief social value, then the best means to attain this goal should be employed. If greater income equality is the goal, then it does not make sense to continue trying to reach this goal with means that do not work and may even increase income inequality. Those with values favoring redistribution must not allow misconceptions about how to attain income equality to cloud their judgment about the effectiveness of taxation as a solution.

There is another way that economists measure standard of living, not based on income. They look at how much time it would take someone to work (their labor) to purchase a good. In terms of the labor hours required for goods and services, instead of cost in terms of money or dollars, the cost has fallen considerably over time. Consider the cost of food for example.

Table 4.4: Minutes of Work[54]

	Cost in Minutes of Work	
Item (Year)	1919	1997
Tomatoes (3 lbs)	101	18
Sugar (5 lbs)	72	10
Coffee (1 lb)	55	17
Bread	13	4

This data indicates that, from 1919 to 1997, the cost of food items, in terms of labor, has fallen significantly. The cost of sugar, for instance, has fallen by eighty-six percent. This decrease in cost, in terms of labor hours, holds true for other goods as well.

Table 4.5: Cost of Various Items by Hours of Work[55]

	Cost in Hours of Work	
Item	1970	1997
King Mattress & Box	156	61
Air-Conditioner	45	23
Range	113	22
Dishwasher	69	28
Refrigerator	112	68
Clothes Washer	72	26

These are just a few examples of how the cost for goods in labor hours has significantly fallen over time. This trend is true of practically all goods. The costs of computers, cell phones, and other items have also fallen significantly. The reason for this drastic fall, in the cost of labor hours, is long-run economic growth, as discussed in the previous chapter. We have also seen how macroeconomic government intervention, for certain short-term benefits, has the opportunity cost of stifling long-run economic growth. Similarly, avoiding government intervention promotes long-run economic growth, at the opportunity cost of forgoing certain short-run benefits.

It would seem that, in addition to measuring increases and decreases in income and income inequality in dollars, ethical considerations of the promotion of individuals' well-being should include other ways to measure standards of living. Does income in dollar amounts really measure happiness when the dollar's value decreases with inflation? Whatever constitutes what is best for all in a society might include considerations beyond dollar amounts of income.

Persons' well-being, measured in terms of how much time it takes for them to work to acquire a good or service, has fallen considerably and will continue to do so. In this sense, despite current inequalities in income, everyone in society, now, is better off than everyone in society, in the past, and this trend will continue. It seems ill-advised to see income levels as equivalent with well-being, or to use income as a complete measure of poverty and income inequality.

SUMMARY

In this chapter, we surveyed the complex area of social values. We have seen arguments for and against prioritizing any given social value, and how social values can and do come into conflict, resulting in necessary trade-offs between them. In this chapter, we have also surveyed several important issues in macroeconomics, like the relationships between income per capita and government assistance, inflation and GDP, government regulations and GDP, and income inequality. In some cases, the data revealed facts that are counterintuitive to non-economists, and some of the numerous and complex ethical questions have been intimated.

In the final chapter, we examine more closely the question of the complex relationship between the government, economies, and ethics, as we look at the pros and cons of free market vs. command and control economies, typically discussed in terms of capitalism, socialism and communism. It should now be apparent that every economic policy comes with opportunity costs and trade-offs. This is also true of the different normative and social ethical systems. One individual's preferred construct comes at a cost in welfare to others. The considerations, in the final chapter, of a total system for government interaction with markets, necessarily build on and include all that has been said thus far in terms of values in general, normative ethical theories, social ethics, micro- and macroeconomics. This discussion will also, of necessity, include revisiting the limit questions concerning the nature and purpose of human societies discussed in the previous chapters.

NOTES

1. We now know that there is indeterminacy in nature at the quantum level, and this becomes a factor in the free will vs. determinism debate. Some advocates of free will, in the libertarian sense of freedom from prior determining causes, appeal to quantum indeterminacy. Some determinists rejoin that because of the ubiquity of causal determinism in nature, there must be such causal determinism at the quantum level, but we do not yet understand the causal laws at work.

2. The debate over free will and determinism in philosophy and religion is a complex one, with a variety of issues to consider, many questions, and different answers that are argued for in different ways. Even a brief survey of the metaphysical limit question of free will and determinism would lead us very far afield, and whole volumes have been written on this topic. For good introductions to this complicated and old debate, see Robert Kane, *A Contemporary Introduction to Free Will* (New York, NY: Oxford University Press, 2005), and Robert Kane, ed., *The Oxford Handbook of Free Will* (New York, NY: Oxford University Press, 2005).

3. Some argue, on the premise that all individuals are risk-averse instead of risk-loving, that in some cases taxation and redistribution of wealth will not decrease market efficiency in producing utility. This does not account for loss due to administrative costs of taxation. Also others would respond by questioning the assumption that all individuals are risk-averse.

4. Pope Paul VI, "Message for the Celebration of the Day of Peace," January 1, 1972, URL = <http://www.vatican.va/holy_father/paul_vi/messages/peace/documents/hf_p-vi_mes_19711208_v-world-day-for-peace_en.html> (accessed February 15, 2012).

5. See, Aristotle, *Nicomachean Ethics*, Book 5, and Aristotle, *Politics*, Book 3, in *The Complete Works of Aristotle: The Revised Oxford Translation*, 2 vols., 6th printing

with corr., ed. Jonathan Barnes (Princeton, NJ: Princeton University Press, 1995), 1729 – 97 and 2025 – 45.

6. John Rawls, *A Theory of Justice* (Cambridge, MA.: Harvard University Press, 1971).

7. Rawls, *A Theory of Justice*, 85.

8. Rawls, *A Theory of Justice*, 85 – 86.

9. Rawls, *A Theory of Justice*, 86.

10. Rawls interacts with and criticizes utilitarianism specifically.

11. Rawls, *A Theory of Justice*, 161 – 75.

12. He says: "Kant is clear that the original agreement is hypothetical," citing references (Rawls, *A Theory of Justice*, 12 n. 5).

13. Rawls, *A Theory of Justice*, 453 –54.

14. Rawls, *A Theory of Justice*, 12, 19.

15. Rawls, *A Theory of Justice*, 18 – 19.

16. Rawls, *A Theory of Justice*, 137.

17. Rawls, *A Theory of Justice*, 137.

18. Rawls, *A Theory of Justice*, 21.

19. Rawls, *A Theory of Justice*, 145.

20. Rawls, *A Theory of Justice*, 120, 136.

21. Rawls, *A Theory of Justice*, 152 – 53.

22. Rawls, *A Theory of Justice*, 62.

23. Rawls, *A Theory of Justice*, 60 – 61.

24. John Rawls, *A Theory of Justice*, rev. ed. (Cambridge, MA.: Harvard University Press, 1999).

25. Rawls, *A Theory of Justice*, rev. ed. (1999), 54.

26. Rawls, *A Theory of Justice*, rev. ed. (1999), 54.

27. Rawls, *A Theory of Justice* (1971), 60.

28. This is related to the economic principle of *Pareto optimality*, discussed earlier: Only those actions that make no one worse of and at least one person better off are justified.

29. Rawls, *A Theory of Justice* (1971), 158 – 59, 248.

30. Robert Nozick, *Anarchy, State, and Utopia* (New York: Basic Books, 1974).

31. Robert Paul Wolff, *Understanding Rawls: A Critique and Reconstruction of A Theory of Justice* (Princeton, NJ: Princeton University Press, 1977).

32. Chapter five discusses the philosophy of Karl Marx, in detail.

33 Amartya Sen, *The Idea of Justice* (Cambridge, MA: Harvard University Press, 2009).

34. "U.S. Bureau of Economic Analysis (BEA)," U. S. Bureau of Economic Analysis (BEA), URL = <http://www.bea.gov/iTable/iTable.cfm?ReqID=9&step=1> (accessed January 10, 2011).

35. Ibid.

36. Ibid.

37. Rebecca Blank, "Distinguished Lecture on Economics in Government: Fighting Poverty: Lessons from Recent U. S. History," *The Journal of Economic Perspectives* 14, no. 2 (2000): 3 – 19.

38. "U. S. Department of Labor," Consumer Price Index, URL = <ftp://ftp.bls.gov/pub/special.requests/cpi/cpiai.txt> (accessed January 10, 2011).

39. Ibid.

40. Ibid.

41. Weidenbaum Center, Washington University and the Regulatory Studies Center, the George Washington University. Derived from the Budget of the United States Government and related documents, various fiscal years.

42 "LNS14000000," Unemployment Rate, URL = <http://data.bls.gov> (accessed February 26, 2010).

43. Harald Uhlig, "Some Fiscal Calculus," *American Economic Review* 100 (2010): 30 – 34.

44. Hal Varian, "Distributive Justice, Welfare Economics, and the Theory of Fairness," *Philosophy & Public Affairs* 4, no. 3 (1975): 223 – 47.

45. Robert Nozick, "Distributive Justice," *Philosophy & Public Affairs* 3, no. 1 (1973): 45 – 126.

46. Varian, "Distributive Justice, Welfare Economics, and the Theory of Fairness," 223 – 47.

47. Bart Wilson, "Contra Private Fairness," *American Journal of Economics and Sociology* (Forthcoming).

48. Bart Wilson, "ReasonTV Interview," URL = <http://reason.tv/video/show/experimental-economist-bart-wi> (accessed October 25, 2011).

49. Nozick, "Distributive Justice," 45 – 126.

50. Varian, "Distributive Justice, Welfare Economics, and the Theory of Fairness," 223 – 47.

51. Nozick, "Distributive Justice," 45 – 126.

52. "Summary of Latest Federal Individual Income Tax Data," Taxfoundation, URL = <http://www.taxfoundation.org/files/ff285.pdf> (accessed October 25, 2011).

53. "P60-238," Income, Poverty, and Health Insurance in the United States: 2009, URL = <http://www.census.gov/prod/2010pubs/p60-238.pdf> (accessed January 10, 2011).

54. "Time Well Spent," Dallasfed.org, URL = <http://www.dallasfed.org/fed/annual/1999p/ar97.pdf> (accessed January 10, 2011).

55. Ibid.

CHAPTER 5: MORAL ASSESSMENTS OF CAPITALISM, SOCIALISM & COMMUNISM

Discussions of ethics and economics often focus on the government's relationship to markets. In the media, politics, talk with co-workers, friends, and family, we see and make value judgments about government involvement in markets. Is capitalism inherently evil, or just and good? Is taxing those with more money to provide for those with less fair and good, or unjust and bad? Do governments have a moral obligation to provide certain goods and services to those who do not get them in free markets? Is more or less regulation of markets right? There are no easy answers to these questions, as there are many complex factors to consider.

Historically, there have been many governmental relationships to markets, or *economic systems*, as economists call them. In our times only a few are prevalent. Since modern western values are shared in many countries, the few dominant economic systems today are really varying degrees across a spectrum that shares common underlying assumptions. "Capitalism," "socialism," and "communism" are attempts to label sections of this spectrum. Economists call many systems today "modern mixed economies," because they have features of both sides of the spectrum: minimal market regulation on one side, and more centralized economic planning and government involvement in markets on the other. No pure form of these three economic systems exists in reality; instead, we have modern mixed economies. Socio-political-economic debates usually are over the end of the spectrum we should emphasize. For evaluative purposes, in this chapter, we treat capitalism, socialism, and communism in their abstract and ideal forms.

There is no one form of capitalism, of socialism, or of communism. These categories emerged in the last few centuries with other modern developments, like industrialization and technologization, which now play major roles in every system. There is a general consensus about some fundamental features of each, but debates continue over the details of each system. Which properties are essential to capitalism? Which properties are essential to socialism? Which features are non-essential to each system, so that if they are removed the system in essence remains? Here, we again broach limit questions about being in general. What makes a particular thing, like an economic system we call "capitalist" or "socialist," that type of being?

We can construe these terms as models for trying to understand the complex actual phenomena of how different governments interact with markets. Models simplify complex entities for representation and understanding. A model car is not as complex as a real car but depicts some aspects of a real car: shape, proportion, color, parts, etc. Models of the same entity vary greatly depending on the parts on which they focus. Every model has some similarities to and some differences from that which it models. The automobile engineers' model, in designing a new car, differs from the plastic model of that car in the hobby shop. The engineers' model may even be schematic, two-dimensional, or computer-generated, and not made of a substance like plastic.

Although simpler than what it models, a model is useful to the extent that the similarities are relevant to understanding and analyzing aspects of what is modeled and, there are no relevant dissimilarities. We can use models meeting these criteria to analyze and predict effects, as is the case in science. Over the years, scientists have used different models of atoms to make accurate predictions, but chemists and physicists know these models do not perfectly correspond to the entities we call "atoms." Thus, in discussing capitalism, socialism, and communism, we regard these as models exemplifying complex entities that focus on a handful of aspects with which we are concerned, especially for ethical evaluation. Here we refer to capitalism, socialism, and communism as distinct categories, but we must remember these caveats.

In this chapter,[1] we first describe generally agreed upon features of these different economic systems, focusing on aspects relevant to moral assessment. Then, we try to show how one's answers to the many questions involved in ethics, discussed throughout the book, lead to different moral evaluations. Different—even diametrically opposed—evaluations can result from different answers to numerous philosophical questions concerning ethics and values.

We must keep in mind, the point made earlier, that this discussion involves three, not two, areas: economics, government, and ethics. We must not assume that, because we can modify how our governments interact with markets, we can also modify economic laws. The agreed upon laws of positive economics are not malleable; they are analogous to natural laws, like electromagnetism and gravity. How governing bodies interact with markets can change, but the economic laws governing resource allocation remain the same. Like other scientists, economists can predict, from these laws, numerous effects that will result from various actions or causes. If a government does X, then Y will result. States can change how their governments interact with the markets, as in the capitalist, socialist, or communist models. Many results of these types of interactions with markets, though, can be predicted by the laws of positive economics.

Because economic systems are complex with innumerable factors, many that are not directly observable, there are unexpected outcomes. When predictive failures occur, these are due to an ignorance of all causal factors involved, not because positive economic laws themselves are uncertain. The laws of supply and demand, market equilibrium, efficiency, utility maximization, types of goods (public vs. private, rival vs. non-rival, excludable vs. non-excludable), etc., are constantly operative. The factors are so numerous and often unaccounted for, though, that at times the reasons for specific effects are not known. All economic systems allocate resources through choices and trade with some medium of exchange, and the positive microeconomic laws, agreed upon by all economists, govern these activities, regardless of how the government interacts or does not interact with markets.

We have seen that choices always involve trade-offs. Resources are finite and therefore possibilities are mutually exclusive. As the old saying goes, "You cannot have your cake and eat it too." This means the choices of market agents and regulators, like governments, involve mutually exclusive effects, or trade-offs. Our answers to a litany of ethical limit questions dictate which trade-offs we value and judge to be good or right, and which we judge to be bad or wrong.

Before applying ethical limit questions to economic systems we must first try to identify features common to the different systems we call "capitalist," "socialist," and "communist." After this, we will turn to the ethical arguments for and against each form, highlighting the answers to ethical limit questions assumed in each argument.

WHAT IS CAPITALISM?

What are the salient features of capitalism? Private property owned by individuals and groups is fundamental, but not constitutive of capitalism alone. Private property owned by individuals and groups, like families or companies, and which property owners can buy, sell, and trade according to their preferences, is essential to capitalism. While socialism and communism have different definitions of ownership, as economic systems, they, too, are grounded on private property. Private property is a necessary assumption of all positive economics; without it there is no market and no allocation of scarce resources. It is a fact that most goods are rival and excludable; this makes them private, not public, goods. Two people cannot eat the same food, and two people cannot use the same PC, cell phone, or IPod at the same time. Two people cannot take the same dose of medicine, and they cannot wear the same clothing simultaneously. Shelters have maximum capacities, and a doctor can attend to only one patient at a time. These things are true in any society: capitalist, socialist, or communist.

Private property has been justified in a number of ways. Using a type of natural law ethics, some argue it is a natural right. They appeal to the historical fact that most societies at all times and places have valued private property. Others claim it is a divinely given right or even command, employing a form of divine command theory. Others use a consequentialist normative ethic to claim that private property maximizes happiness or pleasure.

Another feature of capitalism is that the means of producing goods and services are privately owned. In theory, the whole population could own a factory and its machines. However, both today and at most time and places, private individuals or groups have owned the means to produce goods and services. Capitalism has been defined as an economic system only in the last few centuries, but capitalists argue that private ownership of the means of production has been the foundation of all economic systems. In early hunter-gatherer societies, men who hunted owned weapons to hunt, while women owned and used household tools to make clothing and cook. In agrarian societies, farmers owned land to grow food and would reserve some of the seed produced one year to grow the next year's crop. Raisers of livestock not only traded and sold animals, but kept a reserve of animals to reproduce more animals. Although different from modern manifestations, these are arguably examples of private ownership of the means of production.

Capitalism, as a term, appeared during the technological boom of the early nineteenth-century Industrial Revolution, typically seen as beginning with the widespread use of the steam engine in the AD 1700s. Socialism and communism appeared as terms to describe certain responses to problems attending the Industrial Revolution.[2] We must note, though, that many of these problems, like technology replacing human labor; the need for more natural resources from fossil fuels to run machinery and produce electricity; the need to replace worn out machinery; pollution and waste; physical dangers and safety issues; and the division between skilled and unskilled labor; are issues that all modern industrialized societies face. Every society must choose: (1) what is produced, (2) how it is produced, and (3) who produces it.

Further, the metaphysical limitation of finite resources imposes opportunity costs and trade-offs for all modern industrialized societies. The movement today to switch from paper to electronic documents, for instance, trades off using trees as a resource for other natural resources still needed to produce and fuel other modes of producing, sending, and storing documents. Computers need electricity. Machinery and energy are needed to recycle paper. Coal, oil, gas, and other natural resources are the opportunity costs of replacing paper made from trees.

Private property, private ownership of the means of production, and issues resulting from industrialization are part of all modern economic systems. Hence, many identify minimal market regulation as a defining feature of capitalism. It sees the natural allocation of scarce resources by market systems with minimum interference, or free markets, as best, and promotes them.

Later, we will examine capitalism's reasons for valuing free markets. In summary these include: (1) the positive economic fact that free markets most efficiently allocate and minimize wasting scarce resources; (2) free markets best decide who gets goods and services according to who values them the most; (3) the positive economic fact, related to number 2, that free markets maximize utility (as defined by positive economics), assuming market agents know best what they need and want; (4) free markets maximize the social value of freedom, also highly valued by capitalists; (5) free markets generate the greatest long-run economic growth, benefitting all in society long-term; and (6) free markets provide a natural and non-biased way of maximizing merit-based distributive justice.

Valuing free markets means that capitalism values markets with as little external involvement by governments and other centralized economic planning groups as possible. There should be as few controls on prices, supplies, and wages, as possible; and individuals and groups should be as free as possible to buy, sell, and trade according to their wants and needs.

Limited government is a necessary corollary to promoting free markets. Full commitment to prioritizing free markets means that governments should have a minimalist function. They should only provide public (non-rival and non-excludable) goods and services. These include national defense and enforcing contracts between parties through legal and judicial systems.

There have rarely been pure limited governments providing only truly public goods. In most modern economic systems, governments provide some rival and excludable goods. Most provide personal security through police forces and large-scale public transportation, like roads and bridges. These are judged to be *quasi-public* goods. Strong advocates of free market capitalism urge, though, that these are public provisions of private goods. There have been privately owned toll bridges and roads, which individuals could be excluded from unless they pay.

Some private goods, like education, are judged to involve positive externalities and so require government provision and regulation. Education is rival and excludable. Two students cannot consume the same educational resources, like the same seat and the same units of a teacher's time and energy. Students can be prohibited from consuming educational resources. Yet most free market capitalist governments provide optional or mandatory public education due to externalities. National defense and law courts, by contrast, are not excludable, since no citizens can be excluded from benefiting by them, even if they do not pay taxes.

The profit motive, competition, and valuing risk-taking are also often included among free market capitalism's essential properties. Some judge one or more of these as bad, and, thus, morally telling against capitalism; but others judge one or more of these as good, and so in favor of it. The profit motive means that parties seek to sell goods and services at more than the cost of attaining, producing, and supplying them. This extra value above the supply cost is called *surplus value*, a term coined by Marx.

Some argue that surplus value is robbery. They say surplus value involves suppliers selling a good for more than the purchase or production price, which is the good's "real" value. Surplus value, then, involves suppliers taking more from buyers than the value of the good sold, which means surplus value is bad and acquired immorally. This is predicated on the assumptions, which most—but not all—accept, that private property is a right, and that theft is wrong. Others argue that "surplus value" is a misnomer, because it really represents the value of the time, effort, resources, and risk that the seller invested in acquiring, producing, and trying to sell the good.

Others further argue that surplus value is necessary for economic systems to function. There would be no buying, selling, and trading—and hence no markets and economic systems—unless buyers valued the good more than sellers. People buy and sell based on their preferences, which determine a good's value to them individually. Because different preferences specify different values for a good, there is no absolute and objective value. A seller values the good less than the buyer. By selling it, they gain more value than not selling it. A buyer values the good more than the seller. By buying it, they gain more value than not buying it. Both buyer and seller gain value, due to the different relative values they each place on the good. Microeconomic welfare calculations assume that buyers and sellers value goods differently, increasing consumer and producer surplus in every transaction. In this analysis, there is no one "fair" price, since buyer and seller value the good differently. A "fair" price really means that each gains more positive economic utility, or value, by making the transaction than by not engaging in the transaction, as dictated by different preferences.

Some respond by saying there really is an objective value to a good or service, but either the buyer or seller is wrong in their judgment about its value. Either the buyer pays more than its real value or the seller sells it for less than its real worth. This assumes that one of the parties does not know what is best for her, and does not know the good's real objective value for her. It assumes that one of the parties wrongly judges an *apparent* good to be a *real* good, when she engages in the transaction, but that her judgment is wrong.

Some argue that the real motive behind the profit motive is accumulation of capital in the form of personal and corporate wealth, not to gain happiness in the form of positive economic utility. Sellers try to sell goods at the highest possible price, given the market conditions, in order to accumulate wealth. Buyers try to buy at the lowest possible prices in order to retain maximum personal wealth. Added to this is the value judgment that accumulation of wealth is selfishness at the expense of other market agents and is, therefore, wrong. Such a judgment can be predicated on different normative ethical theories: natural law, theories of human rights, divine command theory, or Kantian ethics in which the profit motive is seen to violate the second formulation of Kant's categorical imperative, to not use others as a means to the ends of one's own betterment.

Others respond that wealth produces happiness as it increases the freedom to attain more of what is wanted or needed; and that greater wealth means greater long-run economic growth, including higher incomes for all. They indicate how aggregate supply requires more investment, or capital, as explained in chapter four on macroeconomics. Profit is required for technological and industrial growth, which increase long-run supply. Greater wealth also means more trade, which similarly generates long-run economic growth. This makes all better off, in the long-run.

Combining these considerations with a consequentialist normative ethic, some justify the profit motive as necessary—even good—in bringing greater benefit to all, in the long-run. Others use a normative ethical theory that claims the pursuit of individual pleasure or happiness is good and thus should be sought, like eudaimonistic happiness-based theories or ethical hedonism.

Market agents compete for value. In competition, sellers and buyers act in the market to maximize their profit and/or utility. Due to the laws of supply and demand, suppliers compete to sell the same good at the lowest possible price in order to sell more units, thereby maximizing profits. Each unit a supplier sells is missed profit or utility for other suppliers. Buyers compete with other buyers to buy the same good at the lowest possible price in order to get more utility for what they pay. Each unit they buy at the lowest price is missed utility for other buyers.

As with profit, some judge competition to be bad, but this value judgment is about how market agents treat other agents not involved in the transaction. Sellers treat other sellers as opponents, trying to get more buyers to buy their goods instead of their competitors' goods. Buyers treat other buyers as adversaries as they seek to obtain the same good offered at the lowest price.

A number of normative ethical theories can lead to a negative moral judgment on competition. Social theories of the origins of ethics say that such behavior is anti-social and not conducive to the maintenance of society. Natural rights or divine command theories may claim that we have an obligation to treat others as we want to be treated, not as adversaries. Although such competition has been characteristic of most socio-politico-economic systems, critics argue that, even though this has been the case, "is does not imply ought," and that this has, in fact, been the case does not mean that this *should* be the case.

Others argue that competition is not bad, or that if it is, then it is a necessary means to a greater good. On social theories, of the origins of ethics, some argue that saying competition is anti-social is wrong regardless of how we personally feel about it, because, historically, people have not abandoned societies in which there is competition. Rather, they have remained and even sought competition. Thus competition does not destroy social relationships and societies. A form of natural law theory could argue that competition, since it is necessary for trade in free markets and free markets are natural, is the way human economic systems *should* be.

Similarly, some reason that, since competition is necessary for free market mechanisms and because free markets promote utility and long-run economic growth, making all better off, competition is actually good, or if it is bad, it is a means to a greater good. Competition also promotes higher quality goods and services, as suppliers seek to improve their goods and services to raise the demand for them. Higher quality goods and services benefit all in society.

Regarding this latter claim, many consequentialist ethical theories argue that some bad is necessary for a greater good. Conversely other theories, like many rule-based ethics and Christian natural law theories, claim that any bad means used to attain a good eviscerates the final good of its goodness. So, any evil means used to attain a good end makes the whole undertaking wrong.

Risk-taking is also part of free markets. Sellers take risks in acquiring resources to produce goods that may or may not sell at a profit, if at all. Buyers take risks in buying goods they believe they need or want, which may or may not be an accurate judgment. Free market capitalism values such risk-taking, which allows all to succeed or fail based on their choices in markets. This value judgment is based on: (1) the assumption that individuals are the best judges of what they need and want; (2) the benefits that successful risks have for the individual and society as a whole; and (3) the necessity of such risk-taking for free markets to function and flourish.

The first is based on the arguments prioritizing individualism over paternalism. Examples of the second include instances of successful entrepreneurship, like those who risked producing automobiles when the automobile was invented and its future was uncertain. Those risks proved greatly beneficial for society, indeed all of humanity, in the long-run. The third is based on the goods judged to result from free markets in general, and risk-taking is necessary in free markets.

In contrast, some judge risk-taking to be bad. They focus on failed instances of risk-taking that have harmed risk-takers. On the supply side, this means instances of business (seller) failure, and on the buyer side, this means instances of buyers making wrong judgments. Examples of the latter include "buyer remorse," where buyers think they want or need a good or service but later judge that they do not need or want it. Many specific examples could be adduced: buying extra insurance, timeshares, and exercise equipment that is never used.

Some add that the profit motive creates false perceptions of needs and wants, phantasms of *apparent* as opposed to *real* goods. Free market capitalism assumes that market agents are honest, disclose all knowledge relevant to transactions, and are "rational." There are times, though, when market agents act on impulse or do not have full knowledge of what the transaction entails. Withholding relevant information and the creation of false wants is considered deception, which most—but not all—normative ethical theories judge to be wrong. Acting on an apparent as opposed to a real good is considered bad, not good, by definition, if the distinction between real and apparent goods is valid.

One rejoinder of free market capitalists is that sometimes market agents do not seek all relevant information for practical reasons, such as the time and effort necessary to do so. This is called *rational ignorance*. By trading off additional knowledge for time and energy, they are responsible for their ignorance. Another response is that competition corrects deceit in free markets. Buyers and sellers want honesty and so naturally avoid deceptive transaction partners.

Free market capitalists may even admit the possibilities of deceit and creating false needs, judging them to be bad or wrong. Perhaps accumulating capital and investment entails deception and creates false needs and wants. They respond that market efficiency, utility maximization, and the long-run economic growth that results from capital and investment growth, and benefits all in society in the long-run, are greater goods justifying these lesser evils. Here, again, others may say that good ends never justify bad means. Many proponents of rule-based ethics and natural law theories judge that the bad means, of deceit and the creation of false values to attain capital, derogates from or nullifies the long-run good of greater economic prosperity for all.

Related to these points is, again, the issue of time and focusing on the short-run or the long-run timeframe. We saw in macroeconomics that regulation and market involvement by governments can be justified to stem short-run economic lagging. Both the Keynesian and Austrian solutions to a recession employ neoclassical economic theory. Keynesian solutions advocate intervention to curb periodic natural downturns in free markets. Austrian solutions advocate non-interference in free markets, riding out the economic slump for the trade-off of greater long-run economic prosperity. Positive economic laws dictate that long-run economic growth is often the opportunity cost for short-run relief caused by market intervention, and a short-run economic downturn is often the opportunity cost of long-run economic growth.[3]

There is also the short term, though. Free market and intervention strategies have the opposite and inverse views of the individual transaction point. Paternalists and advocates of more regulation indicate that short-run choices may seem to, or really, be good for the buyer or seller, at the point of sale, but in the long-run prove to be bad. Again, buyer remorse is the classical example. Even if point-of-sale preferences accurately reflect real needs and wants, these can change across time and so do preferences. Free market advocates focus on the preferences, now, in the short-run, at the point of transaction, but downplay or ignore the long-run consequences of individual choices across time. Time is another important factor in discussions of ethics and economics. Things change across time, but many discussions of ethics and economics treat the data brought to an ethical analysis of economics as if it were puncticular and static.

Another consideration is the nature of the posited free market agent. In modeling markets, neoclassical economics assumes that sellers and buyers at each point on the supply and demand curves are "willing *and* able" to engage in transactions. Each point on the supply curve represents the number of units a seller is willing and able to supply at a given price, and each point on the demand curve represents the number of units a buyer is willing and able to buy at that price.

We discussed the positive economic assumption of the "willing and able" market agent in prior chapters. It is related to limit questions regarding metaphysical (not social, political, and economic) free will and determinism. Neoclassical economics assumes a type of equality of condition of market agents, who are all willing and able to participate in market activities. What if some cannot participate, or do participate in market activities, but against their will?

Advocates of free markets with as little regulation as possible say that this is most efficient and maximizes positive economic welfare and utility. Welfare and utility calculations can go awry, though, if market agents are willing but unable to engage in transactions expressing their preferences, or are able but unwilling to engage in a transaction into which they are forced, against their will. Then the point representing "willingness and ability" on the supply or demand curve might not accurately express preferences, and so not accurately express maximum utility.

A buyer may want or need a good or service, but be unable to pay for it. The crisis of healthcare in contemporary America is one of many possible examples of this. Likewise, a worker—a "seller" of labor—may be forced against her will to work for pay that does not meet her family's basic needs. If she accepts a lower wage than she needs, the labor supply curve does not reflect the price at which she is *willing* and able to sell her labor. We will see that one reason for communism's rise was the claim that workers during the Industrial Revolution were forced, against their will, to work for wages well below what they needed to support their families.

Granted, positive economics must make some basic assumptions—like the supply and demand curves express quantities that market agents are willing and able to supply or buy at a given price—in order to proceed with a mathematically measurable analysis. These assumptions can be questioned, though, and if inaccurate, can change what the mathematical analyses reflect.

A final point regarding free market capitalism is that it has affinities with democratic governments instead of paternalism, as discussed earlier. Free market capitalism values individual liberty and sees individuals as the best judges of what they need and want. Democracy holds that individuals are the best judges of what is best for themselves and society. Regulations and centralized economic planning derogate from freedom, by limiting choices and having others make choices for individuals. This is often predicated on the paternalist assumption that individuals do not know what is best for themselves and society. Since both democracy and free market capitalism highly value the social value of freedom, they often appear together in modern socio-politico-economic systems.

WHAT IS SOCIALISM?

Socialism appeared as a description of various economic systems, in eighteenth-century European philosophy, that were conceived to redress aspects of capitalism judged to be morally wrong. The term *socialism* became more widely popularized through the philosophy of Karl Marx (AD 1818 – 1883), who described it as a necessary step in the evolution from free market capitalism to communism. We will examine Marx's communist theory later, but here only note that communism regards socialism as a "halfway house" between capitalism and communism.

Since the twentieth century, the term socialism has described a variety of socio-politico-economic arrangements existing worldwide. These include efforts to attain communist states in the former Eastern Bloc countries during the Cold War, China, North Korea, and Cuba, as well as economic systems in a number of Latin Americana and European countries today. Some even describe the traditionally free market capitalist system in the U.S.A. as moving progressively toward socialism, since the Great Depression and the Second World War. As with free market capitalism, because of the variety of systems described as "socialist," finding a precise definition that includes its essential features is problematic.

We noted how industrialization is characteristic of what we call free market capitalism, but this is largely an accident of the rapid technological advances of the last few centuries. The latter are arguably, in part, the effects of increased trade due to globalization and better transportation. Issues like technology replacing human labor, an increased need for natural resources to make and run machines and generate electricity, an ongoing need to replace worn out machinery, pollution, waste, physical hazards, and the distinction between unskilled and skilled labor are not unique to free market capitalist societies but arise in all modern societies. What we will identify as salient features of socialism—government ownership of some or all of the means of production and economic planning—existed in some pre-modern non-industrialized societies. Therefore, while industrialization is characteristic of most modern economic systems, we call socialist, it is not an essential feature of socialism.

We also noted how private property has been virtually ubiquitous in a variety of societies at most times and places in history. Private property is a necessary assumption of positive economics, regardless of the specific socio-politico-economic system in which markets function. Socialism does not deny private property. Socialism differs from capitalism not by denying private property but in having some sort of collective ownership of some or all of the means of production. Private property among individuals and groups still exists. Collective ownership of the means of production of at least some private goods and services characterizes socialism.

Sometimes socialism is described as worker ownership of the means of production. This usually does not mean, though, that all workers in a given private company own the company, as with worker-owned companies in free market capitalist systems. Some private, but employee owned, companies in the U. S. A. now include Publix and Food Giant supermarkets, the Herff Jones educational goods company, and W. W. Norton & Company publishers. Avis Rent-a-Car was originally employee owned before being sold to a private corporation.

The ideal of collective ownership of the means of production in socialism usually means that all citizens own the means of production. Pragmatically, the most expedient or only way to attain this has been through the state administering the means of production as the citizens' representative. In practice, state ownership of the means of production, to various degrees, has been an essential feature of what we call socialism.

In theory, all citizens jointly own the means of production, which the government runs as a proxy. In practice, additional factors arise due to the difference between the state on the one hand, and the citizens on the other. Even in the most representative forms of government, the state is never, strictly speaking, identical with the whole population except in a pure democracy, which is rare and does not exist in the modern world. Consequently, the citizens and the state function as two distinct parties, with the citizens as the employees and the state as the employer.

A corollary to common ownership of the means of producing private goods and services in socialism is some degree of collective control over the distribution and exchange of private goods and services, sometimes called *central economic planning*. This entails some degree of engineering and control over the allocation of scarce resources in lieu of allowing free markets, with as little regulation as possible, to distribute them. In central planning, resource allocation is "collective" as opposed to "individual" because individuals freely engaging in trade do not allocate scarce resources, but rather a group or society as a whole does. As with collective ownership of the means of production, the most expedient or only way to implement collective control over resource allocation is through the state.

In order to avoid the many discrete individuals trading in free markets from allocating resources, centralized economic planning must interfere with natural market mechanisms. This typically means that the state is involved in and changes the ways that markets naturally allocate goods and services. States often do this through taxing and redistributing wealth, imposing regulations on production and prices, and distributing resources according to need instead of ability to acquire them.

In summary so far, socialism is not primarily characterized by the abolition of private property or industrialization. Socialism is characterized by some form of collective control over the means of production and the allocation of private goods and services in a way that transcends natural market mechanisms for doing so. These are common denominators of the various socio-politico-economic arrangements that we call "socialist." Both of these duties most often fall to the state or the government, as representative of the citizens.

Why do advocates of socialism value collective ownership of the means of production and the collective and centralized allocation of goods and services? One reason is that they place a premium on the social value of equality of condition over other social values, like freedom and merit-based distributive justice. Free markets naturally produce differences in resource allocation and, therefore, inequalities of condition, so intervention in market mechanisms is required to insure greater equality of condition.

In chapter four we examined arguments for and against prioritizing equality of condition, freedom, or merit-based distributive justice. Advocates of free market capitalism prioritize the social value of freedom, as said above. They also generally see justice primarily as retributive, rewarding merits or contributions to society and punishing demerits or harm to society. The assumption of willing and able market agents, who, because of their freedom are responsible for their helping or harming society, undergirds this view of retributive justice. Along with this, if free and responsible individuals merit the wealth they acquire, then taking some of their wealth and giving it to others who did not merit it is a grave injustice tantamount to theft.

We have seen the manner in which problems for this view of justice arise if one answers the limit questions of philosophical anthropology about metaphysical freedom and determinism in a more deterministic way. Socialism and communism have affinities with holistic theories of societies, in which individuals are shaped and determined by their larger social contexts. If people are determined by prior causes so that their choices are not free, or if their possibilities for freely choosing are severely limited by prior determining causes, then this poses problems for prioritizing the social value of individual (social, political, and economic) freedom.

There is also the question of whether those who do not choose freely can be held responsible for their actions. If a person acts in ways that harm society because of their genes, upbringing, socio-economic background, education, or limitations of their class or social category (e.g., race, gender, religion), then is it fair to punish them for their actions? Should we not attempt to reform them so that they can make positive contributions to society? Again, deterministic assumptions and the conclusions, about lessened responsibility logically flowing from them, are behind the view that penal systems are corrective and reformatory. Such assumptions and reasoning undermine justice, conceived as merit or demerit, deserved due to responsible choices.

Socialism values equality of condition and justice construed as distributive justice akin to equality of condition, not retributive justice, in part because of these assumptions and the reasoning that flow from them. We have analyzed in some detail the arguments in favor of such assumptions and lines of reasoning. Using the same analysis, we could assess the pros and cons of socialism's prioritization of the social value of equality of condition.

Another reason for valuing collective ownership of the means of production and collective distribution of resources is to honor certain rights judged to be absolute and universal, like life, education, food, shelter, employment, and healthcare. Free markets do not guarantee that all will have these, and, in fact, may introduce such disparities in the distribution that some may not have them at all. Different right-based normative ethical systems can justify an obligation to honor such rights. Some natural law theories may conclude that human beings, *qua* human beings and in order to fully "be" human, require the things guaranteed by these rights. A divine command theory may claim that God has given all humans these rights, perhaps by claiming that God has created humans in God's image and has commanded us to honor these rights. A form of Kant's categorical imperative may be used to rationally and consistently universalize some or all of these rights.

Related to this appeal to rights is the claim some private goods and services, again like life, education, food, shelter, employment, healthcare, etc., produce more happiness or pleasure than other private goods and services, and so must be guaranteed, in order to attain the greatest net well-being or welfare of all in society. Happiness or pleasure-based ethical theories, and consequentialist theories like utilitarianism, can justify these claims. A form of virtue ethics may say that it is a virtue of human beings and/or a government to provide such things for others, and therefore doing so is good and right.

Critics say, on the other hand, that such a grading of goods and services, according to the utility they produce, assumes that someone or some group other than individuals engaging in free market transactions "knows better" what will provide them with maximum utility. This again raises the limit question of who knows what is best for individuals and for society as a whole. Do individuals or some person or some group with more accurate knowledge and value judgments know best? This limit question is, again, related to the question of whether democracy or paternalism is the best form of government. We have already examined different arguments for the different answers to these limit questions. The pros and cons of these arguments likewise apply to the present discussion.

Grading the utility of goods and services also assumes that utility is mostly absolute and uniform across different individuals. It assumes all *really* need or want (as opposed to what they might think they need or want) housing, education, employment, etc., instead of utility being different and relative across different individuals. Advocates of free markets respond that utility differs from person to person. A specific example we saw is that taxing and redistributing wealth to produce more net utility is sometimes justified in economics by assuming that most or all people are risk-averse. If more are really risk-loving, then it is not necessarily true that taxing and redistributing their wealth causes them less harm (understood as disutility) compared to the good (understood as utility) brought to those to whom the wealth is redistributed.

Critics doubt the ability of centralized planners to account for the needs and wants of every person in society because of the limits of human knowledge. Enormous amounts of knowledge, regarding many individuals' preferences, are required for centralized planning to correctly allocate resources according to people's needs and wants apart from natural market mechanisms. Central planners would have to be practically omniscient or all-knowing. We discussed this in prior chapters. Critics of centralized planning point to the fact that black markets emerge whenever there is regulation in order to support their view that natural free markets best allocate resources according to individuals' preferences, and that centralized economic planning fails to do so.

Coupled with this is the vast complexity of economic systems so that interventions in markets almost always produce unintended consequences. A common example is how price ceilings intended to help some who want certain goods, but who are unable to get them, always produce a supply shortage and always result in fewer people attaining them, than without the price ceilings. Another common example is that minimum wage laws (minimum prices on the supply of labor) always result in a decreased demand for labor, and hence more people being unemployed. The laws of positive microeconomics dictate these necessary effects and economists can predict such results, depending on a particular market's characteristics, as discussed in the first chapter.

A recent example of unintended consequences concerns universal healthcare legislation in the U. S. A. Economists point to several important unintended consequences. One is that the legislation increases costs for employers. This is similar to increasing the minimum wage. The law of supply and demand dictates that increasing the cost to employ someone decreases the demand for employees, so more go unemployed. A related possible unintended consequence is that uncertainty in the legislation's implementation and effects may make employers more reticent to take on new employees due to increased risk. If true, this also decreases demand for new employees. Even though the legislation's goal is to increase equality of condition in healthcare coverage, unintended consequences may lead to less equality of condition in employment.

Central planners enacting such market interventions, even with good intentions, are often not economists. Even economists do not always predict well all of the necessary consequences of a given action, due the complexity of economic systems. Hence, free market capitalists argue that it is best to let free markets allocate resources in order to avoid unintended consequences.

Adding assumptions about risk-aversion and utility, some advocates of centralized planning claim that some regulations are "costless" and therefore justified on the Pareto optimality principle. Free market advocates respond that in neoclassical economic theory—which almost all economists agree upon—without added assumptions about risk-aversion, free markets produce maximum utility, while any interference introduces inefficiency and disutility.

A consequentialist normative ethical theory, used to justify centralized planning and allocating resources outside of natural market mechanisms, must factor in the inefficiency and disutility that results as a consequence. Deadweight loss introduced through regulation and taxation as discussed in other chapters must be considered. Even if some goods and services, like housing, food, employment, healthcare, and education, definitively cause more utility than other goods and services, we must see if the deadweight loss, introduced by the regulation and taxation necessary to get them to more people, outweighs the extra utility that they generate.

Some of the reasons that socialism values collective ownership, of the means of production and collective distribution of certain private goods and services outside of natural market mechanisms, arose, historically, out of critiques of free market capitalism. As discussed, some allege that the profit motive, competition, and risk-taking are bad and immoral. Others add that capitalism engenders greed, animosity, adversarial relationships between people, promotes dishonesty, and creates false desires for apparent instead of real goods.

They use diverse normative ethical systems to arrive at these same claims. Kant's deontological ethics, divine command theories, and social theories that explain morality as a way to promote and maintain human societies all judge dishonesty and greed to be wrong, but for different reasons. Earlier we examined the issues surrounding the critiques of capitalism with respect to the profit motive, competition, risk-taking, dishonesty, and the creation of false needs and wants. We examine the issue of adversarial relationships in the later section on communism.

We mentioned that, practically, collective ownership of the means of production often involves state ownership of the means of production. Only in a pure democracy, nonexistent today, would the state as owner and the citizens as workers be absolutely identical. So, in practice, there is almost always some distinction between the state as an entity and the individual citizens as entities. Citizens and the government practically function as two different parties, the citizens as employees and the state as employer.

As a result, issues regarding the relationship between employers as buyers of labor and employees as sellers of labor, which critics of free market capitalism judge to be wrong or immoral, also arise in socialism. There are still rival and excludable, or private, goods. For various reasons, including the costs of maintaining the large government required in socialism, the state, as employer, seeks to attain as much value or utility as possible from buying labor and selling private goods and services.

Thus the profit motive arises with its pros and cons, as discussed above. Is the profit the state seeks a theft of "surplus value" from workers? Does the state pay people less than the real value of what they produce, or is profit relative to the preferences and utility of the parties to the transaction, each mutually benefitting from the different degrees of value, which employer and employee assign to what they are trading in the employment relationship? Does the state deserve the value of the profit because of its own time, energy, investment, and risk-taking?

The same issues regarding competition likewise arise. Is there competition between workers? If so, then is this bad? Does the state compete with other suppliers to sell private goods, especially now in our global economy? If so, then is such competition wrong, or is this competition natural, necessary, and even good, as advocates of free market capitalism argue?

Another concern is the possibility of totalitarianism. Here, we once again broach limit questions in philosophical anthropology regarding psychological egoism and psychological altruism, discussed in chapter two. Are people essentially selfish so that all of their actions are motivated out of self-interest, or can people be unselfish, so that at least some of their actions are motivated out of genuine concern for the well-being of others?

If psychological egoism is true, then, in socialism, the state as an entity distinct from the populace means leaders produce goods and services and allocate them in ways to serve their own self-interest. Psychological egoism claims that all apparently altruistic actions, ostensibly performed for the good of others, should be reinterpreted to find underlying selfish motivations. Central planners may say that censorship, intolerance of differences of opinion, limitations of individual freedom, indoctrination, and strict control of citizens' lives are for the good of the citizens and dissidents, who do not know better, in a paternalistic fashion. But if psychological egoism is true, then these are power plays by those in control to justify and retain their privileged positions.

As we also said in our discussion of psychological egoism and altruism, it is inconsistent to hold at the same time that: (1) people can only act selfishly and

(2) make the prescriptive normative value judgment that people should act unselfishly. Many normative ethical systems can judge selfishness as wrong, but not all do. Ethical hedonism makes the prescriptive value judgment that people *should* act in ways that promote their own pleasure and happiness.

Some free market capitalists are psychological egoists, and espouse a form of ethical hedonism where people should pursue their own happiness. They do not judge greed to be bad, but good. They argue that the curious thing about free markets is that as individuals pursue their own happiness or utility through free trade, everyone benefits. Both parties to a transaction gain utility. Free trade at market equilibrium brings maximum net utility at any given time, and free trade brings the greatest economic growth in the long-run, benefitting all in society.

Opponents of socialism point to evidences of totalitarianism and authoritarianism in countries with socialist systems, to prove psychological egoist assumptions, or to fuel pessimism about a centralized planning body that looks out for society's common good instead of its own self-interest. As we saw in our discussion of psychological egoism and altruism, it is impossible to prove an answer to this limit question empirically. Further, psychological altruists can still admit that people are inclined toward selfish behavior, even most of the time. Psychological altruists only claim that people can act selflessly sometimes. As such, psychological altruists allow for consistently making the prescriptive value judgment that people *should* act selflessly.

Just because there are instances of totalitarianism and authoritarianism in socialist systems does not, by itself, prove psychological egoism or that socialism is always totalitarian. Arguably, some societies with what we might call socialist elements, like the medieval Byzantine Empire, seem to have exercised collective control in non-authoritarian in ways that did promote the common good of the people. Thus, some socialists argue that the instances of totalitarianism in socialist states of the twentieth century diverged from the socialist ideal, which can be realized in a truly democratic socialism.[4]

Another consideration is that if a society is socialist, or even communist, it participates in our global economy. This economy involves natural free markets because we do not have one international government or society. Even if a society values socialism, that society, as a whole, still faces what socialists judge to be wrong and immoral with free markets if it wants to participate in international trade, which most socialist societies are willing and able to do.

Having surveyed what many agree to be the essential features of free market capitalism and socialism, and some key values driving both, we will now turn to communism.

WHAT IS COMMUNISM?

Communism as an economic system is often associated with Karl Marx (AD 1818 – 1883). Yet, the features most use to identify communism have been theorized about or partly put into practice at various times in history. These commonly accepted traits of communism include: common ownership of all material resources or the abolition of private property; equal distribution of material resources with no disparities; and the absence of any class distinctions.

Plato described a communist society in his *Republic*. Religious communities throughout history have tried to practice a form of communism, and St. Thomas More (AD 1478 – 1535) described a form of communism in his *Utopia* (AD 1516). The English Protestant Dissenter sect known as the "Diggers" or "Levellers," led by Gerrard Winstanley (AD 1606 – 1676), tried to implement a classless and propertyless society, and European thinkers before Marx theorized about forms of communism. Because Marx's communist philosophy is the most well-known and has had the greatest effects on the contemporary world, we explain it here in some detail.

Marx formulated his communist position as a response to free market capitalism, and as we have said, he viewed socialism as a halfway house on the way from free market capitalism to communism. Marx's exposition of his communist philosophy is instructive in three key ways.

First, it arose out of the concrete conditions of the political climate of the nineteenth-century West and the horrors attending the Industrial Revolution, which many would say represented free market capitalism at its worst. Marx's critiques of free market capitalism were not simply theoretical, but based on actual conditions of the poor in nineteenth-century London.

Second, Marx's exposition of communism exhibits the fact that all philosophical limit questions are interconnected, so that a satisfactory consideration of one limit question cannot be undertaken without consistently addressing a litany of others. That is, Marx's philosophy is a comprehensive philosophical worldview (*Weltanschauung* in the original German). Marx's philosophy is thus more akin to the continental tradition in philosophy today than contemporary Anglo-American analytic philosophy. The latter excels in addressing philosophical questions with logical rigor and exacting precision, but by considering them discretely and independently of other philosophical questions. The former is more systematic and comprehensive, considering numerous limit questions in their interrelationships, but can arguably take a lesson from the robust logical and linguistic analysis of contemporary Anglo-American analytic philosophy.

Third, Marx's philosophy demonstrates the fact that philosophy is eminently practical and that ideas have consequences. Political revolutions of the twentieth century were rooted in Marxism, and parts of the world strove, and are still striving, to attain Marx's communist Utopia. The division between Marxist countries and the free market capitalist states, during a much of the twentieth century, fueled the Cold War. No western philosopher has had so great and global following as Marx, and no philosophy has had more concrete impact on people's lives.[5]

Regarding the first point about the nineteenth-century West, Marx lived when the modern values of liberal democracy were struggling to replace older monarchical, imperial, and class-based political systems. Generally speaking, these two political philosophies roughly correspond to the debate between democracy and paternalism in social and political philosophy, discussed in chapter three. In the not too distant past, the American Revolution had succeeded but the French Revolution had failed, only to lead to the Napoleonic Empire. Some still had hope in modern liberal democracy, but some thought that the "American Experiment" would fail. The camps were evenly divided, and the concrete results of this ideological conflict were wars and revolutions that ransacked nineteenth-century Europe and Latin America.

The Industrial Revolution was revolutionizing society as well. Rapid and epochal technological change in agriculture, textiles, metallurgy, and the invention of the steam engine coalesced to quickly and drastically decrease the demand for unskilled labor. This technological boom arguably resulted from increased trade due to globalization and better transportation. The supply of unskilled labor stayed the same but the demand curve shifted in, moving the market equilibrium to a point of lower price and lower quantity on the supply curve.

With this surplus supply many manual laborers (suppliers of labor) were unemployed, and those who secured employment were forced to sell their labor at a much lower price than prior to the demand curve shift. This led to abject poverty among the working-class poor. Most families had to make their children work, too, in an age when there were no child-labor laws. These unskilled laborers and their families were forced to live in one-room quarters in slums, frequently owned by the factory owners who employed them.

Marx documented a litany of eyewitness accounts from doctors and government workers of the horrible working, living, and health conditions of these working poor of London, in his two-volume *Capital*. He provides a testimony after testimony like the following:

> Mr. Broughton Charlton, county magistrate, declared, as chairman of a meeting held at the Assembly Rooms, Nottingham, on the 14th January, 1860, 'that there was an amount of privation and suffering among that portion of the population connected with the lace trade, unknown in other parts of the kingdom, indeed, in the civilised world. . . . Children of nine or ten years are dragged from their squalid beds at two, three, or four o'clock in the morning and compelled to work for a bare subsistence until ten, eleven, or twelve at night, their limbs wearing away, their frames dwindling, their faces whitening, and their humanity absolutely sinking into a stone-like torpor, utterly horrible to contemplate. . . . We are not surprised that Mr. Mallett, or any other manufacturer, should stand forward and protest against discussion. . . . The system, as the Rev. Montagu Valpy describes it, is one of unmitigated slavery, socially, physically, morally, and spiritually. . . . What can be thought of a town which holds a public meeting to petition that the period of labour for men shall be diminished to eighteen hours a day? . . . We declaim against the Virginian and Carolinian cotton-planters. Is their black-market, their lash, and their barter of human flesh more detestable than this slow sacrifice of humanity which takes place in order that veils and collars may be fabricated for the benefit of capitalists?[6]
>
> William Wood, 9 years old, was 7 years and 10 months when he began to work.

> He 'ran moulds' (carried ready-moulded articles into the drying-room, afterwards bringing back the empty mould) from the beginning. He came to work every day in the week at 6 a.m., and left off about 9 p.m. 'I work till 9 o'clock at night six days in the week. I have done so seven or eight weeks.' Fifteen hours of labour for a child 7 years old! J. Murray, 12 years of age, says: 'I turn jigger, and run moulds. I come at 6. Sometimes I come at 4. I worked all night last night, till 6 o'clock this morning. I have not been in bed since the night before last. There were eight or nine other boys working last night. All but one have come this morning. I get 3 shillings and sixpence. I do not get any more for working at night. I worked two nights last week'.[7]

> Of the witnesses that Commissioner White examined (1863), 270 were under 18, 50 under 10, 10 only 8, and 5 only 6 years old. A range of the working-day from 12 to 14 or 15 hours, night-labour, irregular meal-times, meals for the most part taken in the very workrooms that are pestilent with phosphorus. Dante would have found the worst horrors of his Inferno surpassed in this manufacture.[8]

The first quote compares the situation of children in the lace factories to the chattel slavery of the contemporaneous American south, saying the latter pales in comparison. Indeed during the American Civil War southerners remonstrated that the condition of the slaves in the South was worlds better than that of the free working poor in the Industrialized North.

The question of the reasons for these deplorable conditions still remains. The correlation of free markets with these horrid living conditions of the masses does not imply causation, as there were many other factors at work that could have been the causes. The rapidity of technological growth during the Industrial Revolution—again, probably due to increased trade, which so quickly reduced the demand for unskilled labor—was historically unprecedented. Natural market mechanisms of supply and demand were still at work, but the demand for unskilled labor dropped so quickly and so drastically that the market for unskilled labor suffered an unprecedented low. Thus, some contend that it was not free markets that caused the horrors of the Industrial Revolution, but rather the input for the demand curve. The market mechanism still worked according to the laws of positive economics, as all markets have done and do.

Whatever the reasons for the Industrial Revolution, Marx's philosophy grew out of his lived experience regardless of whether or not he interpreted it correctly. He was clearly concerned about the concrete social problems attending the Industrial Revolution and the larger scale social and political unrest in nineteenth-century Europe.

Regarding the second point about the systematic nature of his philosophy, a variety of philosophical sources and concerns informed Marx's philosophy. His philosophy addresses not only limit questions in social and political philosophy, but also those in metaphysics, ontology, philosophy of religion, epistemology, philosophical anthropology, and the philosophy of history.

Marx was reared in a Jewish family and came from a long line of rabbis. His father was forced to convert to Lutheran Christianity, due to anti-Semitic laws prohibiting Jews from working for the government. As an adult, Marx became an atheist, which plays into his philosophy, but Judeo-Christian religious themes still pervade his writings. Like many modern Jews, he channeled traditional religious zeal into secular modern pursuits with a burning devotion and an indefatigable perseverance. Although an atheist, he lived and worked according to the Eastern European Jewish ideal of the poor religious scholar, devoting more time and energy to study than to mundane pursuits, like gainful employment. He was rarely officially employed, and his family lived on loans and donations from friends like his colleague, Friedrich Engels (AD 1820 – 1895). Instead of Torah and Talmud study, Marx labored tirelessly at documenting what he saw to be the evils of capitalism, and working assiduously on his communist philosophy as an alternative.

Marx was influenced by many modern philosophical developments. He had a robust faith in humanism and the supremacy of reason as touted by the Enlightenment. Instead of the traditional Christian view of human nature, as irreparably damaged by original sin and in need of divine grace, it saw humanity with the unique faculty of reason as able to overcome the challenges of life and history to ultimately attain physical, intellectual, and moral perfection.

The nineteenth century also witnessed the "turn to history" in intellectual circles. This took with grave seriousness the effects of history on all things—ideas, religions, and philosophy as well as institutions—but at the same time saw history as progressive improvement through struggle. Darwin's evolution, social Darwinism, and the Industrial Revolution, which, despite its problems, was seen by many as the path to greater happiness for humanity, confirmed this view. Progress toward a hard-earned utopia was in the air of the eighteenth century.

The dominant philosophy that all engaged, in Marx's day, was that of G. W. F. Hegel (AD 1770 – 1831). We have mentioned Hegel's social and political philosophy. Hegel was as systematic and thoroughgoing as Marx, and contributed to the eighteenth-century turn to history.

Recall that Hegel responded to Kant's epistemology. Kant posited a non-traversable gap between our subjective knowledge (*phenomena*) and the objects of our knowledge as they "really are" "in themselves" (*noumena*). Hegel responded that to be aware of a limit (the limits of our subjective knowledge of objects in the world) is to be aware of both sides of what the limit separates. This means that we know at least something about what lies beyond the limits of our knowledge, most fundamentally its existence. So, instead of utterly divorcing a subject's private knowledge from known objects à la Kant, Hegel reunited the subject's knowledge and the object known.

As an Idealist, regarding the metaphysical limit questions about the fundamental nature of reality, Hegel claimed that knowledge and ideas constitute reality. He famously said: "*What is rational is actual* (has existence, is actually real), *and what is actual* (has existence, is actually real) *is rational*."[9] Hegel applied this to social and political philosophy to argue against revolution in an age of revolutions. He said that an existing society as instituted by law is rational and therefore real, with a right to exist. We must not overthrow the current socio-politico status quo, but rather seek to understand it, because it is real and therefore rational.

As an Idealist, Hegel maintained that Absolute Spirit (or Mind) is ultimate reality. The theme of a continual appearance in history of a *thesis*, an *antithesis* negating the thesis, and then a reconciliation of both in a *synthesis* entered the parlance of German Idealism earlier through Johann Gottlieb Fichte (AD 1762 – 1814). Hegel employed this theme, called *dialectic*, of struggle and reconciliation through sublation (*Aufhebung* in German), to describe the progress of Absolute Spirit in history that moves in process toward complete self-realization.

Humans, as rational, embody or incarnate Absolute Spirit but Hegel's organicist theory of human societies, discussed in chapter three, led him to conclude that the state, not individuals, is the full incarnation of Absolute Spirit in history. He also couched his philosophy in the categories of Christian theology. He saw in the doctrine of the Trinity the idea that all beings, including God, are a union of opposites. He saw in the doctrine of the incarnation, of God become man, the idea that God as Absolute Spirit in history exists in humanity, suffers, and dies with a greater goal in mind, expressed by the doctrine of the resurrection.

After Hegel's death his followers split into two camps, the so-called "right-wing" and "left-wing" Hegelians, corresponding to conservative and progressive interpretations. Those on the right interpreted his philosophy as compatible with Christian theology, belief in a theistic God as ultimate reality, and as justifying the political status quo against the revolutionaries.

Those on the left interpreted Hegel's philosophy as asserting the correctness of philosophy over orthodox Christian theology, which they saw as a primitive mythological system of symbols, rightly interpreted by Hegel's philosophical categories, and replaced by them as superior. They also took Hegel's identity of the real with the rational and his claim, that the Absolute Spirit/Mind manifests itself in history through dialectical struggle, to mean that the Absolute Spirit is the same as the universe. They believed that classical Christian monotheism is incorrect and ultimate reality is just the universe taken as a whole. This led to the theological position of atheism and the metaphysical stance of naturalistic materialism, which says matter and energy are ultimate reality. They also judged the current political situation of Europe to be in an inferior stage of dialectical struggle in the progress toward a greater synthesis. On this claim, they found grounds to question the status quo in unison with the revolutionaries.

Marx became a left-wing Hegelian as a student. Early on, he was enamored with another left-wing Hegelian, Ludwig Feuerbach (AD 1804 – 1872). Feuerbach developed a naturalistic explanation of the origin of belief in God using Hegel's reunification of the "knowing subject" and "object known," which Kant had separated. He argued that, in knowing himself, a human is both the knowing subject and known object. The human then projects what he judges to be his best traits, like knowledge, power, presence, love, mercy, fairness, righteous judgment, etc., making them superlative and unlimited (i.e., omniscience, omnipotence, omnibenevolence, omnipresence). At the same time, the person omits his traits that he judges to be bad and limited (i.e., ignorance, powerlessness, evil, immorality, unfairness, etc.). The person then objectifies this idealized knowledge of his own nature as if it were a real thing distinct from himself—an object—but still in anthropomorphic form as "God." This projection becomes to the human person an independent subject over, above, and against himself:

> Man—this is the mystery of religion—projects his being into objectivity, and then again makes himself an object to this projected image of himself thus converted into a subject; he thinks of himself as an object to himself, but as the object of an object, of another being than himself. Thus here (sic). Man is an object to God. . . God is the highest subjectivity of man abstracted from himself.[10]

For Feuerbach, this idealized and projected human nature becomes an idol that a person worships and serves as if it were distinct from him. By projecting his own idealized human nature, worshipping it, and serving it, the person is alienated from his true self. This is the tragedy of religion:

> . . . in proportion as the divine subject is in reality human, the greater is the apparent difference between God and man; that is, the more, by reflection on religion, by theology, is the identity of the divine and human denied, and the human considered as such, is depreciated. . . . To enrich God, man must become poor; that God may be all, man must become nothing. But he desires to be nothing in himself, because what he takes from himself is not lost to him, since it is preserved in God. . . . What man withdraws from himself, what he renounces in himself, he only enjoys in an incomparably higher and fuller measure in God. . . . The more subjective God is, the more completely does man divest himself of his subjectivity, because God is, *per se*, his relinquished self, the possession of which he however again vindicates to himself.[11]

The individual is subject to an illusory antithesis between himself and God, because God is not real but only a projection of the person's idealized nature. There is a Hegelian antithesis between the real human individual and the projected human nature. Using a Hegelian idea recurring in many reactions to Hegel—like the fathers of existentialism Sören Kierkegaard (AD 1813 – 1855) and Friedrich Nietzsche (AD 1844 – 1900)— Feuerbach speaks of this antithesis between the person and their projected nature as an *alienation*.

This alienation between the individual and the good qualities of their nature causes, argues Feuerbach, passivity and non-activism. Belief in God makes people passively accept and suffer their lot in the present life, without trying to improve it, because of their false hope for a reward in the afterlife, which is not real according to his atheistic materialism. According to Feuerbach, then, belief in God causes oppressed people to accept the status quo instead of trying to change it. Once people realize this antithesis and alienation of their own making, they can embrace and use all of the virtues and powers of human nature to improve their lives in the here and now.[12]

Embracing left-wing Hegelian atheism and materialism, the young Marx was keen on Feuerbach's explanation of the human predicament and projection theory of the origin of belief in God. Playing on the etymology of Feuerbach's name (*Feuer* means "fire," and *Bach* means "stream" in German), in 1842 Marx wrote: "There is no other way for you to truth and freedom, but through a stream of fire [a *Feuer-bach*]. Feuerbach is the Purgatorium of the present."[13]

Very quickly—only three years later—Marx produced a scathing critique of Feuerbach in his *Theses on Feuerbach* (1845). Therein he: (1) criticizes left-wing Hegelianism and Feuerbach for remaining at the abstract and theoretical level of contemplation instead of practical and concrete change (Theses 1 & 5); (2) says the question of truth is pragmatic and truth is proved through experience, not theoretical and scholastic disputes over the reality or non-reality of thinking (Thesis 2); (3) claims that Feuerbach's analysis of religious self-alienation is a symptom but not the real cause of humanity's problems (Thesis 4); (4) faults him for understanding human nature as an abstraction from the individual person instead of correctly viewing human nature as an ensemble of social conditions, because both humanity and religion are social products, not individualistic (Theses 6, 7 & 9); and (5) ends with the famous statement: "The philosophers have only *interpreted* the world, in various ways; the point, however, is to *change* it."[14]

Several ideas that become major themes in Marx's philosophy appear in the *Theses on Feuerbach.* The stress on the practical nature of truth and the priority of the society over the individual—found in Hegel's organicist theory of societies, as discussed earlier—have been identified as seminal ideas for postmodern philosophy, which rejects some key assumptions of modern philosophy. In the *Theses* Marx also advocates a "new" materialism that does not view the determinism implied by materialism as necessitating a passive acceptance of the status quo (Theses 3, 9 & 10), but includes human activity to initiate social change.

As a left-wing Hegelian, Marx accepted the atheistic materialist interpretation of Hegel. Materialism answers the limit question about ultimate reality by claiming it is matter and energy. With the revolutionary philosophical and religious changes of the modern period, materialism rose to prominence in conjunction with the success of scientific explanations for natural phenomena, which had hitherto been given religious and spiritual explanations.

Modern science increasingly explained events in terms of prior efficient causes and rejected the older metaphysical claims about "final" causes that dominated medieval Christian thought. Final causality regards the purposes, goals, and reasons for events and entities. As we earlier pointed out, the metaphysical notion of final causality has functioned in a number of answers to ethical limit questions. Some claim that all human action is goal-oriented, and natural law theories rely on the belief that all entities have a specific purpose or reason for existing.

Modern science's prioritization of efficient causality—temporally prior events as causes solely account for later events as effects—coupled with the success of scientific explanations led to a denigration of final causality. This led to a crisis of values, meaning, and purpose in modernity, which eventually permeated modern societies and cultures. Further, efficient causality combined with materialism leads to metaphysical determinism, an iron chain of cause and effect in nature that precludes indeterminacy and freedom, as discussed earlier in earlier chapters.

Even though a staunch materialist and determinist, Marx pointed out that humans are unique in nature. For Marx, on the one hand, humans are the results of deterministic materialistic processes. On the other hand, humans also "transcend" natural processes, by manipulating and changing natural causes to produce effects different from those which would naturally occur.[15] Technology, which applies scientific knowledge to effect such changes, is an example. Despite the severe problems that attended it, the Industrial Revolution involved technology in action to alter nature and improve humanity's natural lot.

Thus, in good Enlightenment humanist fashion, Marx argued that deterministic materialism should not lead us to passive acceptance of the status quo, but rather motivate us to actively transform conditions we judge to be poor.[16] Economics, as a science, deals with natural causes and effects. We can alter causes and effects through technology, or applied science. This raises the question of whether or not we should change the causes in order to get more desirable effects, and, hence, raises limit questions about ethics and values. This gives rise to normative economics in addition to positive economics. Marx urged that even though in his view determinism is true, our unique ability to transcend and alter nature imposes an obligation on us to improve economic situations, by manipulating the causes to produce effects that are judged to be better.

Hegel had tried to at least partially ground his philosophy of history on the empirical facts of history. As a left-wing Hegelian and materialist, Marx embarked on a scientific interpretation of history that finds the deterministic laws of human economic development with the goal of changing economic causes to bring about better effects. In *Capital* he likens his empirical observation of Industrial Revolution England's capitalism to that of physicists who observe nature to arrive at scientific laws through induction, claiming that "it is the ultimate aim of this work, to lay bare the economic motion of law of modern society."[17]

As a left-wing Hegelian, Marx stressed the "real" over the "rational" side of Hegel's equation of the real with the rational. For Marx, ideas are the products of concrete material forces in history. Using its ideas, human reason can and should understand the material forces at work in human history, but the causes and effects of historical development are ultimately material. We are material beings living in a material world, and so we depend on matter for life, subsistence, and flourishing. This is why, for Marx, the abstractions of philosophy cannot improve humanity's lot. This is what he criticized Feuerbach and other "old" left-wing materialists for claiming.

Marx applied Hegel's dialectical analysis of the progress of Absolute Spirit to the material forces of human history in what was later dubbed *dialectical materialism*.[18] For Marx, ideas are secondary and only mental representation of the material world humans know and contemplate. He did see history as following an iron deterministic chain of cause and effect, just as Hegel's dialectical development of Absolute Spirit followed the deterministic certainty of logical deduction. For Marx as for Hegel, history is the dialectical appearance of a *thesis* later negated by its own contradiction in an *antithesis* to be later sublated in a *synthesis*. Instead of ideas as for Hegel, for Marx these are material forces in perpetual conflict and reconciliation. Yet this dialectical struggle is as necessary and inevitable for Marx as for Hegel.

Because, for Marx, humans are material beings living in a material world and requiring material resources for their existence and flourishing, Marx saw the dialectical struggle as a conflict of classes competing for scarce material resources. Marx saw modern free market capitalism as another instance of the perpetual dialectical class conflict in human history:

> The history of all hitherto existing society is the history of class struggles. Freeman and slave, patrician and plebian, lord and serf, guild-master and journeyman, in a word, oppressor and oppressed, stood in constant opposition to one another, carried on in an uninterrupted, now hidden, now open fight, a fight that each time ended, either in a revolutionary re-constitution of society at large, or in a common ruin of the contending classes. In earlier epochs of history, we find almost everywhere a complicated arrangement of society into various orders, a manifold gradation of rank. . . . The modern bourgeois society that has sprouted from the ruins of feudal society has not done away with class antagonisms. It has but established new classes, new conditions of oppression, new forms of struggle in place of old ones.[19]

A primary concern of Marx was to know why these struggles for material resources occur, causing the rise and fall of dominant socio-politico-economic arrangements in history. In his philosophy Marx divided history into several distinct epochs. He said that earliest history, before the rise of private property, was primitive and communal. With the advent of private property arose a succession of several epochs, each characterized by the dominant technological resources used to manipulate material resources, in order to produce goods and services to meet humanity's material needs and wants. Concomitant with these technological resources, a dominant economic structure arose, dividing those who own the means of production from the unskilled laborers. The economic system of a given epoch was characterized by those who owned the means of production and therefore had power over the laborers. The economic systems of each era were thus founded on class divisions that fueled the class conflicts of that era.

He often iterates these epochs as: (1) prehistoric communal society as ideal without private property and class conflicts; (2) slavery in antiquity; (3) feudalism in the Middle Ages; (4) capitalism in modernity; and (5) the socialist/communist era yet to come, which will return humanity to the ideal state without private property and class conflicts. Determinist laws push humanity through these stages, and so they are inevitable. The fifth epoch is also inevitable, as Marx describes in his analysis of the fourth epoch in which he believed himself to live.

Generally speaking, Marx saw these eras as relatively stable periods in which economic systems correspond to the dominant form of technology that humanity had hitherto developed to manipulate nature in order to supply its material needs and wants. Our unique rational nature, enabling us to transcend nature, and our inherent creativity cause advances in technology across time. When new technological means of production and distribution of material resources arise, they conflict with the extant technological means of production and distribution of resources, or the status quo. An internal dialectical contradiction of thesis and antithesis develops, and a revolutionary upheaval occurs, ushering humanity into a new epoch.

Marx called the private owners of the means of production in the modern capitalist era, the *bourgeoisie*, and the masses of unskilled laborers, the *proletariat*. *Proletariat* comes from Latin meaning "landless," and specified that they do not own property, and therefore only have their labor to sell to make a living. *Bourgeoisie* comes from a French term meaning "town's people," used to designate the new urban class of bankers, craftsmen, and merchants that arose in the late Middle Ages, and who had material resources to engage in trade.

Marx's critique of capitalism centers on profit. He argued that the goal of capitalists who own the means of production is to make profits, which are then reinvested in more means of production, or capital. Increased profits mean increased investment and capital, and hence supply side growth. He argued that the profit motive has no other end or goal than accumulation:

> Accumulate, Accumulate! That is Moses and the prophets! 'Industry furnishes the material which saving accumulates.' Therefore, save, save, i.e., reconvert the greatest possible portion of surplus-value, or surplus product into capital! Accumulation for accumulation's sake, production for production's sake.[20]

In order to make profits to fuel the accumulation of more means of production, the capitalist must pay laborers less than the value of their labor, according to Marx. He held to the early modern labor theory of value, as we described in Locke's political philosophy. The labor theory of value says that all natural resources are the common property of all. When someone mixes their labor with a natural resource to produce an artifact, like making pottery from clay or a weapon from copper, then the product has more value due to the added labor. Marx claimed that, in primitive times, those who made artifacts from natural resources owned and used those same artifacts.

With the rise of private property and advancement in technology during later epochs, the means of production were owned by only a few. Most people did not own the means of production, and so had to trade their labor to obtain the material resources they needed to live. Those who owned the means of production employed laborers to produce goods to be sold. This had the appearance of a free trade relationship in which laborers sold their labor to owners of the means of production. It was not free, though, because laborers did not own the means of production, and had no other way to make a living. Marx thus called this a form of slavery for the worker, sometimes comparing it to the chattel slavery in the antebellum American South.

Marx says that a good's value is a function of the natural resources, means of production, and the labor used to produce it. The owner of the means of production provides the first two components, but the laborer provides the third part. In order to gain value beyond what they put into making the good, owners of the means of production must pay laborers less than the value of the labor they contributed to the good. Hence the workers' wages are less than what they deserve for the labor they contributed, and in effect the capitalist steals some of the value due to laborers in what Marx calls *surplus value*, or profit. The less the owners pay workers, the more surplus value or profit they make, so they try to pay workers as little as possible. In the capitalist era, capitalists reinvest much of the surplus value or profits they take from workers back into means of production, or capital.

Marx uses the Hegelian idea of *alienation* to describe the effect that the profit motive has on workers. Alienation is separation with negative connotations. Feuerbach claimed individuals are alienated from their true selves when they project the good aspects of their human nature out into their created idea of God. For Feuerbach, alienation of the person from her own nature is the problem.

In his stricter materialism and on his labor theory of value, Marx claimed that workers are alienated from the material fruits of their labor, not an abstract idea or nature. Labor is a material thing that workers mix with natural resources. When the capitalist steals part of this labor in order to make a profit, the worker is alienated from her labor, which is part of her.

Marx agreed with Feuerbach's projection theory for the origin of belief in God. However, he characteristically held that the *idea* of God is secondary and dependent on primary *material* causes. The idea of God is symptomatic of the real problem of material alienation. People are really alienated from their material essence, which subsists in their labor and which the capitalist steals. Labor, as alienated material essence, is valued by money, which becomes an object separate from the worker. The worker worships and serves this false God of money. Money is really their own alienated self and rightly belongs to them, in the same way that for Feuerbach people worship and serve their own human nature, which they wrongly believe is distinct from them.

Marx described other forms of alienation that he believed capitalism produces. Instead of valuing workers as human beings who are ends in themselves, the capitalist treats workers as means to the end of profit. This criticism is like Kant's second formulation of the categorical imperative. The capitalist does not treat the worker as a human being but as a tool.

Workers also compete with other workers for jobs, so they do not view each other as human beings who are ends in themselves. Thus, in each other's eyes, workers are alienated from their true human nature. Further, Marx claims that workers view capitalists as mere tools to earn a living, and not as human beings. Thus capitalists, too, are alienated from their true human nature.

Therefore, in Marx's philosophy, the fundamental problem with capitalism is that the profit motive causes human alienation. How does the Hegelian dialectic of thesis, antithesis, and synthesis, play out in capitalism? In the current epoch and on the larger scale, Marx identified free market capitalism as the thesis, the rise and consolidation of the proletarian class in revolution as the antithesis, and socialism as the sublation or synthesis. According to Marx, free market capitalism contains inner dialectical contradictions, which will inevitably lead to its demise.

First, capitalism's individualism, competition, and private property are contradictory. Ironically, as capitalism grows, it relies on more interdependence and social interaction among capitalists. As capitalism grows the social network of capitalists grows, and so all competitors eventually get the latest technology. This eliminates some capitalists' competitive edge over others, which decreases profits. For Marx, capitalists exploit laborers by taking their surplus labor as profit, but as technology increases and the need for labor decreases, the ability to exploit surplus labor decreases as well. Hence profits decrease. Marx also speculated that increased technology would lead to overproduction, and thus a supply increase (supply curve shifts out) while demand remains the same. This results in a lower equilibrium price, which also decreases profits.

Capitalism would thus ruin most capitalists, as eventually most will not make enough profits to survive. The means of production will fall into the hands of fewer and fewer capitalists. Marx also predicted that a combination of globalization and the quest for cheaper labor, to save dwindling profits, would result in capitalists expanding production overseas and internationally.

In Marx's theory the proletariat class rises as the antithesis to capitalism. Free market capitalism necessarily produces great disparities in material wealth. He predicted an increase in the number of the working poor, as failed capitalists join the ranks of the proletariat and wealthy capitalists become fewer and fewer. As the proletariat grows in size, the labor supply increases while the demand for labor remains the same, thus reducing the price of labor (wages).

Marx predicted that the plight of the growing masses of the poor would become so great that they would unify, first on a small scale, like labor unions, but then on an increasingly large—even international—scale, and then revolt. The victorious (by virtue of sheer numbers) proletariat would then rule, at first in a heavy-handed and vengeful way, but then through socialism, where a proletarian state owns the means to production and collectively distributes goods and services.

Socialism for Marx is the ineluctable result the historical dialectic as it passes through the self-defeating capitalist stage. He saw socialism as a good dialectical development but not the final one. Marx believed socialism would be a step on the way to communism, the final consummation of the dialectical materialist process. Communism for Marx corresponds to Hegel's historical consummation in complete self-knowledge of Absolute Spirit. It is the completely rational, and therefore most real, manifestation of human society. Thus communism will bring a complete break from, and cessation of, the dialectical class struggles of history.

In Marx's final communist stage private ownership of the means of production, either by capitalists or by the state, will cease. Private ownership of the means of production is the source of perennial class distinctions so that when it disappears, so will class conflicts. There will no longer be the haves and the have-nots. There will no longer be a working class "enslaved" to their employers. Workers will no longer be alienated from the fruits of their labor and will be valued as ends in themselves instead of means to the end of material gain. Humans, predicts Marx, will cease to live in a state of conflict and competition, instead, living in a state of mutual cooperation, support, and valuing of one another as a family. In the communist state, all dialectical contradictions of history, nature, and humanity are resolved:

> This communism, as fully-developed naturalism, equals humanism, and as fully-developed humanism equals naturalism; it is the *genuine* resolution of the conflict between man and nature and between man and man—the true resolution of the strife between existence and essence, between objectification and self-confirmation, between freedom and necessity, between the individual and the species. Communism is the riddle of history solved, and it knows itself to be this solution.[21]

In his philosophical anthropology Marx believed that people are not intrinsically selfish, greedy, and competitive. He believed that their social conditions make them this way. This corresponds to the Hegelian prioritization of society over the individual. When society changes from the class struggle for material resources to the communist collective, so, too, will individuals cease to be selfish, greedy, and competitive. In some ways, Marx's philosophical anthropology views human nature like Rousseau's, as discussed in chapter three. It sees human beings as essentially good but corrupted by bad social conditions.

Again, for Marx, ideas are secondary to the material world, which alone is real. As a left-wing Hegelian and dialectical materialist, Marx stresses the "real" side of the Hegelian maxim "the real is the rational" and understands this reality as matter/energy. The "rational" is humanity's secondary moment of thinking about its primary material existence and activity.

Thus, for Marx, culture, social conventions, legal structures, philosophy, and religion are secondary products of primary material forces and economic structures. The mental and intellectual trappings of an epoch reflect the dominant economic substructure of the era, and are used by the few in power to control and exploit the masses of people they are oppressing.

Marx holds that those in power use the religious belief in a blissful afterlife to make the oppressed masses passively accept their miserable lot in this life, with a false hope. They likewise use religiously motivated ethical principles for gaining a better afterlife to keep the oppressed masses submissive and passive. Moral injunctions like: "If you want to go to heaven when you die, then do not steal, turn the other cheek, forgive, and do not take vengeance, etc." have the real motivation of preventing the oppressed masses from rebelling against their oppressors now.

Marx calls the dominant mental structure, arising from the material and economic forces of a given period and used by the few in power to subjugate the masses, an *ideology*. Since Marx, and through other thinkers like Friedrich Nietzsche (AD 1844 – 1900) and Sigmund Freud (AD 1856 – 1939), the goal of deconstructing ideologies, to get beyond their apparent reasons to their real reasons of power and control, have become prominent in what has been dubbed postmodern *deconstruction*. We have already noted other adumbrations of postmodern thought in Marx, such as his pragmatic notion of truth and the prioritization of the society over the individual.

Because he believed that the intellectual structures of a society are the result of more basic and real material and economic forces, Marx questioned the practical cash-value of ideas for actually changing the world. On this basis, he criticized his fellow Hegelians, like Feuerbach, for focusing on ideas instead of praxis. We have noted, though, that Marx's philosophy has arguably had more concrete effects on people's lives than that of any other philosopher.[22] The twentieth century witnessed numerous political revolutions that found their justification in Marx's call to proletariat revolution. He ends his *Manifesto of the Communist Party* with these words:

> The Communists disdain to conceal their views and aims. They openly declare that their ends can be attained only by the forcible overthrow of all existing social conditions. Let the ruling classes tremble at the Communist revolution. The proletarians have nothing to lose but their chains. They have the world to win. WORKING MEN OF ALL COUNTRIES, UNITE![23]

Marx's predictions about the dialectical development of capitalism, socialism, and communism include the prediction that the final consummation of the communist state would be international. If ever attained, then, this would obviate the concern addressed in our summary of socialism, concerning how socialist and communist countries still operate in globally free markets, and thus do not avoid the criticisms of free market capitalism on the international scale. Marx's communist utopia is international, and all free market capitalism is abolished worldwide.

There is also the ethical question of revolution. Is there ever a time that violence is morally justified to attain what is judged a greater good? Normative ethical systems that: (1) judge the violence of revolution to be evil and (2) judge that bad means make good ends themselves bad, would judge such revolution as ethically unacceptable. Other ethical systems, like utilitarianism, would conclude that sometimes some bad is necessary for a greater net good to be achieved.

MORALLY ASSESSING FREE MARKET CAPITALISM, SOCIALISM, AND COMMUNISM

In the next sections we raise some considerations for morally assessing free market capitalism, socialism, and communism. These sections presuppose all that has been said in the previous chapters on economics, ethics, social and political philosophy, and philosophy in general. Here we reference concepts, terms, and analyses discussed in previous chapters. Thus, to fully understand the following sections, it is imperative to read the earlier chapters.

As we raise these considerations we present arguments for and against these three economic systems. We try to show how different answers to ethical limit questions addressed in earlier chapters lead to different moral assessments. As we said in the introduction, our goal is not to exhaustively analyze any one consideration. We only want to raise the point with the minimal knowledge required to understand its importance. We leave the task of comprehensive analysis to others to examine each point in greater depth. A book must be written to do justice to any one of these considerations. Here we offer only a modest iteration and summary of the issues involved in morally assessing capitalism, socialism, and communism.

We must keep in mind that a satisfactory analysis of any one system requires identifying moral criteria to pass judgment on the system, including determining which components of the system weigh more heavily in the moral assessment. We do not specify a system or rubric for moral assessment. As an example, one such criterion would include the distinction raised earlier between ethical judgments of moral agents and individual actions. Economic systems are complex with many parts. We can analyze both parts and whole systems. Should we make ethical judgments only about entire economic systems, or their parts too? If the latter, then how do we grade the relative worth of each part in the final overall moral assessment?

Many of the considerations here regard specific ethical questions addressed earlier in this book. Some, though, regard historic economic and political data. When appealing to such data, we must remember that counterfactuals are difficult to settle. It is easy to say that things could have been otherwise had other courses of action been taken. Such claims are difficult to prove.

We examine these systems in tandem because an argument against one is often an argument in favor of another. An argument against free market capitalism, for example, is often an argument for socialism and/or communism, and vice versa. Thus, while we focus first on considerations for a moral assessment of capitalism, we really raise considerations that apply to all three systems. We try to show how different answers lead to different judgments of each.

Early on we said that the goal-oriented nature of human action raises limit questions about values, or axiology. We also distinguished between positive economics as the scientific study of the laws of economic systems, and normative economics as policy-making about what "should" be the case in economic systems. Choices to let economic systems run freely with as little regulation possible, as in free market capitalism, and choices to intervene to alter the way economic systems naturally allocate resources, as in socialism and communism, are goal-oriented and value-informed. We morally assess these economic systems with the goal of judging which is best, and of trying to implement it. The choice for free market capitalism is a choice to not act but it is still choice, based on the value judgment that free market capitalism is best.

Finally, by way of introducing these sections, not only ethical questions but other philosophical questions arise because they are inextricably bound up with ethical limit questions. What is the nature and purpose of a human society? What is the best form of government? Are human beings incorrigibly selfish or can they be selfless? What is ultimate reality? How real are ideas? Are human choices determined or free? How and why should we classify beings according to certain groups? These philosophical limit questions and more arise, at least implicitly if not explicitly, in moral assessing free market capitalism, socialism, and communism.

Some Considerations in Morally Assessing Free Market Capitalism

There are many arguments for and against the morality of capitalism. Each assumes answers to numerous ethical limit questions. Often an argument for capitalism is an argument against socialism or communism, and an argument against capitalism is one in favor of socialism or communism. Specific pros and cons of capitalism, socialism, and communism are related to other pros and cons. Here we raise some considerations for a moral assessment of capitalism, but in doing so we, by way of contrast, raise considerations for evaluations of socialism and communism. Some considerations arise repeatedly because of their close relationship to others.

Some of the greatest arguments for capitalism are consequentialist. Free markets produce the greatest net utility as measured by positive economics, as we have seen. We have also seen that free markets create the greatest long-run economic growth.[24] Long-run economic growth means many long-term benefits to a society, including a higher standard of living for everyone—including the poorest in the society compared to the poor in other societies, longer life expectancy, technological advances to make life easier, better healthcare, lower cost of goods and services (regulations increase supplier input costs and therefore increase prices), and more goods and services to choose from. Free market capitalism is most efficient in using scarce resources and avoiding waste, and many judge wasting scarce resources to be immoral.

Many normative ethical systems can judge maximum net utility, these long-term benefits, and avoiding waste as good. Advocates of free market capitalism point to the higher standard of living in capitalist countries compared to non-capitalist countries, now and historically.

Yet, in some ethical systems, the opportunity costs of attaining these goods outweigh them, or the bad means necessary to attain them eviscerate their goodness. These include things judged to be bad like: (1) income, wealth, and standard of living disparities that free market capitalism produces; (2) competition, the profit motive, and risk-taking as discussed previously; and (3) the greed, dishonesty, and other vices said to result, as also discussed previously. Strictly non-consequentialist rule-based normative ethical systems—be they rational deontological, divine command theory, human rights theories, or other—would add that good consequences of capitalism can never justify the immorality of breaking *a priori* ethical principles.

Free market capitalist advocates often use a consequentialist argument that admits these ethical liabilities of capitalism, but claim that its long-term benefits produce a greater net utility for all members of society, all things considered. Therefore, capitalism's moral liabilities are necessary evils for a greater overall net good, or capitalism is the "least of all evils."

We noted in our discussion of utilitarian consequentialism, in chapter three, that most utilitarians claim some evils are necessary to produce the greatest good for the greatest number. We used the common example of a soldier jumping on a grenade and dying to save his platoon members as necessary to produce the greatest good for the greatest number. A common philosophical thought experiment, used to question this utilitarian claim and to highlight the problem of justice,[25] is to envision a scenario in which it is necessary to hideously torture an innocent infant perpetually, in order to maximize pleasure for an entire society. Without torturing the infant, pleasure would not be maximized.

The problem is that saying it is morally justifiable to endlessly torture an infant for a society's greatest net happiness goes against our moral intuitions. One explanation for this is that we intuitively value certain things, like not torturing innocent children, more than others, and these can be missed in a utilitarian calculus of the greatest net happiness. Remember that Mill made a qualitative distinction between types of happiness in response to Bentham's more strictly quantitative analysis of pleasure in the utilitarian calculus. Similarly, things like food, shelter, employment, and healthcare may be judged to be more valuable than the utility of expressing preferences according to individuals' perceived needs and wants, as does positive economics, and as is used by many free market capitalists to justify the inequalities of condition necessary for other long-term societal benefits in terms of utility and welfare maximization.

Another point is that some who admit the value of the market's efficiency in generating maximum utility and welfare still fault capitalism for wasting scarce resources in other ways. A criticism of free market capitalism is that it creates false wants and needs. To sell more goods suppliers try to convince buyers that they should want, or even need, what they really should not want and do not need. This creates an artificial excess of demand that does not correspond to real wants and needs. This artificial excess of demand is not reflected in an analysis of the supply and demand curves because they represent individuals' preferences already informed by their own perceptions of what they think they need and want, which are apparent, as opposed to real, needs and wants.

This artificial demand fuels a level of consumption of resources above what it would be without the false needs and wants. In this way, more scarce resources are consumed than necessary. This is a different form of waste than deadweight loss and other forms of utility loss, as measured in positive economics, and assumes a distinction between real and apparent goods. Yet, if the distinction is valid and if this does happen, then overconsumption is a consideration.

Another case for capitalism entails the arguments for prioritizing the social value of liberty that we examined. We have seen that capitalism highly values freedom. Free markets maximize the freedom of individuals and groups to enter markets and engage in trade according to their preferences. Further, the maximal economic growth, which free markets insure, means many more goods and services for people to choose from and more choices mean more freedom.

Some critics of capitalism contend that guaranteeing this freedom usually assumes that individuals know what is best for themselves and society, are rational, and have full knowledge of what they are doing when they trade. Hence some use arguments for paternalism and a distinction between *real* and *apparent* goods to gainsay the capitalist prioritization of freedom.

We have also seen how, like material resources in their allocation and consumption, social values can be mutually exclusive. Prioritizing freedom often means diminishing equality of condition. Capitalism will trade-off equality for liberty, but socialism and communism will trade-off freedom for equality. This difference is based on judgments about which social value is more valuable, as we examined in chapter four. For instance, advocates of equality over freedom indicate that Mill's "Harm Principle" is contradictory and nonsensical, since all societies must impose some restrictions on individual freedoms in order for the society to exist.

Free market capitalist advocates also argue that justice is merit-based and retributive, not an equal treatment in terms of an equal distribution of goods and services. Recall from chapter four that, although there are different conceptions of justice, a common denominator between them is the general principle "equal treatment of equal cases." Different conceptions of justice differ in what "treatment" and "cases" mean. In some economic understandings of the justice, "treatment" means "provision of certain goods and services" and "cases" means "every person in society." Various socialist and communist positions construe economic justice this way. In merit-based conceptions, "treatment" means "rewards and punishments," and "cases" means specific actions judged to be meritorious or deserving punishment, regardless of who does the acting.

Economically, merit-based justice means those who contribute to society deserve material rewards that those who do not contribute to society, or harm society, do not deserve. Material rewards should be commensurate with merit. In this view, giving the same material resources to one who has contributed less, not contributed, or brought detriment to society, is unjust.

Free market capitalists also say that the neutral free market mechanism, not a privileged individual or group, should determine merit. Individuals and groups can be biased and have different views of merit. Plus, there are too many agents in the market for any person or group, even if they are nonbiased, to know the contributions of each. Such a judge must be all-knowing. Thus the free market, in which all collectively, and those closest to each agent, "vote" with their money, is alone qualified to judge. This means that some can and will differ from the judgment of the market, but the market determines reward and punishment. Someone may think it unjust that fast-food workers make less money than surgeons, but the collective supply and demand of the markets for fast-food and surgery alone are qualified to judge the value of fast-food workers and surgeons. Some may think it unjust that movie stars make more money than candy factory workers, but the collective supply and demand of the markets for movies and candy are the final arbiters of the merits of movie stars and candy factory workers.

So advocates of free market capitalism define justice as merit-based. For merit-based justice to work, equality of opportunity is necessary. This, again, raises limit questions about the "able" side of the posited "willing and able" market agent. What about those who are unable to participate in market activities? What if someone is willing to be a surgeon but does not have the resources to get the education and training? What of the physically and mentally handicapped?

Free market advocates respond that this is not a question of justice but of charity. One assesses charity's value according to answers to limit questions in a number of areas, including philosophical anthropology (e.g., psychological egoism vs. altruism) and according to one's normative ethics. However, many—including free market capitalists—judge charity to be good and virtuous. Some judge it to be a moral obligation, as in a divine command theory that says "Love your neighbor as yourself," while others judge charity to be good but not obligatory.

Opponents of free market capitalism point to a widespread lack of charity in free market systems without some intervention in free markets. Yes, successful rich persons do give to charity but they are typically the exception, not the rule. Some opponents even point to how individuals and businesses use charity as means to make more money, as in tax exemptions for charitable giving or as means to hide other dealings judged to be immoral. They claim that in capitalism charity becomes a means to cover up the profit motive, avarice, and exploitation.

Socialists and communists, again, claim that it is wrong to assume market agents are "able" as well as "willing," and hence claim that equality of opportunity does not exist as the necessary prerequisite for merit-based justice in free market capitalism. Alternatively, they argue that the state must intervene in markets to insure greater equality of opportunity, or we must drop the conception of justice as merit-based altogether for one that is more like equality of condition.

Some—but certainly not all— free market capitalists question the value of charity altogether. This seems counterintuitive, but they argue that saving increases capital, or the investment (I) factor in the macroeconomic formula for Gross Domestic Product (GDP), as discussed in chapter three. Because increasing aggregate supply is necessary for the long-run economic growth that benefits all in society in many ways, they claim that saving is better for all, in the long-run, than giving money to the needy now, in the short-run. Sanderson[26] speaks of a *tactile fallacy* in which donors think they are doing "good" by giving charity and to the needy whom they see now, but fail to see the countless future individuals who would also benefit if instead the individual saved their money thereby increasing investment and affecting long-run economic growth that requires capital investment now. Thus there is a trade-off to charity today and that is less investment today, and this can have effects on our long-run economic growth.

Using a form of psychological egoism, or at least questioning the motives of many philanthropists, some claim that people give charity now to people they can see because it makes them feel better. They argue that the best thing to do is to forgo feeling good now, save, and invest now, which will benefit all in society in many and greater ways in the long-run.

How one ethically judges charity depends on answers to limit questions about the relative value of long-run economic growth, honoring certain rights and moral principles now, human nature and its motivations in acting, and how time factors into economic value judgments.

Critics of free market capitalism also question prioritizing merit-based distributive justice, because it assumes that players in markets have acted morally in making the contributions that the market has rewarded with material resources. What if a business sells more goods because of false advertising? What of the "robber barons" of the *laissez-faire* post-Civil War U. S. A. and the Gilded Age? What if capital has been accumulated by means judged to be unethical?

Critics of free market capitalism may admit that on capitalist assumptions merit-based distributive justice is highly valuable. However, they indicate that merit-based justice assumes equality of opportunity, as discussed in chapter four. If different market agents do not have the same opportunity to merit, then are the cases "really the same" and is merit-based distributive justice really fair? If minorities or women cannot get an education or a job because of their race or gender, but majority races and men do, then is it right to say that white males' rewards are merited but blacks', Latinos', and women's are not? The minorities and women do not have the same equality of opportunity as the white males. Issues surrounding the limit question of metaphysical free will and determinism in philosophical anthropology surface here as well.

A related problem with the merit-based distributive justice, requiring equality of opportunity, is the claim that capitalism protects the vested interests of the few rich and powerful. Those with more money and power can influence market structures. Smaller businesses can be squeezed out of markets so that monopolies (exclusive suppliers with no competitors) result. Sometimes monopsonies (exclusive demand with no competitors) appear. Those with more money can use their money to attain goods and services that give them an advantage in the market that disrupts equality of opportunity.

The rich and powerful in one market can also disrupt equality of opportunity in other markets, violating merit-based distributive justice in those markets. A software CEO accused of a crime can afford the best lawyers, but a poor minority accused of the same crime cannot. The CEO's lawyer wins the case, not based on justice but on skill, while the poor minority loses his case, not based on justice but due to lack of skill. Can we really say merit-based justice is served in such cases? In such cases equality of opportunity is diminished and, hence, so is merit-based distributive justice.

Similarly, the rich and powerful can use their power to control elected officials to influence governmental legislation in their favor. This, too, disrupts equality of justice and hence merit-based distributive justice. There is pervasive political lobbying by interest groups who use money to influence politicians, who are financially supported by those special-interest groups and "Super PACs." The more money that some elected officials get this way, the better they are able to "buy" their offices. Once in office, they are indebted to their patrons so they pass legislation in their favor. Thus, money and power give certain groups unfair advantages in the marketplace. This applies to elected officials of all major political parties. This is also the origin of the claim that in free market capitalism the government is "in the pocket of big business" and, "corrupt." When this occurs, some gain an unfair advantage over others in their respective markets, equality of condition is jeopardized, and so is merit-based distributive justice.

These considerations also pose problems for the premise that agents in free markets are "willing," or free. Recall that Marx claimed—*pace* capitalist claims to the contrary—that Industrial Revolution workers were forced to work for less than they wanted and needed, which constituted a form of slavery. They were not really free because they had no other choice.

Similar charges can be leveled if the wealthy and powerful gain unfair advantages in markets, as in monopolies. A concern today is that oil cartels control the oil supply. Modern people in industrialized countries, like the U. S. A., rely on gasoline for their day-to-day activities. They need gasoline, and so buy it at prices higher than they really want to pay for it. This means that the market equilibrium point does not really reflect the point at which buyers are "freely" expressing their preferences and maximizing their utility. A utility analysis is inaccurate, because the assumption, that agents in the market are "willing" as well as able, is false.

To these charges, free market capitalists rejoin that monopolies and legislation, bought for vested interests, presuppose the market regulations that free market capitalists so staunchly oppose. It is precisely more government intervention in the markets, not less, that causes these problems. Thus, free market capitalists argue that the responsibility for such corruption lies with critics of free markets who advocate more governmental regulation, not with free markets.

So there are numerous criticisms of free market capitalism that it promotes vices, bad actions, and jeopardizes the value of merit-based distributive justice that it so highly prizes. We will discuss the criticisms that capitalism hides, even promotes, vices, later. Advocates of capitalism respond that an all-knowing moral assessment of every market agent's motives and actions is impossible. There are too many players and transactions to monitor. Although, yes, some agents doubtlessly act immorally—according to a number of different normative ethical systems—the free market is still the best universal, all-encompassing, and unbiased judge of merit, all things considered. Capitalists also retort that when immoral business dealings are found out and made public, they harm those practicing them, as people will not patronize such suppliers. Thus it is in the best interest of suppliers and sellers to act with integrity.

As noted, many essentially free market capitalist societies, including the U. S. A., have implemented more centralized planning and government intervention in markets since the Great Depression and the Second World War. These modern mixed economies have the goal of promoting greater equality of opportunity and condition. Doing so involves unavoidable trade-offs in other things that capitalism values, like efficiency and long-run economic growth.

Free market capitalists also point to the hitherto failures of many socialist and communist societies. The former USSR and her allies, constituting the Eastern Bloc vis-à-vis the "Free World" during the Cold War, collapsed at the end of the twentieth century. Those that have survived and flourished, like China, have adopted more free market capitalist practices. During the Cold War many citizens of these countries tried to emigrate to free market capitalist countries. This shows that they preferred them over the socialist and communist systems where they lived and were unhappy. Today, we see increasing economic and social troubles among western European countries that have adopted more socialist practices in the last half century. In our discussion of socialism we noted the danger of totalitarianism and authoritarianism.

Considerations here include the fact that correlation does not imply causation. Defenders of socialism respond that, yes, many socialist and communist systems have failed, and many that have adopted more socialist policies are now experiencing economic difficulties. However, economic systems are among the most complex that humans study. Thus, a number of other unknown factors were at work. Some of these unknowns were the real causes of the failures of the twentieth-century socialist and communist projects.

Another consideration is that people's preferences may not always indicate what is best for them if there is a valid distinction between apparent and real goods. They may act irrationally, out of ignorance. That citizens of socialist and communist countries sought to move to the Free West does show that they made value judgments, expressed in preferences they acted upon. This does not necessarily mean, though, that their judgments were informed, rational, and / or correct.

Regarding totalitarianism in socialism and communism, this is inevitable only in some answers to certain limit questions about human nature. Otherwise, it is a possible but not necessary corollary of socialism and communism. Recall, also, that Hobbes judged totalitarianism to be the opportunity cost for social benefits, and he was willing to make the trade-off.

In many ways, arguments against capitalism as immoral are arguments for the morality of socialism and communism. Marx targeted the profit motive and his theory of surplus value as the fundamental problem with capitalism. Many early modern economists, including free market advocates like Adam Smith, held to a form of the labor theory of value, as discussed in chapter three. Marx's analysis of profit and surplus value, likewise, relies on a labor theory of value. Economics as a science has made much progress since early modernity and Marx's time. Most economists today do not accept the labor theory of value, and they do not accept the real estate theory of value that dominated earlier theories. If the labor theory of value is faulty, then Marx's critique of capitalism—indeed his dialectical materialist philosophy of history—is questionable.

In identifying essential features of capitalism, we examined Marx's and others' criticism that profit amounts to stealing what rightfully belongs to the laborer. There we noted additional considerations. Perhaps profit is rightly due to the owner of the means of production, not to the laborer, since the capitalist invests time, effort, resources, and risk in acquiring, producing, and trying to sell goods. Laborers do not invest these. We also surveyed questions about value. Is value relative to different individuals and groups or is it objective and absolute? Who determines value? Trade requires different assignments of value by different individuals, otherwise there would be no buying and selling. These value questions lie at the heart of the differences between capitalism, socialism, and communism. Capitalism says individuals alone know what they need and want, as expressed in their preferences, but socialism and communism are more paternalistic.

If the theory of surplus value is correct, the question arises of determining the value of different laborer's work. Some do a good job, some do a mediocre job, and some do a poor job. The goods they produce are sold at the same price. How would the owner determine the value due to each worker based on the value of the labor they input for each good?

Marx's philosophy also judges money to be bad, because it represents the worker's alienated essence which the worker then sets up as an idol, worships, and serves. Free market capitalists respond that Marx's philosophical account of the origin of money, grounding his negative judgment on money, does not correspond to the historical reasons for the appearance of money. Early economies were barter systems that exchanged goods and services, often food and livestock. As humans developed long-distance travel via boats, wagons, etc., it was more difficult to take their goods with them. A farmer could not take his produce or his animals hundreds of miles to trade. Money, in the form of precious metals and coinage, thus developed as a portable value exchange.

Granted the historical origination of money, a variety of normative ethical systems judge certain effects of its use to be bad, like greed, dishonesty, and theft. Others respond that money itself is neutral and can be used for either good or bad purposes, apart from its purpose as a medium of exchanging value. They invoke the legal axiom cited in chapter one: *abusus non tollit usum* ("Abuse does not remove use"). They add that greed, theft, and avarice existed before the advent of money. Answers to limit questions about: being and value, whether all human actions are morally assessable, and philosophical anthropology, inform one's position on this point.[27]

Another element, of Marx's and others' critiques of capitalism, is private ownership of the means of production. Apart from Marx's critique, and depending on answers to ethical limit questions about which social value is most important (e.g., freedom, equality of condition, and opportunity), one might judge private ownership of the means of production to be wrong.

We can ask what gives only some individuals or groups the right appropriate natural resources like wood, metal, and fossil fuels, to produce goods. Do they not belong to everyone? The labor theory of value says that, once persons mix their labor with a natural resource to produce an artifact, then they own it. The advancement of collective scientific knowledge and technology also raises the question of what gives only some individuals and groups the right to use technology to produce goods and services. Who "owns" collective scientific knowledge and technology? Philosophical limit questions, which we surveyed about the nature of societies and individuals' relationship to them, inform answers to these questions. And again, free market capitalism has affinities with answers prioritizing the many discrete individuals, while socialism and communism have affinities with those prioritizing the one society as a whole.

Free market capitalists respond to such queries by pointing to natural markets as the "ingenious" ways humans, as social animals, capitalize on each other's strengths and talents. Some have the ability and skills necessary to appropriate natural resources and technology, while others do not. However, those who cannot appropriate natural resources and technology can trade their labor and their own specialized skills, like welding, with those who have appropriated resources and technology, like iron ore and factory machinery.

Critics also indicate that free markets allocate resources so that there are disparities, often great, in goods and services. They use natural law, rights-based, divine command, and other rule-based normative ethical theories, to say we have an obligation to allocate some resources to all in ways that free markets do not allocate them. Using consequentialist theories, some value certain goods and services more highly than others, like food, shelter, healthcare, and education, claiming that, although free markets maximize utility, they fail to account for the greater utility that these basic resources provide. We discussed this criticism and some responses to it in the previous section on socialism.

Free market capitalists appeal to justice as merit-based, instead of other forms of distributive justice, prioritizing equal condition. The "very wealthy" and "very poor" deserve what they have, based on their respective contributions and lack of contributions to society, as judged by collective, unbiased, free markets. This again assumes that those who have merited wealth have done so morally. We visited some of the questions concerning this earlier.

They also say that value judgments of "wealthy" and "poor" are arbitrary and relative, depending on who makes them. In the 1950s the U. S. government defined the poverty level as three times the amount of foodstuffs needed to feed a family of four in one year. This is arbitrary and relative. Some families of four might need more or different foodstuffs than others, and necessities vary from family to family. Also, those Americans judged to be "very poor" in the U. S. A. are "very rich" by the standards of other countries. Many "poor" Americans have cell phones and televisions, in addition to daily nourishment, but the poor of some countries have none of these.

Other responses to the wealth and income disparity criticism of free market capitalism include income mobility in capitalist societies, and the failure of taxation and redistribution strategies attempted in both the U. S. A. and other societies. The quintile analysis, in chapter four, revealed that, although in the U. S. A. top income earners have been taxed more with the goal of cash transfers over the last few decades, income among lower earners has remained the same or decreased, depending on the quintile, with a slight increase in income among top earners in the highest quintile.

Similar data also show that there is great mobility between income quintiles. Many in the top quintile regularly fall into the lowest quintile and many in the lowest regularly move to the highest. Rejoinders to these facts include: this mobility is the exception and not the rule and, relying on assumptions of metaphysical determinism, most in the lower quintiles are destined to remain there (due to a social, educational, ethnic, and other factors that seal their fate).

Capitalists also respond that the wealth disparity criticism rests on a faulty analysis. Free markets naturally result in differences in what specific material resources people have, but not differences in the value of those resources. In trade, people freely exchange money for goods and services. The goods and services have the same value as the money exchanged for them. Buyers trade money with sellers for goods and services, but they freely choose what and how much they buy. Some buy and consume more goods and services than they sell, so they have less money. Some sell more goods and services than they buy and consume, and so they have more money. The disparity in value is illusory because the money exchanged and the goods and services consumed are of equal value. Thus, the difference is in type of value, not amount of value.

We have also seen critics claim that free market capitalism has adverse moral effects on relationships. Marx spoke not only of workers' alienation from their labor, but also of alienation between people in capitalism. Hobbes viewed the state of nature before societies as one of war. Marx viewed private property as bringing war into humanity's original pristine communal state. Due to competition and the profit motive, the owners of the means of production are at war with workers and other suppliers, and workers are at war with their employers and one another.

Capitalists use workers as means to the end of profit, which dishonors their human dignity; Marx called this slavery. Workers are robbed of their freedom to do as they want for fear of losing their jobs. Treating people as means to ends instead of ends themselves violates Kant's second formulation of the categorical imperative, and is wrong on a number of ethical systems.

Workers are alienated from their employers and each other. They try to work less and for fewer hours, and seek higher wages. They resent their employers' power over them, the limitations on their freedom, and steal from their employers. Workers compete with one another for jobs, status, and promotions. Such ill-treatment of others can be judged wrong in numerous normative ethical theories. Relying on a form of divine command theory, some critics say that capitalism forces people to violate the divine command to "Love your neighbor as yourself."[28]

Free market capitalists have several responses. We have said that some are psychological egoists, claiming we cannot but help acting out of self-interest. So they dismiss, as irrational, any ethical command to do otherwise. They argue, though, that the genius of natural economic systems is that this self-interest brings greater benefits for all, which would not obtain otherwise.

Others are psychological altruists, but say we prefer the benefits of free exchange, capitalizing on each other's abilities and talents. Some indicate that the assignment of mutually beneficial tasks to men and women in prehistoric times—hunting and defense to men, domestic tasks to women—before the advent of private property, money, and markets, attests to this fact.

They also raise the criticism of psychological egoism, we saw in chapter two, that it is impossible to know the inner motivations of anyone else. Perhaps critics wrongly project their own selfishness and negative views of others onto free market agents. The inductive generalization, that all people always and everywhere act only out of self-interest, is difficult to prove. Although such selfishness and viewing of others, as means instead of ends, doubtless occurs sometimes; it may not occur in all or even the majority of cases. Many employees view their employers positively. Many employers provide perquisites for employees, like bonuses and profit-sharing, which are by no means necessary. If some, or many, do not treat others as mere means to selfish ends, then this proves, they say, that private property, private ownership of the means of production, and free markets do not inevitably cause alienation and war among people.

Marx predicted that this alienation and less-than human treatment would eventually lead to revolution. We noted that several revolutions of the twentieth century were consciously informed by Marxist philosophy—and thus subject to the accusation of self-fulfilling prophecy. Other revolutions have taken place throughout history for a variety of reasons, not all economic.

Yet, in the modern western capitalist societies that Marx was criticizing no such class conflict-based revolutions have taken place. Some of these have adopted laws and regulations regarding minimum wages, overtime pay, minimum work hours, minimum employment ages, and health and safety regulations; they have not experienced revolutions based on class conflict. Of course these regulations involved unavoidable trade-offs in efficiency and other things that we have noted.

Even with such laws and regulations, these societies have retained the essential features of free market capitalism that Marx criticized. Further, with the passing of the colonial era many non-industrialized and less developed societies seek out free trade with capitalist countries like the U. S. A. The same is true of many former socialist countries. In expressing these preferences, they reveal that they judge themselves happier and better off by engaging in free trade, than not. In this way, capitalists argue that, despite its failures and limitations, people of all classes and estates prefer free market capitalism, all things considered.

Opponents rejoin, again, by appealing to distinctions between what is and what ought to be, real and apparent good/happiness, and means and ends to say that such facts do not necessarily legitimize what they judge to be wrong on other grounds.

Related to the criticism, that capitalism causes alienation in relationships, is the claim that the competition, it necessarily entails, is immoral. We examined some arguments for and against morality of competition in the section on free market capitalism. What we have just said, about assessing capitalism's effects on relationships, also applies to the question competition.

Also related to the charge that capitalism introduces immorality into human relationships, are the accusations that it fosters specific vices. Critics, here, explicitly or tacitly, appeal to an ethical theory that makes value judgments about the goodness or badness moral agents, like virtue ethics, to claim that capitalism inculcates vices, not virtues. These vices include individualism, greed, dishonesty, and corruption, favoring the wealthy and those in power.

We have seen the way free market capitalism focuses on many individuals engaging in free transactions. Advocates of capitalism often appeal to positive economic utility and welfare analysis. This assumes that individuals are free, rational, knowledgeable, and the best judges of what they want and need. Capitalism's prioritization, of the many individuals of over the one society, is evident in its affinities with social contract theories of society, as discussed previously.

Judging individualism to be a vice, critics assert that capitalism promotes it at the expense of the good of society as a whole. They join to this the criticisms of alienation, competition, selfishness, and free market agents' treatment of other market agents, which we have already discussed. All of these, they say, are detrimental to society's unity and solidarity.

Capitalists respond by indicating, again, that free markets promote the "good of society as a whole," in terms of things already mentioned. These include: maximum utility, welfare, and long-run economic growth with its many long-run benefits to society. And, again, different normative ethical systems will judge the value of these effects differently. Utilitarian or other consequentialist ethics may value them highly. Some non-consequentialist, rule-based, and rights-based theories may value them less, pointing to gross inequalities in wealth, and an unequal allotment of some material resources, judged to be more valuable than others. In addition, certain answers to anthropological, social, and political limit questions will not lead to the judgment that individualism is bad. Different answers will lead to more negative judgments on individualism.

Critics also allege that free market capitalism relies on, and so fosters, dishonesty. Even though some cite counterexamples where dishonesty is valuable to question a negative value judgment of lying, lying is wrong on a number of normative ethical systems. Critics say that making profits requires dishonesty. In order to make profits, sellers must get buyers to pay more for goods than they paid for them (in resources, infrastructure, power, and labor). Marx's surplus value theory says that capitalists pay employees less than the real value of their labor in order to make profits. Employees are dishonest with their employers regarding the time and effort they work, and in giving false impressions about their value to their employers.

All we have said, about absolute objective vs. relative value among different individuals, applies here. Marx's surplus value criticism might be legitimate, if value, between two or more parties, is absolute and objective. However, if value is different, according to each individual or group, then the seller might really value a good less than the buyer. On account of the different values they assign to the good, both buyer and seller gain utility and there is no dishonesty or theft. Similarly, employers who know employees' shortcuts might value them enough to pay what they do for their work, despite the shortcuts.

On the other hand, if the dishonesty involves withholding information or imparting false knowledge about a transaction, then the deceived party's value judgment is not accurate. This is true even if buyers' and sellers' value judgments are relative and different, because the deceived party would form a different value judgment if she had all of the correct information.

A seller could tell a buyer that a watch is a Rolex when it is not, but the buyer believes the seller, and pays what he is willing and able to pay for a Rolex. An antique collector might tell a seller that his antique Currier & Ives lithograph is only a replica when it is genuine; the seller acts on that information and sells it for less than he would, had he known it is authentic. Regulation through bodies, like the U. S. Food and Drug Administration, has the goal of insuring greater seller disclosure through legislation and regulation.

In such cases people form value judgments—absolute or relative to themselves as individuals—based on misinformation, which are different from the judgments they would make with the correct information. Free market capitalism and the assumptions about fully knowledgeable market agents, upon which some arguments for capitalism are based, rely on accurate information and full knowledge. The possibility of such deceit raises ethical challenges for free market capitalism.

One response, we have already mentioned, is that the free market mechanism will correct such dishonesty; but this is debated. What if a dishonest market agent goes undetected for a long time, or is dishonest in ways that are very difficult to detect?

General contractors compete to build houses by submitting cost estimates, or bids, to potential home buyers. In an actual case known by one of the authors, a general contractor would offer competitive bids that corresponded to the building materials he intended to use in construction. Some competitors, though, would *say* their estimates were based on superior building materials, like ¾" plywood instead of ½", #1 instead of #2 lumber, plywood for sheathing and roofing instead of waferboard, 30lb. shingles instead of 15lb., etc. Their estimates were *really* based on the lower prices of the inferior building materials, which they would use if they won the bid. Naturally, their bids were less and so they won more bids. Detecting such inferior building materials can take a long time, if they are ever detected at all. In such cases, the demand for such dishonest but undetected suppliers does not decrease, and the market does not naturally correct their dishonesty.

Some auto mechanics tell customers they need more work than they really need in order to make more money, and some dentists tell patients they need more dental work than they really need. Examples could be multiplied. Depending on frequency, the value one places on honesty compared to other values, and the trade-offs in values one is willing to make, one may or may not judge this as telling against free market capitalism. Some may very well judge the liabilities of regulation and legislation to be worth the trade-off for greater honesty in some transactions.

Another response to criticisms of dishonesty in capitalism we have seen is that market agents may not seek all information for pragmatic reasons. They see some ignorance as the opportunity cost for saving time and energy, and they make this trade-off. Economists call this rational ignorance. Critics respond, however, that market agents should not take advantage of other's rational ignorance, doing so is immoral, and free market capitalism promotes doing so.

Selfishness and greed are other vices in many versions of virtue ethics. Critics allege that private property and the profit motive make people in free market capitalist systems more greedy and selfish than they otherwise would be. They want more material resources than they need, and their dealings with others are not motivated out of concern for others but are rather self-interest. In capitalism, people become doctors, lawyers, and politicians for prestige and material gain, not out of concerns to help the sick and dying, serve the cause of justice, or serve one's country.

In examining the alienation critiques of capitalism's effects on relationships, we summarized how the philosophical question of psychological egoism vs. psychological altruism informs that consideration. This question is relevant here, too. It may be difficult to know a person's true motivations in seeking a lucrative and well-respected career, or their motivations for any course of action, in a free market. Questions of real vs. apparent goods, and who has the right or ability to make value judgments, also apply here. How do we know what people really need and want, and whether or not their own judgments about what they need and want are accurate? Another consideration is that not all in capitalist systems seek high-paying, prestigious jobs, like educators and social workers. Because not all do, it is difficult to conclude that the free market system itself is what causes people to desire and seek material resources and prestige.

We have mentioned the criticism that capitalism instills in people false needs and wants. Critics claim that in order to get more transactions to generate greater profits, suppliers try to convince people they need things they really do not need. Fueled by the greed of potential plaintiffs in such lawsuits, some lawyers create a false need for litigation through frivolous lawsuits. Capitalism causes people to consider luxuries as necessities. It trains people to want sports and luxury cars, designer clothing, jewelry, and exquisite food and drink. In this way, capitalism brainwashes people with a materialistic ideology in which they are taught to think they are free (in the marketplace), but they are really slaves to possessions and the desire for more.

Critics add that these false needs become insatiable. Real necessities like food and rest can be met, but the false need for more and better "stuff" cannot be satisfied. When hungry we can eat and become satisfied; and when tired we can sleep and wake refreshed. Yet, if we always feel we need more and better than we have, it is simply impossible to squelch such an infinite desire.

Along with this, capitalism trains people to have a material sense of value so that their self-worth comes from the number and quality of their possessions compared to others' possession. They want bigger houses, nicer lawns, better furniture, and more recreational "toys" like boats and sporting goods, all to feel superior to others and thus better about themselves. This equation of personal worth with private property creates class divisions, explicit or implicit. This feeds all the concomitant problems of class divisions like alienation, destruction of relationships, greed, envy, jealousy, resentment, contempt, and class warfare.

All of the considerations, about how to determine value in a transaction and who determines it, are relevant here. Another consideration, which applies to the charge that capitalism encourages any vice (dishonesty, greed, individualism, selfishness), is the limit question of the relationship of the many individuals to the one society in social philosophy. This question is itself related to the philosophical question of metaphysical free will and determinism.

As we have seen, libertarian free will[29] has affinities with: prioritizing individuals over society as a whole; viewing democracy as the best form of government; judging freedom to be the greatest social value; and emphasizing personal responsibility. Determinism—hard or soft—has affinities with: prioritizing society as a whole over the individual; advocating paternalism over democracy; judging equality of condition to be the greatest social value; lessening personal responsibility; and viewing prison systems as rehabilitation instead of punitive.

The question of free will and determinism is relevant to the virtue-based ethical theories. If other factors, like society as a whole, determine people's habits (virtues and vices), which in turn determine their choices, then we can change those other factors in order to change people's habits, and hence their choices. Marxist critiques of "ideologies" are partly predicated on determinism; Marx was a deterministic materialist. Changing societal values and patterns of thinking can thus change individuals by changing their habits, or virtues and vices.

Criticisms of free market capitalism, saying that it affects individuals' values, habits, and patterns of thinking to act in immoral ways, thus, can rely on determinist answers to limit questions in philosophical anthropology. Free market capitalists can rejoin that they hold to metaphysical indeterminism and libertarian views of free will. The criticism is based on an assumption about philosophical anthropology, with which they do not agree. They might believe in virtues and vices, but they may claim that habits, values, and ways of thinking *incline but do not necessitate* people's choices. People are truly free in their choices so that nothing finally forces their decisions. This could undercut objections that capitalism inculcates bad values, ways of thinking, and vices, which rely on an assumption of metaphysical determinism.

In this section, we have surveyed a litany of considerations in morally assessing capitalism. We have frequently considered the same points required to assess socialism and communism, by way of contrast. Depending on the answers to a host of limit questions, ethical and other, positive or negative judgments on capitalism, socialism, and communism result. In the next section, we raise some additional considerations relevant to socialism and communism.

Additional Considerations in Morally Assessing Socialism and Communism

In raising considerations for a moral assessment of capitalism, we have, at the same time, raised issues for assessing socialism and communism. One answer to a specific limit question can lead to a positive judgment of capitalism and a negative judgment of socialism and/or communism. The opposite answer can lead to a negative judgment of capitalism but a positive judgment of socialism and/or communism. Here, we raise additional points equally relevant and that likewise lead to different assessments, depending on one's answers to specific questions.

We have seen how capitalists appeal to the fact that free markets promote maximum efficiency, utility, welfare, and long-run economic growth to argue that capitalism makes individuals and society, as a whole, better off in valuable ways, and so is good. The corollary to this claim is that the centralized economic planning, required by socialism and communism, introduces inefficiencies in attaining these aims. It also results in unintended consequences, because economic systems are complex, and so central planners must be all-knowing in order to accomplish their goals. We have examined considerations raised by both sides on this point.

Inflation is also an issue with more government involvement in markets. In chapter three, we saw that the intervention solution to periodic economic downturns (recessions), by increasing aggregate demand through government stimuli, causes inflation. To stimulate aggregate demand, governments increase government spending or decrease taxes to incentivize consumer spending. As aggregate demand goes up while aggregate supply remains the same, prices increase and inflation results. Free market solutions prescribe allowing aggregate supply to naturally fall, so that equilibrium eventually falls to even lower prices than before the economic downturn.

Related to this is the fact that the government debt required for a stimulus also fuels inflation. To enact a stimulus, a government needs more money, so it must borrow and/or print more money. The law of supply and demand dictates that when the amount of money in circulation increases, its value per unit decreases. If a country with fiat currency—not necessarily dangerous by itself—prints more money than its current GDP, currency devaluation and price inflation result.[30]

Negative value judgments on inflation are pervasive. There is widespread popular frustration with inflation that outruns GDP growth, and many normative ethical systems could be used to judge inflation as bad. Say that someone at the beginning of his career aims to save one million dollars for retirement, and does. If the government does not pay off its debt via GDP growth then inflation continues. If such inflation outruns economic growth, then the one million dollars he has saved is worth considerably less at his retirement than when he began saving. Inflation diminishes the value of the money he has saved, by decreasing its value. According to free market capitalists this violates merit-based distributive justice, because the value he has justly merited, as represented by his savings, is decreased against his will.

Those advocating more market intervention may acknowledge these liabilities but judge them to be the opportunity cost for other more valued benefits, like alleviating short-run economic suffering, and so make the trade-off. Answers, to questions about honoring certain ethical principles and promoting certain values in the present, inform the willingness to make this trade-off. Issues of time, too, like what is valued in the short-run and in the long-run and why, inform judgments about the opportunity costs of government intervention that causes inflation.

We have also seen the criticism that big government is necessary for centralized planning, which means resources that should go to citizens are used to support the infrastructure. Free market capitalists favor smaller governments requiring minimal resources to function, so that free market activity can allocate resources to the citizens in order to maximize their utility. They also say that centralized planning promotes waste and careless in distributing resources:

> There are four ways in which you can spend money. You can spend your own money on yourself. When you do that, why then you really watch out what you're doing, and you try to get the most for your money. Then you can spend your own money on somebody else. For example, I buy a birthday present for someone. Well, then I'm not so careful about the content of the present, but I'm

> very careful about the cost. Then, I can spend somebody else's money on myself. And if I spend somebody else's money on myself, then I'm sure going to have a good lunch! Finally, I can spend somebody else's money on somebody else. And if I spend somebody else's money on somebody else, I'm not concerned about how much it is, and I'm not concerned about what I get. And that's government. And that's close to 40 percent of our national income.[31]

Socialists and communists respond that free market capitalism promotes not only inequality of condition but also inequality of opportunity. The rich and powerful control markets for their benefit, at the expense of others. They also say that free market capitalism promotes corruption in government, as political offices and special interests are bought and sold. Thus, government wastefulness is not avoided in free market capitalist systems with minimalist, small government. We discussed both sides of these points in more detail earlier.

We have also seen that the social value of justice, and how one defines and values it relative to other social values, factors into moral assessments of capitalism, socialism, and communism. Free market capitalists highly value merit-based distributive justice. For this reason, they judge taxation and the redistribution of wealth in centralized economic planning to be theft.

Communists, in particular, say this criticism is not valid because in communism private property is eliminated. Moral judgments on theft presuppose private property, but if there is no private property then there can be no theft. In his rationalistic moral philosophy, Kant argued that moral principles must be able to be consistently universalized without contradiction. On this basis he argued that theft, or the principle "you can take another's property," cannot be universalized since then all would steal and no one would have private property.

Recall that Marx's communist philosophy was informed by Hegel. In his responses to Kant, Hegel argued that the maxim "you can take another's property" does not involve a contradiction. Rather, he claims that all Kant proves is that two different principles: (1) "you can take another's property" and (2) "people should have private property" are incompatible. Hegel argues that Kant nowhere proves that private property is good and valuable. Criterion (1) does not establish that people should have private property and so can be consistently universalized. Hegel did judge theft to be wrong, but on the social analysis that theft is not conducive to societies.

Marx took Hegel's hypothetical questioning of the assumption that private property is justified, seriously, however. When there is no private property, as in communism, then there are no grounds for a criticism based on the immorality of stealing. Free market capitalists rejoin that private property is a presupposition of all economic systems since the beginning of human history, regardless of government or lack thereof. Communists admit this but say that in the pristine original state there was no private property. The institution of private property was bad and with it arose the natural economic systems that positive economics studies. In the communist Utopia private property, and the economic systems that economics studies, disappear. Theft will also disappear in the communist Utopia, since without private property there is no theft.

Private property's legitimacy has been almost ubiquitously assumed at all times and places in history. One can undercut the accusation of theft in communism by questioning the legitimacy of private property. Most centralized planning systems, like socialism, include private property. Like communists, socialists do claim that when people have their basic necessities met crime, including theft, decreases. Both socialists and communists claim that free market capitalism promotes theft on the individual level, because disparities in material resources promote envy and many do not have basic necessities. Envy and want, they say, result in stealing.

We have seen that free market capitalists claim that taxing and redistributing wealth violates merit-based distributive justice, because what people have rightly earned is taken from them and given to others who have not merited it. Some socialists respond by questioning the value judgments of the free markets' contributions to society. They say that no sports star, movie star, or CEO has the "right" to earn $10,000,000 when most people, like custodians, factory workers, cashiers, restaurant employees and many others, make exponentially less. This raises the question we have repeatedly broached about who determines value and why. How one answers this question informs one's judgments about the values of different jobs, goods, and services to society.

Capitalism prioritizes the social value of liberty but socialism and communism prioritize equality of condition. In chapter four, we saw that social values can involve trade-offs. Less equality of condition can be the opportunity cost of greater individual freedom, and vice versa. Which is valued more and why determines which trade-off one is willing to make. Advocates of centralized planning judge income inequality, poverty, homelessness, unemployment, and other disparities resulting from free markets to be greater social ills, compared to values like maximizing positive economic utility, welfare, long-run economic growth, and freedom.

Another point made by socialists and communists is that socialism and communism promote individual freedom while capitalism diminishes liberty, but in a different sense. We saw in chapter four the way in which some argue that security is a type of freedom. If one feels secure to walk alone in Central Park at night then one is free to do so. But if Central Park is dangerous at night, then one might want to walk alone in Central Park at night but not have the freedom to do so due to fear.

In a similar way, some argue that the anxiety and inequality of condition caused by free markets reduces individual freedom. People fear not having enough money for their basic needs and losing their jobs in free market systems. This anxiety robs them of their freedom, but in socialism and communism the fear of losing one's job and lacking basic necessities is eliminated. Without basic needs, like food, shelter, clothing, means of making a living, and healthcare, people's individual freedoms are substantially diminished. They may want to engage in other activities, like recreation and personal development, but are "forced" to spend more time procuring basic necessities and have anxiety about doing so. By providing the basic necessities for more people, socialism and communism eliminate these enslavements and fears. Thus, they promote individual freedom in another way, say socialists and communists. Other valuable social benefits also ensue. Again, they argue that crime decreases or disappears if people's needs are met.

This becomes an argument for the centralized economic planning, necessary to insure that more people have these necessities. The greater market intervention necessary to do so reduces market agents' freedom to act according to their preferences, but this is a trade-off for other freedoms. In socialism and communism, people may have fewer choices of goods and services but some are willing to trade-off maximal freedom of preferences, to promote freedom other ways.

This reasoning, again, broaches the question of whether individuals know what is best. If so, then we should create scenarios where they can express their preferences unhindered. If some or many are apt to choose apparent instead of real goods, then perhaps we should limit them so they get what is really good for them. Are people oblivious to an anxiety over securing basic necessities, which enslaves them and limits their freedoms? If so, then maybe someone who knows better should provide their basic necessities so they can enjoy other types of freedom.

There is also the point, raised in chapter three, that at least some limitations on individual freedoms are necessary for people to live and work together in societies. Mill's harm principle tries to maximize individual liberties but still proscribes individual freedom to "harm" others (we saw the problems with defining what "harm" means here) and to take their property. Critics claim that, while it asserts maximal freedom, capitalism in reality reduces people to slaves—again with a large degree of fear—so that they are forced to do things, like pay more money for gas or take a substantially lower wage, other than they need or want, against their will. This, too, reduces individual liberty and is ironic, given capitalism's claim to promote maximal freedom.

A related critique of socialism and communism is that loss of individual identity is the opportunity cost. Equality of condition removes the differences between people that make them unique. It imposes sameness in living conditions and possessions. Some capitalists say, again, that we value the freedom to be different from one another over equality of condition, pointing to how free markets naturally arise even when there are regulations limiting markets. Socialism and communism impose a boring uniformity, causing more harm than happiness, say capitalists.

And again, advocates of equality of condition respond that people do not have a natural tendency to have different material goods than others. This is socially conditioned, they claim, and we can and should condition people to have different values. Social and cultural conditions determine people's values and wants, and we can change these by changing their societal causes. Answers to these questions rely on answers to the limit questions about the priority of the individual over society or vice versa, and answers to the question of metaphysical free will and determinism.

Advocates of equality of condition also say that, just because we want the freedom to acquire better and more material possessions than others, this does not mean that we should. The way things are, does not necessarily dictate the way that things should be. Answers to this question hinge on answers to limit questions about the relationship between ontology (being) and axiology (values), between "is" and "ought."

Hence socialists and communists argue that true individuality does not consist in having more and better possessions than others. Instead, it consists in cultivating one's potential, personality, education, interests, hobbies, and artistic expression, and in fostering interpersonal relationships. Capitalism, they say, imposes false values and the false belief that people are defined by their possessions. As people in free market capitalist societies all get the latest fashionable goods and services, they ironically become more the same than different.

Another criticism of free market capitalism is that classes and disparities in wealth mean that some work little, or even not at all. The very wealthy can choose to work less—they are *unwilling* to work, and the unemployment caused by free markets means some are forced to not work, even when they want to work—they are *unable* to work. Added to this is the claim that as the false wants and overconsumption that capitalism causes are reduced, there is less overall work to be done.

In socialism and communism all are required to work. More people working means less overall time for each person working, assuming the amount of work to be done remains the same. If the workforce is greater and the overall workload remains the same, then the workload per person decreases. Historically, as populations have increased, people have worked less and had more free time. Elimination of false needs and overconsumption further lessens the overall workload. This means more free time for more people to cultivate what really matters: personal development, education, hobbies, recreation, art, and interacting with others.

Thus advocates say that socialism or communism free people from spending most of their time trying to make more money and acquiring more material things. Socialism and communism provide more free time for people to develop that in which authentic individuality and humanity consists. Questions of what "real" individuality and humanity entails are ontological limit questions and questions of philosophical anthropology, of the types surveyed in chapter one. What is a "human individual?" This is a limit question of philosophical anthropology, and entails a host of ontological considerations about classes of beings in general. Once again, answers to one set of limit questions are inextricably bound up with, and presuppose, answers to other sets of limit questions.

Free market capitalists also criticize socialism and communism for promoting laziness and diminishing motivation. If goods and services, especially those essential for survival, are automatically provided, then people will not be motivated to work to earn them. There is no competition; competition motivates people. Lessened competition also decreases quality. All of these factors conspire to promote economic stagnation and failure, say free market capitalists. They point to the failed socialist systems of the twentieth century to corroborate these claims.

Socialists respond that, although we have witnessed these effects in socialist systems to date, they are not its necessary results. They say greater enforcement of work is required; they typically hope that human ingenuity will overcome these hitherto deficiencies of socialism. Further and forthcoming data is necessary for final judgments in this regard.

We must mention an important criticism of Marx's economic analysis. His predictions, regarding how history must move from capitalism through socialism to communism, assume that industry and technology have limits. He assumed that capacity and efficiency would reach a limit. For Marx, technology is like wall; markets move ever closer to the wall. The space between markets and the wall represents value, which is always decreasing. Supply has a limit. To make profits, capitalists must pay workers increasingly lower wages, thus, pilfering surplus labor value. Eventually, the value disappears, resulting in an abrupt and violent change of the entire system.

Since Marx, economists have seen that technology continuously grows, depending on capital investment on the supply side. In reality and *pace* Marx, the wall moves, so to speak. There is no limit inevitably decreasing and eliminating value. The fact that no worker revolution since Marx has resulted from a technological capacity and efficiency limit is also proof of this. The twentieth-century socialist revolutions were informed by Marx's philosophy, and so were arguably became self-fulfilling prophecies.

SUMMARY

Drawing on all previous chapters, this chapter identified salient features of what we call free market capitalism, socialism, and communism, and raised considerations for morally assessing them. Throughout we saw arguments for and against both parts and the whole systems of capitalism, socialism, and communism. We also saw that an ethical analysis of these three models of how governments interact with economies requires a consideration of a host of other limit questions. These include not only limit questions concerning ethics and values, but also limit questions of metaphysics, ontology, philosophical anthropology, and social and political philosophy. Examining the arguments for and against these three models, we witnessed how different answers to these numerous ethical and other limit questions dictate different moral evaluations.

NOTES

1. This chapter builds on all earlier chapters of this book, and presupposes knowledge of their contents. We refer to a terms, ideas, and analyses presented in earlier chap-

ters, referencing them without explanation. Therefore, it is important to read the whole book before reading this final chapter, despite the potential temptation to do so.

2. Popular responses arose, too, such as the Luddites who destroyed factories and machinery in England, as they protested these issues (such as decreased demand for manual labor) attending industrialization and the rapidly advancing new technologies.

3. Some critics of free-market capitalism try to dismiss short run nonintervention as necessary for long run economic growth in neoclassical economic theory, wholesale, because of this temporal factor. They say that neoclassical economics assumes static supply and demand curves, which are really in constant flux. This criticism misses the fact that economists admit that neoclassical economic theory—the one standard set of economic laws and principles agreed on by all economists, no matter what their normative economical persuasion may be—is a theoretical model, with the liabilities of all models, but produces accurate predictions. Therefore, it must correctly depict, albeit in a simplistic and incomplete way, the realities of complex economic systems admitted to be in constant flux in real time. This is similar to the situation in the natural sciences. The limits of Newtonian physics have been realized since the advent of relativity theory and quantum mechanics, however, the Newtonian paradigm is still used to make accurate predictions and "works"—we can get rockets to the moon by using it.

4. See, for instance, Hal Draper, *Karl Marx's Theory of Revolution*, vols. 1 – 4 (New York, NY: Monthly Review Press, 1977 – 91); Hal Draper, *Socialism from Below* (Atlantic Highlands, NJ: Humanities Press, 1992); and Michael Harrington, *Socialism, Past and Future* (New York, NY: Plume Books, 1990).

5. See, for instance, Jonathan, Wolff, "Karl Marx", *The Stanford Encyclopedia of Philosophy (Summer 2011 Edition)*, Edward N. Zalta (ed.), URL = <http://plato.stanford.edu/archives/sum2011/entries/marx/> (accessed January 6, 2012).

6. Karl, Marx, *Capital: A Critique of Political Economy*, vol. 1 (New York, NY: Modern Library, 1906), 268.

7. Marx, *Capital*, vol. 1, 269.

8. Marx, *Capital*, vol. 1, 230.

9. G. W. F. Hegel, *Outlines of the Philosophy of Right*, ed. Stephen Houlgate, trans. T. M. Knox (New York, NY: Oxford University Press, 2008), 14 (Italics in original).

10. Ludwig Feuerbach, *The Essence of Christianity* (New York, NY: Harper and Row, 1957), 29 – 31.

11. Feuerbach, *The Essence of Christianity*, 25 – 26, 31.

12. The direct object of Feuerbach's attack was the Lutheran Protestant Christian view of the relationship between humans and God. In this view there is an "either – or" regarding activity: either God does something or humans do something, but not both at the same time. Other forms of Christian belief do not see divine and human action in as mutually exclusive a fashion as the Lutheran Protestant orthodoxy with which Feuerbach takes issue. Similarly, the conception of Christian theism and divine action informing Marx's philosophy is Lutheran Protestant orthodoxy.

13. Karl Marx and Friedrich Engels, *Werke*, vol. 1 (Berlin: Dietz, 1961), 27.

14. Karl Marx, "Theses on Feuerbach," in *The Marx-Engels Reader*, 2nd edition, ed. Robert C. Tucker, 143 – 45 (New York, NY: W. Norton & Company, 1978). In Thesis 1 he writes: "[H]e (Feuerbach) regards the theoretical attitude as the only genuinely human attitude, while practice is conceived and fixed in its dirty-judaical manifestation. Hence he does not grasp the significance of "revolutionary," of practical-critical, activity" (Marx, "Theses on Feuerbach," 143). The reference to "dirty judaical manifestation" regards the distinction between salvation by "faith alone" and salvation by "works or

effort" in Lutheran Protestant Christianity, which sees the former as correct and the latter as the wrong view held by Judaism at the time of early Christianity. This is based on a certain interpretation of St. Paul's letters. Ethnically Jewish himself, Marx criticized the passivity engendered by this doctrine of "salvation by faith alone, not works" that denied the power of practical, concrete human work to effect important changes. Contemporary biblical scholarship has strongly criticized the misreading of St. Paul's letters that led to this dichotomy between "effort/works" on one hand and "passivity/faith" on the other hand, which Marx is referring to. See, for example, E. P. Sanders, *Paul and Palestinian Judaism* (Minneapolis, MN: Fortress Press, 1977).

15. To anachronistically impose later categories on Marx, Marx was probably a "compatibilist" or a "soft-determinist" on the limit question regarding free will vs. determinism, as discussed in prior chapters.

16. Thesis 3 reads: "The materialist doctrine that men are products of circumstances and upbringing, and that therefore, changed men are products of other circumstances and change upbringing, forgets that it is men who change circumstances . . . The coincidence of the changing of circumstances and of human activity can be conceived and rationally understood only as revolutionizing practice" (Marx, "Theses on Feuerbach," 144).

17. Marx, *Capital*, vol. 1, 12 – 13, 14.

18. Despite common assertions that Russian Marxist, Georgi Plekhanov, coined the term in 1891, German Marxist, Josef Dietzgen, first used the term "dialectical materialism" (*dialektischer Materialismus*) in an 1887 essay. See, Josef Dietzgen, "Streifzüge eines Sozialisten in das Gebiet der Erkenntnistheorie," in *Schriften in drei Bänden* (East Berlin: Akademie, 1965), 3:61, 75, 79.

19. Karl Marx, "Manifesto of the Communist Party," in *The Marx-Engels Reader*, 2nd edition, ed. Robert C. Tucker, 469 – 500 (New York, NY: W. Norton & Company, 1978), 473 – 74.

20. Marx, *Capital*, vol. 1, 652.

21. Karl Marx, "Economic and Philosophic Manuscripts of 1844," in *The Marx-Engels Reader*, 2nd edition, ed. Robert C. Tucker, 66 – 125 (New York, NY: W. Norton & Company, 1978), 84 (italics in original).

22. Deirdre McCloskey argues that not so much material economic forces as ideas and worldviews account for the modern worldwide spread of economic liberalism and capitalism. See, Deirdre N. McCloskey, *Bourgeois Dignity: Why Economics Can't Explain the Modern World* (Chicago, IL: University of Chicago Press, 2010).

23. Marx, "Manifesto of the Communist Party," 500.

24. These points, coupled with a form of virtue ethics, are the basis of Deidre McCloskey's moral defense of capitalism in, *The Bourgeois Virtues*. See Deirdre N. McCloskey, *The Bourgeois Virtues: Ethics for an Age of Commerce* (University Of Chicago Press, 2006).

25. Here the "problem of justice" is a technical term in philosophy for the problem that utilitarianism justifies discrimination against minorities to maximize the greatest net happiness for the greatest number, as in slavery.

26. Rohnn Sanderson, one of the authors of this book.

27. Free-market capitalists, in cultures influenced by the Bible, point out that the Bible never says: "Money is the root of all evil," as some wrongly think. It says: "The *love* of money is a root of all sorts of evil" (1 Timothy 6:10).

28. Leviticus 19:18.

29. Again, in the philosophical debate over metaphysical freedom and determinism, "libertarian" free will corresponds to many people's intuitive sense, that their choices are

not entirely determined by prior causes, and that they have the "power of contrary choice" in the robust that they really can choose from multiple possibilities. Other positions, like compatibilism or soft-determinism, define "free will" in ways that include determinism (e.g., "freedom from external coercion"), and thus go against many people's intuitive sense of what "free will" means.

30. As long as the amount of money per unit—fiat or backed—corresponds to a nation's current GDP, then inflation and deflation do not occur. When the value of what backs currency that is in fact backed (e.g., by gold or silver) increases beyond GDP, then the value of money per unit increases and deflation of prices occurs. Conversely, when a government prints more fiat money units, then there are more units of currency in circulation to account for the whole GDP. This means that the value per unit of currency decreases, and so price inflation occurs.

31. Milton Friedman, interview with David Asman, Fox News, May 14, 2004.

CONCLUSION:

In any endeavor, when we lack information we often do not know the questions to ask. This book has very likely raised more questions than supplied answers. If so, then the authors have accomplished one of their primary goals. By providing a basic introduction to economics as a discipline today, and to philosophy in general and moral philosophy in particular, the authors have sought to educate readers of all backgrounds about the numerous and complicated questions at the intersection of ethics and economics.

In attempting to do this, the authors assumed no knowledge of economics, philosophy, or ethics on the part of readers. They sought to avoid the use of technical terms and ideas without first explaining them in, sometimes great, detail. Those already familiar with economics and/or ethics may have found many of these preliminaries to be a review, but they serve the purpose of fully informing those with no knowledge of one or both disciplines.

As stated in the introduction, the purpose was not to definitely answer any of the ethical and philosophical questions we can ask about economics. Rather, the authors aimed to inform readers so that they may be aware of the many and complex factors requisite for a serious consideration of ethics and economics together.

So many books on ethics and economics advance specific answers for ethical issues in economics, and/or advocate a certain normative economic policy. The authors of this book did not intend do so. Rather, their intention has been to provide the basic tools from both disciplines required to begin to think about ethical issues in economics. If readers leave this book with a greater knowledge of economics, philosophy, and/or economics, as well an increased appreciation of the number and complexity of questions arising at their intersection, then the authors have achieved their main goal. Not definitive answers and closure, but problematizing of ethics and economics, was the aim.

The, admittedly many, questions raised in this book are but a mere sample of the many questions we can ask about ethics and economics. They are the proverbial "tip of the iceberg," so to speak. If, after reading this book, one is left with the impression that there are many issues to consider in ethics and economics, none of which has a simple and easy answer, the authors will have achieved what they set out to do.

Another stated goal of the book was to provide enough information for readers to understand, at least to a greater degree, why individuals and groups arrive at different—even diametrically opposed—answers to questions in ethics and economics. In any specific moral question in economics, there are multiple, different, and frequently opposed potential value judgments. Depending on the answers one gives to a number of philosophical limit questions, one will judge the same action, policy, or state of affairs to be good or bad, right or wrong.

Some claim that acting in a rational and self-interested way in markets is bad, but others say it is actually good. Some believe we should give individuals as much freedom as possible in markets to pursue what they want. Others believe we should limit or even determine their choices for them, because most people are not the best judges of what is best for them and society. Some say competition is bad but other say it is good. Some argue that the pursuit of profits is evil, while others claim it is virtuous. Some say that income and wealth disparity is bad, but others say it is good. Some claim there are "fair" or "just," and "unfair" or "unjust," prices and wages. Others judge the same prices and wages to be eminently just or fair, and may even deny the possibility of any such judgments of fairness and justice except between parties to transactions. Some assert that it is right and good to regulate prices and wages, but others say regulating prices and wages is wrong. If readers leave this book understanding more of the reasons, on both sides, for the different and opposite answers to these and similar questions visited in these pages, then the authors have accomplished one of their chief aims.

Some judge free-market capitalism to be the essence of vice and evil. Others judge it to be virtuous and what is best for the common good of all. Some say government intervention in markets is good and salutary, but others say it is bad and deleterious. Some view justice as a type of equality of material condition in the allocation of scarce resources. Others see justice as rewards for contributions, and punishments for lack of contributions and harm imposed on society. Some aver that all in society should have certain goods and services, such as a certain amount of food, gainful employment, education, and healthcare, and that not providing these for all is gravely evil. Others argue that the interference in free markets, taxation, and redistribution of wealth required to do so are themselves gravely evil. Some claim that it is good and right for governments to provide safety nets for individuals or groups who do not succeed in private markets. Others claim that such safety nets are bad and wrong. If readers leave this book with at least a better understanding of why, depending on their answers to a host of philosophical limit questions—ethical and otherwise, people answer these questions in such diverse and opposed ways, and claim moral justification for doing so, then the authors have accomplished much of what they endeavored to do.

Some, especially those with training in either economics or philosophy, or both, may fault the book for not going into the depth required for a satisfactory treatment of these questions. They may also fault the limited number of examples given in any one case. However, in trying to accomplish their stated goals in one volume, the authors were of necessity limited in the number of examples they could offer on, and the depth of treatment of, any one issue or point. The sheer number of considerations at the intersection of ethics and economics forbids such exhaustive treatments of any one point. As stated in the introduction, other writers limit themselves to a more comprehensive treatment of specific individual issues. The breadth and scope of this book in outlining the fundamentals of philosophical ethics and economics, and discussing numerous questions at their intersection, simply forbids a full, all-inclusive, discussion of any one question raised. The authors hope that their survey, admittedly far-reaching, of the scores of issues to consider will invite others to treat the individual questions more exhaustively.

The authors anticipate that perhaps the greatest criticism—and one which will probably come more from philosophers, ethicists, and theologians than from economists—is the distinction between positive and normative economics. As the most predictable criticism, the authors would like, in this final section, to address it one last time.

The distinction between positive and normative economics is commonplace in the discipline of economics, and the beginning of chapter one attempted to justify this distinction, at length. Some interlocutors in discussions of ethics and economics try to discredit the neoclassical economic theory explained in this book, by attacking some its theoretical assumptions. As also noted in the first chapter, such critics offer no viable alternative economic theory that all objective observers of economic phenomena agree upon, and that has the explanatory and predictive power of the economic theory that they attempt to discredit by assumptions. It is one thing to criticize, but quite another to offer positive ways forward after critique. The former is easy, the latter very difficult.

As explained in the first chapter, the questioning of the assumptions of economics as a science is the task of philosophy, not of economics as a social science. Economics as a social science is limited to what is empirically observable among the phenomena that we call economic. In these pages the authors have raised the questions about virtually all of the assumptions that such critics of economic theory raise, and explained the arguments for and against different possible answers to these questions about its assumptions.

Some of the questions about the assumptions of economic theory that are raised, examined, and questioned in this book include: What is the connection, if any, between fact and value? Can we separate facts from values? Is the distinction between positive and normative economics one grounded in reality or merely a notional distinction for the purposes of analysis? Are agents in markets, whether individuals or groups, rational and adequately informed in their actions? Are agents in markets, again as individuals or groups, always self-interested or sometimes altruistic? Are utility and welfare, as quantified and measured by positive economics, the greatest or only economic values? When should an externality be identified, and to what degree does such an externality affect utility calculations? Are human beings primarily individuals and social groups loosely formed associations of individuals, or are humans so inherently social and relational that social groupings, in some ways, take precedence over, and determine, individuals? Is private property owned by private parties—be they individuals, families, groups, communities, or states, and without which there is no science of economics—good and right? These are all important philosophical questions about the assumptions of the social science of economics. Yet, the authors situate where they·belong, within the purview of the "limit questions" of philosophy, partly because they are non-empirical.

We can certainly ask the philosophical question of whether fact and value can be separated, as has been asked repeatedly in some detail in these pages. Economics is a *social science* and so involves the study of human beings, as do other social sciences. We can also ask such philosophical questions about the assumptions of other social sciences, like sociology and anthropology. Yet these philosophical questions do not gainsay the task of those disciplines. This is the empirical observation of the phenomena they study and the formation of theories and models based on such observations, which have a degree of explanatory and predictive power.

Even if the correct answer to the non-empirical philosophical question of the relationship between fact and value is that they are inseparable, or even indistinct, we can still use the empirical scientific method to study the aspects of phenomena amenable to observation, induction, theorization, and testing. In this case the inextricably of fact and value, or their identity, would apply to *all* empirical sciences. If fact and value are not *really* separable or distinct, they are still at least *notionally* distinct, and *all sciences* proceed on this notional distinction. Even some "hard" sciences, like biology, physiology, and anatomy study human beings, but the imposition of philosophical limit questions in their assumptions, and in the realm of values, does not derogate from their proper empirical tasks in their own limited spheres of inquiry. Even if fact and value are mere notional distinctions, philosophically speaking, we can still isolate and study the empirical elements of human beings, whether in the "hard" sciences, the social sciences in general, or in economic activity in particular. We can observe, measure, make hypotheses, test, and formulate laws about them, which is what positive economics does.

Economic theory is far from perfect, and is always improving. The sheer complexity and number of factors involved in economic phenomena impose limitations on economic theory, but do not discredit it. Neoclassical economic theory, and especially microeconomics, does not have only limited, but rather great, predictive and explanatory power: Regardless of philosophical assumptions about the rationality, knowledge, self-interestedness, or altruistic motives of humans engaging in trade, economists can still observe how humans allocate scarce resources. They have done so, and have come to certain, agreed upon, and nonmalleable features of human economic activity, in the form of economic laws.

The number and complexity of factors involved in economic activity can and do make it difficult to predict with certainty all outcomes. The theory is valid, but the number of factors to which it must be applied is daunting. Nonetheless, using economic theory and laws, economists can predict with certainty some specific outcomes, in the way that other sciences can predict specific effects from specific causes. It is nonmalleable fact, agreed upon by all economists of all normative economic persuasions, that as an increase in supply lowers price, while an increase in demand increases prices. It is a nonmalleable fact, agreed upon by all economists, that almost all interventions in the way that a market naturally allocates a good introduce deadweight loss and inefficiency.

Supply and demand are economic laws. Private property—meaning private ownership not only by individuals but also by groups like families, private firms, communities, and societies as a whole—is a necessary assumption of economics as a science. The economic laws of supply and demand have been firmly corroborated by innumerable observations of how humans naturally allocate scarce resources, as they assume private ownership. The right to private property is not an empirically observed fact and is therefore not law of economics, but rather a necessary assumption of economic theory and laws.

In debates between "conservative" and "liberal" normative economic policies, *all* economists aim for maximum positive economic efficiency, because it is mathematically pliable and measurable. The reasons for this were explained in chapter two. Even economists with "liberal" normative economic leanings advocate market inefficiency in dealing with externalities, because they believe it will produce maximum positive economic efficiency. The noted socialist economist, Abba Lerner (AD 1903 – 1982), is one among many examples.

Questioning philosophical assumptions about the science of economics cannot discredit the agreed upon data and laws of the science. There is much that is still debated in the discipline of economics itself, but there is also much that is certain. Critics who do not like the agreed upon data, theory, and laws of economics cannot "make them go away," by merely raising philosophical questions about its assumptions. Those who do not like the agreed upon facts of other sciences engage in such tactics. This strategy is possible because *all* sciences proceed upon assumed answers to certain philosophical limit questions, as discussed in the first chapter. Empirical observations and the theories gained by them, however, have led to many practical certainties in all sciences. These facts must be reckoned with in any dialogue of ethics with those sciences. For this reason, one can learn the contents of the discipline of biology in distinction from learning bioethics, and one can learn the contents of the discipline of sociology in distinction from learning social ethics.[1]

In summary, it is quite impossible to consider the intersection of ethics and economics without taking economics as, at least notionally if not really, a distinct endeavor in its own right. To deny at least a notional separation of positive economics from normative economics would utterly remove the "economics" part of the discussion. Again, there simply is no other plausible economic theory, agreed upon by all objective observers of economic phenomena, that has the explanatory and predictive power of current economic theory. All economists, regardless of their normative persuasions, agree upon a body of essential facts and laws.

In closing, again, the stated purposes of this book have been to: (1) inform all non-economists about the basic principles of economics; (2) inform all non-philosophers about philosophical ethics; and (3) show how these two disciplines begin to interact at a variety of points. If readers leave this book with some greater degree of knowledge of the disciplines of economics, philosophy, and ethics, and some greater understanding of the many and complex ways in which they intersect at various points, then the authors have achieved what they hoped to do.

NOTES

1. It is a curious fact that critics of economic theory champion the conflation of the positive and the normative in economics, but, with apparent inconsistency, readily admit this distinction—be it real or notional only—in other sciences.

www.ingramcontent.com/pod-product-compliance
Ingram Content Group UK Ltd.
Pitfield, Milton Keynes, MK11 3LW, UK
UKHW041830240926
475560UK00017B/33

9 780761 859581